Watercolour action study by Ian Wright.

Return of the

Clown Prince

A Personal, Retrospective Anthology

by

LEN SHACKLETON

("From a game with a business in it, to a business with a game in it!")

First Printed November 2000
Re-printed April 2001

First Published in 2000 by
GHKN PUBLISHING LIMITED
8 Ryelands Way
Rosemount
Durham, DH1 5GR

ISBN 0-9538244-0-3

Cover design and production by Rufus Abajas, Byron House, Seaham.
Printed & bound by Bookcraft (Bath) Limited

GENERAL ATTRIBUTIONS

Soccer Research/Advisor: Graham Hedley
Information Technology/Preparation: Colin Saxton
Editorial/Project Management: Roger and Catherine Shackleton.

Dedication

This book is dedicated to the memory of my father,
Leonard Price Shackleton (1898 - 1972), an ardent
amateur sportsman himself - cricketer, footballer and
track athlete. It was his enthusiasm, encouragement
and support that enabled me to become a
professional sportsman.

4

Foreword
by MICHAEL PARKINSON

(Broadcaster - Journalist - Writer - Sports Enthusiast)

Sincerely
Michael Parkinson.

~ Preface ~

It is now over 40 years since I hung up my boots, prevented from playing by a chronic ankle problem despite much pre-match strapping-up by the club physio, Johnny Watters. Increased likelihood of a poor contribution to team performances and the risk of permanent disability made retirement inevitable. This book has mostly been written abroad in Tenerife, which has become as dear to my heart as the North East. Until, that is, the day when the late Bob Maxwell jumped into the sea (it's a wonder that he didn't miss) not far from our apartment in Los Cristianos together with part of my Mirror Group pension!

The title of this book comes from a spoof retirement presentation (a headline from a back page mock-up) made by my former colleagues at *The People* where I 'worked' for the best part of 25 years. It follows two earlier books, *Clown Prince of Soccer* (1955) and *Shack's Guide to Soccer* (1956). The second was tongue-in-cheek and gave the late David Jack and I many humorous hours writing it. *The Clown Prince*, in particular, had been very well received - an August publication with several reprints before Christmas attracting much attention due to a certain blank page!

Although this new book is primarily intended for the older football enthusiast with an understandable bias toward the North East of England, it has been put together in a way intended to help readers of any age get the full flavour of the times in which I played. In my retirement I have been very fortunate to enjoy good health and plenty of golf. That is perhaps why this third book has been so long in the offing. What follows is not intended to be detailed "memoirs" as I have found those of others sometimes disappoint by expectations which prove to be too high. I thought I would avoid that format and instead put together a selection of anecdotes combined with extracts from period articles. I have added a radio interview by the great Jimmy Armfield (the ex Blackpool & England full-back), some art work and contemporary photos. I am also indebted to my friend Brian Leng of *The Wearside Roar* for the second, previously unpublished, interview, additional photos, illustrations and his most welcome proof-reading services.

This book would never have seen the light of day without the support of many people. I take particular pleasure in acknowledging the support of John Feast, as archivist, David Bull, for publishing advice and my friend and fervent fan, Ted Little, for all his kindness and vital I.T. support.

There has been magnificent support for this book from SAFC Chairman, Mr Bob Murray. His long-term admiration during my playing career has now culminated in his personal encouragement and the general advice and support from the club. Perhaps it is all the more fitting that he has provided the *Introduction* to this book - as his near namesake Club Manager, Bill Murray, did in my original book *The Clown Prince...* Coming from him, the embarrassingly generous sentiments expressed are very greatly appreciated indeed!

I have been very fortunate in having a sporting career - it almost goes without saying that being paid to keep yourself fit is much better than working. I hope that the reader enjoys this collection of anecdotes, opinions and supporting information as much as I have enjoyed my own personal trip down memory lane whilst writing it. I was not certain that there would be sufficient interest in a follow-up book of this type as, sadly, I represent a generation diminishing in numbers with each passing year, but time will tell.

To quote from a favourite comedy source of all three of my sons:
"...nostalgia is not what it used to be..." *(Monty Python)*.

In the past I have often been accused of being controversial but this has always been out of general conviction and I have never, deliberately, set out to be sensational. I do not regard myself as a rebel although, because of the set up of the professional game in my time, I certainly believe that I had a cause...

Len Shackleton
Los Cristianos & Grange-Over-Sands
1999/2000

Introduction
by BOB MURRAY

(Chairman - Sunderland AFC)

It's quite mind-blowing to think of the impact Leonard Francis Shackleton would be making right now had he been born 50 years later with the same prodigious talents.

In an age when his kind of ball wizardry, trickery and magnificent individuality is in such short supply in English soccer, would his transfer value be so huge that only the world's wealthiest club could afford to sign him?

Imagine how much more entertaining games would be as he unfurled his skills. Just think how TV pundits would drool over repeated action replays of his mouthwatering repertoire of skills. To what lengths would bone-crunching defenders go to try to prevent him making them look silly?

On the other hand would his maverick nature and unorthodox style put him at odds with modern coaching methods and condemn him to the role of unfulfilled genius? The fact he was only capped five times for England during his glittering career was often attributed to his outspoken nature. Would he be even more isolated today?

What is absolutely certain is that "Shack", who scored 101 goals in 348 league and cup appearances for Sunderland, stands out among a handful of truly legendary players during the club's 121-year history - and I was lucky enough to see the great man play at Roker.

Supporters' memories inevitably build up mental stocks of great goals, super saves and perfect passes, but with Roker regulars during *1947-57,* only one name springs to mind when it comes to sheer, all-round entertainment.

It was the forthright Yorkshireman bought from Newcastle for the first £20,000 fee in soccer history. Len became known as the Clown Prince of Soccer. It meant that as well as thrilling crowds, he could make 'em laugh - and we could certainly do with a lot more of that in these deadly serious times.

His retirement through injury after the first game of the *1957-58* season coincided with a major turning point in fortunes for this great club, which then slid to its first-ever relegation. Apart from the 1973 FA Cup win and the occasional false dawn, it seemed doomed to 40 years of underachievement.

But the tide has turned for us again with the move to the Stadium of Light, 1998-99 promotion to the Premiership and going on to finish the following season in the highest top level position since Shack's heyday. Fans are smiling once more - and feeling confident that those good times are back to stay.

So it's an ideal time for an updated version of this charismatic inside forward's famous autobiography to be re-published. Len Shackleton is one of the pillars of this club's history - and it is a great honour to be invited to contribute. I hope you find it every bit as entertaining as older supporters enjoyed watching the author in action.

BOB MURRAY
(Sunderland Stadium of Light, July 2000)

~ CONTENTS ~

Foreword
Preface
Introduction by **Bob Murray**

Chapters

1 Autumn 1996 Radio 5 Live - from Jimmy Armfield's "Football Legends" Series.
2 USA & Canada - Summer 1955.
3 The Brian Leng/"The Wearside Roar" Interview.
4 East Africa 1956 - Closed Season Exhibition Tour.
5 Critics and Contemporaries.
6 Hong Kong Trip 1966 & the Most Important People in the Game.
7 Humorous Characters and Anecdotes.
8 North Eastern Sporting Club's Las Vegas Trip 1968.
9 No Longer Blank!
10 Full Circle - From a Game with a Business in it to a Business with a Game in it.
11 New Freedom of Contract.
12 My Friend Barney Ramsden and Other Great Players of all Eras.
13 The Football League - 100 League Legends marking the 1998/9 Centenary.

Bibliography & Acknowledgements

Appendices

I The Football League "100" League Legends. Photographs of all 100 players from the first century of the English League - cross reference chapter 13.
II Editor's 'out-takes'.
III "Clown Prince of Soccer" (1955)

~ Chapter 1 ~
Radio 5 Live Autumn 1996 -
Jimmy Armfield's "Football Legends" Series

Presenter, Eleanor Oldroyd - In the first of our new series Jimmy Armfield talks to a real North East icon. Fifty years ago on Saturday, Len Shackleton made his debut for Newcastle United and scored 6 goals, which is still a club individual scoring record but apart from his goal scoring feat, Len Shackleton was known to one and all as the Clown Prince of football:

Who's a Clown? *(Len Shackleton Collection)*

Len   I probably got the name of the Clown Prince because I used to go out and enjoy the game. That's what it was - I used to enjoy myself just like clowns do to provide the entertainment. I wasn't as good a competitor as I might have been or should have been but results weren't too important - I used to enjoy the game, and that was what it was all about to me, i.e. enjoying it.

Jimmy   Len Shackleton Clown Prince, soccer genius, entertainer, call him what you will. Whatever, for those who love the unorthodox he was a big attraction on football grounds throughout the country in the period just after the last war. Shack, that was his nickname, played for both

Newcastle and Sunderland - the Geordies loved him - and here is one of them, the late Brian Redhead, recalling an early memory of his favourite player.

Brian   The man I liked the most of all, I suppose, when I was a teenager, was Len Shackleton. A man of immense wit. I once saw him take a penalty against Manchester City, when Frank Swift was still alive. He put the ball on the spot and he then walked almost to the halfway line and he ran like a train at the ball and took a tremendous kick, and Swifty dived, but the ball was still on the spot! He hadn't actually touched it, and he turned round and he back heeled it into the net and the crowd went raving mad! And old Swifty walked out and he took Len Shackleton's head in between those great hands and he kissed him!

Jimmy   Well that was typical Shack, born in Bradford, in 1922, he developed an almost carefree style of forward playing. He tormented defenders and frustrated managers but no one, however critical, could ever doubt that here was a self-taught 'ball artist'. Arsenal were the first lot to spot it when he was just 16.

Len   George Allison and Arsenal came for me when I was a kid. So I went down to join the ground staff of the Arsenal before the war until (after a period of months) George Allison, the manager, told me one day that he was going to sack me - he said that I wouldn't make the grade.

Jimmy   What did you think about it, when he told you you wouldn't make the grade?

Len   Well what do you do? He said: "Before you go back to Bradford I want to show you television". This was in 1938/39 - as much as to say you can go back to the 'country cousins' and tell them that you have seen television! We didn't even know what television was Jim, in those days. It really rankled me that, but somehow it used to work a little bit better for me at Highbury against the Arsenal, because I used to play particularly well there and cut out the clowning a lot!

Jimmy   So it was back to Bradford where he started out, alongside men like mighty legendary goalkeeper Chick Farr and Ron Greenwood. But the Yorkshire Club were never going to hold on to such a talent. Although when the move actually came Shack knew nothing about it!

Len   Fred Emery, the manager, told me after training, he said: "Report to the 'so and so' hotel in Bradford at 2.00pm." So I went home to see my wife, told her that I had to go into town. At that stage I don't know what I'm going for but I assume that I am being transferred, but I don't know. I

A young Shack and Bobby Daniel - brother of Ray - August 1938 *(Len Shackleton Collection)*

Park Avenue c. 1945. *(Len Shackleton Collection)*

went into the hotel and Bill Murray came over to me and he asked, "Are you Shackleton? And I said "Yes;" "Well," Mr. Murray replied, "I just wanted to wish you all the best wherever you go to, because you are not coming to our club!"

Jimmy   Where was that, Sunderland?

Len   Yes, Sunderland. "They want too much money for you." (Mr. Murray stated). So Stan Seymour and a couple of Directors came down the steps – they were from Newcastle United - and Stan came over to me and said you are coming to Newcastle! I didn't have to sign but I didn't know that, I was only a kid and I didn't know that. He said you are going to Newcastle - so I'm going to Newcastle! I didn't even know the transfer fee and I had to wait for the evening paper coming to find out that the transfer fee was £13,000, which was the joint top fee at that time. Albert Stubbins had just been transferred to Liverpool for £13,000 - and I thought "I'm not as good as him" - and I said to Mr. Seymour (thinking I'm going for about £5,000 or something like that): "Okay Mr. Seymour, what do I get out of it?" He said he would give me £500, so I said that was great!

Jimmy   £500 at that time, what was your actual wage at Bradford?

Len   It was £8 (per week), I think.

Jimmy   So, really, that must have seemed like an absolute fortune?

LFS, Wilf Taylor, Stan Seymour (MD), George Rutherford (Chairman)

Len   It was a fortune, yes Jim it was, and that is the be all and end all of the thing - Seymour didn't even give me the £500, I never even got that from him.

Jimmy   Well that started the fractious relationship Shack always had with football club directors. He never trusted one of them, and in his autobiography the chapter entitled "What Directors know about Football" consisted of a blank page! So he was off to Tyneside and incredibly on his debut against Newport he scored 6 goals and that is still a scoring record at Newcastle!

Len   Six goals on your debut in 'Geordieland', or anywhere, is brilliant but on

Newcastle debut v Newport *(Newcastle Chronicle & Journal)*

reflection that was the worst thing that happened - because if you score 6 goals in your debut they expect it the week after, and you are a comparative failure if you only get a couple of goals!

Jimmy Did they give you the ball?

Len No, that was another thing - they wouldn't even give you any new laces for your boots. You had to provide them yourself. No, I would have liked that match ball because I think it might have been worth a few quid now!

Jimmy On Tyneside, Shack still had his critics, but he had his fans as well and one of those was Bob Stokoe, the former United central defender and still a golfing partner of this soccer legend.

Bob I remember him in 1947 when I had just joined Newcastle and Len was the big star at that particular time. Len was without any doubt one of the greatest showmen, I think, you have ever seen on the football field. I remember him playing in a game one day taking the ball around the goalkeeper only needing to knock it in the net. But rather than do that, he has a little sit on it and then back heels it in, you know! Which was typical of Len, he loved spinning the ball, he loved tempting wingers against fullbacks to tackle with the ball, squeezed between Bobby Cowell and Billy Elliott and people like that. He is just a one off, I cannot make a comparison with any of the current players? If they had been able to

Stokoe and Shack - after their playing days together - still friends *(Len Shackleton Collection)*

18

record like they can now with slow motion things and that, I tell you he would never have been off the screens!

Jimmy   But there was no television and Newcastle weren't without inside forwards either. So Shack, because of his individual style, was sold off yet again. This time just up the road to Sunderland.

Len   The record for that time was £20,000; I think Tommy Lawton had gone to Notts. County from Chelsea for £20,000 and Sunderland wanted to beat that fee, so when I was sold from Newcastle, Sunderland nipped in with an extra £50 (to make the new record £20,050).

Jimmy   You've been involved in these record transfers, you told me a lovely story about a Newcastle Director throwing a threepenny bit on the table?

Len   Well that was to be the Stubbins' fee (on my first transfer) - Bradford wanted to beat the Stubbins' fee so one of the Newcastle Directors, Wilf Taylor it was, threw a threepenny bit on the table and said - there you are we've beaten the Stubbins' fee!

Jimmy   So you were transferred for £13,000 and threepence?

Len   Basically, yes.

Jimmy   So Shack joined what was described then as the 'Bank of England Team' - Bill Elliott, Billy Bingham, Ted Purdon, Ken Chisholm, Charlie Fleming, Ray Daniel all bought for big fees - but still, Sunderland won nothing? (...apart from a corner at Wolverhampton once - LFS!).

Len   We had a good lot of lads - a great lot of lads - but the names and things don't make a team. You have got to have some kind of blend and that was what we didn't have. And I don't know why because the public up there Jim... I've told people till I'm fed up of telling them... that the best sporting public in Britain are in the North East! If Newcastle or Sunderland had done what Manchester United and what Liverpool have done over the years, well that would have really proved my point.

Jimmy   Because you, of course, were in the very famous FA Cup defeat at the hands of Yeovil, they were a non-league team in 1949, can you remember it?

Len   Can I remember it? We will never forget that - we were never allowed to forget that! We travelled the length and breadth of Britain, it was to go to the west-country and we stayed there on the Wednesday and it was hot and sticky and humid. I'm not making excuses mind but I did... and I'm sure

RAY DANIEL £30,000

TREVOR FORD £30,000

JIMMY COWAN £9,000

BILLY ELLIOTT £26,000

LEN SHACKLETON £20,000

all the rest of the lads too… felt so lethargic and how the hell they beat us? They beat us in extra time - because at that time we couldn't replay - and Yeovil scored in extra time - oh gee!

Jimmy   So what happened when you got home?

Len   We never lived it down! They still keep raking up the past (blood-and-sand)!

Jimmy   Well he was there 10 years, and Sunderland were attractive to the fans but frankly they were a 'nearly' team. They reached two semi-finals, in 1955 and 1956, where along the way they beat Newcastle and Bob Stokoe.

Bob   We had won the cup in 1955 for the third time and I had established myself in the Newcastle team in 1954/55 and we were drawn against Sunderland in the sixth round. He came to St James' Park, 62,000 - the biggest crowd I ever played in front of at St. James' - and he put on one of his acts and beat us 2-0 and I would have loved to kick him all over the stand that day! He always paid me a compliment that if I had been his manager - this is in later years because he knows how disciplined I was in my way - I would have probably got more out of him. I would have tried to kick his backside on certain things. If Len had been more of a dedicated team player than an entertainer, he would have been a world beater!

Jimmy   Well, few would doubt that and here is one of his old Sunderland team mates, former Northern Ireland International, Billy Bingham, describing the raw talent that could torment defenders and team mates alike.

Billy   He was a law unto himself, who must have been difficult to handle because he was a pure individual player. He would irritate you a little bit because maybe he would take too much out of it. And, of course, people would maybe accuse him of not playing for the team but playing for himself and in terms of this he was an individualist. But when I say an individualist I mean that he was a brilliant dribbler. At the height of 5'8" he had size 9 or 10 boots so he could dribble the ball. I've seen him catch the ball coming out of the air, where a guy would 'thigh it' or get it on his chest. Shack would actually catch it 'midstream', his control was brilliant! He was playing at Highbury having a brilliant game and he had already scored for us. And he would run the ball along the touchline tempting the linesman to wave his flag that it was out, but he would hold it in all the time. And Tapscott was playing on the right wing for Arsenal and Shack actually beat Tapscott - made a lovely cross to our attacking left side - and then turned round and started to coach Tapscott on how to cross balls because Tapscott wasn't crossing the ball too well!

Jimmy   During the game?

Billy   During the game, right under the main Arsenal Director's Box!

Jimmy   He once gave you a goal in a match?

Billy   Yes, I was about 19 at the time, small star among a team of stars. There were 9 Internationals in the side. In this particular game the cross came in, so I went up to head it. The goalkeeper went up with me, George Swindon, it fell and we had to scramble to get the ball. And Shack actually got it first and with Swindon on the ground and me beside Swindon, Shack was actually holding the ball on the goal line!

Proof that we did practise - sometimes. *(The Len Shackleton Collection)*

Jimmy   He could have scored easy?

Billy   Easily, and he called me to get up and I scrambled up first because I was a bit lighter than Swindon and poked it in.

Jimmy   So what did the crowd do then?

Billy   They were in absolute raptures because nobody had ever done that before! Most forwards are selfish - they want to get their own goals, don't they?

Jimmy   Well naturally Shacks' humour created humour and his room mate at Roker Park was Welsh International central defender Ray Daniel, and he soon joined in the party spirit.

Len   We used to call him 'Bebe' (after Bebe Daniel & Ben Lyon) and he was my room mate and he had a tremendous sense of humour did Ray. One day we were playing away from home and he asked one of our Directors, one of the leading surgeons in the North East, to come and cut his chicken up for him at the dinner table - that was Ray! Another day we were playing at Villa, Ray goes down and he's hurt - goes in a crumple - and I dashed over to see him, because he was a mate of mine, to see if he was hurt badly, but he was winking at me and I was wondering what he was winking for. The trainer comes on and takes his stocking off and there is a little bit of a 'trickle' on his shin.

Shack with Billy & Ray wondering why the interest in the underside of the ball? *(Courtesy of The Daily Mirror)*

Jimmy   Blood?

Len   Yes, blood and George said, is that all it is? And he said yes - but it's red! It's red and it should be blue! Because he was known as a 'blue-blood' - he was one of the aristocrats and he called the trainer on, to have a private joke with me, in front of 40,000 - and that was the kind of sense of humour that Ray had!

Jimmy   Well Shack did get a handful of England 'call-ups', and he'll never forget his first International, that was against Scotland in the victory match at Hampden just after the war.

Len   We had been married for about 3 years so I paid for my wife to come up. There is a 136,000 people there Jim, they paid me 30 shillings, which in today's terms is £1.50, we got a 3rd Class travel fare. We got beat in Hampden 1-0, travelled back to Bradford on the train, had to stand up in the corridors because the train was full, and I got an 'Illuminated Address' - we didn't get a Cap for that!

A couple of years after that when I had been to Sunderland the first year, I got picked against Denmark. We played in Denmark: Tommy Lawton, Billy Wright, Swifty, Bobby Langton. I think we drew but we should have beaten them easily. But we didn't and we sat in the dressing room after the match and Billy Wright was saying to Walter Winterbottom - I can hear him now - "…Walter can we keep our shirts…?". And Walter said: "…No you can't keep your shirt…!". As it happened I was lucky because I played a few more times for England after that and I was able to keep my shirt but I felt sorry for one of the greatest inside forwards that I've seen, who was Jimmy Hagan.

Jimmy   From Sheffield United.

Len   What a brilliant player Jimmy was - and that was his one and only Cap - and he never even got a shirt!

Jimmy   There is one match when England beat West Germany (see copy of match programme in chapter 7), who were the World Champions, 3-1 at Wembley. The quotes that I read at the time say that Shackleton was the outstanding man of the day - can you remember the game?

Len   Well I can remember it but it (the quote) wasn't strictly true. I wanted to prove to myself, mainly to my family, that I could hold my own at that level. And that level was that Germany had won the World Cup. The summer before that they had beaten Hungary at the finals of the World Cup. I wanted to play against them and prove to myself that I could live in that company - which I did and I scored what I felt was a super goal.

Jimmy   Well many said that Len didn't win as many Caps as his talent merited. Here is the England manager of the day, Walter Winterbottom.

Walter   He was a solo merchant, you know; he played the way he wanted to and therefore he might not be helping other players with their fortes, with their strengths as you would have expected him to. Because one of the things you had to do when you got a team together was to see better ways of linking. And if a wingman like Stanley Matthews was there, you knew very well the best way to help him to play was to give it to him to his feet. Not to pass through the ball for him to run onto because he didn't like that. So you knew how to play with him, but if you were not going to do those things then Stanley Matthews wouldn't have a good game, he would be out of the picture. Len was the type of person who could take the stage himself and wanted to more often than not. And therefore, possibly, the selection of Billy Woodfield? Well, it's all right, he's putting up a show

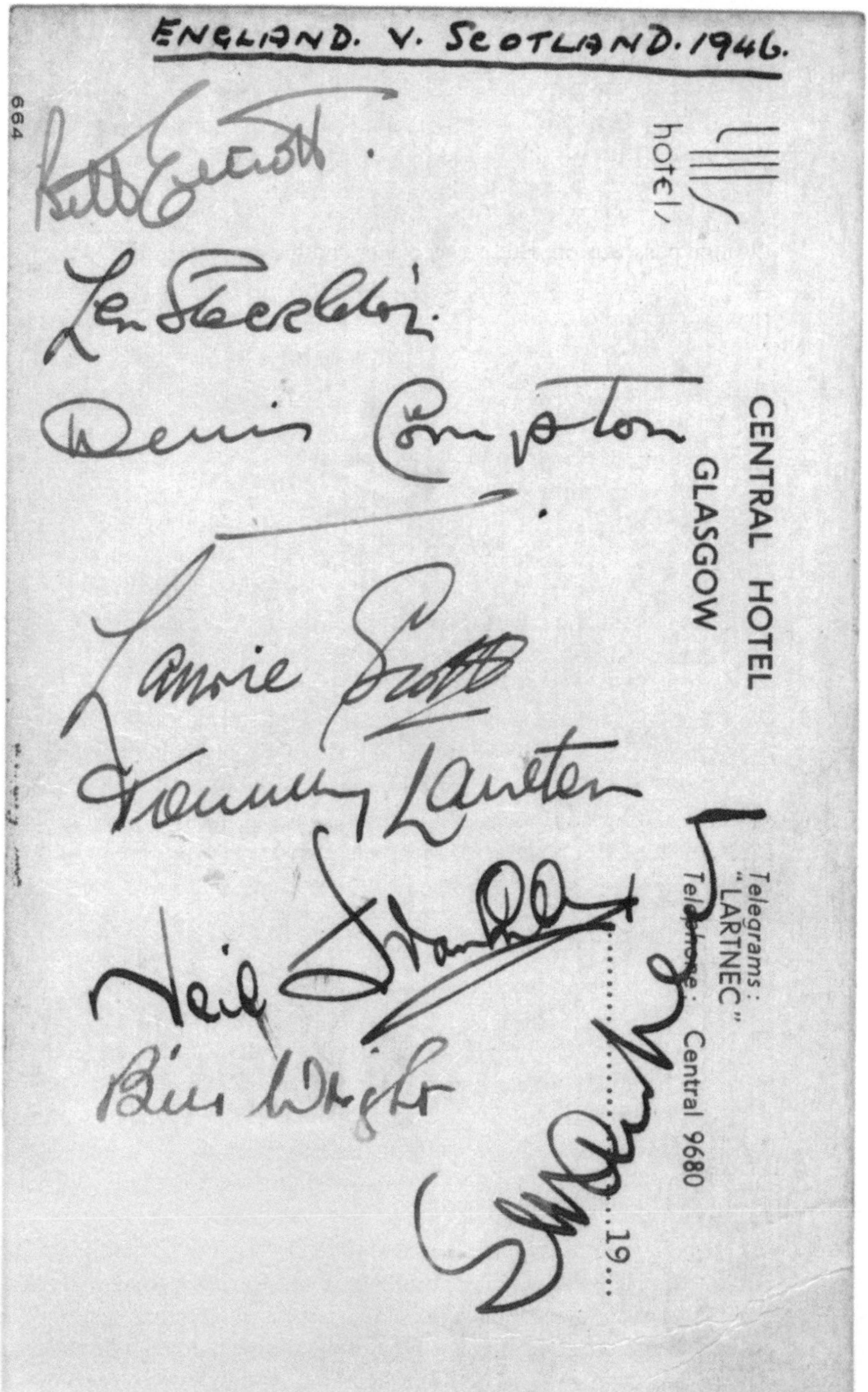

ENGLAND. V. SCOTLAND. 1946.

664

hotel

CENTRAL HOTEL
GLASGOW

Telegrams:
"LARTNEC"
Telephone: Central 9680

19.....

Reg Attwell

Len Shackleton

Denis Compton

Laurie Scott

Tommy Lawton

Neil Franklin

Billy Wright

but we're getting nowhere with it, we're not scoring goals. If there's a challenge for a position and a lot of players are there going for it, then you are bound to have changes. And if one player starts to knit-in better than others it's your bad luck to get out of the picture at that time even though you're good enough to be playing in an England team and that was the case. He could link up alright but he would do a lot of personal skills which were purely isolated from the game.

He'd trick a player and then he'd turn around and beat him again, there's no need to do it! And he would try fancy tricks when a good straight through pass was on. But it was clever and the crowd loved it too, let's be fair! When he played against Germany I do remember the crowd just rising to him almost like the feat of 'Gazza' when 'Gazza' scored against Scotland in the recent European Cup. He could produce tricks in that order and that giftedness which is quite exceptional!

Jimmy But Len Shackleton wasn't going to change his style, he always wanted to be a crowd pleaser, he wanted to tease defenders and he even used the corner flag as part of the act. Here he is again, followed by Stokoe eulogising about Len's incredible ball skills.

Len Big Peter Sillet, remember Peter Sillet at Chelsea?

Jimmy Yes.

Len Well we get the ball into the corner flag, there (gesticulating) about a yard off the corner flag, Peter over with me, kick it on the corner flag and if you hit it in the centre it comes out. It did and I'm nearly in the penalty box. Peter is wondering what's happening? But that to me is a plain tactic. Not difficult to do really but it gets misconstrued as 'showmanship'. Against Holland 'B', I was at St. James' one day and just before the match starts they're throwing the practice balls out to me. There is one rolling to me and it's got to be rolling at the right pace mind, you know this Jim? It's rolling to me on the ground, so I hit it underneath - like you do with the snooker shot - you hit it on the bottom - and it goes forward about 15 yards and then it comes back. And I'm calling the ball to me with my finger and it stops just by me. And we still get people who talk about that particular game. Now I cannot understand why everybody doesn't do that?

Bob Stokoe Many is the time that I, as a young lad after I had seen him do this sort of thing, used to go on the training ground on my own with a few balls to try and do it - it was such an embarrassment, the ball went further the other way! I mean even when he played cricket I've seen him lift his left leg up and knock a four through his legs. He was an excellent cricketer. Yes, he was a good bowler and as I say batsman, he had a good eye for everything.

Good golfer, played squash, badminton all these sort of games that he could handle with no bother.

Len   I used to get more cash playing cricket, as a professional cricketer in the North East, than what I got from my football. I played for the Minor Counties - when I was at Newcastle for Northumberland for a little bit, then I got transferred to Sunderland. I played Minor Counties for Durham and professional for Wearmouth. And what a good club it was - most of the other clubs in the Durham Senior League came to sign me but I wouldn't move from Wearmouth because, once you get a good club, you stay there, i.e. I had a good football club at Sunderland, so I stayed there. I had to finish playing football with a bad ankle eventually and I had to quit cricket as well for the same reason.

When you're 'in' you're also 'out' - watching, accompanied by son, Graham. *(The Sunderland Echo)*

Jimmy   When you actually finished playing at Sunderland because of your ankle injury, what were you going to do with your career then?

Len   I didn't want to go into coaching or into management, so I went onto the *Daily Express* and I had six happy years with them. They were a good firm.

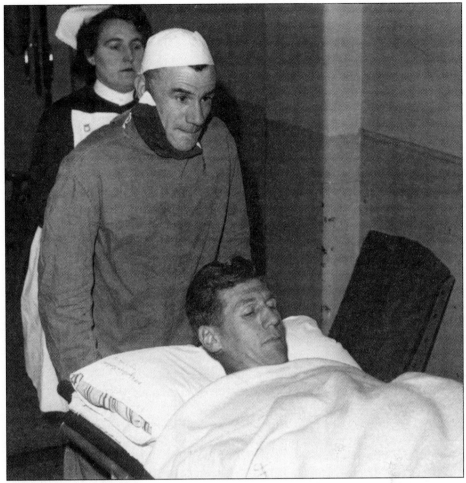

All treatment proves ineffective. *(Courtesy of The Sheffield Star)*

Jimmy   How long were you a journalist?

Len   In addition to the *Express*, I was a journalist for about 20 years with *The People* but I didn't like the job. My wife summed it up the best when she said "It's like schoolboys telling tales". And that's basically what it is. But it paid good expenses, it paid good wages. I was associating with people that I knew and I liked and it was better than working!

Jimmy   How do you feel about the present day players? Let's talk first all about the money - do you get envious of the money they earn?

Len   Not really. There's no sour grapes with me. My eldest boy is a solicitor, my middle boy is a chartered surveyor, my youngster is a doctor and an osteopath. So that's what football has given to me, to give to them - so it's not sour grapes when people are earning (1996) £12-15,000 a week - it sounds ridiculous doesn't it!

Jimmy Coming back to where we started about the Clown Prince of football, do you think if you had not been the Clown Prince you would have got more Caps?

Len I would have got more Caps probably, but nobody gets a lot of Caps who plays in the North East you know. You look in the records, it's a little bit out on a limb?

Jimmy Why is that Len?

Len I don't know, but they don't. But as I said, you look at the records. Jackie Milburn, tremendous centre forward - and he just got a few, I don't know how many (about 7) but just a few. A little bit different now perhaps because of the television. If I had my time to do over again and I wanted some Caps and I wanted to get the best from the talent that they had given me I would have moved to London, but it would have been at the expense of moving away from some great people. If it had come to the crunch, I wouldn't have done it, you know? Life was about people, basically it's all about people. I'm not a Geordie, I'm a Yorkshireman but I class 'going home' as the North East because they are brilliant people!

Jimmy Well today Shack lives in retirement at Grange-over-Sands on the north side of Morecambe Bay. And when I called to see him, frankly it was one fun story after another. Today golf is his game, but forever, for most of us, he will always be the ball artist who helped to put a smile on the face of soccer at a time when the country needed it. Max Miller, the old great cockney comedian, would often include in his act the words "There'll never be another" - probably the same could be said about 'Shack'!

Eleanor Oldroyd:
Len Shackleton in conversation with Jimmy Armfield, and next week we will be featuring the Burnley and Northern Ireland legend, Jimmy Mackelroy.

Reproduced with grateful thanks to both Jimmy Armfield and BBC Radio.

~ Chapter 2 ~
USA & Canada Trip - Summer 1955

Sunderland's closed season tour began properly for the players when we arrived by airport bus at the team's hotel in Midtown Manhattan. It was off the world famous Broadway, not far from both Madison Square Garden and Times Square. New York City immediately presented a marvellous collection of sights, foreign smells and noises and a stunning skyline - literally appearing as a different world with a movie-like atmosphere.

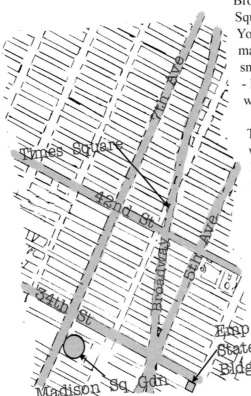

The team got booked-in and four of us went out to test the air and stretch our legs. There was Ted Purdon, Ken Chisholm, Ray Daniel and myself ('Chis', 'Purdy', 'Bebe' & 'Shack'). We went walking in the streets around Madison Square Garden and Times Square between the Garment & Theatre Districts. Almost immediately, it seemed, there was an enormous commotion. Lots of noise with police cars arriving, sirens sounding, the whole neighbourhood in uproar. There was a bank raid in progress; as the squad cars arrived police officers spilled-out onto the pavement with their guns drawn. Two guys ran out of a nearby bank, watched by the many members of the public present, including ourselves. The cops went down on their knees, took aim and started shooting at the robbers! They hit one in the shoulder and a bystander as well! We had been there barely five minutes and had already been plunged into this excitement! It seemed quite surreal. The sort of larger-than-life episode frequently portrayed in the movies or on TV. A memorable introduction, where fortunately none of us had had to 'eat lead' or suffer any other harm!

Purdy

The team had been paid for the 3 or 4 weeks' tour, based on about $2 a day plus spending money. I am not certain what my team mates got (my 'cut' certainly wasn't $100s!) but I do remember that Chis and Purdy asked for theirs in $1 bills to make it look a real 'wad'. Purdy went up towards the Bronx to see Harlem for himself. He soon discovered what a very rough place it really is and was lucky to return with only his 'wad' stolen – and that was within about the first twenty four hours! We all had a whip-round for him. But desperate times called for desperate measures. Chis, Purdy and some of the others had spotted a notice outside an apartment block announcing $5 to $10 payments given to blood donors. Anyone was eligible, so trust Ken and Ted to be generous with theirs! And for $10 a shot why not, New York was/is an expensive place to go out on the town at night. They attended quite a few sessions during our stay under false names! Fortunately, to supplement the spending money, bonus payments were also made by the club, for each of the games we played. I imagine the club received a percentage of the gate money, so this worked out well all round. We played Huddersfield Town 4 games plus several local American and Canadian teams, for something like a total of about ten or eleven games.

In New York we soon discovered World Heavyweight Boxing Champion, Jack Dempsey's Bar & Restaurant, not many blocks from the team hotel. Jack Dempsey himself would sit in a window seat every day, on display as it were. Opposite JD's was another restaurant where none other than Marilyn Monroe made daily visits because she was working in a Broadway show at the time. Thinking back I realise how lucky we were to have come across such circumstances and even more so for Chis - because he used to go in just to chat her up! Not many people would ever attempt that and even fewer would be able to carry it off. But Chis and Purdy were very charismatic operators. Whilst still in New York they even managed to get themselves invited into a filmstars' party, involving a 'date' with Joan Crawford. Exactly what

INTERNATIONAL SOCCER

SUNDERLAND F. C.
of ENGLAND
(ENGLISH FIRST DIVISION)

VS.

PHILADELPHIA
UHRIK TRUCKERS
—CHAMPIONS—
AMERICAN PROFESSIONAL SOCCER LEAGUE

SUNDAY, MAY 22, 1955
SOUVENIR PROGRAM   KICK-OFF · · · · 2:30 P. M.
TWENTY-FIVE CENTS

CONNIE MACK STADIUM
TWENTY-FIRST ST. AND LEHIGH AVE. • PHILADELPHIA, PA.

Bebe

Chis

SUNDERLAND of ENGLAND'S FIRST DIVISION

Front (left to right): Jack Hedley, Len Shackleton, Ken Chisholm, Bill Elliott. **Insets:** George Aiken, Charlie Fleming.
Back: Ray Daniel, Joe McDonald, Ted Purdon, Willie Fraser, Al Snell, Stan Anderson, Bill Bingham.

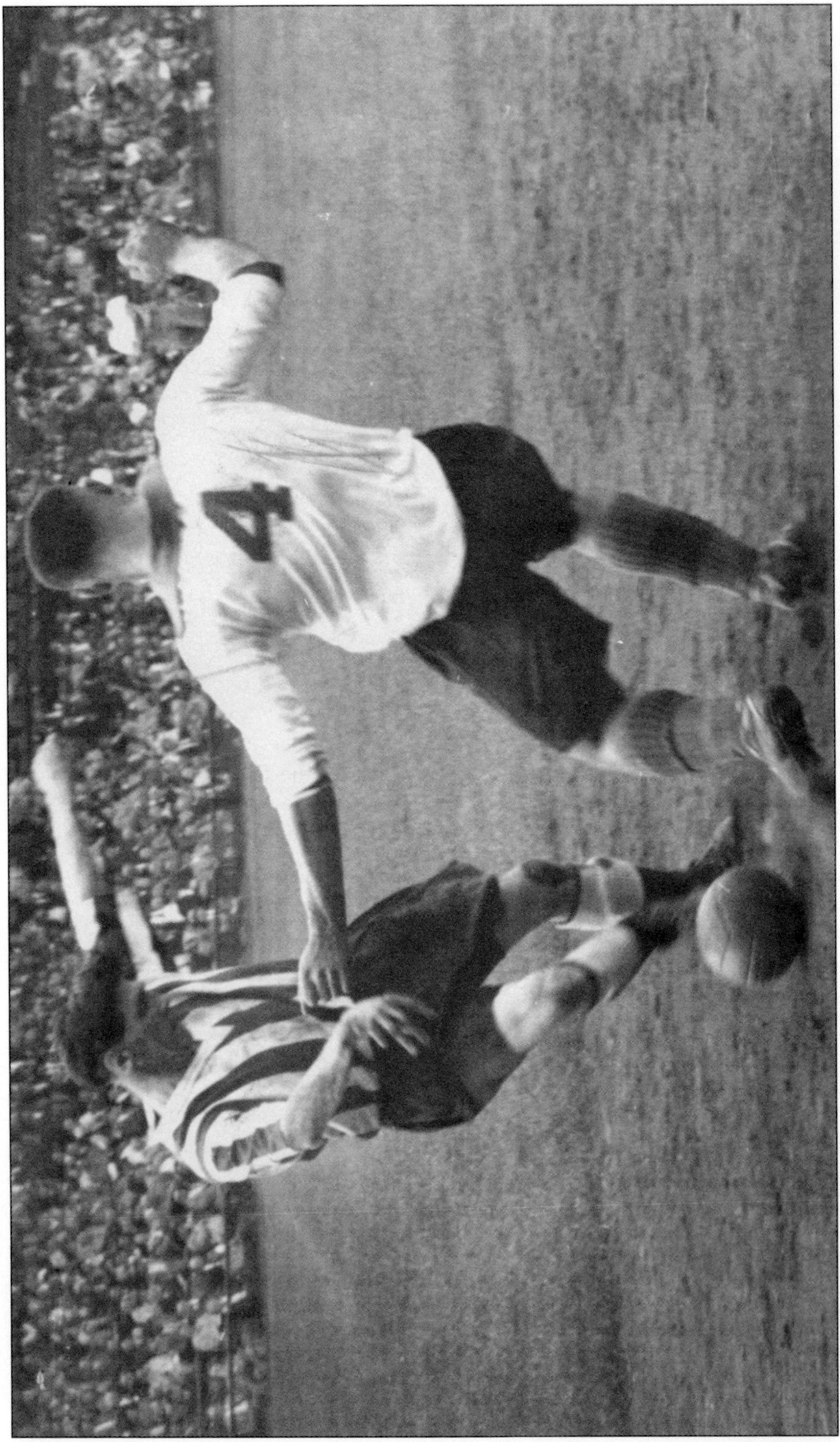

Ebbets Field - New York, May 1955

the circumstances were, no one was very clear about at the time. But knowing Chis, his reality was often far less believable than most people's fiction. Together with his partner in romantic exploits, Purdy, they made a successful 'double-act'. There's probably no real secret to it except either having 'it' or not? A bit like commercial acumen - for those who have it, the exploits seem to follow some invisible and inevitable hidden path, usually leading to general success. Whereas for the rest of us, it's not at all like that - on occasions we can only stand back in wonderment and admiration - just how did they make it seem so easy?

Moving on a little, the sport of boxing featured in ways other than just JD's bar when we were in New York. We met the British Heavyweight Don Cockell who had just come across the continent from San Francisco, where he had been famously in contention for the Championship of that time. Unfortunately, he was defeated by Rocky Marciano but of course this was no disgrace against one of the best undefeated fighters of all time! I remember Don seemed very pleased to meet us when we encountered him as a 'fellow Brit.' in New York. And he really was quite a character to meet. Maybe not so surprising when you consider it must have taken some pretty extraordinary talent and energy in that era to make it that far, both professionally and geographically, remembering that we were not part of the so-called 'global village' of today. That trip saw another link with professional boxing, which in its own way was also quite remarkable.

We were out together with our trainer Bert Johnston when all of a sudden we were stopped by this guy who recognised him. The odds must be heavily against something like that in a crowded foreign city. It turned out to be another boxer - one whom Bert had met several years before, called Gus Lesnovitch. Bert had last met him at a bout in Leeds where he had fought Freddie Mills, who was later to become a murder victim said to have 'gangland' connections. We enjoyed Bert's surprise meeting with Gus, being brought up-to-date on the then current fight scene in New York. Looking back, those were great times and to quote one of my late-mate Chis' favourite sayings: "…face it guys, this really is living it up…"!

Robert (Bert) Johnston Alva Albion Rangers, Sunderland and Scotland, centre half. As with many of his contemporaries, Bert's career was cruelly interrupted during his prime years by the war, but for which, surely, many more honours would have been in store?

LFS and Bert Johnston *(Courtesy of the Daily Express)*

Born north of the border 2 June 1909, Bert joined the English First Division club from the Scottish junior club at 19 and steadily worked himself through the ranks to a first team debut in April 1931, replacing injured Jock McDougall, in a 3-0 win against West Ham United. A regular place came by 1933-34, having made 7 appearances in each of his two post-debut seasons. Full international honours followed his consistent performances at the heart of SAFC's defence. He was a member of the squad who won the First Division title in 1936 and played centre half in the 1937 F.A. Cup winning side. By the outbreak of war, Bert had accumulated some 164 League and Cup appearances for SAFC.

At the end of the war, having guested for Lincoln during it, Bert joined the training staff at Sunderland as assistant trainer, before quickly becoming the first team trainer. Like manager Bill Murray, Bert became a victim of a clear-out at the club – after 29 years' loyal service in Bert's case - following the infamous 'illegal payments' enquiry and suspension of several directors, in the wake of the so-called 'Bank of England' side.

Not generally known was the fact that, during the four close seasons after the war, Bert coached in Norway and even turned down a lucrative offer to coach the Norwegian international team due to family considerations here at home. Just like my friend Barney Ramsden, who took on a similar post-war role for the Norwegians (see chapter 12), Bert would certainly notice a difference were he still alive today! Starting with the amateur sides he helped foster, the Norwegians have gone from strength-to-strength and achieved a level of proficiency out of all proportion to the meagre size of the country's population. In no small way this is testimonial to the expert guidance provided all those years ago by Bert and his colleagues, at a vital stage in the development of Scandinavia's modern game!

... and finally, Belmont Park, Long Island, New York, May 10th 1955, photo on club house terrace - SAFC with First FC of Nurenberg, Germany, German American FA and hosts. At a race meeting where there is full access to all jockeys and trainers, you would think that you could win a good few bucks - but never have I lost so much money, in as much comfort, in all my life!

Bert's FA Charity Shield Winner's Medal 1936 *(Courtesy of The Johnston Family)*

Bert's FA (English) Cup Competition Winner's Medal 1936-37 *(Courtesy of The Johnston Family)*

HIGH GUN
WINNER OF
THE BELMONT
JUNE 12, 1954

BELMONT
PARK

Westchester Racing Association

PRICE FIFTEEN CENTS

FOURTEENTH DAY
TUESDAY, MAY 10, 1955

WESTCHESTER RACING ASSOCIATION

250 PARK AVENUE, NEW YORK 17, N. Y.

DOUBLE ON FIRST AND SECOND RACES
WINDOWS WILL OPEN AT
12:00 AND
CLOSE AT 1:05 SHARP

$2 DAILY DOUBLE TICKETS SOLD IN
Grandstand Area CASHIER'S WINDOWS 46 to 82
Mezzanine Area CASHIER'S WINDOWS 225 to 238
Lower Club House Area CASHIER'S WINDOWS 416 to 430
Upper Club House CASHIER'S WINDOWS 504 to 509

$10 DAILY DOUBLE TICKETS SOLD IN
Grandstand Area CASHIER'S WINDOWS 7 to 9
Lower Club House Area CASHIER'S WINDOWS 411 to 413

JAMAICA uncashed winning tickets should
be sent by registered mail ONLY to
METROPOLITAN JOCKEY CLUB
Room 1350, 60 East 42nd Street, New York 17, N. Y.

AQUEDUCT
QUEENS COUNTY JOCKEY CLUB
250 Park Avenue, New York 17, N. Y.

SARATOGA
THE SARATOGA ASSOCIATION
250 Park Avenue, New York 17, N. Y.

PLEASE DO NOT DESTROY OR DISCARD PARI-MUTUEL TICKET UNTIL RESULT IS <u>OFFICIAL</u> AND YOU ARE CERTAIN IT HAS NO VALUE. CONSULT MUTUEL INFORMATION CLERK IN ANY CASE OF DOUBT REGARDING YOUR PARI-MUTUEL TICKET.

PLEASE CHECK YOUR MONEY BEFORE LEAVING WINDOW

Belmont Park, Long Island, New York, May 10th 1955 *(Courtesy of Brian Leng)*

41

~ Chapter 3 ~
Shack after Newcastle United days -
The Brian Leng interview

Introduction

The 1950's have long been regarded as the golden age of British football. It was an era which produced many of the greatest players in the history of the game and who the crowds flocked in their thousands to see, knowing that they would probably be watching something so special, that they would still remember it in 30 or 40 years time. Performers who even now, almost half a century on, still enjoy legendary status in football circles - the likes of Matthews, Finney, Mannion, Lofthouse, Wright, Milburn and, in my view, the greatest of the lot - Len Shackleton.

In actual fact, I was a Shack fan even before I had seen him play, such was his reputation whenever I overheard football being discussed. As an eight-year-old football fanatic eagerly awaiting his first visit to Roker Park, just listening to my father and his pals recalling the great man's performances, was sufficient to convince me that here was a player who was very special indeed.

When the day of that very first pilgrimage to Roker finally arrived, I wasn't disappointed. Even though the lads in red and white lost 2-0 to Spurs, Shack was absolutely outstanding and for years afterwards I, along with countless others, marvelled at the great man's unbelievable talent with a football. My only regret is that I never managed to see him perform away from home, particularly at Highbury, a ground where he produced his most extravagant displays of showmanship just to remind 'The Gunners' how wrong they were to reject him as a youngster!

I was delighted to be introduced to Len a few years ago and I'm proud to say that we have remained good friends ever since. As a footballer, Shack was a unique talent who will never be forgotten by those who were fortunate enough to see him play. As a person, you really couldn't meet a nicer man.

(Brian Leng - The Wearside Roar)

Brian   Once you had made your mind up to leave Newcastle there were a number of clubs chasing your signature, when did you first discover that Sunderland were interested in signing you?

Len   We were living in Gosforth at the time, when one night there was a knock on the door. My wife Marj went to answer it, and discovered a funny little man with his collar turned up and his trilby pulled down over his face. The guy didn't say who he was, just that he wanted to speak to me.

When I went to see for myself, he introduced himself as Jack Hall, team scout for Sunderland. He continued: "I've got Bill Murray, the Sunderland manager, in his car just around the corner and he wants to speak to you."

I had to think quickly so I told him we were going out. We weren't of course, but I reasoned that if he was keen enough to come at night it would do no harm to make him wait another couple of hours. So we

Manager Mr Bill Murray hard at work
(*Courtesy of the Sunderland Echo*)

went out, although I have to confess we couldn't get back quickly enough!

It must have been after 10 o'clock when there was another knock at the door. Sure enough, it was Jack Hall again, still with his collar up and his hat pulled over his face! He took me to the next street where Bill Murray was waiting in his car. It wasn't parked under a lamp-post but in the shadows in between, so there was less chance of being spotted, it was real cloak and dagger stuff!

Bill Murray came straight to the point and said: "We want you to come and join us at Sunderland." Well, you have to remember in those days nobody was supposed to talk to the player first but United must have made it known that there was to be an auction, and they were going to take the best price.

Brian   How had Sunderland gained advance knowledge that you might be available?

Len   I later discovered that Colonel Prior, the Sunderland chairman, had learned this from a 'contact' at St. James' Park and also that the highest bidder would get the first opportunity to talk to the player. Apparently they had told Colonel Prior that the bidding was expected to be around £20,000 and if Sunderland could beat that figure then they could discuss a potential interest in me without any binding commitment. It transpired later that Sunderland had bid £20,050 which is where the extra £50 is accounted for. Hence Bill Murray had effectively squared-up the transfer by talking to me, to establish if I wanted to come, about two days before the deadline.

Brian   At the time the fee was a British record, just as it had been when you joined Newcastle from Bradford.

Colonel Prior, Chairman only a short time after LFS's arrival *(Courtesy of the Sunderland Echo)*

Len   That's right, but the ironical thing was, Sunderland had pulled out of the bidding when I was at Bradford because they thought the fee was too high. Yet, within 18 months, they had to pay another £7,000 for me!

Brian   How did the Sunderland fans react to the club signing a player from their arch rivals?

Len   To be honest the fans were absolutely brilliant, just as they had been at Newcastle. In fact, that was one of the main considerations when I decided to join Sunderland. The people in the North East are really smashing and I certainly didn't want to leave the area, so moving to Roker Park was ideal in that respect.

Brian   How different was the set-up at Sunderland compared to what you had experienced at St. James'?

Len   Sunderland was a great club and really looked after its players. As well as that, of course, they were in the First Division, so the quality of opposition was much higher. Having said that, my first match in red and white stripes was against Barnsley in a friendly at Roker Park which had been arranged after Sunderland were knocked out of the F.A. Cup. If I remember rightly, it went quite well and we scored four or five.

Brian   Your first season at Roker turned out to be something of a struggle, with the club only avoiding relegation by the narrowest of margins. How difficult was it for a new player joining a club in that situation?

Len   My first game in the First Division was against Derby County at the Baseball Ground and we ended up getting walloped *5-1*. When I arrived home late that night I told Marj: "I'm afraid I've dropped the biggest clanger in my life joining this club. I think they've just bought me to try and keep them up, but there's no way I can save them, they're bound to be relegated!"

Brian   The following season saw a significant change in the club's fortunes, however, and a year later they almost clinched the championship.

Len   That's right, we went very close that season. In fact, we were in pole position for most of the campaign but lost a vital home game against Manchester City towards the end of the season that effectively cost us the title. It was one of those games that stays with you for years - an absolute nightmare! City hadn't won away from home all season and actually ended up being relegated. We, on the other hand, were undefeated at Roker Park so the game looked to be a formality. Unfortunately it turned out to be one of those days when nothing went right and we ended up losing 2-1. We even missed a penalty, and when the referee ordered the kick to be retaken because the goalkeeper had moved, poor Jackie Stelling missed again!

Jackie Stelling *(Courtesy of the Sunderland Echo)*

Brian   It was during this period that the club began to invest heavily in the transfer market. How did you feel about the club trying to buy success?

Len   They had the right idea certainly, but they carried it out in the wrong way. Buying the best players is fine but you have to blend them into a fully balanced side. Unfortunately, Sunderland didn't manage to do it.

Brian Sunderland's spending power earned them the nickname 'The Bank of England Club'. Did other teams resent the club because of that?

Len   I think they did, yes, but they couldn't resent it too much because we didn't win anything, although we did come close on a number of occasions.

Brian Losing at the semi-final stage and missing out on an F.A. Cup final appearance in consecutive years must have been a bitter experience.

Len   It certainly was and on one of those occasions, 1955, we would have met Newcastle in the final which would have been a fantastic day for the North-East. Unfortunately, it was Manchester City who beat us again in the semi-final on a quagmire of a pitch at Villa Park. It may sound like sour grapes, but that game really shouldn't have been played. There was so much water lying on the pitch that the players could hardly move the ball more than a few yards, and as a contest it was a complete farce.

LFS putting the ball between Messrs Barmes and Paul at the Villa Park semi-final.

For me personally though, the following year when we lost to Birmingham City at Hillsborough, was an even greater disappointment. Our eldest son, Graham, was just a youngster at school at the time and I promised him that if we managed to get to Wembley, he could go too and see the Queen at the Cup Final. Naturally, he was very excited because the papers were full of it so you can imagine the level of disappointment when we were beaten. With hindsight though, it probably taught him a very important lesson - that you can't win everything and you have to learn to lose and, more importantly, learn to lose properly. So, if nothing else, that semi-final defeat gave one member of my family a very important lesson in life.

Brian Even though there were some great players in the game in those days such as Matthews, Finney and Mannion, you were widely regarded as the most skillful of the lot. Was that a natural talent or did you have to practice regularly?

Len No, not really, but I did play quite a lot of head tennis with one or two of the lads and that certainly helped perfect the art of ball control. Some afternoons, instead of going back to training, we would set up a game under the main stand at Roker Park. Normally I partnered Ken Chisholm against Ray 'Bebe' Daniel and Ted Purdon. Now 'Chis' was the sort of player who had the knack of always playing to his capabilities.

He was never a great player but because he performed consistently in just about every game, he was successful. To be honest, he wasn't particularly fast and couldn't shoot brilliantly but he was quite skillful and could head a ball - so I'd chosen my partner well! We would play for 'five bob' a time and, on average, we'd win about five out of seven games. To be honest, we could have beaten them every time but we had to let them win a couple otherwise we'd have cleaned them out!

Our 'head tennis' opponents 'Bebe' and 'Purdy' *(Courtesy of the Sunderland Echo)*

Brian   Compared to the ball used in the modern game. How difficult was the old leather 'casey' to control?

Len   I would have really loved to have played with the ball we have today. I was pretty good with the old leather ball but with the modern ball I would have been an absolute sensation, believe me! You also have to remember that in my day the weight of the ball varied dramatically depending on the weather conditions. For example, whenever the fixtures were announced, I would always check to see when we were playing Bolton away. If it was in the middle of the season around February say, then Shack wasn't playing!

Burnden Park was a notoriously heavy pitch at the best of times and Bolton used to soak the ball in a bucket of water from the Thursday to Saturday and by kick-off time it was like a ball of lead. And then you would have Tommy Banks, the Wanderers' full-back kicking seven bells out of you. No, if it was Bolton in February, no way was I playing!

Brian   Bearing in mind that there were quite a few hard men around in those days. Didn't anyone try to hammer you during games?

Len   Of course they did, in fact, in just about every game we played, there was always someone who would set out to kick Shack, but fortunately very few did. Roy Paul of Manchester City was a typical example. He was a fearsome looking character who wouldn't shave from a Wednesday and would frighten the living daylights out of you. He would kick an opponent over the stand if he got the chance - he never managed to kick Shack though!

Mind you, probably the hardest of the lot was one of my own team-mates at Roker Park, Billy Elliott. Billy and I had played together as kids at Bradford and I recommended him to Bill Murray, the Sunderland manager. Nothing happened for a while so I got in touch with Billy and he said he would be keen to come, but then Burnley appeared on the scene and he ended up signing for them. It was another two years before he eventually joined Sunderland and by then Bill Murray had to fork out £30,000 for him!

Two very 'hard men' - Billy Elliott and Roy Paul. *(Courtesy of the Sunderland Echo)*

Billy was a great player to have on your side and, in my opinion, was every bit as good - if not better than - the likes of Roy Keane, Norman Hunter and Billy Bremner. He stopped other players playing - that was his strength - to stop those that could play. Billy could play in a variety of roles but I reckon left-half was far and away his best position. Having said that he was capped for England at outside-left, although that didn't really prove anything, such were the talents of the England selectors at the time!

Brian   Throughout your career you were always something of a showman, hence your nickname, 'The Clown Prince of Soccer'. Were you conscious that the crowds were turning up in their thousands just to witness your special brand of football skills?

Len   I used to love to entertain the fans, certainly, but more often than not it was a time-wasting tactic. For example, when I sat on the ball at Arsenal, it was my way of saying to the home fans: "We've got the ball, we're winning and if we've got the ball, your lot are not going to score!" So it was a tactical thing, not just playing to the crowd.

Mind you that sort of thing can sometimes backfire on you. I remember one year playing against Charlton at The Valley and receiving the ball on the touchline in front of the massive open terracing packed with home supporters. So I dribbled up the line, showing a bit of ball control and just keeping the ball in play. I was enjoying myself, having a bit of fun and really annoying the supporters when the blinking linesman flags for a throw-in, anticipating the ball going out of play, even though it never actually did. Now, what can you do when the linesman makes a decision like that? I looked a right Charlie in front of the 30,000 or so fans on The Kop, I can tell you!

The sequel to that story happened a week later against Arsenal at Roker Park. Our right-winger, Billy Bingham, managed to break through just before half-time and fire in a shot which George Swindon in the Arsenal goal could only parry. The ball broke to me inside the six-yard box with an open goal in front of me. All I needed to do was stick it into the empty net but I noticed George, on all fours, scrambling towards me in the mud. So I took the ball to the goal-line, beckoned him towards me saying: "Haway George, it's not in yet!" Then, as he lunged for the ball, I rolled it over the line.

Now, that was my way of paying-back the linesman for the week before. And, as if in confirmation of the point I was making, the referee had already given a goal and was heading back to the centre-circle. He'd anticipated the ball was in, even though it hadn't crossed the line.

Unfortunately, when we returned to the dressing room at half-time I was immediately confronted by Bill Murray who was really annoyed. "Hey Shack," he shouted, "If the referee had only been half as clever as you thought you were, he would have given a bounce-up, because once he had blown the whistle the ball was dead, and that was before it had crossed the line!"

Well, you do things sometimes and you learn by your mistakes when you realise how they can rebound on you. Fortunately, the referee hadn't been as quick as Bill Murray!

Brian Apart from your tricks with a football, you were also famous for one particular piece of skill with a half-a-crown. How did that come about?

Len It was actually when Don Revie arrived at the club and he was in the dressing-room bragging to the lads about his latest trick. He was flicking a sixpence

Sometimes 'the showman', Don Revie in SAFC colours
(Courtesy of the Sunderland Echo)

up in the air, catching it on his foot and, after about the third attempt, flicking back up in the air and catching it in his blazer pocket. Ray Daniel was having a go, because his ego was enormous, but he couldn't manage it because you've got to practice it.

So, after a few days Revie says to me, "Hey, Shack, are you not going to have a go?" He must have imagined I would be keen to have a go the first time he demonstrated it, but I didn't want to, not until I had practiced it first! So I practiced at home for a few days using a half-a-crown. Then, one morning when all the lads were in the dressing room getting ready for training, I said to Revie: "Hey Revie, have a look at this will you, what about this?" I wasn't flicking it a foot-and-a-half in the air as Revie had, but right up to the ceiling, catching it on my foot, then lobbing it back up into my blazer pocket. That was great - stealing the thunder from Revie, 'the show-off'.

The follow-up to that story is that many years later I was invited to do an interview on the 'One o'Clock Show' at Tyne Tees Television. Before the show the interviewer asked: "Can you do the trick with the sixpence?" I corrected him joking: "It's not a sixpence, it's half-a-crown - do you mind?" I agreed to do it though, and during rehearsals decided to have a bit of fun. Two or three times I tried the trick and failed, on purpose of course, just to see the reaction of the interviewer. I assured him that I would be okay, but because the show was live, the poor guy was worried sick. Fortunately, when the show went out everything went to plan, but I would have looked a complete chump if I hadn't done it properly!

Brian As well as being football's greatest showman during the 1950's you also had a reputation for being something of a rebel. Would you say that was a fair description?

Len Not really a rebel - frustrated, yes - because the game was wrongly run, wasn't it? I can remember that I played one season for £17 a week and that was the biggest wage I ever received as a professional footballer. Now, money didn't motivate me then and it doesn't motivate me now, but it's all about fairness. I would say that nobody fought harder than I did to get the maximum wage lifted, because it was wrong, it's a simple as that.

Brian You weren't exactly popular with the authorities, particularly after the 'blank page' hit the bookshelves. Did that bother you?

Len Not in the least, in fact, I think they were half expecting me to have a go at them. I remember Bill Murray pulling me to one side and asking: "I hear you're writing a book Shack, I hope it's not going to be too naughty?" When I asked him to elaborate, he told me that Alan Hardaker, the secretary of The Football League, had been in touch and had indicated that they were going to come down on me really hard if my literary efforts were 'over the top', as he put it.

But that didn't deter me, I was determined to write what I felt, what I believed in. I told Bill the book was intended to be constructive, not destructive but if they didn't like it they could do what they liked, even if that meant putting me out of the game.

Brian How did the idea of the blank page come about?

Len Completely out of the blue really. A journalist called David Jack helped me by editing the book and we used to meet up at our house in Seaburn every Friday night. He would stay with us over the weekend and we would do a few pages together. One weekend, after we had been working at it for a few weeks, I said: "Hey David, we're going to have a break, let's take the day off and go out somewhere." I then threw a blank sheet of paper onto the table. "What's that supposed to be?" he asked, to which I replied, "The average director's knowledge of football!" He thought that was a great idea even though I had only intended it as a joke. But he had the journalistic mind about the situation and insisted that we include the blank page in the book.

Brian How much interest in the book do you think the blank page generated?

Len I don't think it was just the blank page that created the interest, it was also the first book that had been written by a footballer playing hell about the game. Sales were phenomenal really but, unfortunately, the publishers had not anticipated such a huge demand and had printed insufficient copies. They were printing it as fast as they could. This was in the September and by Christmas they were on the 5th Edition!

Brian How did the people running the game react?

Len There was a load of publicity about the authorities putting me out of the game and stupid stuff like that, but whenever I met directors from other clubs their reaction was just the opposite. For example, shortly after the book was published we played Portsmouth at Roker and before the game I went down to the foyer to meet one or two of their players who I knew personally. Then one of the Portsmouth directors came over and introduced himself and then added: "I think the book is great Len, absolutely brilliant!" At first that surprised me but then it suddenly dawned on me what was happening. He obviously didn't think of himself as the *average* director - none of them did. They obviously thought: "Oh, he's not talking about me, it's the other lot."

Brian On reflection, do you think your outspoken approach cost you the England caps your talent clearly deserved?

Len Without doubt, and whilst I did manage to win five full caps, I have always felt I should have won more. To be honest, the England set-up was a complete shambles in those days and the manager, Walter Winterbottom, was absolutely useless. I remember he always wore a tracksuit with 'WW' on the front - I used to call him 'Washer-Woman'!

As a typical example, we were playing the League of Ireland in Dublin and on the morning of the match Walter proceeded to give us his tactical talk. Starting with our keeper, big Frank Swift, he said: "Frank, when you get the ball, throw it out to Eric Westwood... Eric you pass it to Harry Johnston, Harry move it up to Peter Harris..." He went through the entire team, mimicking all the playing actions as he spoke, until finally the ball ends up in the box. "And you Shack," he nodded to me, "You kick it in!" Can you credit it, at such a level, "You kick it in!", he couldn't even say shoot! Apart from that he'd ignored one minor detail - the opposition, where were they in all this. So I couldn't resist it and replied: "Which corner would you like it in, Walter?"

If I remember rightly, we won 5-0, I scored two goals, but it was another four years before I got a cap!

Brian Of course, you were playing in a team of internationals virtually every week at Roker and it was widely rumoured that Sunderland were able to attract the best players simply because they paid a little extra. Was that the case?

Joe McDonald and fellow Scotsman 'Chis' *(Courtesy of The Sunderland Echo)*

Len Well, I have no idea what the club might have paid the rest of the lads, but I'll tell you of one little incident and you can draw your own conclusions. It happened just after Joe McDonald, the Scottish international full-back, had joined us from Falkirk. Joe was a lovely guy but very naive and one morning before training, Ken Chisholm decided to wind him up about his signing-on fee. Of course, Joe hadn't actually received a penny but Chis was telling him that all the lads had received substantial sums when they joined Sunderland and he should demand the same.

One by one, Joe went around the dressing-room asking each player how much they had received. Of course, by now all the lads were joining in on the joke until eventually Joe says: "I'm going up to see the boss and demand a signing-on fee, how much should I ask for Chis?" Chis replied: "A grand, you've got to ask for at least a grand!"

"Right, I'm going up to see him now!" said Joe, storming out of the dressing room. As you can imagine, all the lads were waiting for the raised voices from Bill Murray's room when suddenly Joe pops his head around the door and says: "Er, sorry Chis, but what's a grand?"

Poor Joe was so naive - I mean you've got to be naive to try for a signing on fee three weeks after you've signed!

Brian Eventually, however, Sunderland's alleged 'under the counter payments' to players landed the club in serious bother with the authorities. What do you recall about the events surrounding the so-called 'illegal payments' scandal?

Len I can remember the Football League held a commission which resulted in our chairman, Bill Ditchburn, and the players involved being banned from the game sine die. I wasn't involved personally because the investigation didn't go back as far as the time I joined the club.

Brian How do you think the scandal affected the club?

Len Most of the players involved had already moved on to other clubs, so it didn't affect the playing side too much. Soon afterwards, of course, the bans were overturned by the courts so the players were able to resume their careers. Unfortunately, Bill Ditchburn never managed to regain power because, by then Syd Collings had taken over as chairman and eventually went on to become chairman of the England International Selection

Messrs. Ditchburn and Collings, Directors/Chairmen *(Courtesy of the Sunderland Echo)*

Committee as well. I remember upsetting him years later when I called him a 'laundry-man' in one of my newspaper articles. Well, he owned and ran a laundry, and as far as I was concerned, that's exactly what he was - a 'laundry-man'. Imagine that qualifying him to be in charge of the England set-up! In my view, such things are too important to be operated as someone's hobby.

Brian Your final season with Sunderland also coincided with the arrival of Alan Brown as manager and the club being relegated to the Second Division for the first time in its entire history. How much of a disappointment was that to you personally?

Len A big disappointment, naturally, although I only played one game that season, against Arsenal at Roker Park, so you can't blame me!

As far as Alan Brown was concerned, I thought he was a terrible manager and events proved it - he took them down in his first season, and as if that wasn't bad enough, he came back 12 years later and did it again!

New 'Brown' sweeps clean at SAFC
(Courtesy of the Sunderland Echo)

Brian It was a troublesome ankle injury that eventually forced you to quit the game. When did you first realise that your playing career might be coming to an end?

Len I'd had the bad ankle for about five years before Brown joined Sunderland. I suppose you could say I was only functioning by using my natural ability and, basically, that's what kept me going. As I mentioned earlier, the last match I played was against Arsenal on the opening day of the 1957-58 season and my ankle 'went' completely in the first-half. After the match, Johnny Watters, our physiotherapist, assessed the damage and recommended I should see a specialist consultant in Barnsley the following Monday.

As soon as I returned home that night, I called my family doctor, Dr Rodger George, who was also a personal friend and asked for his opinion. To me, Barnsley was a strange location for a so-called expert and, seeing that my career was on the line, I wanted to make absolutely certain I was getting the very best advice. But our doctor advised me, that not even the best Harley Street specialist could tell us anything we didn't already know. He also suggested that if I didn't follow the club's advice and see their specialist, then it could be misconstrued as a way out of the game of my own making.

So, on the Monday, I headed down to Barnsley to keep the appointment but the specialist decided that I should come back that Wednesday for a manipulative operation under anaesthetic. I received the results of the operation on the Thursday and it really came as no surprise when I was told I must quit the game immediately. "If you don't..." the specialist concluded, "...you'll almost certainly end your days as a cripple."

I tried to be philosophical about the situation. After all, at 35, I had lasted for a good while and had enjoyed a marvellous career.

Brian   Having been a great servant to the club for ten years. How did Sunderland reward your efforts?

Len   In those days you didn't qualify for a testimonial match automatically as they do today, it was very much at the discretion of the club. I had asked Alan Brown about the prospects of a benefit match, as they were called in those days, and he said he would enquire about it, but I soon formed the impression that he was stalling. I then went to see one of the directors, Jack Parker, whom I believed to be a decent sort and he said he would put it to the board, but never did.

Finally, somewhat in desperation, I decided to approach the chairman Syd Collings. I had remembered that when I was transferred from Newcastle to Sunderland it was Collings who had approached me and said: "Look, you'll be paid a fee but, if you don't get it by any chance, come and see me and I'll sort it out." I thought it was very decent of him at the time but I had never had the need to put him to the test. They might have been empty words, perhaps?

I actually confronted him in the dressing-room in front of one or two of the lads and, having stated my case, I reminded him: "Mr. Collings, isn't it fortunate that the Football League enquiry didn't go back as far as when you and I joined the club?" I can still see him today as I looked right under his collar button and watched him begin to sweat visibly. "Well, Mr. Collings," I continued, "What about a benefit match?" And, would you believe, it was passed by the board within a week!

But don't you think it's terrible when you have to resort to those sort of tactics with the so-called pillars of respectability in the establishment simply to claim something that you should be entitled to as a matter of course. And can you understand why, having discovered what really lies behind that apparent respectability, I have become labelled as something of a rebel? It's quite ironical, because I'm not really - but fortunately God-given talent enabled me to win back a little against the otherwise quite blatant exploitation.

Brian   Finally, does the man who began his football career in Bradford all those years ago have any regrets about moving to the North East and spending the best part of his playing career with Sunderland?

Len   Not in the least. I love the place and, more especially, I love the people. Even though I was born in Yorkshire and now live in Cumbria, I still consider the North East to be my home. The only problem is, whenever I return to the area, the Newcastle fans always accuse me of being biased towards Sunderland, but I always tell them: "Listen, I've nothing against the Newcastle fans, it's the set-up at the club - I don't care who beats them!"

(Editor's note: "someone mentioned the War then, but I think we got away with it!").

~ Chapter 4 ~
East Africa 1956
Closed Season Exhibition Tour

Another splendid time that really stands out in my memory was a tour of East Africa.

BI s.s. 'UGANDA'

A wonderful trip, on a cruise ship, taking three weeks from the Royal Albert Dock in London out to Mombasa, on the S.S. "Uganda".

To start at the beginning though, during that football season I received a letter from the Football Association of Kenya inviting me to go out and play some exhibition matches during our country's closed, summer season. This was also in association with the Tanganyika F.A. and promised to provide some interesting football in an exotic setting. I asked permission from my club (Sunderland), which was forthcoming, so I wrote back to accept the invitation, little expecting the extent of the official disapproval which descended upon me, proving me to be a slave to the FA system (see Annex to this chapter for supporting details). I was happy with the combination of expenses and the playing fee offered but, having thought about their proposal, asked for a favour. I explained that, at home, a lot of my time was spent in winter travelling to away matches usually over whole weekends. This was

because SAFC was somewhat 'out on a geographical limb'. Because I lost a lot of time in this way, I wanted to make up for it by travelling to East Africa by ship, rather than by air, and to be accompanied by my wife and eldest boy, Graham who was then only about 9 years old.

B. I. s.s. 'UGANDA' — 1st CLASS 2 BERTH BATHROOM CABIN

Fortunately my request was well received, without any problems at all. The deal became all expenses (travelling, hotels, etc.) paid, plus about £250 as a playing fee. There were about eight exhibition matches involved. It may not sound so, but this proved to be really quite demanding - following the hard, home season's soccer - and also involving some coaching.

Looking back to the mid-1950's now with hindsight, what caused me most surprise at the time was the general high quality of play. Given the relatively rudimentary facilities available to those African people and the early level of the game's development on that continent, this level of quality was all the more of a surprise. I

soon discovered that the original idea of playing for the 'expat' Europeans *against* the African teams was going to be a positive disadvantage. This was because many of the Europeans had spent little time training, but a lot of time 'living-it-up'. They

were mostly unfit as a result. However, the native East Africans were much more impressive. In fact they were quite brilliant! They were as fit as the metaphorical 'butcher's dog' and had great natural ability. I felt that all they were lacking was some improved facilities, combined with expert coaching to get their talents properly harnessed to the game. It struck me at the time that black people were going to form future teams to be feared by the rest of soccer. I believe this view has been borne-out, when you consider the subsequent achievements made in international tournaments?

One particular match I recall was played at Dar-Es-Salaam. The stands were packed - a complete 'full house'. Indeed even the tall, coconut palms around the ground were full of spectators - and they really *were* tall trees out there! Some locals had climbed up to get a better view, particularly behind the goals. I remember taking a penalty and made out with a really long run-

up, that I was intending to shoot hard and squared-up to shoot to the left. After the run-up though, all I did was push the ball in to the other corner of the goal with the inside of my foot! Well, when the (European) goalkeeper dived the other way the African people went wild, cheering and shouting. A good few of that end's spectators even fell out of the trees in their enthusiasm!

Unfortunately, some were injured and had to be taken to hospital to get 'patched-up'. A great shame, particularly as they were such lovely, friendly people who were obviously so keen on the game.

Another incident concerns a match played in Zanzibar. A beautiful little island we were fortunate enough to visit. Part of the itinerary involved a match against the prison team! The whole party was taken to a gaol and my wife, Marjorie, was even shown around the women's section by the female governor of that part of the prison. It was a pretty eye-opening experience. Inmates were identified with their, sometimes gruesome crimes, including murder. The same was, of course, true of the male inmates and general conditions were harsh. It seemed that the prison had a wide selection of robbers, murderers and drugs-peddlers. The planned match was staff v prisoners. Playing for the former meant facing formidable opposition - or so it appeared to me, being a natural-born-coward with a low pain threshold! I remember thinking that I really didn't want to be in the middle of all that. I didn't want to face a frustrated murderer venting his pent-up emotions and seeking revenge on society by kicking 'hells bells' out of Shack! That wasn't a good idea as far as I was concerned. Very fortunately all passed-off well, without too many 'red cards' or trips to the infirmary, but I was still mighty relieved when it was all over.

When the time came to return home, the closeness of the start to the next home season posed a problem. When we were still in Nairobi the K.F.A. Secretary, Bob Whittingham, offered to arrange for a special car to take us all the way to the northern end of the continent. He suggested it should meet the ship at Port Said so that we could still return by sea. However, the plan seemed too tight and, in the end, our return had to be by air. With this though, came another problem, to arrange for the shipping of the many 'souvenirs' for family and friends. We had bought these throughout the several African countries visited, using the playing fees. So much had been gathered on this trip-of-a-lifetime, that we had to buy additional luggage to supplement outward journey's cabin trunk and small suitcases. There were all manner of things. Ornately carved small tables (one each for my sister and sister-in-law), a large leather drum and many carved, wooden ornaments. We ended up with a full cabin trunk plus about seven or eight separate cases. Bob Whittingham kindly offered to send it by air freight to London, for later collection out of Customs 'bond' and I think the bill was something like £40 which was 2 or 3 weeks' top football wages at home. Our hosts had been very hospitable and their continuing generosity really was the icing on a very special cake for my family and I. We had been given VIP treatment wherever we went and I'll always be grateful to the people of that time and place.

When we landed at Heathrow the luggage was brought out of 'bond' and laid-out on a long trestle table in the Customs Hall. We were approached by a uniformed officer who enquired about the identity of our luggage, by now about a dozen or so large items. The officer asked where we had been - I hoped that he was interested in football - and so I explained that I had been on a footballing exhibition tour. Fortunately, he recognised my surname, but he still demanded to know the contents of our luggage. Well, I had to be honest and said that it was more or less a case of 'you name it, we've got it'! There was no contraband and we were not attempting to smuggle anything illegal. But any lack of co-operation could have meant hours of delay and we were all very tired. So we were relieved when he went along the line and chalk-marked everything! By the end of this I had to hire *two* taxis to get the three of us (and all our luggage) to Kings Cross, Great Northern. It was hectic getting everything across London to catch the train but people were helpful. Which just goes to show the nature of the 'perks' from playing football at a certain level. Even though wages were nowhere near what they are now (it was before today's mad celebrity excesses), it was a sort of 'VIP treatment' greatly appreciated then and since. I can certainly have no complaints about what football gave to me and my family when you consider experiences such as these!

...and now for a few souvenir snaps to remind everyone of that special trip:-

From meeting the various officials...

64

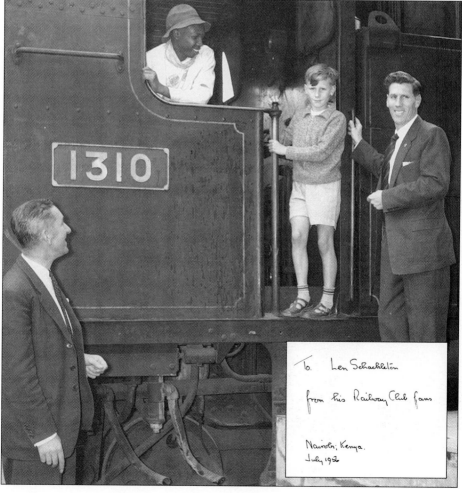

To   Len Shackleton
from his Railway Club fans

Nairobi, Kenya.
July 1956

...to sight-seeing over the Serengeti and Mt Kilimanjaro

...and collecting some new silverware!

~ Annex ~

(The tour that nearly didn't happen!)

FOOTBALL ASSOCIATION OF KENYA
(Affiliated to the F.A.)

Telephone 58031 ext 14
Secretary J.R.Whittingham.
Treasurer

22nd Sept 1955

P.O. Box 234
NAIROBI
Kenya Colony

Mr L Shackleton
C/O.Sunderland F.C.
Roker Park

Dear Sir

I am writing on behalf of my Association to enquire if you would be interested in a short tour of Kenya, say four to six weeks. The tour to take place during the close season of English football.

If your interested we are quite prepared to make the tour well worth your while. The tour would consist of playing games with the Kenya National side in selected parts of the Colony such as Mombasa, Zanzubar and Nairobi. All accomodation and travelling expenses would be borne by my Association and a guarantee of so much per game would be payed to you.

On the receipt of a reply from you we can discuss terms more fully as it is our intention to bring out two star forwards each year to play exhibition games in the Colony.

Tom Finney was here last year and was a great success. All our soccer is played under amatuer status but according to Tom Finney we rate Div three standards.

You will find our terms quite liberal and our hospitality first class and I am sure you would enjoy the sights of our delightfull country which abounds in all types of wild life.

In closing let me congratulate you on your book, I have just read it and think it is a fine example of outspokeness and contains a great deal of truth, perhaps thats why there is a lot of truth in the old saying that nothing hurts so much as the truth.

Hoping to hear from you soon
I remain
Yours Faithfully

Hon. Sec.
F.A. of Kenya.

THE FOOTBALL ASSOCIATION.

PATRON:
HER MAJESTY THE QUEEN.

PRESIDENT:

SECRETARY:
SIR STANLEY ROUS, C.B.E., J.P.

TELEGRAPHIC ADDRESS:
"FOOTBALL ASSOCIATION
PADD. LONDON."

Any reply to this letter should be
addressed to The Secretary and the
following reference quoted.

SLW/MT

22, LANCASTER GATE,
LONDON, W. 2.

27th October 1955

J.H.Whittingham,Esq.
The F.A. of Kenya,
P.O.Box 234.
NAIROBI.

Dear Mr.Whittingham,

Enclosed is a newspaper cutting which suggests
that you do not require us to help you to find a Coach to
visit Kenya during the summer of 1956.

We are not sure that we will give permission for
Mr.Shackleton to act as a Coach to your Association in view of
his attitude to governing bodies. However, this report in the
newspaper may be premature in which case I shall be pleased to
hear from you and to know if there are any other developments in
connection with your proposal to invite one of our players to
Kenya.

Yours sincerely,

Secretary.

Enc.

FA may ban Shack's trip but club do not object

CLOWN PRINCE'S TOUR OF KENYA IN DANGER

Sketch Soccer Reporter

'F.A. censured us—trip off'

By GEOFF WHITTEN

SOCCER NEWS by JAMES CONNOLLY

Shackleton tour mystery- F.A. 'refuse permission

FOOTBALL ASSOCIATION OF KENYA
(Affiliated to the F.A.)

Dear Len. This is purely personel but conveys the feelings of the whole of our members ~~BJ~~

Telephone
Secretary
Treasurer

P.O. Box 234

NAIROBI

Kenya Colony

Mr L Shackleton

15th December 1955

Dear Len

I am in reciept of your letter of the 5th of Dec and the copy of your letter to the F.A. and I fully agree with your sentiments in regard to the whole affair but I would like to point out that the remarks made in the Sunday Graphic are not quite the true state of things as they stand and that the offer to Matthews made not one atom of difference to your case in any shape or form. I wish you to know that the only reason we had for curtailing the negotiations was the objection instituted by the Football Association and whether it was our plan to bring out Matthews, either before, or after, or with you, is irrelevent to the case.

The offer to Matthews still stands although up to the time of writing he has not accepted direct to us and the only intimation we have that he will come is in the reports we see from time to time in the press in England. The most he as ever said is "I hope to be able to make it" but nothing has ever been finalised, but dont think I am trying to avoid the issue , if Stan accepts we are ready and willing to have him here at the terms offered last year when he was in South Africa.

In your case the focal point is whether the F.A. are prepared to lift the ban or no. Depending upon their blessing is the whole case and I am sure that if they gave consent the deal could still be brought to a sucessfull conclusion. We are blamed for muddling the whole affair, that is incorrect for at the time the F.A. lodged their objection we had recieved no reply from either you or Matthews and I have dated letters from you and the F.A. to substantiate that. We are quite in the position to invite two stars out and I am sure we are quite able to asses the profits that would accrue from such a venture. I regret I cannot give you any official dope on the subject at the moment nor until after our next meeting but I can tell you this , If the F.A. raise their objections we are duty bound to stand by our offer moreso in view of the fact that you have cancelled all your own committments in anticipation of making the tour.

I would like the English press to hear both sides of the story before they committ us as muddlers, then perhaps it would be the F.A. who had cause for regret and not us. Dont forget Len, that we alone are in possesion of the true facts relating to the whole unsavoury affair. Despite our poor financial status(to quote the Graphic) we were also making strenuous efforts to obtain the F.A. touring side on the way

Continued overleaf

70

back from their tour of the Union but after months of negotiation with the
South African F.A. who finally agreed to our offer Rous wrote us and said
it would make it hard work for the players but he would see what he could do,
        These offers take money but our main aim is to bring the best to Kenya
and we do all in our power to do this.
        Remember , Len , before you condemn us here that we do not accept the
blame for the hitch that occurred, the onus of that lies with the F.A. and
the next move is up to them, we would love to see you here as well as
Matthews and our offer is still subject to their approval before I can
promise to resume the negotiations.
        Your letter will go before the A.G.M. in January and I personnaly
feel that we must respect our offer and I feel sure that it will also be
the feeling of the majority of the Members of the Council.
        If the reported threat to sue us becomes reality then that is your
affair and we shall have no alternative but to defend ourselves and see
that the blame is placed where it rightly belongs and that is definitly
not here in Kenya. Due to the close season just starting it has not been
possible to convene a meeting to discuss the problem and the misleading
press reports as most of the Members are holidaying at the coast and the
matter has had to be deffered till our meeting of the 5th of Jan. next, it
is also on the agenda for the A.G.M. of the following week.
        Until then I cannot give you any official gen on the subject except my
own feelings in the matter and if it were left to me the trip would definitly
take place as scheduled . I have wrote the F.A. asking why we are being made
the scapegoats for the mix up when but for them there was no mix up at all,
        Our only sin has been that we accepted their ruling in good faith and
for that we are being labelled "blunderers"
        I will let you Know immediately the outcome of our meeting on Jan. the
5th and trust you will see the real side of the matter. If the F.A. relent
I cannot see any other snags in the deal.
                        Yours Faithfully
                                    Hon Sec.

P.S. For the sake of Graham I hope everything turns out as you wish it and
that, Len. is from the bottom of my heart.

THE FOOTBALL ASSOCIATION.

PATRON:
HER MAJESTY THE QUEEN.

PRESIDENT:
H.R.H. THE DUKE OF EDINBURGH, K.G., K.T.

SECRETARY:
SIR STANLEY ROUS, C.B.E., J.P.

TELEGRAPHIC ADDRESS:
"FOOTBALL ASSOCIATION
PADD. LONDON."

Any reply to this letter should be
addressed to The Secretary and the
following reference quoted.

22, LANCASTER GATE,
LONDON, W.2.

SLW/MT

25th January, 1956

L.Shackleton,Esq.
9, Seaburn Terrace,
Sunderland.

Dear Mr.Shackleton,

We have been asked by The F.A. of Kenya to pass
on to you the following offer for a short coaching engagement,
for your consideration:-

> The sum of £250 for a four-week tour, partaking in
> four to six games arranged by The Kenya Football
> Association.

> The dates of the tour to be finalised at a later date
> when it is known at what time Stanley Matthews is
> going to Kenya as they wish to have both Stanley Matthews
> and yourself at separate times.

> The F.A. of Kenya undertake to pay all your expenses
> and those of your wife and son from home to Kenya and
> return and also your accommodation and travelling expenses
> whilst in Kenya - they will also take out the required
> Insurances as stipulated by your club.

> You must give an undertaking that you will not partake
> in any game or attend any Function whilst in Kenya
> without the full sanction of the Kenya F.A.

We shall be pleased to know if you are prepared to
accept the above offer - subject of course to the approval of your
club.

P.T.O.

I assume that the dates of the visit to Kenya will be in May or June after the completion of the playing season in England.

Yours sincerely,

Secretary.

P.S. The Football Association has not publicised this matter and I would suggest that you keep the matter confidential and leave the publicity to this Association after the matter has been finalised.

You will remember that it was the publicity which was given prematurely to your previous invitation which caused complications and embarrassment.

Shackleton delights spectators in first Nairobi game

Fans flocked to watch at Morogoro

By SEASIDER

THE TANGANYIKA STANDARD

SHACK PULLS HIS GAGS, BUT AFRICANS FORCE A DRAW

By FLOTSAM

~ Chapter 5 ~
Critics & Contemporaries

What follows are the views and opinions of some of my contemporaries. These cover my playing career in outline (and briefly afterwards as a journalist, i.e. as part of the *Brian Clough Story*) with the intention of giving an 'outside' perspective on things. Comments are not always favourable but have been included in the interests of balance. The quoted extracts are not ranked in any particular order other than general chronology and subject. Much research has gone into putting this section together and, in choosing extracts from the many books and articles reviewed, I have attempted to fashion a common thread to the story. In order to ensure that the respective authors' views are set, as far as possible, in their original context I have sometimes included quite large extracts.

In making my selection of quotes, I sincerely hope that I have done full justice to their original intentions as well as supplying the reader with an additional, interesting perspective. After all, in making reference to stories about my own career these people were merely making *their* views known as they saw them at the time. Readers will be well able to judge for themselves whether what has been said accurately reflects the truth about the author - one way or the other.

* * *

To start at the beginning. My early career is covered in Malcolm Hartley and Tim Clapham's statistics-packed, 1987 book *'The Avenue (Bradford PA Pictorial History & Club Record)'* with the following brief and relatively uncontroversial description:-

> *"...Shack captained Bradford Boys and gained three schoolboy international caps. He left Carlton School in 1938 and was taken on to the Arsenal ground staff. He* (me) *recalls:* 'One day George Allison came out to do some training with the staff. He put his foot on a railing and called out to me - here boy, come and do these - meaning his laces. I looked at him and I thought, well, I'm only a ground staff boy and he's the manager, **(but I didn't like his patronising attitude)** so I said - tie them yourself - because no one was going to speak to me like that.' *Arsenal did not keep him in May 1939. He made his first appearance for Avenue as an amateur on May 20, 1940, scoring on his debut in a 2-0 win against Hartlepool.*
>
> *Shack turned pro on Christmas Day 1940 and became Avenue's outstanding personality during the war when his great skill and impudent confidence resulted in entertainment in excelsis. He scored 166 goals for Bradford in the wartime period. No one ever hit more for the club..."*

Author's note: Someone once told me that a *Guinness Book of Records* joint entry was earned during those days: "On Christmas Day 1940 two players turned out for two different football clubs on the same day. (**My friend**) Tommy Lawton played for Everton against Liverpool in the morning, then made an afternoon guest appearance for Tranmere Rovers against Crewe Alexandra. Len Shackleton played for the two Bradford Clubs, Avenue (own side) against Leeds in the morning, then guested for City at Huddersfield in the afternoon."

Bradford v Barnsley, FA Cup Tie *(Len Shackleton)*

* * *

Mike Kirkup's 1990 biography of Jackie Milburn provides some interesting comments on other Newcastle players' views of my attitude to the set-up during those (not-always-so) United days:-

"...Bob Stokoe reflected many years later: 'There were so many of us in those days who only wanted to play for Newcastle United; we were black 'n' white daft!... ...But Seymour recognised that the Geordie public, starved of the big time for so long, craved the star attractions... ...chequebook in hand, Seymour plundered the British Isles of the best footballing talent that was available.' The list of players was impressive:

Joe Harvey in 1945 from Bradford City for £4,500
Len Shackleton in 1946 from Bradford for £13,000
Frank Brennan in 1946 from Airdrie for £8,500
Roy Bentley in 1946 from Bristol Rovers for £8,500
Jack Fairbrother in 1947 from Preston for £7,000
Frank Houghton in 1948 from Ballymena for £6,000
George and Ted Robledo in 1949 from Barnsley for £26,500
Bobby Mitchell in 1949 from Third Lanark for £16,000
Alf McMichael and George Hannah in 1950 from Linfield for £20,000

...on 5 October 1946 when the Clown Prince of Soccer took centre stage at St. James' Park, Len Shackleton had arrived! Newport County were the unfortunates to be mesmerised by the magic repertoire of the irrepressible Shack. United's team that day was: Garbutt, Cowell, Graham, Harvey, Brennan, Wright, Milburn, Bentley, Wayman, Shackleton, Pearson. Newcastle thrashed a bedraggled Newport 13-0, with Shack getting six goals! This amazing goals bonanza equalled the highest ever Football League score, and still remains Newcastle's biggest win and record score for the First and Second Divisions (1990). Other scorers were Charlie Wayman (4), Jackie Milburn (2) and Roy Bentley (1). Incredibly, Shackleton (it was actually Wayman - Editor) *had missed with a first-minute penalty..."*

My relatively short time with the club was marred by what I - and many of the fans - believed was wasteful in-fighting between members of the board and inept man management, of which I was not the only victim. This even extended to what should otherwise have been only minor 'domestic' matters:-

"...Yorkshiremen Harvey and Shackleton had still not been housed to their satisfaction in Newcastle, despite numerous promises. Both aired their grievances to Seymour. Inexplicably, on the eve of the 1946-47 semi-final match, top goal-scorer Charlie Wayman was dropped in favour of

Two Yorkshiremen at Newcastle United, 1947 *(Len Shackleton Collection)*

Stobbart. No explanation was given, but there were rumours of a dressing-room rift, hastily refuted afterwards... ...Roy Bentley, living in a flat belonging to the sister of a director, complained that his bath was in a bad state, and requested a new one. It shows much for George Martin's status that it was he, the team manager, who came to inspect Bentley's suspect plumbing. He decided that Roy's plea was a frivolous one, and suggested a new coat of paint would do the trick. Bentley was indignant, and within two months was transferred to Chelsea. That was in January 1948, and one month later Len Shackleton exchanged his black and white cap and bells for the red and white of Sunderland as he took his clowning from Tyne to Wear. Shack's move was brought about by devious player power behind the scenes at St James's..."

Mike Kirkup then goes on to quote directly from Jackie himself giving his own feelings about me at United at that time:-

" ...Shack was unbelievable! If he had had the guts or the will to want to do well, instead of joking and carrying on, he was untouchable as a footballer. He was my labourer at Hazlerigg workshops when I moved there after I left Ashington Colliery. We both had to go there because of this reserved occupation lark. I used to have a motorbike and we went back and forward to St James's three times a week for training. Shack was on the back, both with "wor" pit gear on.

He was absolutely the tops in ball control. He was doing these things all the time in training, making mugs of goalkeepers. I've seen Jack Fairbrother dive at his feet in training, and Shack would just let him come, then just ease the ball away. Whey, the ball was only inches away from Jack's fingers, and Jack was wild-eyed. He would've killed him if he'd got him.

Him and Tommy Pearson gave an exhibition one day at Newcastle against Cardiff when they kept the ball between them with six or seven defenders around them, frightened to death to tackle. And this happened for ninety minutes, before we beat them 4-1.

It was sheer entertainment with Shack. He admitted later on that he had no interest (I had become de-motivated and lost my natural enthusiasm for the game because of surprisingly poor management - represented by board-level disputes and the financial 'racket' that operated even at such a 'top' club - combined with the hypocritically-presented and artificially 'respectable' façade - in effect, both fans and players were being conned) *but he just wanted to feel that he'd entertained the public. Oh, he was unbelievable - but hopeless! Joe Harvey says to George Martin 'We'll never win anything with Shackleton in the team. We've got to get rid of him.'*

And it was true! I've nothing against Len, he was a smashing fella, but he had no interest other than entertaining the crowd. He would rather beat three men than lay on a winning goal. And we got rid of him! He signed for Sunderland..."

There were, however, certain differences between the management styles of the Boards of Newcastle and Sunderland. An insight into this is perhaps best illustrated by Jackie's continuing comments:-

"...Every year in the late forties and early fifties they (Sunderland AFC) *were fighting against relegation. Although they knew what they were doing. 'Cos players used to get a hundred pounds a man for staying in the First Division, for the last six or seven games, stuffed into their boots! It was worth it to the club. Whey, aye! Whereas we never got a penny..."*

Later, to take-up Mike Kirkup's own telling of Jackie's story, we, two former team mates were to find ourselves on the same side again, albeit only temporarily:-

" ...Milburn was chosen to play for the Football League against the Irish League at Liverpool on 20 September 1948. Also in the team was Len Shackleton, by now playing for Sunderland. **(Please see picture on back**

A decade after playing days, journalists and friends *(Courtesy of The Daily Express)*

of dustcover) *To say that Milburn made a great start would be to understate the facts. He scored a brilliant hat-trick, and was dangerous every time he got the ball. Jackie pays tribute to Shack for his own display that day, and says that, leaving his clowning aside for this match, Len gave a service to him that could not fail to produce the three goals he scored..."*

The answer to the question of whether either Jackie or myself would ever get among the caps again in the 1949-50 season - and if England made it to the 1950 World Cup Finals, the prize of a trip to Rio - was answered when we both read in the sporting press:-

" ... 'Milburn and Shackleton picked for England'. Some papers expressed

The Author at 'Wor Jackie's' testimonial *(Courtesy of The Daily Mail)*

surprise at Milburn's inclusion in the side after being released from England's continental tour to go to America with Newcastle and being passed over for the first game of the season against Eire which England lost... ...Jackie joined up with his old pal Shack at the Seabank Hotel, Portcawl, in Glamorganshire; the game was to be at Cardiff. It was a case of the most expensive player in England - Shackleton had moved for £20,050 - playing alongside the Ashington pitman who had cost Stan

Seymour only a tenner. They should in fact have been playing in opposition that Saturday instead of as team-mates. A Sunderland v Newcastle derby took place but, without the two stars, the expected gate never materialised.

Len Shackleton had a great game as England trounced the Welsh 4-1 in front of their own crowd. But if Shack was great, Milburn was tremendous, scoring 3 goals - two of them from headers and making the other goal for Mortenson..."

Jackie later raises the wages issue, which many other players believed was one of my own favourite hobby horses, as demonstrated in the following extract:-

"...That's why I came to admire Shack more than anybody. He insisted that we were playing for buttons. He insisted on this, way back to the war years. Aye! In fact, he came over just before the '51 Final - he was playing for Sunderland at the time - and spoke to the lads. 'Hey, you want to refuse to go on the bloody pitch,' he says, 'because they're making nearly forty thousand pounds on the gate' It was three and a tanner for a ticket then, and about a couple of quid for a seat, or something. And he went through the whole routine of what they were clicking, the FA, and how much they were making, and what we were getting.

Len Shackleton was a man before his time, not only with his inimitable style of play, but also his foresight into what was happening in the game at that time. A great deal of money was being made, with attendances holding up very well, although not as high as in the immediate post-war years. That the money wasn't going to the players was obvious, when the maximum wage at that time was only £12 in season and £10 in summer. Shack, together with players' champion Ernie Clay, (see the George Eastham story and Bosman ruling details in chapter 11) was later to be instrumental in the FA taking a closer look at the whole idea of the maximum wage. The Newcastle lads decided not to take Shackleton's advice, however, the consensus being that if they refused to play, the board would soon draft in another eleven lads more than eager to pull on a black and white strip in a Cup Final..."

Perhaps, based on this final extract (from Mike Kirkup's book), it is easy to understand why I had such disdain for team talks and tactics in that era - when misused in the hands of those with less than a full understanding of what they were about:-

"...Team talks from trainer Smith and manager Seymour tended to be short and to the point... ...Coaching was looked upon as something of a joke by the long-serving pros. Walter Winterbottom had been giving an

England side some slide-rule advice, and ended with: 'When it's on, I want Wright to transfer the ball to Finney, then Finney to Mannion. Mullen and Milburn will then go on dummy runs, and the ball will be switched back to Finney who will get to the bye-line and cross for Shackleton who will put it into the net.' Biding his time, Shack paused before quipping: 'Ah yes, Walter, but what side of the net should I put it in?'

Charlie Crowe, who later became a qualified coach, remembers the coaching jargon that Winterbottom himself coined. One such piece of gobbledygook went: 'On getting the ball use your peripheral *vision.' Charlie says what he meant was: 'Watch your back!...'"*

* * *

This brings me nicely on to a couple of humorous quips from Charlie's own book '*A Crowe amongst the Magpies*':

"...I recall one day that as I was about to take a throw-in, Len pointed at his backside so that he could knock it back to me. He always wanted to do the difficult things. One particular game at St James' Park against Cardiff was typical of the way the supporters were treated to the Shack Magic. After a spell of inter-passing with Tommy Pearson which demoralised the Cardiff defence, Len actually hitched up his shorts, sat on the ball and brought the game to a temporary halt. The crowd were ecstatic. In the same match he tried to do a one-two off the corner flag!

Shack found himself in favour (rarely) *with England coach Walter Winterbottom in the late 1940s, winning a smattering of England caps. But Len did not suffer fools gladly… …The Baseball Ground at Derby was notorious for being nearly all sand. Taking a free-kick, Len teed the ball up on a mound of sand. 'You can't do that,' said the Ref, 'it doesn't say you can do that in the rules'.*
'Ah, yes,' said Len. but there's nothing in the rules to say you can't do it either…"

* * *

My 1955 book *Clown Prince of Soccer* (reproduced as Appendix III to this book for ease of reference) attracted plenty of adverse criticism. Clearly not everyone agreed with my views, frankly expressed as they were, on the then set-up of our national game. To continue with the theme started on the dust cover of this '*Return…*' book, the *Daily Mail* (August 1955) published readers' reactions to their own book review. These included a retired former player, then a director, hitting-back at the blank chapter 9 but firstly some of the readers' letters:-

--- 0 ---

"Shackleton has been a fortunate young man - he has set up three businesses on money received from the game which directors, the object of his scorn, help to finance. If he had been on active service during the war he would have had many shocks far worse than descending a coal mine and he might never have returned to play football - or write a book."
*- **A. E. Shuttleworth, Shipley, Yorkshire.***

--- o ---

*"What a pity that after carefully pin-pointing many of the faults of our football system Shackleton must exaggerate them out of all proportion, thereby destroying the power of his criticism. What a pity his capabilities could not be harnessed and guided in the right direction - he would be the deadliest footballer of his day." - **A. J. Lord, Blackpool.***

--- o ---

After those, now for the director's views referred to. Under the heading of: 'Director Hits Back - At The *Clown Prince* of Football', Mr. Jack Diffin, described as a former professional footballer (Belfast Celtic, Linfield and Shelbourne) with international and inter-League honours; had also been a Board member at Port Vale since 1943. He wrote an open letter from which I quote extracts, as follows:-

" Mr. Shackleton,

First of all, I would like to associate myself with those 'fans' of whom you say: 'They called me the clown prince of football. They called me irresponsible. They called me big 'ead and lots of other uncomplimentary things.' But, believe me, I'm no fan of yours.

Like you, Mr. Shackleton, I have earned my bread and butter as a professional footballer and was proud to do so... ...There's an old saying about 'biting the hand...' Remember it?...

...I feel just as proud of being an 'average director'... I have been on both sides of the fence... forgive me then, if I assume that I do know a little more about these things than even you...

...But ask yourself, Mr. Shackleton, does your prominence in the game give you the right of being unpardonably rude to those 'average directors', the men whose interest in football and footballers has, no doubt, helped in some measure to your present affluence in the business world?...

...I can tell you now that it isn't necessary to have been a footballer to become a successful director. I know directors who have never played football but their knowledge of the game will challenge even yours!...

...Directors provide for the club the most important thing of all ...the cash to enable it to carry on... and you don't, the sportsmen who are continually dipping their hands into their pockets shouting the odds about it...

...Without the 'average director' there would be no need for the Shackletons or the rest. There just would not be any League football clubs...

...You may think it was gracious of you, Mr. Shackleton, to 'mean no disrespect' with your remarks questioning the ability of English Selectors to do that job because of their weekday occupations. Those remarks were cheap and unworthy...

...Think again, Mr. Shackleton! Keep off the trouble-shooting and save your shooting for the football field. You might then even improve your last season's record of eight goals in 32 League games... blank days as well as blank pages, eh?...

...I say hats off to the average directors. Shame on you, Shackleton.
Jack Diffin."

Phew, to use a certain tabloid's favourite expression - what a scorcher - after that little lot, a further couple of readers' letters tending towards the adverse to bring this part to its close. (But before that, a brief reflection). What a pity that the invitation for readers' views was, at that time, in response to the paper's own review, i.e. readers were being invited to send their comments on a book which none of them had yet read! Trying to be as fair-minded and objective as possible, I should not have been perturbed by adverse criticism. Indeed, again at that time, I wrote to the paper myself to say that there was nothing I would like more than to read the reactions of the public to my book, whether good or bad. In responding to what had been printed, the main point I sought to make was this: it would have been fairer to me, the publishers and the paper's readers, to have allowed those readers to see my book *before* asking them to condemn or applaud it, according to their own individual views.

--- 0 ---

"League football needs a thorough spring clean from top to bottom, or maybe a surgical operation would be nearer the mark. Shackleton has diagnosed many symptoms but, unfortunately, he has made it difficult for

the patient to have faith in the doctor. Len! You could have written a book many would have enjoyed. What a pity you have spoiled it." -
A. G. Cross (Rev.), Darlington.

--- 0 ---

*"The fact that Shackleton has two successful confectionery businesses and is now branching out into hairdressing should be sufficient answer in itself to criticism of football directors who have never kicked a ball. Has he ever made a toffee apple or cut a lock of hair?" - **H. Fay, Liverpool.***

* * *

In his 1962 book entitled: '*SOCCER WITH THE STARS*', Billy Bingham raises a point that I would like to develop, when he reflects upon the ability of clubs to buy success, quote:-

Billy, SAFC 1948
(Len Shackleton Collection)

"...As the late Bill Murray used to say when he was manager of Sunderland: 'Success can be earned but it can never be commanded.' ...Aston Villa before the war and Sunderland after it are the two examples most often quoted, though it is conveniently forgotten that Sunderland also successfully bought their way out of trouble at least once before their eventual crash..."

"...Nor has wealth always been merely a means of assuring survival to fight another day, important as that is in itself in a competition where one bad season can put the game's highest honours out of a club's reach perhaps for years..."

"...Newcastle bought big and bought often in the decade after the war. They didn't always buy well, but usually they had the good sense to cut their losses by discarding the misfits in good time. And the list of their good buys in those years is as long as your arm - Frank Brennan, Len Shackleton, Bobby Mitchell, Alf McMichael, the Robledo brothers, Joe Harvey, to mention just a few..."

Later he talks about how to blend these expensive players in the interests of team performance, which does not always go as smoothly as one might hope:-

"...The flaw in their thinking, however, was the assumption that every star player must be potentially a good player for Sunderland, irrespective of his style or of his known limitations.

They were not to know, of course, that two such outstanding players as Len Shackleton and Trevor Ford would never be able to fit in with each other..."

Corroboration of this view comes from Trevor Ford in his 1957 book: '*I Lead The Attack*', for example:-

"...But Shack and I weren't the only misfits at Roker Park. Any club which lays down a policy of spending to the hilt for the stars is bound to end up with a team of individualists. There's no one in the side prepared to do the fetching and carrying..."

NB:- again to help with context, on the inside flyleaf of Trevor's book his publisher records the following promotional description, partially quoted here to remind the reader of his (1957) top status. The latter is supported now, 40 years later, by Trevor's inclusion in top 100 players of the Football League's first century, namely:

"...one of Britain's most discussed post-war footballers... His transfer trail from Swansea Town to Aston Villa to Sunderland and then back to his native Wales... cost the buying clubs a total of just under £70,000 to make him soccer's costliest player... he tells the behind-the-scenes moves preceding each of his transfers. So far Ford has secured well over 30 caps for Wales and is renowned as one of the game's greatest centre-forwards..."

Sometimes in life, through no particular fault of either party, a situation of mutual dislike arises from the beginning. Perhaps this may be the opposite of love at first sight? Whatever, in Trevor's book his feelings towards me were clearly expressed:

"...Shackleton... is described in official handbooks as a slightly erratic genius of inside-forwards, and is probably the greatest ball-player in British football, but some inborn desire to turn every game into a music-hall comedy has earned him the tag 'Clown Prince of Soccer'...

...another Roker Park nickname... in my opinion, more allied to the truth, because it is based on the heartbreaks, the frustration and human suffering of a string of players. The tag: 'centre-forwards' graveyard'......Since the war more centre-forwards have 'bit the dust' playing for Sunderland than any club I know...

Sunderland had started the 1948-49 season with their new inside right signing from Newcastle - Len Shackleton - and straight away his dazzling dribbles and individual ball jugglery became the hub of nearly every attacking move. From this moment on, Sunderland centre-forwards wore a worried look on their brow. What could they do? Here was a style of inside-forward play completely foreign to them - and few of them found the answer...

...You can't blame Shack for the type of game he plays. For him clowning seems just as much a part of the game as scoring goals. But you can blame the club for permitting it..."

Notwithstanding his general feelings about me, not all of Trevor's criticisms were adverse:

"...Shackleton is amongst the immortals as a ball-player. His dazzling dribbles, his weaving and bobbing with the ball at his feet, is a heart-break to opponents and a joy to watch, but what a pity his clowning has been allowed to nullify much of the co-ordination of the forward line...

...Twenty-one other players on the field were transfixed as Shack did tricks with that ball the like of which I'd never seen before. The crowd loved it. This was the clowning Shack at his best, but where did it get us? Precisely nowhere. The result was that when he did make a move, the opposing defence was in position and the attack broke down. Time and again when I thought Shack was going to slip a goal-scoring pass to me he would veer off..."

Billy's view on the 'Trevor Ford v Len Shackleton debate' of that time provide a contrasting view to Trevor's; this additional perspective is quite an interesting one:

"...The situation between Shackleton and Ford had never been a happy one and now it deteriorated. They appeared to dislike each other off the field and never seemed to strike up an understanding on it. Each blamed the other for this state of affairs and I suppose there were faults on both sides. Trevor, supported by most of the Press, claimed that Shack wouldn't play to him.

I remember that after one spate of criticism on this subject, we went out to Holland to play the Dutch 'B' team and won 7-3. Len made one of the goals by going right through the Dutch defence with an amazing dribble, finally sending the goalkeeper the wrong way with a feint. Then, when he had only to tap the ball in, he instead rolled it back to Ford, somewhere near the eighteen-yard line. 'Here you are, Fordy,' he shouted, 'don't say I never give you a pass.' Trevor Ford controlled himself well enough to be able to crash the ball into the back of the net.

Trevor Ford and the author - not always confrontational *(Courtesy of The Newcastle Chronicle and Journal)*

Considering what a great footballer he was, it can hardly be denied that Shack should have been able to give any centre-forward a reasonable service. 'Fordy', of course, wasn't just any centre-forward, he was the most dynamic spearhead in the game at that time. Yet he had his shortcomings, too…"

* * *

… Trevor continues with his own version of events:

"…It is all right if during the pre-match tactical talk moves such as this are considered and approved, but I seldom knew what Shack was going to do next…"

* * *

… whereas in relation to Trevor's positional awareness, Billy had this to say:

"…When Trevor complained that he never knew what Shackleton was going to do next he wasn't telling us anything new, because most of us

thought that half the time, Shack didn't know what he was going to do next himself. But you didn't have to play with him long to realise that one of his favourite moves was the reverse pass.

Thus, if I saw Len set off on a diagonal run carrying the ball towards me on the right wing I could be fairly sure that his final pass wouldn't be to me, in front of him, but somewhere to his left and behind him. Poor 'Fordy', who wasn't a great positional player at the best of times, never seemed to cotton on to this, and consequently if he was in the right place at the right time it was more by accident than design."

* * *

Trevor however, had believed that goal scoring records would have been possible at Sunderland, had tactical play emerged differently:-

"...By comparison Ivor Broadis may not have reached Shack's heights as a ball-player, but he was a prince to centre-forwards, for he would invariably draw his man and then send a pin-point pass to the advancing leader. As inside-forwards, Shack and Broadis were devastating in the way they could bamboozle the defence and if we had been able to combine in the orthodox way, I'm sure Sunderland would have set up goal-scoring records. Perhaps we might have helped the club to their most elusive target, the championship of Division One..."

Ivor Broadis *(Courtesy of Provincial Press Agency, Southport)*

... and following my earlier, published criticism he responds:

"...Shackleton in his book, Clown Prince of Soccer, wrote that the only thing of note I did whilst playing for Sunderland was to get myself fined £100. Thanks, Shack, for bringing this to light. I thought it had got by unnoticed! I would now like to say to Shack that the only thing of note he did whilst I was with Sunderland was one season when he pipped me at the post by one goal as leading scorer for the club!

But I don't care what Shack believes. The record books say I was top scorer for two out of the three seasons I was there..."

The scoring record may well be correct as Trevor says but, unlike Trevor, I was not a striker, i.e. primarily a goal-scorer in today's idiom, rather an 'all rounder'.

...matters eventually came to a head:

...then came the first big moment of decision in my football life... ...there had been rumours that I was not hitting it off with Shackleton. They said it was our avowed policy not to combine together. This is not altogether true, but I had reached the stage of make or break. And the break came in that game at Villa Park. I refused to play the following week. I told Mr. Murray that if Shackleton was in the side he could count me out.

Was I right? As far as I was concerned I had never made a better move. I felt myself coming back to life and I had only one answer when Mr. Murray called Shack and me together in his office and asked us to shake hands and make up. The answer from me was - not on your Nellie!...

...Shack and I were as different as chalk and cheese. We had developed our own styles of play - Shack as the ball-playing clown; myself as the tearaway centre-forward. Shack preferred to toy with the ball and the opposition; I preferred to steamroller the defences and blast for the net. It was impossible for Shack to change his style to suit me, and impossible for me to change mine to suit him. In that, and that only, we came out of the same melting pot, and to me, at any rate, there never seemed any chance of us hitting it off as part of a team. I never played with Shackleton again..."

* * *

Billy, again, provides an alternative view of events:

"...Eventually, the only remaining remedy, short of transferring one or the other, was to play them in alternate matches. This ridiculous state of affairs clearly couldn't last for long and one Saturday evening in November, Ford was quietly transferred to Cardiff City. The consolation for the shattered dream of the Sunderland board was that at least they got back the £30,000 they had paid for him three years earlier..."

To change the subject to a somewhat more light-hearted one, Billy describes some of the 'extracurricular' activities then enjoyed by the Sunderland players:

"...Living it up, for a good many players of those days, was typified by the regular card school on trips to away matches. Situated as we were in the far North East, we spent long hours in trains and hotels and card-playing for high stakes seemed to grow on us like a fever. Poker was the all-time favourite and often the stakes were frightening. Some players thought nothing of writing I.O.Us for fifty pounds or more, and I myself lost a whole week's wages more than once, before I saw the light and dropped out.

Cribbage and dominoes also had brief periods of popularity, but brag and poker were the staple diet and at both those games the almost invariable winner was the shrewd Len Shackleton. Len even had the odd game in Willie Watson's more select bridge school, but he was soon back behind that familiar pile of money on the poker table. **(But for my feelings on gambling for high stakes please see chapter 8).**

Anyone who ever saw Shack play football can take it from me that he was as quick-witted off the field as he was on it. As a footballer, of course, he was a genius, a master of ball-control, the most wonderful dribbler I have ever seen - and that includes Stanley Matthews. Naturally gifted with agility and balance... he nevertheless worked at his game with an intensity that might have surprised those who sometimes accused him of shirking some of his inside-forward duties.

One thing that I am quite sure developed his extraordinary talents was the game of football-tennis, which was a regular feature of our training in the Roker Park gymnasium. In this game the ball could be played over the net with any part of the anatomy except the hands and arms, and as a rebound off the walls still counted as a good return, you had to be really adept at ball-control. If you've seen Shack pull down a shoulder-high ball using an outstretched foot as if it were a hand, you can imagine what it was like trying to beat him at football-tennis.

Whenever Len perfected a new trick he was always eager to try it out in a match, even sometimes when the circumstances weren't quite right for it. A case in point was his famous chip-shot at goal, which eventually became almost an obsession with him. When it came off, of course, it was brilliantly spectacular, but there were times when he exasperated both the fans and his fellow-players by trying his chip when a simple ground-shot could hardly have failed to score...

That is what is called 'entertainment' Billy, LFS.

> *"...One great goal he scored by the overhead method was in a fourth-round Cup-tie at Preston, but the one I remember most clearly was against Aston Villa in a League game. Len, who had been slacking a bit in his usual inside-forward role, was having a spell at outside-left at the time. I can see him now moving down the touchline, beating the full-back, drawing the centre-half, then beating him and another defender, too, until he was right on the by-line approaching the near post. The goalkeeper, Keith Jones, started to come out, and when he was about five yards away, Shack figuratively drew out his No.9 iron and delicately chipped the ball over the goalkeeper's head and into the net, from a ridiculously narrow angle.*
>
> *The whole stand rose to this fantastic goal and poker-faced Len merely walked back to the halfway line with that unmistakable gait, shoulders hunched and head modestly bowed..."*

That was very flattering of Billy, for which I am grateful, especially as I was previously unaware that he held such highly complimentary views. Just to ensure that I don't get too swelled-headed, though, Billy continues:

> *"...Mind you, Len had some peculiar ideas about tactics, too. Some of them were to do with how to hold on for a draw or a win in the closing stages of an away game. He didn't like Sunderland to win corners in those circumstances, because he said that automatically meant we had one man virtually out of the game at the corner-flag, making it easier for the opposition to break away and score a goal that would cost us a point.*
>
> *I remember one match at Huddersfield in just those circumstances when we did get a corner in the dying minutes. As it was on my side of the field, I went to place the ball at the flag, but Shack motioned me away and put the ball down himself. Then, to everyone's bewilderment, he proceeded to roll the ball down the touchline and eventually out of play for a throw-in to Huddersfield.*
>
> *If we were all a bit mystified, the Huddersfield defenders were plain baffled, and it was quite some time before one of them had the sense to trot out of their goalmouth and go and fetch the ball. By the time the throw-in had been taken, two or three valuable minutes had gone by and the final whistle sounded almost immediately. Shack, for once, grinned like a Cheshire cat at the success of his inspired unorthodoxy..."*

Billy makes an interesting point here, and it wouldn't be the first time that such behaviour has been attributed by critics as 'clowning'. However, as is explained in Brian Leng's chapter 3, I have always seen this as tactical. I can readily see why many others see it differently but that was as intrinsic part of the tactic itself - and it must surely have worked if the opponents *were* baffled?

* * *

Next, as part of this critique - on Shack as others see me - an examination of the views of my contemporaries comes in a slightly different perspective. This time courtesy of that often-capped soccer knight, the now late, Sir Stanley Matthews. In his 1989 authorized biography by David Miller there are several references to my relatively short post-war international career:

> "...By the time of the Victory International of 1946... ...Matthews was about to experience the fluctuating and fickle mood of the re-established FA selection committee... ...the selection committee in its wisdom fielded an experimental team, dropping Carter and replaced him with Shackleton, then still at Bradford; and England lost by only one goal, their first defeat by Scotland in 10 matches... ...Delaney of Manchester United, playing at centre-forward, scored the goal from a free kick just outside the penalty area awarded for obstruction by Shackleton, the conjurer of the ball who would inexplicably play only five peace time matches for England..."

> "...(In 1948) Following a draw against the then outstanding Danish side, in Copenhagen, England moved onto Belfast where they thrashed the Irish 6-2. 'Denmark was my last game, I had a stinker,' Lawton reflects 'Len Shackleton missed about four, and so did I. After the match, Winterbottom told me that Milburn would be picked next time'..."

(Another real tragedy in my view was that this match also saw Jimmy Hagan, the **outstanding** Sheffield United inside-forward from Washington, win his only cap. After that match Walter Winterbottom wouldn't even let the players keep their shirts. PS - Jimmy later went on to successfully manage the world famous Benfica!).

In Sir Stan's biography, commenting on the 1954 England v Germany Wembley International in which we both played, Geoffrey Green of *The Times* is quoted as saying:

> "...The prince of all was Matthews. Majestically he glided across the afternoon. Poor Kohlmeyer, supported by Harpers and anyone else at hand, tried to play him all ways: sliding tackles, lunging, retreating. But always that outside flick, having anchored the defender on the other foot, would carry Matthews clear. As a variation, Matthews would go inside, or

merely beat him by acceleration. Here was a tour de force by the greatest player in football... Not far behind Matthews was Shackleton..."

"...Absurdly, this would be the last of Shackleton's five caps spread over seven seasons: a player of almost unlimited technique who profited or ultimately suffered, according to your view, from a belief that the game was as much about entertainment as a victory. On this occasion he scored one of the goals, Bentley and Ronnie Allen the others.... ...'Stan and Shack were poetry, they didn't just play football', reflects Jack Matthews."

* * *

To move forwards in time to my days as a journalist, I happened to have enjoyed some direct involvement in the careers of several in the game who subsequently became 'household names'. My involvement in Brian Clough's early managerial career for instance is referred to Patrick Murphy's 1993 book: 'His Way - The Brian Clough Story':

"...The man oiling the clanking wheels that brought Clough and Taylor to Hartlepool United was one of England's greatest individualists as a player, Len Shackleton. Clough still laughs at the mention of Shack, whose impudent skills for Sunderland entranced Wearside. Occasionally Shackleton was selected to play for England; on skill and technique alone, he ought to have been an automatic choice for years but the committee which picked the team in those days was wary of a footballer who actually had a brain and a provocative turn of phrase...

...Clough lapped-up Shackleton's iconoclastic opinions and when he became a soccer reporter for the 'Sunday People' in the North East, he found a ready source of gossip and opinion from the brash self-publicist at Middlesbrough. They were good together and Shackleton also noticed the same applied to Clough and Taylor. Bouncing ideas off the other, finishing the other's sentences, they appeared to Shackleton to have an intuitive, telepathic understanding. Shackleton saw them as a managerial partnership long before Clough and Taylor, and it was he, doing the rounds of the clubs, who heard that Hartlepool was looking for a new manager. Ernie Ord, the club's diminutive chairman, was won over to Clough by Shackleton's persuasive tongue, who then told Clough to appoint Taylor as his assistant. Clough contacted Taylor, they met at an hotel in York and the older man was persuaded that the offer of a new, three-year contract at Burton paled in comparison to working together in the Football League..."

ENGLAND
(Red Shirts, White Shorts)

Goal
B. WILLIAMS
(Wolverhampton Wanderers)

2 *Right Back*
R. STANIFORTH
(Huddersfield Town)

3 *Left Back*
R. BYRNE
(Manchester United)

4 *Right Half*
L. PHILLIPS
(Portsmouth)

5 *Centre Half*
W. WRIGHT (Capt.)
(Wolverhampton Wanderers)

6 *Left Half*
W. SLATER
(Wolverhampton Wanderers)

7 *Outside Right*
S. MATTHEWS
(Blackpool)

8 *Inside Right*
R. BENTLEY
(Chelsea)

9 *Centre Forward*
R. ALLEN
(West Bromwich Albion)

10 *Inside Left*
L. SHACKLETON
(Sunderland)

11 *Outside Left*
T. FINNEY
(Preston North End)

GERMANY
(White Shirts, Black Shorts)

Goal
FRITZ HERKENRATH
(R.W. Essen)

2 *Right Back*
JOSEF POSIPAL (Capt.)
(Hamburger Sport-Verein)

3 *Left Back*
WERNER KOHLMEYER
(F.C. Kaiserlautern)

4 *Right Half*
HERBERT ERHARDT
(Fuerth)

5 *Centre Half*
WERNER LIEBRICH
(F.C. Kaiserlautern)

6 *Left Half*
GERD HARPERS
(Soddingen)

7 *Outside Right*
GERHARD KAUFHOLD
(Offenbach Kickers)

8 *Inside Right*
MICHAEL PFEIFFER
(Alemmania Aachen)

9 *Centre Forward*
UWE SEELER
(Hamburger Sport-Verein)

10 *Inside Left*
JUPP DERWALL
(Furtuna Duesseldorf)

11 *Outside Left*
ALFRED BECK
(St. Pauli)

Referee
V. ORLANDINI
(Italy)

Linesmen
B. M. GRIFFITHS (*Wales*)
Flame Flag

C. E. FAULTLESS (*Scotland*)
Orange Flag

If the match is a draw at the end of 90 minutes' play, no extra time will be played

No matter how talented, a little bit of luck can often prove vital. Perhaps the following will put Brian's situation at that time into perspective:

> *"...To Clough the job was a lifeline after several grim months of wallowing in self-pity and worrying how to care for his growing family. 'In the North-East, we have this fear of not having a job and I couldn't do anything other than work in football. I was absolutely thrilled and delighted to get the Hartlepool job.'..."*

As is well known to everyone, once initially established, the combination of Clough and Taylor soon became very strong. Whereas the Hartlepool Chairman may have wished his own direct control to prevail, this was not how it was seen by the new partnership. Despite a change in chairmanship, the partnership's ambitions continued to grow - once again I was instrumental in engineering matters 'behind the scenes', this time to arrange their move to Derby:

> *"...Not for the first time, he saw the openings quicker than his younger partner and Taylor continued to nag away at Len Shackleton, to see if he could land them a better club. In the summer of 1967, he set up a meeting with Derby County to start a remarkable six-year period at the Baseball Ground, a leap of two divisions to a club with a great tradition of skilful football...*
>
> *...Sam Longson, Derby's chairman, was putty in the hands of those two cheeky chappies, Len Shackleton and Brian Clough, when they started negotiations...*
>
> *...For his part, Shackleton told Longson he had better move swiftly, because West Bromwich Albion were casting covetous eyes at Clough and were about to make a formal offer. Shackleton was being economical with the truth, but he rightly reasoned that the bluff old boy who made his fortune in the road haulage business would not follow up that piece of information..."*

...and for good measure, one final quote also to demonstrate that similar views were often shared by Brian and myself. However, just as I was *not* at all instrumental in Brian's move *from* Derby County to Nottingham Forest, neither was I instrumental in his *not* getting the England job - which I believe represents one of, if not *the* single biggest travesty in English International soccer history:

> *"...Clough never believed that he would have fretted at the lack of England matches and pined for the glut of games that prolong an English season. 'I remember Len Shackleton making me laugh in the old days up*

'Cloughie' in action during his Roker hey-day *(Courtesy of the Sunderland Echo)*

in the North-East when he said that if he could, he'd get away with working one day a week for his newspaper for the same money as six days a week.* I understood that. I wouldn't have missed attending 40-odd first team matches, 30-odd reserve games and watching the kids 40-odd times in a season - not one bit. The England job would've suited me down to the ground. I'd even have learned to ski!'…"

* Footnote - Brian was referring to the position when I moved from being a daily columnist with the *Daily Express* to a weekly one with the *Sunday People*.

Please also see Brian's more recent views within chapter 10.

~ Chapter 6 ~

Hong Kong Trip 1966
(...and the 'most important people' in the game - Goalkeepers and Referees)

I feel that an often formerly overlooked but critical member, if not *the* most important player, on any football team is the goalkeeper. My story is from February/March 1966 when a friend of mine, Arthur Gayne, asked me to help him arrange a tour. It was for an English team to help celebrate Hong Kong's *British Week* and Arthur was Coach to the Hong Kong F.A. The proposal was for an all-expenses-paid, two match exhibition tour lasting about 10 days. Obviously, candidates would be from successful teams of the time of the ilk of Manchester United or Stoke City. But because of timing, a team would have to be selected from those knocked-out of the 3rd or 4th Round of the FA Cup. However, as much time as possible would be required at the Hong Kong end to arrange the itinerary, accommodation bookings and general programme. It was therefore decided that the selection would be made from a team knocked-out at the 3rd Round. That year Stoke had been knocked-out at the 'appropriate' stage so I approached a friend of mine, the Stoke City manager, Tony Waddington. Tony was a nice guy, as well as a good friend. In fact the club was also a good one and the whole tour began to take on the air of a very good arrangement for all concerned.

An early interesting development was the discovery that we were sharing our flight with H.R.H. Princess Margaret. This added interest to otherwise mundane landings at Frankfurt, Bangkok or wherever, to collect more passengers or for refuelling. It was very interesting to see the treatment afforded to members of the Royal party at quite close quarters. It certainly worked out very well for me as I was afforded almost 'VIP status' in my role as intermediary between our Hong Kong hosts and the visiting team! We were collected from the airport and taken to the hotel in a 'motorcade'. When there, my room proved to be a suite and it really was magnificent. I began to think that this was too good to be true and that there had been a mix up. Fortunately it wasn't and I was very fortunate and really couldn't have been treated better!

The day after our arrival, our hosts had scheduled 'dinner' in the form of a twelve-course, Chinese banquet. It was absolutely marvellous food, together with appropriate wine courses and champagne. It certainly beat the usual pilchard or

'Marmite' sandwiches, taken on many of my journalistic away-match assignments! Following the dinner, the HK Chief of Police took our party on a guided tour. This really was almost first class treatment! Afterwards when Arthur, his colleagues and I were having a drink, Tony Waddington came over to pass-on his Chairman's delight at the level and standard of hospitality. He added that the treatment was so good, that if I could arrange any further trips of this calibre, I would be invited to join the Board! To underline what a good club it was, I was even allocated the same expenses as the directors. Originally it hadn't been good for Stoke to have been knocked-out of the FA Cup, but it was indeed the proverbial 'ill wind' situation for them to get away to a much warmer climate during February/March. Then, to be given such remarkable hospitality was more than ample compensation for Stoke's F.A. Cup defeat!

One of the main social events was a Gala Charity Film Premiere at King's Theatre, Hong Kong of "The Spy Who Came In From The Cold", attended by Princess Margaret and Lord Snowdon. My friend Arthur Gayne had obtained two tickets and suggested that I should go in his place to accompany his wife, Joyce. We even ended-up seated just behind the Princess - which didn't normally happen when I went to the cinema back home in Sunderland too often!

Goalkeepers

During the trip we talked about many different aspects of football. I remember making the point to Tony that I could not understand managers who would pay then top-money of about £70,000 for a striker, yet overlook the most important man on the pitch? My point was that, if we were talking in terms of results, the most important man *must* be the goalkeeper! I suggested that, as a manager, he should consider paying a lot of money to get the best possible goalkeeper. I felt that given the *importance of results*, then the logic of this must be compelling. I think Tony had agreed that this was a common sense analysis when we were talking. Then, later when Stoke returned from the Hong Kong tour, he went straight into the market and bought a new goalkeeper (I think Gordon Banks, from Leicester?) for a record sum. Many thought he was crazy for paying such a lot of money. But Tony's courage in doing this was vindicated, as subsequently they won the Football League Cup (now called Worthington Cup, former Milk Cup or whatever).

Soo Kum-Poo Stadium, Hong Kong 1966
(seated capacity 28,000)

J. M. Windsor R. G. Dewar A. J. Gayne J. Howard W.McAllister R. E. McIlvride A. D. McTavish

J. P. Boyd J. Mair R.Beevor L. F. Shackleton
(England & Sunderland F. C.)

As a 'footnote', strangely, the goalkeeper deal may never have happened. We were returning from Hong Kong and scheduled to land at Bangkok for refuelling. When the plane was about half way there, the captain made an announcement to say that he had a cracked windscreen in the cockpit. He added that we were at about the 'point of no return' and that it would be better to continue rather than turn back! I happened to be sat next to Dennis Violet and quickly remembered that Dennis had been a survivor of the Manchester United, Munich air disaster! Everyone in football and the general public beyond, knew of what a devastating tragedy it had been. At the immediate time though, I was not aware of the fatal implications of decompression, should the cracked windscreen fail altogether. It wasn't until later that I fully realised the true gravity of the situation when the famous incident of the, then recent, James Bond movie 'Goldfinger' was related to me - cabin occupants had been sucked-out! Nor do I know whether Dennis had been fully aware of the horrendous implications at the time? I recall he was sat next to me not moving or saying much, but it all turned out safely. Dennis was a good friend of mine but sadly he is not with us anymore as he died recently, though fortunately not as prematurely as it might have been!

Referees

My next point is that one of the other most important people in football, often overlooked, is the referee.

A good referee should be able to recognise the intentions of players and apply the laws consistently and correctly. The game forms part of the entertainment industry, so referees must play their part by enabling the game to flow whilst identifying on field infringements correctly. It should be remembered that, even in today's climate, not every tackle is a foul nor is every foul a caution - the referee can impart his opinion when determining and applying the laws. Reading the situation and understanding the players' actions properly leads to correct decisions which, in turn, is then accepted by players, and so also improves the game as a spectacle.

I also understand that, very recently, the Football Association has introduced a new code of punishment for players seeking to remove those type of incidents involving either harassment, man-handling or just intimidatory and aggressive confrontation towards officials on the pitch. It almost goes without saying that this didn't happen to the same extent years ago. It seems to have evolved as society has itself, rapidly changed in recent times. Referees used to be respected more but, perhaps, the pressures and demands in the game of the past were less? Decisions were more readily accepted and questioned far less often than now. I see these moves as a step forward in trying to bring back what has been lost, and it may also help referees to be more effective in other aspects of their on-field performance. It sends the right message to the players and managers, warning of the likely consequences of such negative and destructive behaviour. It also transmits to those lower down the football ladder - having been seen and repeated right down to the 'grass roots' of football - that this kind of behaviour is unacceptable. Maybe after a couple of backward steps, those charged with enforcing the rules of game are now trying to make a giant leap forwards. Another needed in today's 'big money' climate, would be to ensure that referees are properly paid. In other words much better paid in relation to the responsibility they carry in the modern commercial game. At present the reality is that they are not but it is vital that their status should be kept in touch with developments in the game because they control the matches.

There has also been much recent debate about whether referees should become 'professional'. In my opinion the argument ought to be whether they should become full time, since their preparation, dedication and commitment adequately demonstrates that they are already highly professional. However, as most have other jobs or business commitments they are not yet able to be 'full time' because of their need to earn a living elsewhere. Such moves towards independence seem increasingly likely as it would enhance the standing of referees with the public, media and, more importantly the players.

The game has developed rapidly in recent years and with the advent of the F.A. Premier League and Sky TV, there is now more money than ever before within the game. The introduction of digital broadcasting has also seen Football League clubs sign multi-million pound deals for broadcasting rights. Some of this media money could be used to enable referees to become financially independent from their current jobs and concentrate on officiating full time. Perhaps the next major hurdle to overcome is the question of who will be the match officials' employer? To avoid a conflict of interest, it seems logical that it should be the Football Association, because the Premier and Football Leagues are run by the member clubs.

Becoming 'full time' may not be immediately appropriate for all match officials. The 'full time' option should first be available only to those suitably qualified. This is the most important proviso, since paying them more would not in itself make for better officials. Giving them the opportunity to prepare thoroughly and professionally should, however, reap benefits. Full time officials could use their spare time effectively by visiting clubs for training and liaison purposes. For those who haven't played at a high level, they would have the chance to see players in their 'natural habitat' on the training ground. The benefits of co-operation and dialogue should help both players and referees alike to integrate more than previously. This will surely help foster a better understanding between both, working to prevent unsavoury on-field events.

Refereeing is a very difficult job to do properly. If I were seeking to be adversely critical, I guess it would be that many give the impression that they don't really know the game - either in their decision-making or body language. A closer working relationship between players, managers and referees is called for to make this perception change. One possible solution would be for ex-players to become referees as they already know the game well enough to make the correct and difficult judgements often required. It sounds like a good idea to me and there should be no major reason, in principle, why ex-players cannot referee at the highest level. Indeed, I understand that there are referees already on the National List who have played League football.

The door is always open to ex-players although few make this move when their playing days are over because, I suggest, the financial rewards are too poor, bearing in mind the difficulties, problems and confrontations faced. Sadly, also, in today's society these problems are not only on-field with intrusions into personal and private life by both the media and, more worryingly, the public! By way of corroboration, it may interest the reader to know that most National List referees earn less from football than a poorly paid, lower division first year professional. It is only in the Premier League or on the international circuit that salary levels are anything like 'good'. At present, it is likely that only a small minority would express a positive preference until a correct professional package is eventually formulated.

Whilst it is critical that all officials are impartial, it has been suggested that there could be a possible conflict of interests where a former player officiates at a game involving one of his ex-clubs. I do not see this as a problem in practice as players, being the professionals they are, routinely play against former clubs throughout their career. It would be a retrogressive step to throw out the refereeing baby with the ex--playing bath water.

The knowledge and understanding of players and their actions plays a pivotal role in refereeing. Consider the common on-field scenario of determining whether there has been an ill-timed tackle or a deliberately bad one. Imagine a forward with the ball, encountering a defender intent on stopping him. The forward's idea would be to try to beat the man. To do so he will move the ball slightly ahead, to make the defender think that he has lost control. The ball will then be pushed a little further still, to make the defender think that he could get it, so enticing him to challenge. The defender will then commit himself to the tackle, while the forward (if he has gauged things correctly) will nick the ball away to beat the man. But if the forward doesn't get his foot out of the way at the same time as the ball, he will get kicked! In such a situation, a defender could hardly avoid kicking the forward and this position is a familiar one to any experienced defender. He may not tackle but, if he holds back, he will be castigated by both team mates and manager for not doing his job properly! Alternatively, if he makes the tackle, he couldn't really be blamed for the foul, although under the current laws of the game he will run the risk of receiving a caution should the tackle appear late and dangerous to the referee. Hence, as far as the question of ill-timed tackles is concerned, a referee's detailed knowledge and understanding of the game is essential, otherwise the future of the game is in jeopardy.

Considering developments, and with the future of the game in mind, perhaps one of the worst things faced by referees of the modern era is the TV action replay. In every tackle, whether it is ill-timed or badly intended, there is always contact. The TV highlights that contact, but it is for the referee on the spot to adjudge whether or not the player is a fair or unfair victim of the tackle and so, whether the rules have been infringed. Unfortunately, today's players tend to 'simulate' an offence. Such behaviour (acting) is understandable in the context of commercialism now being so important but it is obviously not in keeping with the true spirit of the game. Indeed, the referee's job of identifying and preventing challenges such as 'simulation' or shirt pulling, and dealing with them correctly, is vital. On-field position is also vital, as is reading players' body language and reactions. Attempts to 'manufacture' a free kick by 'simulating' an offence (such as holding or tripping) does not go down well. Players' reactions therefore often act as a good guide in assisting a referee to understand what has actually gone on. Likewise, as the tendency has evolved to slyly hold back on the blind side of the officials, players' reactions and body language act as a good guide to establishing the presence of an offence.

If the referee gets it wrong or misses it, then TV will highlight the event and if possible develop it as a controversial talking point. In live 'Sky' games, for example, the number of cameras covering almost every angle runs into double figures. This makes sure that every possible 'talking point' is covered. I am sure that referees are doing their utmost to eradicate problems prevailing today but players' help is vital. It does the game no good to see players deliberately trying to gain unfair advantage. Increased TV coverage means that everyone is put in the position of 'armchair referee', so it is even more important that the calibre of referees is as high as

possible. As I have mentioned, I don't think that there is any substitute for true knowledge and experience in this connection. What exactly this represents in practice is the most important facet of the whole debate.

It is for this reason that I have drawn upon the up-to-date knowledge and accumulating experience of one of the youngest and most progressive of referees in today's Premier League. Colin Webster of County Durham has collaborated with me in this part of the book, for which I am very grateful. I believe it is always a good idea to introduce

Colin H. Webster

'new blood' into any sport. Whereas most fans' attention is quite understandably fixed on the footballing skills of the players, the skills and abilities of the officials are overlooked to the long-term detriment of the game that we all enjoy so much. So, thank you Colin for your contribution in keeping me right on the most recent developments and I look forward to seeing your own performances in many games to come. I will complete this section by including a biographical summary of Colin's career. Remember his name, it may become quite famous one day as - who knows - he may become the first ever £1 million referee if the commercial realities of today's soccer industry finally filter through to professional (i.e. commercial) terms for full-time officials.

Personal - age 33; Occupation - Senior Valuer in the Valuation Office Agency; Married to Jacqueline, with two sons Matthew Thomas (4 years) and Jamie Alexander (2 months).

Refereeing - career began in 1985/86 (aged 19), progressing through the Wearside and Northern Leagues onto the National List of Assistant Referees in 1994 (aged 27); also appointed to the National Panel List which covers the Nationwide Conference, FA Premier Reserve and Pontins League; selected for appointments in the FA Premier League as Assistant Referee in 1997; promoted onto the National List of Referees in 2000 to receive appointments as Referee in the Nationwide Football League.

Honours - Assistant Referee, The FA Trophy Final 2000; Worthington Cup Semi Final and The FA Youth Cup Semi Final 1999-2000; awarded the Northern League Silver Whistle 2000 (Referee of the Year award); refereed the Northern League Cup Final, the Durham County Sunday Cup Final; Minor Cup Final and Trophy Final and the Wearside League Cup Final.

~ Chapter 7 ~
Humorous Characters and Anecdotes

Ray Daniel

I well remember the first day he arrived from Arsenal and it was one of those situations where we immediately hit it off together. He had a marvellous sense of humour, which fortunately for me, corresponded with my own. He also had 'an ego' as big as a house but a lot of his bragging and exaggerations were tongue-in-cheek. For instance, with future new arrivals he used to wind them up by pointing and saying: "…Scottish Internationals change over there, English Internationals there, Welsh Internationals here, Irish there…". He would say this to new players who probably wouldn't immediately understand his sense of humour - and invariably thought he was being serious! He was, though, a good lad who also often made jokes at his own expense.

I remember an occasion when a smart young man introduced himself to our manager Bill Murray as the boss's son at 'The Daily Mirror' (or some similar popular newspaper of the time). He arrived at the club ostensibly to do a series of feature articles on both the club and players. Bill Murray detailed trainer, Bert Johnston, (see chapter 2) to accompany him and allow free run of the club's facilities. Unfortunately this young man was not as able as his ambitions - he was newly out of university (so probably possessed of a Director's full knowledge of football) and simply wasn't up to the job. Lads like Ray (Bebe) and Chis were having a field day at his expense - one of them suggested that Shack (of all people), had divulged that he wanted to become the first Player/Chairman! Bebe and company were feeding him with horrendous rubbish which he was lapping-up, believing he had a series of scoops! When Bert Johnston cottoned-on to this he went off to inform Bill Murray and warn him of the potential consequences but, initially, Bill decided not to take any action. Matters eventually came to a head when we were on an away trip, travelling by coach - somewhat unusually as trips were often by train - probably to somewhere like Huddersfield or Derby. (*Aside:* incidentally, travelling by bus ruined our 'poker school' as there was less room than on a train).

By this time Bill Murray had fully digested the severity of the situation, should such bogus stories appear in the national press. He stopped the coach and went to find the nearest 'phone box to contact Fleet Street and demand that the smart young man's copy be immediately pulled!

Bebe was full of jokes about all sorts. I have already mentioned elsewhere (Radio 5

Shack, Ell and Bebe trying to take money off each other. *(Len Shackleton Collection)*

Live interview - chapter 1), the story where Ray once asked club director and eminent surgeon, Stanley Ritson, in the dining room of a 'posh' hotel if he would mind using his skill to carve his chicken for him! Despite the fact that, in those days it was 'taboo' for the players to mix with the directors, Mr. Ritson took it well and everyone enjoyed the joke! Mr. Ritson was also quite a character of the old school, being something of a fitness fanatic well into his seventies. For example, when we played Arsenal, staying at the Great Northern Hotel, Kings Cross, he would walk to the ground. When we returned from away matches on the overnight sleeper train, he would walk back from Newcastle Central Station - all the way to his home in Sunderland!

Ray's sense of humour could often be misconstrued, but I and *most* of the other players, greatly enjoyed his company. Hotels became suitable venues for these humorous antics. On one occasion we were playing Aston Villa and the team stayed in the top class 'Midland Hotel', Birmingham. We assembled for dinner, directors and players on one big table. There was a most impressive band - nearly an orchestra - kitted-out in full evening dress. The music was light classical and gave a rather formal atmosphere to the place. Ray and I decided to have a joke and quietly summoned the maitre d' to ask if 'the band' played requests? They did and some time later when we had almost forgotten our request, it was played: The "Woody Woodpecker Song" - with full strings accompaniment - and this was surprisingly well received by all diners!

On yet another occasion, when the team booked into our hotel during a foreign tour (Copenhagen), the players were all registering at the reception. With false

Rare action study of Ray - December 1953 *(Newcastle Chronicle & Journal)*

seriousness, I gave my occupation as 'Company Director' (at the time I had two or three shops in Sunderland, run as a limited company). Ray immediately called the manager over and said: "Boss, have *you* seen what Shack has put here in the register?" Mr. Murray was most upset, pointing out that, first and foremost, at £520 per year, I should regard myself as a professional footballer! But nevertheless Ray and I enjoyed the joke. Perhaps most of all I admired Ray's nerve and attitude towards the hierarchy. At the time it was the norm to start training by doing eight or nine laps around the field. On one particular day, Ray, who was known not to be an ardent trainer, spotted a rare sight: Chairman, Mr. Billy Ditchburn making his way onto the ground from the tunnel. In those days in was unusual to see the manager at training sessions, never mind the Chairman. Ray summoned Mr. Ditchburn over to him and asked: "Hey Mr. Chairman, does this red stuff (pointing to the red cinder track round the perimeter) go all the way round to the other side?"

The last time Marje and I saw Ray and his wife Joyce, was at a players' reunion at Sunderland FC in the early 90s; we miss him, Joyce.

Ken Chisholm

'Chis' was as bright and equally humorous a character as Bebe. For instance, on one occasion I remember Sunderland playing on a summer tour, abroad somewhere. Chis, weighing-up the opposition spotted one player - the one who was to mark me - and called me over, saying: "See that big guy over there with the mouth full of gold teeth? Well Shack, when I go up for a corner, the big guy will be marking me. When I hit (head) him, he'll be stunned, pull the gold out of his teeth and we'll split it!"

Then there was the time when Sunderland were playing Spurs at White Hart Lane and it was *very* important that we won - such an important match that we were offered a £25 'bonus' at a time when we were only paid £16 per week. During a private, pre-match chat, Chis suggested: "Shack, when Sunderland get a free-kick around the halfway line, on the touchline, you take the kick and aim to place it just outside the six yard line, in front of the goal and I'll do the rest". Big brave Chis did exactly that - as I said, we were on £25 per man! The planned situation happened, just in the right place we were awarded a free-kick. I placed the set-up 'pass' exactly where Chis wanted it. As the Spurs 'keeper ('Big Ted' Ditchburn) came out to collect the ball, I could see Chis was timing his run just right and there was bound to be a collision between these 'big men'. I put my hands over my eyes and… CRASH! When I looked up, there were both Chis and Ditchburn in the back of the net together with the ball! Chis was sat down, grinning and holding his shoulder - he had broken a collar bone - but, just like Chis, he said: "We've done it Shack" - he meant that he had won the game for us (and the £25 'bonus', although then 'illegal' per F.A. rules) and the whole team netted an extra week-and-a-half's wages. Having recounted this tale I wouldn't want to portray a false impression. Chis wasn't a thug; indeed a Glasgow University degree man and Pilot Officer in the R.A.F. True to

'Hard Man' Chis in action. *(Len Shackleton Collection)*

type, when Chis was telling of his R.A.F. days training in South Africa and Canada, he told me: "Just call me 'lucky' Chis - as soon as I qualified as a Pilot Officer, the war finished, so I didn't have to fly bombers in action!"

On another occasion Sunderland was playing Arsenal at Roker Park on one very cold and frosty day. Chis was injured very early on - we hadn't all had time to finish our warm-ups - he had been kicked between his legs and went down as though dead! None of this writhing about in false agony like some players today. Trainer George Gray came on with his cold sponge and proceeded to do his bit. Chis, in his very real agony said: "Don't rub 'em George, count 'em!"

Chis really was a great guy to have as a hard and humorous team mate, but because of his great charisma you wouldn't really feel very happy for him to be married to your sister! We kept in touch over the years, occasionally playing golf together and he is now *greatly* missed. Naturally we would laugh about old times which always acted as a tonic. Like Bebe he could also take a joke, because I would remind him of one of my favourite observations from our playing days together: I used to joke with him and say "Chis, your speed is *deceiving* - you're slower than you look!"

Tommy on tour with SAFC in Turkey, 1950
(Len Shackleton Collection)

Tommy Wright

Tom wasn't as naturally funny or charismatic in the same way as either Bebe or Chis, though he was most certainly 'a character'. I recall a SAFC summer tour in 1953 involving a couple of games in both Denmark and Sweden. The second game of the trip was in Gothenburg in which Harry Threadgold was the goalkeeper. He was one of Sunderland's young, reserve 'keepers substituting for regular first team man, Johnny Mapson.

Though this was a 'friendly', things got a bit rough, everyone more or less kicking 'hells bells' out of each other. In one incident, there was a classic 'goal mouth scramble' and Harry went down having received a nasty kick on the head from one of the Swedish opposition. During the skirmishing Tommy, our outside right, tore into the scrimmage. 'Little' Tommy was a bit of a firebrand but wanted to help his pal who was on the deck. He quickly emerged from all this though and shouted to me nearby: "Hey Shack, come and have a look at this, Harry's got another mouth!" He had been badly kicked on the shin, whilst his lip had been even *more* badly split - and it looked like he had another mouth - and that was all Tommy could focus on in the heat of the moment! He wandered off, in surprised shock, repeating this to all the other players as he came to them. Poor Harry found that the 'friendly' had not quite lived up to the name!

Tommy's room mate, brother John
(Len Shackleton Collection)

Tommy soon got himself a reputation as being 'the brave little Scots lad'. He was a great character but was often a little wild - although, in his defence, who isn't at times - especially energetic young men? Tommy was in lodgings at Fulwell, Sunderland, shared with my younger brother John. He had been signed-on by Sunderland as professional for a couple of years to see if he could make the grade. At the 'digs' their landlady kept a goose. She kept it in a pen in the back garden and the plan was to fatten it ready for Christmas. Tommy and my brother had nicknamed the goose 'Argus'. The local *Sunderland Echo* 'Argus' reporter of that time was Jack Anderson. He was well noted for giving abrasive comments about some of the players. His Saturday night sport's column carried comments from the previous week's match. On one particular occasion I remember finding Tommy fuming about Argus' comments on our last match. These were to the effect that Tommy had only one way of beating a full back - by kicking the ball past and chasing around him - but wasn't capable of any greater a variety of moves (per Argus)!

Tommy was still fuming when we played our next game at Bolton, which was in front of a crowd of 40 or 50,000 people. The goalkeeper, Johnny Mapson, kicked the ball out to Tommy on the outside right - who then *caught* it! He took it like a rugby player, side-stepped the full back and drop-kicked it over the bar! As he came back, he was chuntering to himself and any players within earshot: "I'll show Jack Anderson, I'll show Argus that there's more than one way of beating the full back!"

On his way home to their 'digs' with my brother, Tommy had called by to the local paper shop, for that night's sports report on the match. He was still furious and the first thing he did (after tripping over it), was to get hold of the landlady's cat and fling it into the pen with - you've guessed it - the goose Argus! That seemed typical of Tommy; basically he was a good lad but a demonstrative character at times!

Ernie Taylor

Readers may remember Ernie as Newcastle United's very small inside forward - I believe he had served his National Service in HM Navy submarines - who was later to star with Blackpool in a F.A. Cup Final at Wembley, known as the Stan Matthews Final.

The Stan Matthews Final *(Courtesy of Newcastle Chronicle)*

Once, whilst I was still at United, he came into training one morning looking rather grumpy and miserable. Immediately spotting this, one of the players enquired: "What's the matter Ernie, have you had a row with your wife? Did she put your breakfast in the middle of the table where you couldn't reach it?" Ernie took it in good part, seeing the funny side of things and certainly didn't display any of the present day's knee-jerk, politically correct reaction, claiming height-ism or such like! All of which reminds me how important creating a good team spirit really is. In turn this, of course, highlights the importance of good *people managers* (as well as football *coaching*), to the real success that only comes with a correct, overall blend.

Bob Hardisty

During the 1960s era I used to go up to Bishop Auckland regularly to play golf with Bob Hardisty. He will be well remembered in our region as the England amateur and Bishop Auckland wing-halfback player who joined Manchester United just after the Munich disaster. Bob and a few others had been recruited to help them out in the aftermath of that terrible tragedy. Bob was a very good, indeed a fine, player and he was also a keen gambler. One of his good friends was Dennis Smith, the racehorse trainer, of over-the-jumps fame, also from the Bishop Auckland area.

On one occasion I had heard that Bob was in hospital with a heart problem. To put this in perspective, my story goes back a good number of years before heart-transplants were as commonplace as they now are today. Any surgery to remedy a condition like Bob's was very serious. It's pretty serious now, of course, but in those days it was especially so. A friend and my usual golfing partner, Tommy Mervin, and I went to visit Bob in the hospital. The visit was about a couple of days after he had had the operation. Bob seemed well given the circumstances and he recounted his own funny story. He explained that Dennis (Smith) had visited him on the day of his operation and given him 'a good tip' for that day's racing. Bob explained that he had been eager to participate and had 'put three grand on it'! As you can imagine £3,000 was certainly a lot of money then, as it's hardly small change now. So I asked Bob what his idea had been and he replied: "…well I looked at it this way, if I go into the operating theatre and it doesn't turn-out right, well …I'm none the wiser. But if I come back from the operation and everything is okay and the horse has lost, well I'm still pleased to be alive and kicking!"

This story about Bob reminds me of the kind of guy he really was - an extraordinary character, quite happy to take risks to prove that he was alive! All the sadder that he too is no longer with us. One of those people that I will always remember with great humour and fondness. It also reminds me of the quote attributed to the recently departed actor and lifelong gambler, Walter Matthau, under similar circumstances: "If I get lucky, I'll die before I go broke."

Willie Watson

A rare double international

Willie will always be remembered as one or those very rare and talented individuals, a double international, who played both football (right-half back) and cricket (batsman) for his country, England. There haven't been many others, just odd ones spring to mind, such as Dennis Compton and Arthur Milton, for Gloucester and Arsenal, I think?

Whilst Willie and I were both playing football for Sunderland I remember one particular joint visit to see the Greyhound Derby. It had become the custom of some players when the team was playing away in London to go to 'the dogs' at White City. One of the key figures, Major Brown, had become a good pal and we had a standing invitation any time we were 'down in the smoke'. On this particular occasion to which my story relates, it was the semi-final of the 'Greyhound Derby' - one of the biggest events in greyhound racing. Soon after our arrival we were invited to draw the trap numbers for the final due to be run the next week. So Bill and I agreed and there was an announcement over the public address system to the large crowd attending.

About half way through the meeting we went down onto the track so that Bill could draw the trap and I the dog, or vice versa. We even had the spotlights on us as we walked down the steps to the track! Now, it's relevant to mention that both he and I were 'skint', as we hadn't backed a winner all night. Following the draw, people were clapping as we returned to our seats, amidst the glare of the spotlights and I remarked to my co-celebrity: "Hey Willie, people will be saying 'I bet those two get their cards marked and will make a few bob tonight'...". But the reality of it was that all we could do was to jingle our house keys in our pockets - to make it sound as if we had some money left! Just a small insight into what it was really like sometimes, even for so-called celebrities - in those days. In reality not quite as glamorous as it may have been imagined to be but still fun for all that, to be afforded some 'celebrity status' and be part of events like that - quite special really.

Jack Fairbrother

Golfing Story

Towards the beginning of my career, during playing days at Newcastle United, we

Tommy Pearson and the author in 'black & white' days
(Courtesy of C Rawlinson, Burnley)

played a Cup game at one of the London clubs and happened to visit Letchworth, in Hertfordshire to the north of 'the smoke'. We stayed in a large and well-to-do hotel. It cannot have been very long after the war and life outside places like this was still quite austere for most people of my background. The surroundings were both impressive and unfamiliar, not least because, by that stage, I had played very little golf. My good friend Jack Fairbrother and I had been encouraged to play by outside-left Tommy Pearson who was also a 'scratch' golfer. He was very good and once 'did 66' in the qualifying round of the British Open Golf Championship, although, unfortunately, failed to qualify in a second-round 'blow up'.

Anyway, we started to play and about half-way around Tommy was beating the pair of us in a 'better ball' game. To beat two in a better ball takes some doing, testimonial to his 'scratch' ability. So with us both trailing, Jack said something to him like: "Hey Pearson, it's okay for you - look at your clubs, you've a matched set - but look at my clubs, they're old and are all wooden-shafted." So Tom said: "Right, but it's not the tools…". With that he gave Jack his clubs in exchange for the wooden-shafted ones. We continued with the round and he finished the second nine holes - on a golf course he had never played on in his life before - in level par using Jack's old wooden clubs! The point to this must be that it really isn't the tools but the man who uses them that is the most important thing. Well done Tommy - he and Jack were great characters and very good friends too - sad that we lost him just a few months ago (Autumn 1999), but we've all got to go I guess…

Jack and family in Newcastle Cup days (*Len Shackleton Collection*)

Another story involving Jack occurred shortly after my move from Newcastle to join Sunderland. Jack, fans will remember, was Newcastle's goalkeeper and our respective wives were also very good friends. One day we all decided to go for a day trip to Hexham, the Northumberland market town some miles to the west of Newcastle.

We drove over from Sunderland to collect the Fairbrothers from their Newcastle home in our 'old banger' of a car. It was not many years after the war and still difficult to get a new car (as well as the money to buy one), since new cars went mainly for export and were not widely available on the home market. My driver's door was even tied to the steering column as it had no lock! We made it to Hexham by which time it was starting to spot with rain. Jack remarked that he thought my car appeared to be on fire - but my response was that it was probably just steam from the rain and that we shouldn't worry about it and spoil our day out with the 'girls'. We drove around the town a little but couldn't immediately find a parking place. We ended-up in the centre of Hexham on what must have been the main street. Then we spotted a vacant space, just beside a wholesale grocer's premises; we parked in it and left for a look around town and to have some lunch.

When we returned there was a big crowd gathered around a car - you've guessed it - it was my car. We made our way over to where it was parked outside the grocer's. Just alongside it there was a pedestrian passage into the main building for deliveries. On the bonnet of the car was a big pile of 'white stuff' and my first thought (not being technically minded about cars) was that the grocer must have had a flour delivery and some had dropped off onto the car. Anyway, I made my way to the front of the crowd to enquire about what had happened to my car? One of the crowd suggested I go to the opposite side of the street, where there was a commercial garage, and ask the man there to explain all about it.

I went across and introduced myself as the unfortunate owner of the car across the street. I asked what had happened. The chap in charge called to one of his mechanics and introduced him as the young man who had put the fire out! My reaction was to say: "...you put the fire out ...on my car, over there...", pointing to the crowd still assembled around it. He acknowledged this and explained that he had just caught it in time, as the smoke and flames had begun. I replied a little crossly: "Thanks, but you should have minded your own business!" At that the garage manager joined in to agree, and said to the young mechanic: "There you are, I told you what the man would say!" He could see without any difficulty that it would have been more valuable to me as a 'write-off' than as the dilapidated wreck in a semi-cooked condition! We've laughed about it a few times since and I feel a little sorry for that young mechanic who was just trying to help; still, good days, good memories.

FOOTBALL ASSOCIATION INTERNATIONAL

ENGLAND
v
GERMANY

WEDNESDAY, DECEMBER 1st, 1954   KICK-OFF 2.0 pm

EMPIRE STADIUM

WEMBLEY

Chairman and Managing Director   SIR ARTHUR J. ELVIN, MBE

OFFICIAL PROGRAMME   ·   ONE SHILLING

England v Germany Story

There are a lot of things that go on connected with a match of football, behind the scenes so to speak, that the public doesn't get to hear about. One such instance springs to mind, when I made a post-war appearance for England against West Germany. It was in December 1954 and Germany were the reigning World Cup Champions.

We played the Germans at Wembley and pre-kick-off we were all lined-up to meet the assembled dignitaries. Amongst others, the Rt. Hon. Sir Anthony Eden was introduced to both teams. The players for each side stood facing each other and, naturally, members of both teams were 'weighing-up' the opposition. I had been introduced to the VIP who had then moved on. By the time he was 3 or 4 players away from me I looked across to my counterpart in the German side - and what a 'whacking big' guy he was!

I looked at him and then looked at the ground. What a beautiful pitch it was at Wembley, almost rivalling 'Lords' and would have provided a marvellous wicket. So, looking at him, I called over: "Hey Fritz, if we win the toss today we're going to bat." He, naturally enough, looked at me in puzzlement. I then added by way of a general explanation: "It might be a bit green, the ball might move about a bit on the grass." Well, of course, it fell on deaf ears. The Germans didn't know what I was talking about. Somebody on my right - I think Ronnie Allen or Roy Bentley - was killing himself laughing! That's just one of those things that makes for a 'great moment' during times of high tension before a big game. Obviously in those days, without today's TV coverage, such incidents were never communicated to the fans or spectators and would otherwise remain firmly 'behind the scenes'.

Late 1950's Dublin Charity Match

Shortly after I had retired from playing professionally, I was invited to play in a charity match at Dublin. It was organised by Billy Morton; the invitation was all-expenses-paid plus a suggested £20.00 in 'appearance money'. To put it into perspective, this was around the time when top playing wages were less than £20.00 per week, so it was quite a reasonable proposition from my viewpoint.

Other players invited included John Charles, Ivor Allchurch, Jackie Milburn and Ernie Taylor. In other words, quite a lot of well known players of that time. On our arrival at Dublin I asked Billy Morton (whom I didn't know all that well, had not previously met but had just spoken to by telephone) to clarify what the event was for? Was it for a cancer research charity or something of that sort? He told me that the charity had been established to raise funds for a sports stadium - Santry Stadium, Dublin as it later became known. So I made the point that, had it been for a medical or similar charity, I would not have asked for any 'appearance' money, merely played for my expenses. However, as it was for something different then, naturally, I would expect to receive an appearance fee. I also asked him about the expected 'gate' size. He wasn't sure but in the event there was a 'full house' at the ground where the game was held, Daleymount Park, with about 40-45,000 paying customers.

After we had been playing for about 10 minutes, there was a message over the public-address system, announcing that the scorer of the first goal would win a gold watch, presented by Dublin jewellers, Murphys of O'Connel Street. The echo from this announcement had barely died-down when I managed to get the ball. It was at the half way line, just inside the centre circle; the defence was pretty square so I went round the first defender. I continued to go forwards and there was the centre-half coming at me and I beat him. At about 10 to 15 yards outside the penalty area, the two full-backs were converging inside, so with the goalkeeper coming out to me I lobbed one into the far corner. It couldn't have been stage managed better because, as I mentioned, the Tannoy announcement had only just been made before I was able to make this goal-scoring move! As I went back to the centre circle I held-up my arm pointing to an imaginary watch on my left wrist. This gesticulation was in the direction of the Directors' box (also containing our organizer) and, to complete the joke, I also mouthed: "What about my watch?" Perhaps some in the crowd would think 'these guys' must be able to score whenever they liked whereas, of course, it was a complete fluke. It must have been more than a thousand-to-one against. One of those things that you cannot just engineer.

Afterwards, I went to see Billy and asked him if there had been the expected good gate and whether he was satisfied? He agreed with some enthusiasm that it had been and he was. So I reminded him that I had left it to his honour to pay me accordingly. But his response was that I had won a gold watch - and that was it - no match fee! Anyway, that's really incidental because Billy Morton did a lot of good work for football in Ireland - he made a magnificent stadium in Santry, which I believe is still going to this day.

--- 0 ---

Spherical Objects

Ball 'Sense'

I am personally convinced that all moving-ball games are about a *feeling* for the ball and timing. From an early age it became apparent that, very fortunately, I had the natural blessing of *ball sense*. I believed during my playing career and still do now, that if you have been given such a gift, then:-

1) You shouldn't be bigheaded about it, and
2) It should be possible to play *any* moving ball game for a living, such as football or cricket at top class level, provided you *apply* yourself to it.

To support this contention, allow me to recount some personal anecdotes.

Anyone for Tennis

Towards the mid-to-late 1940s, my wife and I, managed a short holiday break to Morcambe with the wartime captain of Scotland and Bradford fullback, Jimmy Stephen and his wife Mary. We were both playing for Bradford P.A. at the time and I knew that Jimmy was quite a keen tennis player as indeed was his wife, Mary.

Jimmy announced that he was going to join the 'open competition' in the park and invited me to join him using Mary's racket. Well, at first I was very reluctant, admitting that I'd never had a racket in my hands before. I didn't even know how to score - in those days there wasn't the TV coverage there is today. Nor had I been exposed to the sport as a child; I was really very ignorant about the game.

But Jimmy proved very persuasive and coaxed me into entering. After the first few 'knock-ups' I discovered that I had a feel for the ball but I still felt 'a bit of a chump'. I wasn't even sure where to stand and had to ask the opponent I had been drawn against about this! He must have thought that I was 'taking the mickey' as I had a pretty good start and gradually began to take the lead. Indeed, I went on to win the tournament but I'm not trying to be at all bigheaded about it. What I

Jimmy Stephen 1944 *(Len Shackleton Collection)*

believe was responsible was my *ball sense*. As a natural phenomenon, it means that moving ball games present a common opportunity, to certain lucky individuals such as myself, who are naturally well fitted. I don't think the same is as true of 'still' ball games such as golf or snooker? Cricket though, in a slightly different sort of a way, does seem to fit into the same, intangible phenomenon. To continue with the theme, some years later I experienced American baseball firsthand and hope that the following anecdote helps to support my belief.

Painted Post

In 1957 I made a second USA visit, when Marjorie and I went on holiday with friends and then business partners, George and Dorothy Childs. George had been a talented amateur boxer in his day and was keen on sports generally. We had become friends during my early Sunderland days and had gone into small business

Grandfather 'Shack'
"Leonard Francis"

Father 'Shack'
"Leonard Price"

One country's cricketing family, another continent's baseballing one?

127

partnership together - ranging from hairdressing to confectionery and ice cream. We were staying with relations of theirs at a place about three or four hundred miles from New York City called Corning (of *Pyrex* glassware fame). Our hosts hadn't met many foreign soccer players but told us that they used to listen to the Saturday teatime results on the radio. It must have been something of a novelty in those days to have foreign visitors of our sort and they made us all feel like VIPs. We had what could only be described as a *brilliant* time! At a nearby little place called *Painted Post* we were introduced to the owner of the local baseball team. He was a nice guy and when he discovered my interest in sport, we were invited 'uptown' to the stadium and into their version of the directors' box, to witness my first 'all American' live, baseball game.

I was also playing professional cricket at that time and was curious to see in which ways baseball compared. During the whole match, which was quite lengthy (however many innings there were, I wasn't certain but there were lots of them), we never saw a *single* 'home run'! Though very sketchy in my knowledge of their game, I was aware that in the Major League games these were prized. They involved knocking the ball right out of the stadium - like a spectacular version of a *six* in cricket. After the game we discussed not having seen a 'home run' that day. After witnessing that game, my view was that 'our' cricket players, such as Brian Close or Willie Watson (the latter also then a Sunderland team-mate), could make a fortune playing in the Major League because of their cricket playing skills. I also felt that *even* I could play reasonably well in this, Minor League, class which I guessed would compare to, say, about Third Division level in soccer terms.

Our host, however, wasn't at all certain about *this* limey's frequent references to cricket! When we went down to the dressing room to meet the players, he pointed to several and 'ordered' them, including the 'pitcher', out onto the field. As he was the team owner they all complied. They took me out with them but I didn't immediately realise what his intentions were. He suggested that I should have a turn with the bat to see what I could do - and I thought 'now you've done it, Shack'! I went out on to the plate and stood with my feet wide apart in preparation. Well, the first pitch whizzed past before I'd even seen that it had left the pitcher's hand! The pitcher did the same again whilst I was trying desperately to work out what was wrong? I felt I *knew* that I ought to be able to deal with it because of my cricket playing experience but was non-plussed as to the real cause of the problem? Then, it dawned on me, when you play cricket you play with the bat *on* the ground, marking the crease. But batsmen in baseball face the pitcher with bat held at the ten-past-two position, shoulders turned ready, watching the ball. The penny had dropped just in time, because had it not, I would have looked a 'right Charlie'! Anyway, I managed to get the hang of it and then found it immediately possible to knock the ball into more or less *any* part of the ground I wanted. This *placing* of the ball wasn't the result of a practiced skill, of course, because I'd never played baseball before. It must have been due to a natural *ball sense*, in the same way as the tennis example.

Incidentally, that trip was towards the end of my playing time at Sunderland. Based on the suggested offers, I could have made a *very* good living over there, even at 34 or 35 years of age. However, the foreign way of life didn't appeal to me as much as that in the Northeast of England - and I've never been motivated just by money. Perhaps the salient point of this story is, if you have a natural *ball sense* then you can use it to make a living at more or less any (moving) ball game. That has to be better than working at something you don't like doing; in short, I consider myself *very* lucky to have been born that way!

Run Rabbit

The presence of a natural gift can, however, crop-up in other unexpected ways. As mentioned, it is nothing to be bigheaded about. What I learned to recognise was how I could adapt the ability of being naturally adept with moving balls sometimes to other things.

This brings me to another 1950's story, again with the late George Childs. He was quite keen on shooting and even had medals to prove it from his days in the services. We used to go shooting early in the mornings on a friend's land in Teesdale. Up to that point I hadn't really had any experience of any sort of firearms. But as soon as I became familiar with the single-shot 2-2 rifle, I realised what a really good 'instrument' it could be. We used to go to the riverside near Cotherstone, in very picturesque surroundings. At that time the place was plagued with rabbits, regarded by landowners as vermin needing to be controlled. We learned how to follow their movements in an attempt to develop a hunting technique. We noticed that the rabbits would run then stop, cock their ears up, test the air to be alert for predators, then move off again - as signalled by the white of their tails.

George's medals as a 'crack shot' were for *stationary* target shooting. I hadn't any experience of any sort of target! As a newcomer George would correct me on the right way to use 'our' gun - we only had one between us. Unfortunately, his stationary target ability didn't seem to help George; he had great difficulty - in fact could hardly hit a moving rabbit to save his life - which was as remarkable as it was frustrating for someone used to a higher proficiency!

George found that he couldn't react quickly enough to get the constantly moving rabbits properly into his sights. Fortunately for me, I was able to anticipate the way of their movements. When we discovered the habits of the rabbits (if the reader will forgive the pun), it seemed to go naturally from there. I would get the rifle up and wait; then when the rabbit stopped, I would shoot - and about nine-out-of-ten times I would hit it, directly in the head, without any real problem. Having said that, such a 'sport' seems barbaric and perhaps it is. But being able to make a relatively clean kill, we were helping the farmer to control a growing pest and I also remember Marje became good at making rabbit stew! What I'm trying to illustrate is, that by comparison to someone like George who was a well-practiced shot, I found I was able to more than 'keep my own'. I can only conclude that this had something to do with a natural reflex and sense of timing - like *ball sense* with football or cricket - but I'm obviously no scientist and can only speak from practical experience, i.e. as I have found things.

Golf Balls

During my sports reporting days I used to enjoy a 'working' game of golf. Many footballers and managers were keen golfers, as well as personal friends, so this provided an ideal opportunity for all. Sometimes managers or players would wish to promote a certain story in the press and my livelihood depended upon a regular supply of topical copy. It was mutually beneficial and regular playing arrangements were established with many friends over the years, e.g. Joe Harvey & Jackie Milburn, Bob Stokoe & Arthur Cox, Len Ashurst to name but a few. There were also club directors and other 'media' people; you could say we were all part of an unofficial sporting 'grapevine' - what is now termed in the modern business idiom as 'networking'.

Shackleton & Ashurst *(Len Shackleton Collection)*

One such example, which brings me closer to the real topic of this story, was the regular game with George Bailey, who had been Radio Newcastle's Sports Reporter from the early days. George was a good player with a 'scratch' handicap. He was a county standard golfer and knew all the technically correct ways to hold the different clubs for the different shots needed. By comparison, I didn't, I just did my best to hit the ball without getting too bogged-down in the technicalities or theory of the sport. For the want of a better expression, I learned to 'fiddle' my way around a course and, from time-to-time, managed to get my handicap down to about six or seven. This was not so much through natural ability or judgement, or anything like that. Because the *ball sense* discussed in this section is not much use in a 'still' ball game. However, I played golf so often that I became reasonably proficient at it *despite* the lack of doing it by the proper method.

When I played golf with George we discovered that I could match his driving-distance by, of all things, throwing up the ball into the air with my left hand, quickly grasping hold of the driver with both, swinging and then hitting it on the half-volley. Now, if my life depended on being able to drive further than George Bailey (who was a truly accomplished player) with him driving-off from the tee, I would have to do it by driving-off as described. Purely for amusement, we tested this frequently and I was usually able to knock the ball straight down the middle to out-distance George. Unfortunately, you can't legitimately do that in golf (i.e. and stay within the rules), so it didn't do my overall game a lot of good! We played in a regular 'four ball' and in many competitions. Quite often, on some of the more remote tees, George would say: "Hey Shack, show 'em your *party trick*." And I would do my best to oblige with a three-hundred-and-odd-yards half-volleyed shot! We used to enjoy ourselves with this unorthodox but harmless 'trick' shot but it all comes back to that 'God given' *ball sense*.

LFS, George Bailey & Jackie Milburn - happy days indeed.
(Len Shackleton Collection)

Cricket & Snooker Balls

I remember during the War, as a relative youngster of 17 or 18, playing cricket for Lidgett Green in the Bradford League. All the teams had Test players then because there was no County cricket during wartime. It really was a great learning opportunity for a youngster - at Lidgett Green I played on the same side as Cliff Gladwin, the England fast bowler. It was Cliff who first showed me how to 'swing' the ball; with hindsight I now know that up to that point, I hadn't previously had a clue, really. Again on that same side, was another England player, Tommy Mitchell, the leg-spinner and 'googly' bowler for Derbyshire. Something that has stayed with me, in the years since, is what remarkable talents Tommy had.

His skills could be compared with those of top class snooker players and the many ways each treat the ball; almost charming it to their will. Tommy's *party piece* also involved snooker; he would put a black snooker ball down on the spot with the white ball in balk. He would then (using his fingers in bowler's fashion) spin the white ball around the black so that it would come back to balk without touching! Even though 'unbelievable' is a rather over-used expression, the sheer degree of control of that feat when witnessed first-hand, was truly amazing! I saw it a few times but even now, all these years later, I remain enormously impressed by Tommy's skills. I've certainly never seen anyone else do anything anywhere near comparable. I don't think Tommy is with us anymore but I can pay his personal skill no better compliment than to say that the level of his ball-controlling ability has lived with me ever since.

Benwell v Benwell Hill (02-08-47); LFS 117 not out & 8 wickets for 35 runs - an unchewed survivor!

(Len Shackleton Collection)

I recall a day when my middle boy was about 10 years old. I was working as a journalist from my study at home. The room was on the ground floor, overlooking the front garden. I was working on my column for the newspaper, when I thought that I must be hearing things. I couldn't believe that what I heard was the sound of leather-against-willow. My wife didn't play cricket; the baby was too small; the eldest son was away and that only left the middle son, Roger, who as far as we were all concerned wasn't interested in sport.

But I kept hearing the distinctive sound of a bat and cricket ball. I knew that Roger was playing with his friends from the next door house in our back garden, but I thought - no, Roger can't be playing cricket - he's not ball orientated at all - he's just not interested. So, I continued with my work, although still kept hearing the sound of bat-and-ball, bat-and-ball; and shouting; and bat-and-ball, bat-and-ball. After about a half-an-hour of this Roger came in to my office and started to rummage in the glass-fronted bookcase. So I asked him what he was doing and what he was looking for? He said that he was looking for another of *those balls* and he showed me. In his hand he had the remains of a leather cricket ball. He explained that the dog from next door has chewed it up, whilst fielding!

I asked again why he was looking in the bookcase? Then I realised, we had several cricket trophies on display in those glass-doored, book shelves. In all, I had three or four of these trophies (silver shields affixed to leather cricket balls, mounted on a wooden base with miniature wickets supporting). They were good leather-case balls. The silver shields depicted some of my best ever professional cricket scores. One was from a Newcastle derby match, 02-Aug-1947, Benwell Vs Benwell Hill (117 runs not-out and 8 wickets for 35 runs). I had others from Sunderland AFC days, when I played professional cricket for Wearmouth, a local cup tie, 04-Jun-1952, Vs Whitburn (a 'hat trick' within 4 wickets for 32 runs). Another was 04-Aug-1952, Vs Philadelphia (9 wickets for 12 runs) and then another versus Chester-le-Street on my debut - that was the one the dog had chewed!

I couldn't believe it, I just couldn't believe it (shades of Victor Meldrew), that Roger had been using one of these balls to play cricket in the garden! As far as I was concerned they were irreplaceable, priceless. He then asked: "At least I took the shield off... can I have another?" To which I replied with words to the effect: "Of course you can't... you really shouldn't be using my trophies anyway." And with that I chased him away back to the garden! But I had to laugh; I couldn't help laughing - after all, I still had three of them left - maybe, if I hadn't been in working from home, the dog would have chewed them all? Then I wouldn't have the remaining ones to hand-down to my grandchildren - in fact, on that day, we nearly lost the prospect of any grandchildren at all from that source - absolutely priceless they are!

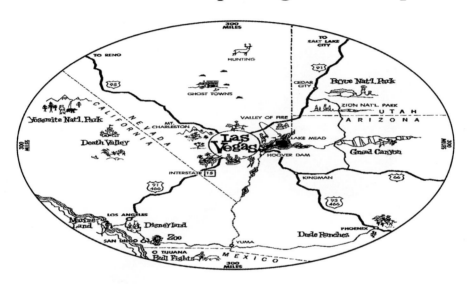

~ Chapter 8 ~
Las Vegas 1968 -
North Eastern Sporting Club's Trip

During the late 1960s, when I was still earning my living as a sports journalist, George Hardwick and I were invited to be guests of the North Eastern Sporting Club on its 10 days' trip to Las Vegas. George, now a robust octogenarian, will be remembered as a noteworthy England & Middlesbrough full back, as well as an entertaining batsman and enthusiastic fielder. The party contained a blend of interesting characters, including a young John Gibson of the *The Chronicle and Journal*. In the party was William McKeag - Alderman McKeag, then Chairman of Newcastle United. When abroad on trips like this, it was his custom to let it be known to the hosts that he used to be a British Member of Parliament (I think he was a Liberal MP but I'm not sure), as well as a football club Chairman.

In Las Vegas the word got around to the local dignitaries that there was another in town, namely Alderman McKeag. It was not very long before a 'phone call was received in our hotel from City Hall, asking to speak to him. The City wanted to bestow 'an honour' upon him and he was asked to accept the Freedom of the City of Las Vegas with a symbolic silver key as the official gift. Billy McKeag soon explained what had been proposed and that an official car was to be sent to take us to City Hall. He also suggested that a small number of us should accompany him for the ceremony. I was amongst that small number of whom he asked support. I agreed to go as I had not witnessed such an 'out of the ordinary' ceremony before and it seemed likely to be 'a bit of an education'.

So, around 10.00 a.m. the next day a big limousine drew-up at the Hotel, complete with about six police motorcycle outriders - all very grand! We whizzed down *The Strip* in Las Vegas to the City Hall and were met with all ceremony. Alderman McKeag was officially greeted by the Mayor or Chief of Police but, whoever it was performing the ceremony stressed how proud he was to be making the presentation to the Chairman of a football club and ex-member of HMG - quite a spiel in fact!

So then it was Alderman McKeag's turn to respond to all this. He obviously felt it important to address the gathering fully and, after spieling-on himself for some not inconsiderable time, our hosts seemed to be getting a little tired. There was lots of shuffling about, changing from one foot to the other, because although he was a very good speaker, he could go on a bit! After he had finished, a couple of guys came over to me and one asked (with a nod of the head in Billy McKeag's direction) "...say bud, how many are there in your party besides him...?" I replied that there were just a few of us, so the official asked if we too would also accept the keys he produced from his pocket? This was immediately after Billy McKeag had been spieling-on, at great length, about how proud he was to receive the self same *Key to the Freedom of Las Vegas*!

What was that about "spieling on"?
Anyone spot a young John Gibson?
(Pictures courtesy of the Las Vegas New Bureau)

Now to me, that was funny! I'm not absolutely certain what the moral to the story is - perhaps some people take themselves rather too seriously? 'Important' people like to be associated with other 'important' people. Chairmen of football clubs seem to be no exception. Indeed, some would say it's almost a pre-requisite for the position? Unfortunately, there seem to be very few true enthusiasts like Sunderland's present incumbent, Bob Murray!

This story about Mr McKeag reminds me of another. It was during Newcastle United's Fairs Cup run a year or so later. Still working as a journalist I was staying in the team's hotel, somewhere in Germany. It was at breakfast time and our table was joined by Mr McKeag. "...Have you heard what Mr Seymour has had for breakfast?", I enquired. He paused for a few moments before giving his reply and said: " ...there has got to be an innuendo in there somewhere Shackleton, if it is coming from you". So I rejoined: " ...Yes, well *I heard* what he had for breakfast, because I was sitting opposite him... it was porridge (slurp! slurp!). This joke suited Mr McKeag right down to the ground because of the long-standing rivalry and the differences in the background of these two directors.

Another thing that I won't ever forget from that Vegas trip, perhaps not surprisingly, is related to gambling. As you can imagine, the glittery spectacle of all the casinos and hotels, with their twenty four hours' service for, seemingly, anything (for anyone who has the money to pay for it) seemed all the more impressive in those days. Nowadays it is still as 'glittery' but with the hardness removed from the edges by the broader attractions of a national, 'family' resort.

At the time of our stay, one of the NESC's well known members turned out to be both a racehorse owner and professional gambler. I was familiar enough with the usual card games of brag and poker. We used to have a regular card school on the many trips to distant away matches, during my playing days **(see Billy Bingham's reference to this in chapter 5)**. But this, in Las Vegas, was on an altogether different scale! The gamblers, sat around the many tables, had stacks of colourful chips piled in front of them. In real money terms these often represented not just hundreds or thousands but sometimes tens or hundreds of thousands of dollars! Seeing this in real life was quite something. Being amongst those actually gambling on this scale, as one of our party was, was an even greater eye-opener! I recall one evening when most of us had circulated, risking a few dollars here and there, coming across this shrewd and courageous member at one of the poker tables. It was just like a scene from a Hollywood movie, except this was real. Our friend sat behind a considerable pile of chips. The game progressed slowly, amongst the general hubbub of the smokey surroundings in a very casual, yet businesslike way. It was quite exciting to follow but I soon decided that the company was literally too rich for my purse - and besides Marjorie would have killed me if I had arrived home with a sorry gambler's hard luck tale - however exciting taking part would have been at the time!

By about one or two a.m., I was becoming tired. So, I retired to my room leaving our friend to continue with his expensive battle-of-wits with the other 'high rollers'. I came back down for breakfast the next day at around nine or ten in the morning. I don't know whether I was really surprised or not to see that the poker game was still in full progress, as the whole thing was quite unreal. But it was and they must all have been pretty evenly matched, as our friend's pile of chips appeared little changed in size from the large pile of the night before.

Again, I'm not absolutely certain about the moral here, except that in real life the shrewdest professional gamblers most certainly 'play the percentages'. Wild risks potentially gaining high rewards are for the amateurs. Anyone taking part in such professional schools must first and foremost be able to afford to lose. At the same time he or she must be clever enough to work successfully on tight margins. Then, backed-up by steely reserve and the ability to bluff, know when to take advantage of the opposition as opportunities are engineered or present themselves. That, to me, seems the only sensible way (if there is such a thing) of managing what in other respects can be a damaging mental condition. It must be fun to be sufficiently wealthy to enjoy a less serious flutter for its own sake. But as far as encountering the 'pros' is concerned, the most entertaining thing to do is to watch!

~ Chapter 9 ~
No Longer Blank!
The Michael Parkinson Foreword

In Michael's *Daily Telegraph* article of Monday 12 October 1998, he reflects upon differences in the game attributable to today's lightweight ball, by comparison to the heavier one in use during my era. He illustrates this by mention of many older players, ending with myself and a reflection on my blank chapter 9 from *Clown Prince...* describing it as:

> " *...the most famous chapter in football biography... the idea every football writer ever since wished he had thought of first.* "

I was very flattered by Michael's view of my blank chapter and have tried hard to think of a follow-up joke of a similar kind for this book.

My son Roger asked Michael about the possibility of contributing to this, my third and final book, he said he would, work permitting.

Naturally I was very pleased at the news and replied to thank him and tell him so, whilst I also proceeded apace with work on the new text.

Then Michael suggested that instead of writing a foreword we use extracts of articles he had written about me over the years. From his public appearances and his views on chapter 9, I think we must share a similar sense of humour. So, I'd now like to reciprocate by thanking Michael for being the first football writer ever to have produced a blank foreword.

* * *

The reader will hopefully gain an appreciation of Michael's views on my playing career and abilities - which I reproduce here with all humility from the following:

The Sunday Times, 22 November 1970: Michael's piece, also mentioning the 'immortal Skinner Normanton', reflects upon his concerns about the modern (sic) game, illustrating his point using the playing exploits of his, then young, sons Andrew and Nicholas:

"It's when I play soccer with my children that I really feel the generation gap. We both love the same game but in very different ways. They and those like them are custodians of the future, and we who worshipped Shack are guardians of the past."

Another *Sunday Times* article, c.1971, refers to my first professional club, Bradford Park Avenue, then unfortunately in trouble:

"Bottom of Division Four, no gates. Strange to reflect that this was the Park Avenue of my childhood, the team that in those distant days feared no one because it was a marvellous blend of strength and skill... it was altogether different when Len Shackleton played for Bradford PA against Barnsley.

He was an artist and recognised as such and therefore allowed the licence his gifts demanded. He once came to Barnsley for a cup-tie in the days when the teams played home and away and the result was decided on aggregate.

Barnsley had held Bradford to a draw at Bradford and when the next leg was played at Barnsley it seemed certain that my lads would be through to the next round... But my biggest disappointment of all was that Bradford won the game with a goal scored by Shackleton in a manner which told me much about the man.

Bradford were awarded a penalty which was hotly disputed by players and crowd alike. After the confusion had cleared and the pitch swept clean of spectators it became apparent that the only player not standing in the Barnsley penalty area was Len Shackleton who was sitting on the ball at the far end of the field with his back to the dispute.

In his own time he strolled downfield, placed the ball on the spot, sent the Barnsley goalkeeper diving after an imaginary football and rolled the real one into the corner of the net. He bowed solemnly to the infuriated crowd and spread out his arms to signify that the game was over. And it was.

That was Bradford Park Avenue when I knew them a long time ago. Today it's just plain Bradford. Minus the Park Avenue, minus Shackleton and like many teams today minus the stuff which memories are made of ."

Next, extracts from one of Michael's articles dated Monday, December 16, 1991:

"I only watched Len Shackleton four or five times, but I can see him clearly against the hazy background of a thousand forgotten games and players.

He was one of the greatest entertainers our game has ever produced.

He illuminated the dark, drab days of post-war Britain. He gave the vast crowds who came to see him something to remember and to dream about. When modern techniques of close control are debated as if they are something new, I remember Shackleton more than 40 years ago taking the ball from any angle, at any speed and taming it in an instant. His control was so sudden and subtle that you didn't realise what he was doing. He didn't trap a ball, he hypnotised it."

And finally… back to the article first quoted above, the *Daily Telegraph* in October 1998:

"What is different now is the way the players can bend the ball. The leather job tended to go in a straight line although there were one or two who could make it dip. I would give anything to see the masters of my youth with the modern ball. What would Wilf Mannion, Tommy Harmer, or the wittiest of the lot, Len Shackleton, do with it? What tunes would they play? In his prime Shackleton could take the lace out while beating his man. Nowadays he would make the ball disappear."

Once again Michael, many thanks for sharing your memories of my playing days over the years, portraying my efforts in such a favourable light and so eloquently put too! What a good job that necessity *is* the mother of invention and we *both* ran out of time!

~ Chapter 10 ~

Commercially a full circle -
from a game with a business in it -
to a business with a game in it

"There's Money in this Game" - Stan Seymour, MD Newcastle United, circa 1949.

"Yes, Mr. Seymour, so you say but we players don't get to see much of it!" - LFS in reply.

It is a 'beautiful' game this national one of ours. At its most fundamental level this cannot be denied. It *was* before I was born as well as when I was learning to play as a tot. It *will be* after I have gone. Sir Stan is no longer with us but the finer points of the game, which he and all other 'legends' of all eras espoused and tried constantly to practice, are still there. But will they eventually be fully overwhelmed, becoming buried by the sheer weight of commercialism?

This seems to be the present danger; a risk of over-exploitation and burn-out. Fanciful, perhaps - but far-fetched, no. I also see the current problem epitomised by accelerated polarisation in the commercial fortunes of clubs. Successful, Premier League clubs go from strength-to-strength, whilst those of the lesser divisions suffer from an ever-widening gap. That's business I guess but as some would say – to quote the late Bill Shankley – our game is "more important than life and death". Very dry and humorous though 'Shanks' was, there was also a hidden axiom within his quip, because to-date the game has always transcended each and every playing generation. Has this altered for good as a result of metamorphosis into a branch of communications media-cum-entertainment industry? Like so many other things in life, it is an instance of something's greatest strength also being its greatest weakness.

It is only a *game* and people should enjoy it as the 'many splendid' and skilful sport that it is. However, it is now also inextricably linked with the world of big business, where the stakes could hardly be higher. This is not totally unique to soccer of course. All 'major league' sports in the USA now generate undreamt-of sums to their top practitioners. It's also not something too new either in the States. They have done so there on a different scale, light-years ahead of the money available in this country for many decades - this was apparent to me personally when I first visited the States in the early 1950s. And it was hardly a new phenomenon to them then. It is all a question of scale; the USA is a continent, not just a country and it has natural resources commensurately greater than our small country's. Hence, mass spectators' sports being high-up in the consumer 'food chain', have attracted a larger proportion of the wealth in a place like the USA, by comparison to here. The new commercial order in our country's game is seen as something of a revolutionary position. But I think that is just confusing the issue with the rapid growth of the commercial 'band wagon' it is now hitched to, i.e. the development of worldwide TV and other communications media. The overall process has been a more gradual and, if you like, insidious one, not half as revolutionary as it may first seem - more evolutionary. Bearing the latter aspect in-mind, of course the game has to change - like anything else in the natural scheme of things - in order to assure its own survival. But have things gone too far and are the game's true fans now being cynically exploited in most quarters?

My playing contemporaries and I all fought for the freedom of contract and to abolish the maximum wage, because the football powers-that-be from the clubs to the F.A., used to deliberately trade on the popularity of the players. What aggravated so much was that they were not doing this in an especially open way. Only occasionally would there be any 'sops' to players, usually in the form of illegal signing-on payments during transfers. There was then much hypocrisy surrounding this as many 'establishment' figures would either not comment, or worse, disavow all knowledge! Clearly, they were happy to cash-in on the popularity of the game but without recompensing the players in a *proper* manner.

At least arrangements these days *are* on a commercial footing for players, though whether overall this is for the good of the game, I don't know, only time will tell. I talk with my wife, as a football fan of long-standing herself, quite often about this. She is absolutely against what she feels are the 'obscene' wages commanded by top players today. That is not to say that she is especially bitter about it on my behalf, because she realises that we had a very good living overall from the game. I'm certainly not aggrieved about what the lads get today because it is simply the commercial outcome of a long-fought and now past struggle. After all, nobody gives 'telephone number' weekly pay simply because they *like* the player as an individual - it's a commercial decision. Obviously, though, from a personal viewpoint it is also rather a pity that it was not as commercial in my time but that's life and "the rub of the green" for you.

Let me repeat an example I have often used in the past. The first England International I played in just after the War was against Scotland, at Hampden Park, in front of crowd of 100-130,000 people! This was at a time before football returned to a normal footing, following all the wartime privations. Even given that, I remember I was only paid about 30 'bob' (shillings), or £1.50 in today's denominations, plus second or third class travelling expenses from my home in Bradford to Glasgow. I had to pay my wife's train fare and then, on our return it was so crowded that we had to stand! This struck me as wrong (economically), after having just performed in front of such a vast crowd bringing in what must have been a fortune to the organizing authorities! But this was all that I and the other 21 players were entitled to at that time. By contrast, there is now VIP treatment for all players and management staff. It is more professionally and commercially set-up for those who provide the entertainment. Let me reiterate, I'm not bitter about this as I believe it is a perfectly correct, commercial outcome. Players now command commercial 'clout' not possible in my playing time - and good luck to them!

To continue the theme of the above subject, I contacted a small cross section of people whose views I greatly respect and invited them to make a small contribution to this section of my book. This was to ensure that I was not presenting things 'in a vacuum' but rather with the broader perspective of those with up-to-date experience in both a footballing and commercial field. They span from the end of my playing time right up to the present date, in one capacity or another (players/managers/ director), namely in alphabetical order a player and manager/director sandwich:-

Brian Clough

Former Middlesbrough and Sunderland striker, described by many as the 'goal machine' (also see chapters 5 & 12) who managed nearly a goal-a-game in his

shortened career, at 250 goals in 271 appearances. This is even more productive than the renowned Messrs. Greaves or Lineker. One of football's greatest tragedies was the injury that ended Clough's career, a cruciate knee ligament was torn. In that playing era such an injury *automatically* put paid to a footballer's career. Not so today (e.g. Paul Gascoigne in the early 1990s), thanks to modern operating techniques; in fact, playing after such injuries is almost commonplace now! But it wasn't to be for 'Cloughie'. I can confirm from my recent discussions with him that he is still the same outspoken leader of men he has always been! If I could change just one thing, I

Everybody's doing it - Cloughie at SAFC's new stadium with his new book. *(Courtesy of the Sunderland Echo)*

would have Brian Clough as manager of England. He wanted the post more than anything else but it never happened – thanks (again, ugh) to the almost clueless hierarchy at Lancaster Gate. Had Clough been made manager of England we would be one of the supreme nations in the world game. But that is one of the penalties - one with which I don't find it too difficult to empathise - of being outspoken!

The present day version of the game in Brian Clough's eyes: "Football is going berserk..." he told me, "...money rules and, indeed it's getting out-of-hand, I'm afraid...". "The players are getting greedier and greedier and what's more important is the 'infection' of the player's agent - greed, pure greed. Yes, the game has gone berserk!"

Brian Clough is/was one of football's pure gems. Unfortunately he is also now almost crippled. "That's my legacy from the game. My knees are very, very bad and I can't drive a car anymore, but so what! I have the best family anyone could ask for! I hardly get back to my native Northeast now - the only connection I have is with my brother Joseph. Sometimes I get up to see him but I have had a very good career in the game - and don't forget, my door is always open to you!".

Bob Murray

Mr. Robert S. Murray is the best thing that has happened to SAFC during the past few seasons. How I wish that he had been chairman when I was a player. But… what will be, will be.

SAFC Chairman, Mr R S "Bob" Murray *(Courtesy of the Sunderland Echo)*

"As you know, Len," he told me, "it's a far different game today. Take Sunderland's Kevin Phillips; when he scores a goal on a Saturday the world sees it on Saturday night. Television is a very good thing; it has brought money into the game - but we have to use it properly."

Talking about Sunderland and Chairmen, there is a story that I cannot remember ever having told in print before: The Chairman during my first few weeks at the club was Colonel Joe Prior - he was one of the real 'old school' - he was Sunderland football daft, if you will pardon the expression for such a noble gentleman as he. On the weekend that the colonel died there had been a Sunderland home game at Roker. Some weeks afterwards his widow came into my shop in Durham Road, near to the (now demolished) Sunderland Royal Infirmary and said: "Len, I've come to tell you - the very last thing the Colonel said (he was on his 'death bed' on a Saturday afternoon) was that he asked 'how are the lads going on, how is Shack playing?' and then he died!"

What a 'real gent' I remember him to have been; what a great guy for Sunderland. The story goes: before the war he went to Ireland in search of 'fresh blood' as a centre forward for the team. But he brought back a racehorse – yes, a *racehorse*! Like Bob Murray and his near namesake Bill Murray (manager in my time at SAFC), he was a gent – H'way the lads!!

Bobby Robson

I managed to catch-up with Newcastle's Bobby Robson - an old friend whose playing career was mostly after mine - just before the start of the new 2000-01 season. What an auspicious date line that reads. As might be imagined his existence at that level in today's game is more than just hectic and I'd like to formally thank him for putting himself out to come back to me in the way he did. Anyway, Bobby told me:-

"The curse of Premiership football is, without doubt, the soccer agent. They are the parasites, the spongers who only 'take out' of the game. They put nothing back. Indeed, the agents cause me, as a manager, more problems than any other thing in the game! I have to put up with them, though. They unsettle players, extract money out of the game and the players they are supposed to be working for! I reckon it takes *four* agents to complete a transfer of a player from one club to another these days - and they each want a cut out of the deal - pure greed!

Tactical 'supremo', Bobby Robson, now manager of NUFC. *(Courtesy of Newcastle Chronicle & Journal)*

"Relatively speaking to what you and I had in our playing times, it is probably true that soccer players have too much commercial clout - again, today's lot really are just plain greedy - but like I've said, the players' agents are the real villains and encourage this in players."

In our playing time, *football was a game with a business in it*. Now it is purely and simply *a business with a game in it*. For example, Premier League clubs receive £8 to 10 million each by way of media driven support. Bobby rates the Premiership the best in the world of football. And 'Robbo' can speak with real authority after successfully managing clubs in the Football League, the Spanish La Liga, plus Dutch and Portuguese soccer. Indeed, Bobby Robson should never have been forced-out of British football - but that's another story.

To me, 'Robbo' is a very talented manager of men, one of the best tactical brains in world football with an extraordinary eye and judgement of a young player. Indeed, he 'found' perhaps the best foreign centre forward I have ever seen - he spotted Brazilian Ronaldo, when the player was a young teenager. He 'managed' him in Dutch football and to back his judgement, he took him to Barcelona (Barca), when he became boss of the Spanish club.

I watch Barca regularly and can honestly say that I have not seen a centre forward to better Ronaldo's abilities. He is certainly the equal of his near namesake, Rivaldo. Ronaldo has the 'lot' - blistering pace, he's fast and quick and brave - what else is there? Also, using my experience of Spanish football (as a spectator, that is), now that Ronaldo is playing in Italian football - when he is not injured - I rate his fellow Brazilian, Rivaldo. The best centre forward in the world at the present time?

A wider consideration of the 'greats' of many eras is covered in chapter 12; to link these observations - and for the record in my opinion - Dixie Dean, Tommy Lawton, Ted Drake and Alan Shearer are not in the same class as Rivaldo - although I realise how unfair it is to compare past with present - but as has been said elsewhere, football is a game of opinion. That's how all fanatics are able to share in the experience and what keeps it truly vital, far more than just monetary considerations!

Penalty Shoot-outs

I hope my observations on the general topic of the financial pendulum having fully arced from a player's viewpoint, over the last 40-50 years, appear positively based as they were intended to be. After all, when one considers what agents and commercial sponsors would make of moves to turn the clock back and reintroduce a maximum playing salary and abolish freedom of contract, it is clear that the progress has been real. That is not to say that the situation is without its abuses; don't just take my word for it, rather refer to the comments of Messrs. Clough and Robson above.

Changes do not always have to be all that radical to bring about real improvement. For instance, it has long been my view, as a spectator, that every game I witness should preferably have a positive result at the end of it. Whereas, the laws or rules of the game have undoubtedly stood the test of time, there should always be room for changes of an 'evolutionary' nature. As considered elsewhere, modern soccer is part of the entertainment industry - it always has been but thanks to satellite coverage extending flexibility so much (there are literally many millions of

Manchester United followers in China, of all the otherwise inaccessible places for it to occur) everything has become greatly magnified. People seeking to be entertained will not be, if a game ends in frustration due to a drawn result.

Hence, my suggestion that with slight modifications to the rules by the introduction of mandatory penalty shoot-outs, in the event of a draw, throughout the whole of football. This could be considered as a way to always ensure a *positive* result. The full time score would still count for the purposes of the football pools but, otherwise, a shoot-out would then follow to overcome the staleness of a draw. That is not to say that there would be no disadvantages - and that on some occasions fans may not find the outcome fully to their liking - but one game's final defeat by these means could be turned around on the next occasion. That, I believe, would be the key to the idea's success, i.e. that the change would be a *positive* development.

It would also help to improve the penalty-taking skills of our country's soccer players - and how many times have we all suffered great angst at the worst possible moment during a 'big' international or foreign tournament occasion? Practice makes perfect and what better way of properly improving proficiency than to develop greater live or real-time opportunities. The world's most highly paid sportsmen and women come from America where their own version of football has 'special team' elements. Perhaps soccer is seen as not as complex as American Football, so we could make do with a 'quasi-special team' set-up for penalty-takers. This would comprise those players with the most fitted temperament and naturally good shooting skills. I'm sure that the coaching regime could easily adapt to meet such a challenge. I'm not about to start a formal campaign for this, although any readers interested enough to support my idea are hereby invited to send me a postcard to the address shown on the verso page of this book. Alternatively, the "lenshackleton.com" website will forward e-mail to me! I'd be *very* interested to hear from you all, either for or against!

~ Chapter 11 ~
New Freedom of Contract
Fairer to Players after the George Eastham Case

Ernie Clay & Fulham Board

I came into contact again with Ernie Clay several years after the George Eastham case (see details of latter below) at his hotel in Portugal. It was the year after Newcastle United had won the Fairs Cup (1969). They went out to play one of the Portuguese sides as part of their Cup defence. We stayed at Ernie's hotel in a place called Sintra, about 30 or 40 miles from Lisbon. As he was on the Board at Fulham we talked quite a lot about football. I knew that Ernie, as a self-made businessman was astute in his dealings. I made my thoughts and feelings about the game quite plain. Fortunately for me, Ernie seemed to be 'on the same wavelength' although I also got the impression that he was none too familiar with all the 'ins and outs' of the game, even as a director. It was possibly true to say that, as a wealthy man, he was probably in the game for the kudos of directorship as much as any direct interest in the game. Perhaps, not so ironically then, that at that time, Fulham was a poorly run and not very successful side.

Having re-established our acquaintanceship, Ernie later came to visit me on several occasions at my Sunderland home. He asked me if I would like to become a member of Fulham's Board - but I had no aspirations or ambitions of that sort and at first declined. It was all very flattering but, being candid, I felt what he really wanted by the offer was to call upon my experience of the game and 'pick my brains' as a sort of unpaid consultant as it were. I don't really think that this reflected anything bad about him and overall I believed that he was a good guy. He persisted trying quite hard to talk me into it; he explained that it would only require a weekly meeting, not a full time 'position' at Craven Cottage. He even went as far as offering a helicopter 'collection service' for me to attend meetings - from the field opposite our house at Cliffe Park in Sunderland! Somewhat against my better judgement, I eventually agreed to go along with his proposals.

I flew down to London (though by plane from the airport) for my first board meeting. I remember that I encountered some very interesting people; these included Ted Drake (former Arsenal centre forward and Chelsea manager) and Birtie Mee (whom I think had been Arsenal's manager when they achieved the post war *double*). As a 'one off' it was an interesting enough experience but I couldn't describe myself as being thrilled by it. Apart from anything else, I didn't really *like* the idea of a weekly trip down to London because this would cause a significant break in my established and practical journalistic routine, working from home. On reflection, when I first returned home, I really should have told Ernie that I wasn't very comfortable with the overall 'board situation'. At the same time I felt that I couldn't just baldly say to Ernie: "Thanks, that was okay but, no, I don't really want to be on the board after all." Fortunately, however, my newspaper employers made it easy for me. The editor of *The People* 'ruled' that it was likely to be against the terms of my employment agreement. I was apparently at risk of bias in my reporting, if I was associated with one club in particular. Whereas I thought I was still capable of functioning accurately and objectively, this editorial decision provided me with a way of withdrawing that would not cause personal offence to Ernie. So - that was that, a single board meeting - but without any 'sour grapes' whatsoever, I was quite relieved really!

Ernie Clay & The George Eastham Case

Coming back to develop the theme of Ernie's earlier role in relation to freedom of contract: - We had shared concerns about the unfairness of football clubs being able to hold a player by the device of *his* (irony) annual contract. The position had been

Messrs Eastham, senior & junior - both friends of Ernie Clay *(Courtesy of George Eastham)*

that each year after expiry, the club could hold-up any renewal, whereas the player could not sign for an alternative club! This due to a player's *Registration* being held by his club. In my view this was a stupid and inefficient practice that could only alienate and not best utilise the talents it was designed to secure. It was simply unfair to players, not least because it could not be imposed in other occupations. For example, if a motor mechanic's contract has expired he would be quite free to go and work for any (rival) garage prepared to pay him. Not so the system of footballers' contracts and registration, which was part of what I (and surely any reasonably-minded participant or enthusiast of the game) regarded as a patently unfair one.

In the early 1960s George Eastham was one of the game's 'leading lights', playing for Newcastle United as an inside forward. As a journalist I had had discussions with George about the unfairness of the contract in English football and we were in general agreement about the problem. Ernie Clay had heard of George's views and asked me to put him in touch. He had also known George Eastham senior during his wartime service. George senior had been a top class player himself, for Bolton before the war. This seemed a good idea since Ernie was not only a person with like views on the topic but also the resources to back them up! So, I performed the introductions and the rest, as they say, is history! Ernie gave him a job and George later took the issue of the unfair, 'slaves' contract to court. This can now be seen as the forerunner to the eventual 'Bosman ruling'. For ease of reference, I have looked into the details of these cases and provide summaries immediately below.

The George Eastham Case

A new deal for footballers, the football Association and Football League. The Rules of the Football Association, concerning the retention and transfer of professional football players, were found to be not binding and were an unreasonable restraint to trade. This as found in July 1963 by Mr. Justice Wilberforce, when George Eastham took Newcastle United F.C. to the Royal Courts of Justice as a challenge to the system. The situation had come about when George Eastham wanted to leave Newcastle United to accept a lucrative job offer outside football and play for another club. Newcastle United had forbidden him to do any of these. The decision in this case became a crucial factor, in that all the contracts signed by 2,700 members of the Professional Footballers' Association were thereby deemed illegal; the system that had tied them to their clubs when a player's contract ended had done likewise! For the first time in 60 years players achieved a 'new deal' in football.

Prior to the findings of the Courts of Justice, George Eastham had fallen out of favour with Newcastle United. He wished to leave the club and had not signed a new contract. But under the Regulations of the Football League Newcastle United could retain control of his services for as long as they wanted to with no liability for paying wages! The result had traditionally produced an impasse with a player having no financial choice but to give in. George, however, refused to submit and give his continuing services to the club. Enter Ernie Clay; an old family friend who offered assistance which changed the whole financial situation for George. Ernie, a Yorkshireman, was a cork manufacturer based in Reigate, Surrey and a long-standing family friend - Messrs. Clay & Eastham Senior had been in the army together. From the resultant publicity Ernie Clay became one of the best known businessmen in the country.

As the dispute widened to serious proportions the newspapers, national and local, gave extensive coverage. Ernie Clay's assistance took the form of employing the player in his firm at wages of £20.00 per week. Hence, alternative employment changed the situation considerably and Newcastle United no longer held all the cards. Up to that point, any player attempting to fight the system came up against an insurmountable economic barrier, for if he no longer wished to play for his club, he was also prevented from continuing with his career elsewhere. (Such had famously also been the case of Wilf Mannion, his earlier dispute with Middlesbrough ending in his financial failure).

Newcastle manager Charlie Mitten's negative attitude towards the transfer request had stiffened George Eastham's resolve. On the 4th of July 1960 George left the club and joined E. J. Clay Ltd as an employee working in Reigate. George then made contact with the Professional Footballers' Association. He sought advice on " …the validity of the extinct contract with Newcastle United… ", reasoning that there was a legal flaw in the system that would not allow a footballer the inalienable, democratic right to choose his own employment. Cliff Lloyd, the well-informed Secretary of the P.F.A., agreed to help by suggesting that an appeal be made formally to the Football League against Newcastle's refusal to transfer the player in accordance with the terms of his request. The Football League replied that it had no power to adjudicate on what was considered a 'domestic' matter between the club and the player.

The decision scrutinised by the P.F.A. appeared to be in direct contradiction to Regulation 19 of the Football League. That is, if any dispute or difference should arise between a club and any of its players, the Management Committee shall, upon application made by either party, consider and adjudicate upon the matter or the question in dispute. The regulation was invoked and George Eastham immediately appealed against the Football League's ruling. Similarly, the Football League took immediate action by asking Newcastle United for representations. Eastham was interviewed again by Newcastle's manager - to encourage him to re-sign his contract - but quite rightly of course, no progress was made! The League then attempted a conciliation process, by asking the player to take his advisors (Cliff Lloyd and Ernie Clay) to meet with the Chairman and Manager of the club but the result of this was continued stalemate. With no satisfaction derived from appeals to the Football League and following much deliberation, George Eastham's solicitors sent the Football League a history-making letter. They gave the League a third and final opportunity to adjudicate in accordance with their own regulations. The League was given seven days' notice to reply, failing which their client had instructed them to take whatever steps counsel may advise, to enable him to continue in pursuit of his livelihood as a professional footballer. This unprecedented move met with no reply. So, on the 13th October 1960, a writ was issued against Newcastle United, the Football Association, the Football League and the individual Directors and Manager of Newcastle United, by the Chancery Division of the High Court. This quickly spurred the club into action, although no communications were directed towards George himself! In November 1960 George Eastham was transferred to Arsenal for a fee of £47,500. Later, in July 1963, Mr. Justice Wilberforce found George Eastham's case *just* and history was made in professional football!

The Bosman Ruling

In 1988, R.F.C. Liege signed Jean-Marc Bosman for approximately £66,000 equivalent. Only two years later after his contract expired a renewal was offered but involving a 60% cut in wages as part of the new deal! Bosman's counter was a preferred move to Dunkerque but Leige's requirement was a transfer fee demand in excess of £250,000 equivalent. This was more than double what Dunkerque felt able to pay and left Bosman stymied. Which situation prompted him to take court action claiming to be the victim of unfair restraint of trade. It was fought all the way to the European Court of Justice, eventually finding in Bosman's favour.

Existing transfer regulations were deemed in *breach* of European Law governing workers' freedom-of-movement between EU member states. This ruling also expounded as illegal, the restriction in the number of foreign players able to be fielded in European competition. Perhaps naturally, there was much consternation as smaller clubs' lifeline in the development and later sale of young talent was a primary source of income. In this country the P.F.A. thought that many of its members could be put out of work as a result of a likely influx of foreign players from elsewhere within the EU. However, within a week the ruling was accepted by the Premier League with clubs being advised that they were free to field numbers of EU nationals as they saw fit! The Premier League's Chief Executive could be said to have displayed shrewd diplomatic tactics. He suggested that the British system would be the model for the EU, i.e. that an out-of-contract player is automatically granted a free transfer if any new deal offered is not *at least* on the same terms as his expired one.

From the ruling it became clear that neither deals between British clubs nor transfers between countries outside the EU were affected. The Court's decision had only concerned out-of-contract EU nationals transferring between member states. Agents' predictions were that players would reap great windfalls, namely: signing-on fees' bonuses *combined* with higher wages to attract the out-of-contract stars or potential ones. In other words, a diversion of the money that would formerly have been spent on transfer fees. Perhaps this will also mean much lucrative work for lawyers, when players attempting to exploit the ruling via transfers between English clubs through an intermediary, temporary transfer to an EU one?

There has been mention of planned EU legislation to compensate small clubs for talented players they have helped to develop should they leave under the Bosman rule. It will be interesting to see just how things develop from here? If nothing else, it also emphasises one long-standing aspect of the game, that without such controversy fans and enthusiasts would soon find things rather dull. Football has always been a game of opinion and it will continue to be the case!

As a complete aside and bringing this book up-to-date there is a tenuous connection with a current problem beyond my professional era. Namely, 'drugs in sport'; that is not to get too serious about things but merely that I'd noticed an interesting legal report. Apparently, Messrs. Christie, Walker and Richardson - together with other athletes from this country mixed-up in the 'Nandrolone' issue - have been on the receiving end of news potentially helping them in this matter. Evidence had been presented by a certain Belgian lawyer, named Jean-Louis Dupont, that could help swimming's world governing body *FINA* to clear two positively-tested 'Nandrolone' swimmers. The connection? Monsieur Dupont represented Jean-Marc Bosman in his landmark case – what was it about lucrative work for lawyers concerning controversy in sport again?

~ Chapter 12 ~
My friend Barney Ramsden and other Great Players of all Eras

As my sister's husband, Alan, is fond of saying: "Your friends you can pick, relations you're stuck with". Well a very, very good friend of mine was Bernard 'Barney' Ramsden whose career was ending at Sunderland as mine was just starting. He joined Liverpool from Sheffield Victoria in March 1935 at about 17 years old. As everyone now knows, Liverpool's greatest sustained success did not come until after the second war by which time Barney's best years were about passed. The 'stats' show he made 23 appearances for Liverpool's post-war Championship side, continuing his wartime links with Jim Hartley - a Scot and right back who had also joined Liverpool as a 17 year-old but in 1934, the year before Barney. At the time of Liverpool's post-war Championship success Barney was about 30 years old and, by that time, feeling the combined adverse affects of wartime service and injury on the field.

Barney

So, unfortunately for Barney, it was the turn of international events that saw him at Liverpool either too soon or, at least, without sufficient continuity for what would have been the prime years of his career. In pre-Sunderland days Barney must go down with members of the older generation as one of Liverpool's best ever left backs. I'm sure it's no exaggeration to say that he was indeed amongst Liverpool's 'all time greats' in this position. One of Barney's closest mates from his Liverpool days was later to become famous as their manager - Bob Paisley. Barney rated Bob as a genuine and reliable friend, recommending him as someone to turn to if ever help was needed in bad times. This must strike a chord with many of Bob's native North Easterners, I'm sure.

Barney's arrival at Sunderland may have marked the closing stage of his playing career but what a good team-mate he was! He was a fellow Yorkshireman and reliable friend as well as team stalwart. To those who knew him personally he was also quite a 'character' possessed of many a colourful tale. Perhaps one of his most remarkable, concerns wartime exploits in the Mediterranean, Barney was involved in raids on Italy at the infamous assault on Monte Casino. He was a sergeant major and during this campaign he and one of his men captured an enemy vehicle loaded with art treasures plundered by the Germans from France. They captured the enemy complete with their plunder. Barney and his comrade were sufficiently tempted to plan burial of the 'treasure' for later liberation. However, his tale did not have the hoped-for prosperous outcome. Despite 'X marks the spot' methodology, they were unable to find it during later searching! This was probably for the best as Barney was basically a good and honest guy. He was certainly no rogue or vagabond which otherwise the nature of this tale may suggest? What he would have done with the 'art treasures' if he had found them again, I don't know? Maybe it's easy for someone like me who has not been as close to the equivalent of a big lottery win, to say this. But I'm sure it worked out 'right' in the end as he wasn't permanently tainted by it - and it was always a fascinating experience to hear him tell the tale over a few drinks! Just like 'Chis' (who was a character-and-a-half for other reasons), friends like this are rare indeed and I consider such friendships to have been priceless and, in that sense, the 'maximum wage' didn't get a look-in!

SAFC full squad 1949-50 *(courtesy of the Sunderland Echo)*

As mentioned, when I first came to Sunderland, Barney's career was about at an end. The biggest upset of Sunderland's century came at that time when we were knocked out of the third round of the FA Cup by Non-League Yeovil. All long-term Sunderland fans will recall this with much pain - when we, the then First Division's so-called 'Bank of England' club played the Somerset side. According to both informed critics and their own form, Yeovil shouldn't have stood the metaphorical 'cat in hell's chance' - but they beat us nonetheless! To this day in Sunderland, whenever cup-ties arise we never seem to hear the last of that particular match and the unexpected result! Barney played fullback and was given a lot of 'stick' for the defeat. What I suspect is that the Directors, knowing that his playing career was more or less finished, decided that 'shouldering the blame' on Barney would help get them off the hook - whilst doing the minimum damage to the other 'first-teamers'. But I felt that that was unfair on Barney who was effectively 'scape-goated' simply because of the stage he was at in his career. That may be part of life but not a very fair or pleasant outcome for such a great bloke!

Well, sometimes when one door closes another opens. When he left Sunderland, Barney became one of the Football Association's first-ever qualified coaches. He was a wonderful coach with a good attitude and ability to handle men - as proven by his sergeant major's wartime rank - with a big and powerful stature in every sense of the word. He did a remarkable job in Scandinavia for the Norwegians, who really didn't know a football from a cricket ball at that time. A small country and we know what strides they have made since, but it was Barney who helped to sow the seeds and paved the way for the present day Norwegians to perform as they do.

--- 0 ---

Career Statistics

I am particularly grateful to the grandson of Teddy Doig (SAFC 1890-1904), Eric Doig, as a member of the Association of Football Statisticians for providing the following details on Barney's career. After all, it's the least I can do by way of tribute to my late friend - to ensure that the facts have been checked via an authentic source! As Barney knew, I was never anything of a Leslie (Mr. Memory) Welch at the best of times and now that I'm approaching 'the big eight' things aren't getting any better! So, thanks again Eric, your contribution as hereunder:

Full Name:	Bernard Ramsden.
Nickname:	Barney.
Birth:	Sheffield, England, 08 November 1917.
Died:	March 1976, Terminal Island, Los Angeles, California, USA.
Early Career:	Hampton Sports (Sheffield), Sheffield Victoria.
L/Pool F.C.:	Signed March 1935, age 17 years, 4 months.
League Debut:	28 August 1937 age 19 years, 10 months at left back v Chelsea (away); lost 1-6.
Wartime:	37 L.F.C. appearances, also guest ones for Brighton & Hove, Leeds Utd. and York City.
Div.1 Seasons:	1937/38, 1938/39, 1946/47, 1947/48 (4 appearances).
L.F.C. Apps:	League 60, F.A.C. 6; Total 66; no goals.
Honours:	First Division Championship Medal 1946/47.
Last Game:	L.F.C. 25 December 1947, age 30 years, 1 month v Arsenal (home); lost 1-3.
Sunderland:	Signed 15 March 1948 v Stoke (away), lost 1-3 (Shackleton No.10).
Seasons:	1947/48 (2 appearances), 1948/49 (10 appearances); Total 12 League, 1 F.A.C.
Last App:	29 January 1949, age 31 years, 2 months in F.A. Cup v Yeovil; lost 1-2 (aet).

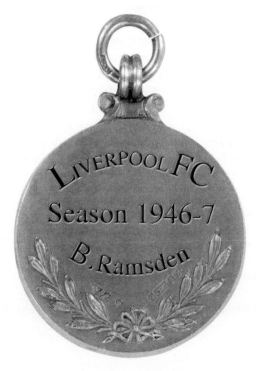

Thanks to John Charles
Ramsden (San Pedro, CA),
for providing these medal
photographs.

Other Great Players of all Eras

In considering the best players I've seen over the last 50 years or so it becomes really clear what a very subjective thing this is. It's very difficult to try and assess the many relative characteristics and also hope to be definitive at the end of it. Football is a game of opinion and so my summing-up of the situation is simple:- a great player would be a great player in *any* era! Apart from that, you can't pretend to be too objective - by just the same token that you can't compare a Rolls Royce with a Jumbo Jet.

I've tried hard to gauge, as fairly as I can, the best players to my recollection - and I can go back quite a long way. There are players like:- *Alex James* (Preston and Arsenal), *Cliff Bastin* (Exeter City and Arsenal), *George Male* (Arsenal), *Eddie Hapgood* (Arsenal) and *Wilf Copping* (Leeds United and Arsenal). So we *are* going back a long, long time here. To refresh the memories of those as old as me, I have researched the archives to paint accurate 'pen pictures' of these stars of a time long ago. But I make no real apology for this on the grounds that in my opinion, they would be deserving stars of today, had the timing of their birth been more recent. I am convinced that with today's media coverage all these people would be household names, rarely off our screens. The biographical details can be found at the end of this section.

Forwards & Play Makers

Having considered all these I think *the* best player, or in the top 'echelon' so to speak, for all round ability has got to be **George Best** of Manchester United. I know he's a character regarded as 'a waster' by many but *George* had everything. He was fast, he was quick, he never seemed to stop running; he had a real 'engine' inside him and he could play, I would think, in any position in the forward line as we used to know it. Even comparing him to *Maradona*, or *Peter Doherty* (Blackpool, Manchester City, Derby County, Huddersfield Town and Doncaster Rovers) - he was at Derby County when I started; a great player was *Peter*, he could run for 90 minutes and then be ready for another 90!

But we're talking about 'ball-players-cum-footballers' now and so *Tom Finney* (Preston North End) comes next. *Tom* could play at outside-left, outside-right or centre-forward and I suppose he could play inside-forward if he was asked to do so. He was one of the absolutely outstanding players in my era, plus being a great guy and valued personal friend.

When we come back to the present day, there is 'Gazza', *Paul Gascoigne* is or was very, very talented. Again he too was fast and quick, he was brave, he could head it; he knew the game but… well we all know what happened to *Paul* in his private life, a bit like 'Besty'.

Coming back to the other 'all time greats', the best goal scorer that I have ever seen (and I can go back to *Ted Drake* at the Arsenal just before the War, I could go up to *Gary Lineker*, I could go up to all of the 'modern day', for the want of a better term, goal scorers) and there has never been a better one in my view as *Jimmy Greaves* (Chelsea, AC Milan, Tottenham Hotspur and West Ham). He was *the* perfect goal scorer. We've had some brilliant ones to compare to, like *Geoff Hurst* - with his 'hat trick' in the World Cup Final (and anybody who does that deserves to be classed as one of the 'all time greats'). But *the* best goal scorer must be *Jimmy Greaves* - he was especially quick and had two really good feet. When you saw *Jimmy* going through the centre of the field with just the centre-half or the goalkeeper to beat, such was his ability that you felt that his only problem was who he was going to shake hands with first, after he had scored! I must put *Jimmy Greaves* in my top echelon as a goal scorer.

Another of the goal-scorers worthy of emphasis is *Gary Lineker* (Leicester, Everton, Tottenham and Barcelona), not least as you can't argue against facts - his goals' record for England is summarised in the 'biographies' section towards the end of this chapter. To me *Gary* was *the* typical successful opportunist cum 'tap-in-merchant'. Whereas it is easy to tap-in the ball from a few yards out, the secret lies in getting into that position in the first place. On many occasions, his critics would claim that anyone could have scored 'from there' and yes they could, if they had put themselves in that position in the first place! *Gary* must be handed full marks for the skill and effort involved in being in that position for the 'tap-ins'! *Gary* was what I term 'quick', and he was 'fast'. The distinction between the two is that the former is very, very 'pacey' over a few yards, say 3 or 4, whereas the latter means that the player can go at great speed over a greater distance, say 20 or 30 yards.

I must now bring in *Maradona*; he was an absolute wizard - the infamous 'Hand of God' goal that he scored against England will never be forgotten. In the context of that particular match (i.e. cheating apart), though, his first goal was absolutely brilliant! Indeed, I think it is the best goal that I have *ever* seen! He went through, beating several men, picked his spot to slot it in. That must bring us to *Eric Cantona* (Marseilles, Paris St. Germain, Leeds and Manchester Utd.) who has got to be one of *the* 'greats'. Again, see more details in the biography part. However, the moral to the *Cantona* story I would like to emphasise, is that to have a truly successful career, not only do you have to have the necessary skills but, perhaps more importantly, you have to be part of a really good side. The converse of this is that it can be soul destroying for any player of ability and flair to play as part of a bad side - he can also take the blame for not performing miracles! So the best combination of all is as it was when *Eric* stepped onto the Old Trafford field.

To the immediate modern day, young *Michael Owen* (Liverpool), whom I don't know but, again, he seems to have the 'makings' of being one of *the* 'greats'. He hasn't yet passed the test of time at his age or at this stage in his career. But if he can continue in the same vein, he ought to be able to join the ranks of names like *Dennis*

Law (Aberdeen, Huddersfield, Manchester City, Torino and Manchester Utd.), *Eric Cantona, Tom Finney, Gazza, George Best* - time will demonstrate it one way or the other - and I hope I'm still here to see if my prediction is proven!

Not to be overlooked is *Brian Clough*, whose record of goals-per-game speaks for itself. Some critics have argued that, as most of them were in the Second Division, then it is not as impressive as it might be. However, that is very unfair as it was not *Brian's* fault that he was not always in the First Division. His record of top (Second Division) scorer for three successive seasons surely demonstrates his contribution to the team effort to win promotion. Sadly, therefore, premature retirement due to injury prevented him from silencing critics of this sort, by going on to emulate Messrs. *Lineker* or *Cantona* in their highest division scoring records.

Back Four Defenders (Centre-Halves)

There are a selection of these that must be mentioned in an 'all time greats' context; they are the 'back four' of the defence to put it in the modern idiom. Without a doubt, *the* best that there has ever been was 'big' *Frank Brennan* (Newcastle Utd.). *Frank* had 'the lot'. He was big and tall (6ft-odd); he was tough - he would let the ball get past or the man get past but never the two of them together! Big *Frank* was my ideal centre-half and he was fast. Even as big as he was, and as a middle-of-the-park-defender, he could do the 100 yards in 10 seconds! In my book he was *the* best in his position, i.e. as a forward you *didn't* want to play *against* 'big' Frank!

We can also come back to other contemporaries of mine like *Raich Carter*, although being older than I, he had nearly ended his career when I played against him. He was one of the best and certainly deserves a place in 'the hall of fame' or *my* version of it. I hope this helps to support my original contention that a *great* player would be so in *any* era.

Now, going from beyond my own playing time, *Charlie Hurley* must rate as one of the top centre-half players. When he was still playing I used to joke with him by claiming that 'anyone' could play at centre-half and why 'the hell' not try at centre-forward? It is the 'glamour' position as *Alan Shearer* has proved. *Charlie*, who was a guy of very likeable temperament, would get his own back on me every time we met by talking about playing centre-forward, knowing that this would 'stir it up'! In my view he was far too good a player to be a centre-half. As an opposing inside-forward or centre-forward, I *would* want to play against centre-halves like *Charlie*. I certainly mean no disrespect to *Charlie's* ability because as far as I am concerned he had all the talent in the world! But it really was quite an enormous waste of a good centre-forward! To explain this view a little further, what a waste for a potentially *great* centre-forward to play in a 'negative' position - because stopping the other guy from scoring *is* negative. But *Charlie* was built for the job, he had an ideal build, although perhaps he wouldn't have been 'quick' or 'fast' enough to get right to the absolute top? But his skill alone would surely have got him 4/5 of the way up 'the ladder' to being one of *the* great centre-forwards of all time, certainly in my estimation. I'm not quite sure just how many goals he will have scored from 'set pieces' by using his head? The record books will have to be closely scrutinised to answer that but he must have scored quite a few that way. Further, what could he achieve with today's ball - the 'goalkeeper's nightmare'! I'm sure *Charlie* would be certain to score a lot more goals than he did with the old ball. So, whereas we used to joke together about the centre half/forward situation *Charlie* in my book (literally) was one of the best players I've ever seen - and I certainly like to classify him as 'a mate' of mine!

Arthur Wright, the wing-halfback, really was a classic example at this position. I don't think that I've seen a better ball player, ever, than *Arthur Wright* in that position. He would have been *absolutely* perfect, in my view, but for being a little short of aggression. It seemed he did not have quite sufficient 'devil' or 'bite' in him when it came to getting 'stuck in' to the opponents, as he didn't want to fall foul of kicking the opponent off the park! By contrast, the converse of *Arthur* must have been *Billy Elliott*. I was actually instrumental in bringing *Billy* from the direction of Bradford. He came to Sunderland via Burnley in the end. He and I played together in Bradford as youngsters. When I was transferred from Newcastle to Sunderland, I talked to Bill Murray about this young talent from Bradford. I mentioned him quite a lot - not that I really expected him to take very much notice of my views - but I felt strongly enough about Billy's abilities that I was reasonably persistent. He really should have taken a trip to Bradford to see the player. However, instead of coming straight to Sunderland he was transferred to Burnley, where he played at outside-left. Now *Billy* was no more an outside-left than I was. He was completely out of position - but he played for England at that position as well! I don't know what that proves, other than a certain lack of correct judgement on the part of England's management at the time, especially if old 'WW' had anything to do with it.

Eventually Sunderland did acquire *Billy* from Burnley but for a lot more money than he was originally transferred from Bradford! He was a top class talent and the fee from Bradford hadn't exactly been inexpensive but Sunderland's final price reflected the earlier lost opportunity. I'd like to think of *Ell* as we all used to call him as a mate of mine and I have a lot of time for his natural ability as I hope the above testimony illustrates? He played at Sunderland as outside-left and left-back but still didn't play in his proper position. I hope the remaining fans from those days can remember *Ell's* range of talents and appreciate the point I'm trying to get across? He would, for me, have been one of the best in the world as a wing-halfback stopping the opposition's inside-forward from scoring - a lot like *Roy Keane* (but with a left foot) at Manchester United. Given the talent of players of this ability, they can still come up and contribute to the score sheet and knock a few goals in when it's required. Well *Ell* was in that bracket to me and would have been one of the greatest ever wing-halfbacks. What would England, post Euro 2000, now give for a left-sided player a la *Elliott*?

Another comparison would be *David Batty* of Newcastle, Leeds and England. Whereas I think it is true that he doesn't often make a bad pass, some would say he doesn't often make a good one but where he predominates is by stopping the opposition from playing and this is vital to the balance of a team. *Billy Bremner* was a great character and footballer of talent but his main role, under Don Revie at Leeds, was to stop the opponents from playing! The opposition's inside-forward 'danger man' would be identified and if the object of the exercise was to prevent positive play in the opposition, *Billy Bremner* was the man to do it! That brings me back to what was just mentioned above, a question of balance or blend.

A wing-halfback of a different calibre was *Stan Anderson* of Sunderland, Newcastle and Middlesbrough. Another good friend of mine and what a good player - what a skilful wing-halfback he was, though totally opposite to 'Ell' or *Roy Keane*. A beautifully well-balanced player who fully deserved to be capped internationally a lot of times. (Stan was the converse of my quip with *Ken Chisholm* that his speed was deceptive - *Ken* was slower than he looked - whereas *Stan's* speed truly was deceptive as he was *faster* than he looked). Being geographically 'isolated' in the Northeast, in a time before today's sort of TV coverage was available, meant that he didn't get the sort of opportunity to come to the attention of the selectors which his talent really warranted.

Similarly, 'little' *Billy Bingham*, the Irish outside-right. He was a 'canny' winger but to me he almost gave the impression, when he went over to take corners, that he might not have the strength to get it over to where it was needed, to the far post or wherever. He certainly was a 'little terrier' prepared to chase lost causes. This all comes back to the sort of blend that a truly able and balanced team should have. Truly a case of a small player with a more-than-ample heart. A good and effective player, the sort that can make a difference to the overall team performance. Many full-backs knew that they had been in a game after 90 minutes on the field with *Billy*!

Players of today? Well, *Alan Shearer* - his goals speak for themselves in the League; they certainly do for England for that matter. Although he has probably now 'had his day', to put this in perspective there are not many top class players - scorers even more so - that last very many years at their peak. At his peak, I felt that *Shearer* was/is as good as there has ever been. To compare him with players of a former time, i.e. my contemporaries, *Tommy Lawton*, *Ted Drake*, people like that, *Jackie Milburn* even. As I said, at his peak *Alan* certainly was a very exciting player, one that you want on your side to get results and he'd certainly do for me in this personal selection of *greats*! Going back to *Jackie Milburn*, what a good centre-forward he was. He wasn't the robust *Nat Lofthouse* type, *Jack* would use his skill, represented by his speed - he was fast and had a never-say-die spirit without being a 'hardcase' to play against. He was a gentleman, just like *John Charles*. The latter was too much of a gentleman to play at centre-forward; too much of a gentleman to play at centre-half but *such* a good player with *such* good ball control that he *could* play successfully as a centre-forward! And we all know what *John Charles* did, especially in his Italian days - again, please see the biographical section below.

Biographical summaries:-

Alex James: Inside left at Preston and Arsenal; there must rarely have been a bigger star in the game, a genius at inside left. His legendary skills and characterised by long, baggy shorts made him become fondly known as the 'baggy trousered Napoleon' at the Arsenal. Only 5'6" in height, a magician with the ball and mastermind to Arsenal's 1930's dominance at the time of the also legendary managerial skills of Herbert Chapman.

From Mossend in Lanarkshire, his footballing days began with Raith Rovers, before moving to Preston in 1925. Thence to Highbury for £8,750 in 1929 where his inch perfect passing with mazy dribbles paved the path for hundreds of goals.

Alex retired in 1937 and I had been a great schoolboy fan of his before following him, though not as auspiciously as it turned out by 1939, to the Arsenal. He worked some time as a Sunday newspapers' match reporter and then Arsenal coach. He died in London 1953; the Obituary Notice by the late Don Davies, an old International of *The Guardian* said Arsenal was a team of talents and James was its mastermind. Some held that Alex's slovenly appearance was natural, others said that it was a pose, but if it was a pose, it was in sharp contrast to what must have been one the tidiest minds in football. Alex hated wasted effort, to him it was the surest mark of an inadequate technique. "Let the ball do the work" was his motto! Funnily enough, Don Davies likened him to me - for which I ought to be very flattered - but for the natural 'comic streak' that made this perky Scot one of the beloved characters of football.

Alex's career record: 1922 to 1937; League only 476 appearances (231 Arsenal), 106 goals. Scotland 8 appearances, 3 goals. Major club honours - Football League Champions 1931, 1933, 1934, 1935, 1937; F.A. Cup Winners 1930 and 1936; F.A. Cup Finalists 1932. (Shades of today's Manchester United?)

Cliff Bastin: Exeter City and Arsenal outside left, he more or less cruised onto the football scene as a teenager, another in Arsenal's formidable side of the thirties. Cliff was an outside left and England schoolboy of distinction. Cliff started with his home team club Exeter City before being snapped-up by Herbert Chapman for the Highbury side in 1929, when barely 17 years old. He was nicknamed "Boy" Bastin for his precocity and had won every honour in the game by the age of 19, being the youngest player ever to win a Cup medal. Cliff played for *The Gunners* until 1947 when he returned to Devon to run a café and report matches for the *Sunday Pictorial*. Cliff was known for an ice cool temperament with a natural talent for scoring many great goals from the wing position.

Cliff's career record: 1928 to 1946; League & Cup 408 appearances, 183 goals. England 21 appearances, 12 goals. Major club honours - Football League

Champions 1930-31, 1932-33, 1933-34, 1934-35, 1937-38; F.A. Cup Winners 1930 and 1936; F.A. Cup Finalists 1932.

George Male: Arsenal, right back and widely considered one of the finest full backs of the inter-war years; in my opinion a very good, reliable full back worthy of a place in *any* team! Along with his left-side partner, Eddie Hapgood (see immediately below) in Arsenal side, *The Gunners'* defence was almost impregnable.

Under the management of Herbert Chapman it was little wonder that Arsenal won so many honours with such a sure Male/Hapgood defence. George joined the *Gunners* from the Isthmium League club Clapton, whilst still a youth, signing professional forms in May 1930. Seven months later he made his debut against Blackpool. It took, however, a couple of seasons before he could fully establish himself. By 1932 he became a regular defender, going on to win 4 League Championships and a F.A. Cup Winners medal, plus a Losers medal in 1932. Interestingly, the 1932 Cup Final was against Newcastle United as George's F.A. Cup debut. Not only did George make captain of the *Gunners*, he also skippered England on six occasions, gaining 19 International caps in all; his first was against Italy in 1934 at Highbury and his last was May 1939 against Romania, shortly before the breakout of war. After it, fortunately he was still active on the soccer field, playing eight games during the 1947-48 championship season. But, unfortunately, this was not enough to earn a fifth championship medal. He retired at the end of the season and took-up the appointment of youth-team coach, which he held until he retired in May 1975, no less - he had been with the Arsenal for 45 years, one of the club's longest ever 'servants'!

George's career record: League & Cup 285 appearances; England 19 appearances. Major club honours - Championship medals 1932-33, 1933-34, 1934-35, 1937-38; F.A. Cup Winners 1936; F.A. Cup Finalists 1932.

Eddie Hapgood: Initially playing for Kettering Town, brought to North London in 1929 by Herbert Chapman and became the Arsenal's left back. Accurately described as an 'elegant' and 'graceful' player who controlled *The Gunners'* rear line in a masterly and organised style, that saw trophies galore arrive at Highbury during the 1930's. A Bristolian, Hapgood retired after World War II and was appointed briefly as manager of Blackburn Rovers before succeeding to Shrewsbury Town, Watford and finally Bath City.

Eddie's career record: 1928 to 1939; League & Cup 434 appearances, 2 goals; England 30 appearances. Major club honours - Football League Champions 1931, 1933, 1934, 1935, 1937; F.A. Cup Winners 1930 and 1936; F.A. Cup Finalists 1932.

Wilf Copping: Leeds United and Arsenal, wing half-back; a Yorkshireman from Barnsley and something of a 'hard man', renowned for his tough and aggressive tackling. Thought of widely as one of the finest wing half-backs ever in an Arsenal shirt. He had trials for his hometown Barnsley, was rejected and headed a little further north to join Leeds United in 1930.

After 160 appearances for United, Wilf moved south, signing for the Arsenal in June 1934 for a fee of £8,000 - already with 6 England International Caps, the rest of the Football League must have winced at the thought of Wilf, now famous for his shoulder charge and tackle, signing for Arsenal, England's then top club! He also used to frighten the opposition (including me seeing him when I was a youngster) by his very appearance - he was very dark and never used to shave for a day or two before a match! A further 13 England Caps came Wilf's way whilst at Highbury. Perhaps the most memorable game for England/Arsenal was in beating Italy - World Cup holders, 1934. After some 200 appearances for *The Gunners* Wilf returned to Leeds United in March 1939, making one more England appearance before the outbreak of war. As for so many, this effectively brought his career to its close - he was considered too old afterwards. He went into coaching, enjoying a period with the Belgian national side and later spells with Southend, Bristol City and Coventry.

Wilf's career record: Leeds United 160 and Arsenal 200 combined League & Cup appearances, respectively. England 20 appearances. Major club honours - 2 League Champion's medals; F.A. Cup Winner's medals and also played in 2 winning Charity Shield sides.

Ted Drake: Southampton, Arsenal, Reading; centre forward. Ted was born in 1912 and joined his home town club in 1931. He quickly continued the goal scoring feats he had made as a schoolboy by netting 48 goals in 72 games, before becoming an Arsenal acquisition in March 1934 for £6,500. Ted is considered by many to have been perhaps the greatest striker to have worn the Arsenal colours. He will always be remembered for the 7 goals he scored against Aston Villa in December 1935. On that day, Arsenal won 7-1 and Ted's goals equalled the long-standing First Division record for most goals in a game. The same season he had also set the Arsenal record for the highest number of goals in a season, having scored 42 in 41 appearances - a record which I believe still stands?

In 1936 Ted scored the only goal in the Cup Final; his first International Cap, at the age of 22, was against Italy at Highbury - this was the day that seven Arsenal players in all lined-up to play the Italians who were the then current World Cup holders - Ted also scored that day! He appeared five times in an England shirt, scoring six times - somewhat surprising that he did not win any more. During the war he suffered a spinal injury playing for Reading and this effectively ended his playing days. He had enjoyed just six seasons with Arsenal, making 197 appearances and scoring an amazing 150 goals during the process! When the war was over, Ted went into management, firstly at Reading, then later on to Chelsea, where he guided them to the first League Championship in their history in 1955. In 1961 he left Chelsea to become a Director at Fulham.

Ted's career record: League & Cup 72 appearances, 48 goals (Southampton); 197 appearances, 150 goals (Arsenal). England 5 appearances, 6 goals. Major club honours - two Division One League Championship medals, two charity Shield medals; F.A. Cup Winner's medal.

George Best: Manchester United, Dunstable Town, Stockport County; Cork Celtic (Republic of Ireland); Fulham; Los Angeles Aztecs (USA); Hibernean (Scotland); San Jose Earthquakes (USA); Bournemouth; Brisbane Lions (Australia); forward - most positions. George Best is unquestionably one of *the* most talented footballers ever to run onto a pitch in the British Isles. Without doubt, his speed, balance, ball control, were incredibly good to the point of appearing 'magical'; his vision and invention dazzled fans and commentators alike throughout Europe and beyond. For ten years these skills truly illuminated the soccer world and that great Brazilian legend, Pele, also declared him to be " ...the best player in the world...". It is indicative of the glamorous times in which he performed, that he was also the first 'pop star' footballer. At the same time it was also said that in many ways he was the natural successor to Billy Meredith, the Manchester United and City right winger at the turn of the twentieth century - enigmatic, rebellious and, most of all, an individual.

Born in 1946, Belfast, Northern Ireland, George's early football was played in Belfast itself. At the age of only 14, the Manchester United, Bob Bishop, famously spotted the Best talent and brought him to Old Trafford. He became unhappy, though, missing home comforts and his friends and returned to Belfast. Matt Busby went in hot pursuit, believing that this youngster had the potential to recapture the same passion and flair displayed by his famous "Busby Babes", before the Munich tragedy had literally killed things.

George turned professional for United on his seventeenth birthday and made his League debut in September 1963; 15 appearances later he won his first international cap for Northern Ireland. Many have said, of course, that it was only this accident of birth that denied him the privilege (and undoubted glory that would have ensued) of competing on the World Cup Finals' stage. Northern Ireland at the time had a below strength side; when their 'golden age' dawned - in qualifying for the Finals in 1982 and 1986 - George's career was already sadly on the wane. For a player who described himself as one for the 'big occasion', it is indeed doubly tragic that he was never able to demonstrate his spectacular skills on the biggest soccer stage of them all.

Best was part of Manchester United's championship side in 1965. It was, however, the European Cup quarter final against Benfica at the *Stadium of Light*, where his image transformed itself world-wide overnight. A stunning performance with two memorable goals in the 5-1 demolition of the Portuguese giants made him the centre of attention; with his haircut and the spirit of the age styling, came the "El Beatle" headlines. George had become the first football 'pin-up'.

On the field, his high point must be the European Cup Final at Wembley in 1968, some ten years after the Munich disaster. United became the first English club to lift the coveted trophy and George was on spectacular form. He scored the second goal in extra time by rounding the Benfica goalkeeper and finishing with panache as only he could on such occasions, United beating Benfica 4-1. This was also the year of his most-goals-scored in Division One and his becoming European Footballer of the Year.

Off the field, of course, he was a restless character known for his love of 'the good life', in the form of parties, women and drink - not necessarily in that order. He owned several trendy clothes boutiques and dated *two* Miss Worlds. He turned to drink with great seriousness of purpose when the one person who had managed to keep his wayward ways in-line, Matt Busby, retired in 1969. By the early seventies he became more erratic and difficult for the club to manage by disappearing for weeks on end. There were still odd moments of magic on the field - after a month's suspension he returned to score *six* goals in a F.A. Cup match at Northampton, a feat yet to be surpassed by *anyone* since in the competition!

George finally left United, the club and supporters he loved, in December 1973 and, after a series of come-backs with glimpses of the 'Best brilliance', he quit the game in 1981 and later admitted he was an alcoholic. With his natural Irish charm he managed to win back supporters with his perceptive views on football on both radio and TV. To this day, still troubled by a drink problem, it will be that decade of magic with Manchester United that the world will remember George Best as probably "*the* best player in the world".

George's career record: 1962-1981, League & Cup 466 appearances, 178 goals (Manchester United); Northern Ireland 37 appearances, 9 goals. Major club honours - Football League Champions 1965, 1967; European Cup Winners 1968; English & European Footballer of the Year 1968.

Diego Maradona: Argentinos Juniors, Boca Juniors (Argentina); Barcelona (Spain); Napoli (Italy); Seville (Spain); Newell's Old Boys, Boca Juniors, Deportivo Mandiyu (Argentina); forward - born October 1960 as one of eight siblings to an impoverished family in Buenos Aires. His life and career are a classic 'rags-to-riches' story with the gradual decline to drink and drug dependency and also fire arms! Few players have made as many headlines in world soccer as Diego Maradona, a prodigious talent, lifting above his contemporaries, classified by many as *the* best player of his generation. Whereas Maradona's temperament was undoubtedly suspect at times, the stocky forward's ability to change the game in a flash with remarkable skills, is beyond question.

In 1976 he played for Argetinos Juniors before his sixteenth birthday, winning his first international cap the following year, 1977. In 1978 the National Coach, Cesar Menotti, surprisingly dropped Maradona from the World Cup squad on the eve of the finals. Argentina went on to win on their home ground (River Plate Stadium, Buenos Aires) with a 3-1 triumph over Holland. Subsequently, Maradona was invited in the next four World Cup competitions. Mexico 1986, a triumph again for Argentina beating West Germany 3-2, Maradona setting Jorge Burrichaga free with an exceptionally timed pass, for Burrichaga to calmly draw goalkeeper Schumacher and place the most important goal of his life into the far corner - the goal that won the 1986 World Cup! Prior to the final, Argentina met England in the quarter finals, the score was 2-1 to Argentina. This was the game with the infamous 'Hand of God' goal. The newspaper headlines "Maradona wins the Cup single-handed".

Maradona the world's greatest football talent in the 1980s scored one of the greatest World Cup goals against England but, sadly, will be remembered more for the one he fisted in. Maradona had scored a total of 5 goals throughout the competition although *Gary Lineker* with 6 was the overall top scorer!

In 1994, his fourth and last appearance in World Cup football, he was expelled from the competition having failed a drugs' test and was sent back home in something of a cloud of controversy. From thereon his football career was virtually over, his life characterised by the fight against drugs' dependency and the withering away of an exceptional talent.

Maradona's career record: 1976 to 1994/5, clubs as shown above; Major honours - World Cup 1986; World Footballer of the Year 1986; UEFA Cup 1988 (Napoli).

Peter Doherty: Manchester City and Derby County, inside left - considered the finest inside forward produced by Ireland with his marvellous swerve, acceleration and shot. With flame-coloured hair and Peter's abundance of skills, energy and tactical brilliance it seemed that he was impossible to mark out of the game.

Born at Colerane, Northern Ireland, Peter was barely 15 when the local Irish League club gave him a trial and then a signing when he was 16 years of age. He served Glentoran, Blackpool and Manchester City before the war and joined Derby County in 1945, teaming-up with Raich Carter. He moved to Huddersfield Town a year later and when 36 years old became player-boss at Doncaster and obtained his last International Cap in 1951. He also managed Bristol City before taking charge of the Northern Ireland International side and leading them to the 1958 World Cup.

Peter's career record: 1933 to 1953; League only 403 appearances, 197 goals. N. Ireland 16 appearances 3 goals. Major club honours - Football League Champions 1937; F.A. Cup Winners 1946.

Tom Finney: A one-club man with Preston North End, he was slightly built and being a naturally two-footed player he was able to wreak havoc with opposing defences along with his ability to find the net with apparent ease. Tom first signed for his boyhood heroes at Deepdale - but not before he learned his trade as a plumber - where he remained to play his last game at 38 years old. He has also remained loyal to the club to the present day and is now Preston's Club President. In 1961, Tom was awarded the O.B.E. and has more recently been knighted. (I remember seeing Tom shortly after when I told him it was "...about bloody time too..."). During his playing career he was twice voted 'Footballer of the Year', in 1954 and 1957.

Tom's career record: 1946 to 1960; League & Cup 473 appearances, 210 goals. England 76 appearances, 30 goals. Major club honours - Football League Division 2 Champions 1951; F.A. Cup Finalists 1954.

As Ken Abram said in one of the national newspapers in September 1956, quote:
"...Preston experimented with star winger Finney at centre-forward. Soccer genius that he is, Finney adapted himself so well, that the Preston crowd left Deepdale saying that Tom was the finest centre-forward since Hughie Gallacher. He scored one and assisted in all the other four first-half goals. He got the other in the second-half from a penalty. (But true to type, Finney said:) "...I still prefer playing in my wing position... ...but if it helps the club I am willing to play anywhere...".

My mate Tom Finney *(Courtesy of The Lancashire Evening Post)*

In the author's view, comparisons can be odious but two of the greatest outside rights, as different as chalk and cheese, were Stan Matthews and Tom Finney. Normally trying to compare opinion and fact is difficult although in this case it should be easy. (*Editor's note* - pen was put to paper on this *before* Sir Stanley unfortunately passed away and no offence is intended). What surprises me most is why, over the years, the footballing press have not debated this issue? With hindsight I now wonder why I did not do this myself, although in mitigation, my column was Northeast orientated. It is not my intention to merely raise something as a *controversial* issue rather as a general point for debate. The facts are simple and speak for themselves:-

·   **Finney** was brave; he had two "good" feet and a good head; he was both fast <u>and</u> quick with good balance; he could play either outside left or right, centre or inside forward, successfully at *any* level.

·   **Matthews**, too, was quick but in football jargon, had only one-foot. Although he had tremendous balance, he couldn't and didn't head the ball. He was none-the-less, a great maker of goals for others.

Who had the more talent? It surprises me that, by comparison to Matthews, Finney has sometimes been less kindly treated by the footballing world - who perhaps didn't know the real men as well as I did? Like Tom, Stan neither drank nor smoked and he carefully watched his diet and maintained a rigorous fitness routine. From what I knew of him over the years, Stan's approach to his profession was reflected in his way of life. He very shrewdly managed his innate talents to produce maximum results (and was honoured as soccer's first knight in 1965 accordingly). In some ways it is remarkable to consider the lengths Stan would go to in preparing himself. For instance, in 1954, for what proved to be my last international appearance, I roomed with Stan. When asked to pass him his everyday shoes I was surprised to find that I could hardly lift them! They had been *weighted* - so that, by comparison, his match-boots felt like 'dancing pumps'! One might almost say, in fact, that he took great care wherever possible - the hallmark of the man as a *professional* - to ensure that *everything* was weighted (pun intended) in his favour!

Geoff Hurst: West Ham United, Stoke City, centre-forward. Born at Ashton-under-Lyne in December 1941, the son of a competent Third Division centre-half, Charlie Hurst. Geoff did not have exceptional skills but rather enough instinctive ball control to be more than a competent schoolboy footballer at Chelmsford and later a promising young professional on the books of West Ham United, winning six youth international caps in 1959. Further, no man in football has achieved a more certain place in the history of the game than Geoff, as he still remains the *only* footballer ever to score a 'hat trick' in a World Cup Final!

In his initial two seasons (1959-60 and 1960-61) he played only 8 games at wing-half back; he became disillusioned and was ready to change clubs. 1961 saw my old Bradford colleague, Ron Greenwood, become West Ham's new manager and he immediately sparked new enthusiasm in Geoff with his lectures on football strategy. Ron also saw in Geoff a strength of character and an eagerness to learn the tactical revolution that he was to introduce in West Ham's game. Hurst had the strength that his impressive physique suggested, he could shoot with either foot and head the ball. Naturally, all of these were required by Greenwood; much more though, he also wanted a forward with the brain and vision to be mobile. To be a target for passes from defence; to be an elusive and unpredictable 'wall' from which attacks could be made in the opponents' half. Then the ability to become an unmarked and late-arriving finisher, who could slip-in on goal and deliver the ultimate finish; a pretty tall order but one Geoff proved able to meet!

Geoff happily pressed himself to the task of learning the role from scratch, there being no obvious role model to copy. In this sense then, by painfully acquiring his own precepts he slowly developed, demonstrating by his giftedness, proof of Ron Greenwood's theory. Geoff had developed into a quick, intuitive and reliable forward well able to compete at the highest level - as Alf Ramsay saw and appreciated and was proven in the 1966 World Cup tournament. He made his England debut in February 1966 at Wembley with a 1-0 win over West Germany. Five months later, in his eighth international appearance, came his unique contribution to World Cup Final history:-

Wembley, 30 July 1966 - who will ever forget England's 4-2 victory over West Germany in extra time? Those immortal words of Kenneth Wolstenholme's TV commentary " ...and there are some people on the pitch; they think it's all over... it is now!", as Hurst ran up the left wing and crashed the ball with his left foot, from just outside the penalty area, high into the top right-hand corner of goalkeeper Tilkowski's net in the one hundred and twentieth minute! The game was not without controversy. England's third goal (Geoff's second), for example, receiving a pass (from Alan Ball) near the angle of the six yard box, Hurst turned and hooked the ball past Tilkowski onto the underside of the bar. The ball bounced down, almost straight out of the goal - both Hurst and Charlton were convinced the ball was over the line. Then came the anxious, heart-stopping delay, whilst the Swiss referee Dienst consulted his Russian linesman Bakhramov, who signalled to the centre spot - England led by 3-2. To this day, that goal is still hotly argued about but, in the last minute, the ever-cool captain, Bobby Moore, floated a long clearance to his clubmate Hurst who ran and hit England's fourth goal, so completing that famous 'hat trick'. History was made and Alf Ramsay's prophecy of the first of May 1963, the day when he took over the managership of the national team, had been fulfilled!

Two years after the finals, Geoff was the subject of the first ever £200,000 transfer bid by Manchester United - it received an immediate response of "No"! His consistent international performances guaranteed a place in England's front line, where he remained until late 1972. Ironically at Wembley but, this time, England lost to West Germany 3-1; he was withdrawn from play after the fifty eighth minute and that was it - his final appearance for his country.

Domestically, most of his career was spent with West Ham United, where he led "The Hammers'" attack in their 1964 F.A. Cup Final victory of 3-2 over Second Division Preston North End. He scored the equalising goal at 2-2 which, ironically, was a header that hit the crossbar to rebound against goalkeeper Kelly and then slowly rolled over the line. In the following year, the 1965 Cup Winner's Cup Final was played at Wembley, West Ham beat Munich 1860 by 2-1 in front of a crowd of 100,000 but this time Geoff did not make the score sheet. However, on the 19 October 1968 at Upton Park, he achieved a double 'hat trick' when "The Hammers" hammered our Roker side by a disastrous 8-0. Hence the World Cup hero thereby equalled Vic Watson's club record for a league game, set almost forty years earlier way back in 1929 (to put this further into perspective, the then last six goals scored by an individual in a league game had been Bert Lestar, for Oldham Athletic against Southport, a Fourth Division match in 1962)! Hurst hit a 'hat trick' in each half and completed the six in seventy five minutes - just failing to equal (another of my all time great favourites) Ted Drake's First Division record of seven goals, scored for the Arsenal at Aston Villa in 1935.

By 1972 Geoff felt it was time to leave West Ham and he joined First Division Stoke City, signed by my mate Tony Waddington (see chapter 6) for a fee of around £80,000. In the early weeks of that 1972-73 season (16 September), in a niggling game at Ipswich Town, Geoff was sent off for the first time ever in his career for arguing with the referee.

On retirement from playing in 1975, Geoff quit the game completely and concentrated instead on a flourishing sports goods business. He was knighted in 1998 in the Queen's Birthday Honours List for his services to football. To bring us fully up-to-date, it was Sir Geoff Hurst along with Sir Bobby Charlton who were key figures in England's 2006 World Cup bid. This sadly failed amidst a fair degree of controversy about hooliganism, richly mixed with behind-the-scenes political pressure for withdrawal from the final round of the contest - where England were perceived already to have failed by some - due to the heavily highlighted mindlessness of a minority element of so-called fans during the Euro 2000 competition. Paradoxically somewhat this emphasises all the more, the extraordinary feat that was Geoff's World Cup Final 'hat trick' - the odds of a repetition are long indeed!

Geoff's career record: 1959 to 1975; League & Cup 448 appearances, 190 goals. England - 49 appearances, 24 goals. Major club honours - F.A. Cup Winners (West Ham United) 1964; European Cup Winners Cup (West Ham United) 1965; League Cup Finalists (West Ham United) 1966; World Cup Winners Medal 1966.

Jimmy Greaves: Chelsea, A.C. Milan (Italy); Tottenham Hotspur, West Ham, forward. Jimmy is considered by many in addition to myself, as *the* natural goal scorer; a true craftsman especially in the penalty area. His speed of thought and cool efficiency to put the ball in the back of the net, despite his dislike of training (and to some also his lack of work rate) and a diminutive stature, made him the supreme taker of chances - his international career of 44 goals in 57 appearances speaks volumes!

Born in London in 1940, Jimmy joined Chelsea at the age of 17 and very quickly acquired a remarkable 124 goals in 157 matches, which led to the Italian giants, A.C. Milan, agreeing to transfer terms in 1961, at which time he also scored a 'hat trick' in the 9-3 crushing defeat of Scotland at Wembley. Despite scoring 9 goals in 14 appearances in the Serie A League and being a big hit with the Milan fans, Jimmy was not able to adjust to the Italian style of play or life. The extremely strict discipline and the defensive style of play within the club were anathema to his creative skills. Additionally being very unhappy about being prevented from playing for England (as a disciplinary measure), it was good fortune indeed that the then manager of Spurs, Bill Nicholson, brought about what could be described as the coup of the season. Jimmy was brought back to the UK, to White Hart Lane, in the process breaking the British transfer record, at a fee of £99,999 which also avoided saddling Greaves as Britain's first £100,000 player. With a third of the 1961-62 season over, Spurs were chasing the European Cup as well as domestic honours; they eventually went on to win the F.A. Cup, beating Burnley 3-1 with Jimmy scoring the first goal!

His time at Spurs was the most rewarding of his career, winning *two* F.A. Cup medals, 1962 and 1967, the latter against his first club, Chelsea, also being the first 'all London' Cup Final of the twentieth century. Perhaps Jimmy's most rewarding achievement of this period was on 15 May 1963, when Spurs beat Athletico Madrid 5-1; he scored the first and fourth goals to carry off the European Cup Winner's Cup - the *first* European trophy to be won by a British side. In the same year, on 23 October at Wembley, Jimmy scored the winner when England beat the 'Rest of the World XI' 2-1. The latter had two British stars, Dennis Law and Jim Baxter of Scotland, in their side and Law was the scorer of their goal.

Despite his reputation as a supreme craftsman in the penalty area with an outstanding goal-scoring average, a bout of hepatitis severely affected his game and subsequently his international career suffered under the management of Alf Ramsey. An injury forced Jimmy to be replaced by Geoff Hurst in the 1966 World Cup Finals and was a further blow to his self esteem. It seems that thereafter, Jimmy never really recovered from missing-out on England's truly famous World Cup triumph.

March 1970 saw Jimmy transferred to West Ham in a 'make weight' part-exchange deal that brought Martin Peters to Spurs for an estimated £200,000. At the end of 1970/71 season, he retired from football at the same time as his fellow England colleague, Jimmy Armfield. He had been battling with alcoholism and overcame it to subsequently become a much loved TV personality, combining with fellow soccer star Ian St John, in the very popular "Saint & Greavesie Show".

Jimmy's career record: 1957 to 1971; League & Cup (England) 517 appearances, 357 goals; Serie A League (Italy), Milan 14 appearances, 9 goals. England - 57 appearances, 44 goals. Major club honours - F.A. Cup Winners 1962 & 1967; European Cup Winner's Cup 1963. To highlight Jimmy's *outstanding* goal scoring ability, he topped the Football League Division 1, top scorer on *five* occasions, namely: 1961, Chelsea - 41 goals; 1963, Spurs - 37 goals; 1964, Spurs – 35 goals; 1965, Spurs – 29 goals; 1969, Spurs – 27 goals.

Gary Lineker: Leicester, Everton, Barcelona (Spain); Tottenham; Nagoya Grampus 8 (Japan), striker (centre forward). Born at Leicester, Gary turned professional at 18 for his home city club in 1978 and led them out of the Second Division in 1980. In 1981 Leicester were relegated but in 1983 he boosted their promotion campaign with 26 goals. Thus started the career of a great goal scorer, rather than a scorer of great goals! A hero of the 1980s, often criticised for his work rate (haven't we all been) he nevertheless knew where to be and when with quiet precision, yet an ever-present threat to the opposition. His role was to simply put the ball in the back of the net - which he achieved on a very regular basis.

1984 saw Gary make his England debut as a substitute against Scotland at Hampden Park, so starting an illustrious international career as one of England's deadliest-ever finishers. In July 1985 Lineker joined Toffeemen, Everton and in his first year at Goodison Park he was top scorer in the Football League with 30 goals. He scored his side's goal in the 1986 F.A. Cup Final, losing to neighbours at the other end of Stanley Park, Liverpool by 3-1 but Gary became Footballer of the Year. Then the World Cup Finals in Mexico turned him into a World Star with his 'golden boot' performance, scoring six goals - a record for a British player - which included a 'hat trick' against Poland and formed one of the most fruitful partnerships with the mercurial, slick-footed Geordie Peter Beardsley. This international partnership flourished to yield 28 goals in 30 matches, 24 of them Gary's!

The Mexico performance led Terry Venables, the then Manager of Catalan giants Barcelona, to sign Lineker for an estimated £4.25m, a new Spanish record, where he went on to win a European Cup Winner's medal in 1989 and become immortalised in Catalonia in scoring a 'hat trick' against their old enemy, Real Madrid.

Before the 1990 World Cup Finals in Italy, Lineker moved back home to join Tottenham Hotspur for an estimated fee of £1.1m. From here he became the first player to top the First Division goals-scoring charts with three different clubs and went on to lead England's attack in the most successful World Cup campaign since 1966 by scoring *the* goal in the 1-1 draw with West Germany in the semi-finals and then losing in a penalty shoot-out (West Germany then went on to beat Argentina 1-0 in the final). Television most ably caught the tearful Paul Gascoigne 10 minutes before full time, when receiving a yellow card - looking for a silly foul which he knew would bar him from playing in the final - and Lineker trying to attract the manager Bobby Robson's attention to make him aware of Gazza's distress. Subsequently Pearce and Waddle missed penalties and England were out - their only consolation, they received the 'fair play' award and Gary once again appeared in the leading scorers' table with 4 goals. The following season Lineker gained a Cup Winner's medal, Tottenham beating Brian Clough's Nottingham Forest 2-1 after extra time. This was a final full of incident; after 15 minutes Tottenham were down to 10 men, Paul Gascoigne was stretchered-off the field with a serious knee injury. Later, Lineker had a goal disallowed and a penalty saved by Mark Crossley, the Notts. Forest goalkeeper, after being brought down. In 1992 Gary's international career ended somewhat suddenly in the European Nations Championship held in Sweden. Graham Taylor, the then England Manager who made Lineker his captain on his appointment, decided to substitute the captain in the match against Sweden which England lost 2-1, finished bottom of their group table and eliminated them from the competition! At that time Gary was one goal short of Bobby Charlton's national record of 49 goals, though Charlton had worn the England shirt 26 *more* times. (In fairness to Bobby, of course, his forte was as a goal maker every bit as much as a scorer). Yet with all the disappointment, Lineker was again voted Player of the Year.

Gary's final playing days were spent in Japan, where he played for Grampus 8 in the Japanese League before returning home again to England to start a new career in journalism and TV (*Match of the Day*). Like Sir Stanley Matthews, Gary will enter the record books in that in a career of 16 years at the peak of the game, he did not collect a *single* booking!

Gary's career record: 1978 to 1994; League & Cup (including Barcelona) 631 appearances, 322 goals. England 80 appearances, 48 goals. Major club honours - Everton, Division One League Winners, F.A. Cup Finalists 1985; Barcelona, European Cup Winners Cup 1989; Tottenham Hotspur, F.A. Cup Winners 1991; Footballer of the Year, 1986, 1992; Golden Boot Award, World Cup 1986.

Eric Cantona: Auxere (Martigues), Marseille, Bordeaux, Montpellier, Marseille (France); Sheffield Wednesday, Leeds United, Manchester United, forward/striker. Eric, as a French striker came to Britain with a 'bad boy' reputation, his erstwhile career littered with many controversial incidents both on and off the park. Tall with distinctly Gallic looks, he was well versed in "The Arts" - claiming to be an artist (no pun intended), a poet and philosopher - his footballing skills were undeniably audacious and breathtaking at times. These characteristics combined with his fine physique made for a truly 'explosive' performance potential. These ingredients are a legend-in-the-making combination, so not surprisingly it was said of Cantona that whilst he was on the pitch a game was rarely lost!

Eric Cantona came to the UK from a self-imposed retirement to join Sheffield Wednesday but the club was unwilling to sign him without first a trial period. Msr. Cantona was not himself impressed by this and left to join Howard Wilkinson's Leeds United, for about the final third of the 1991-92 playing season. He was usually a substitute but helped Leeds to win the Division One Championship. August 1992 saw the start of the new F.A. Premier League - on 20 February at Lancaster Gate, the F.A. Council gave the official go-ahead to the formation of the new Premier League, thereby breaking-up the 104 years old Football League. Eric seemed to be settled at Leeds but struggled to hold a regular place and in November 1992 he was transferred to Manchester United for a fee of £1 million. This sensational transfer across the Pennines had arisen from a somewhat chance conversation between Messrs. Wilkinson and Ferguson. Without any shadow of doubt, it was the signing of Cantona that gave Manchester United the additional dimension and flair that made them the first Premier League Champions in 1993. This had been the club's first championship win in 26 years!

As for Eric himself, this success meant he became the first ever player to win Championship medals in successive years at different clubs! Not surprising then that he soon became a cult figure amongst Manchester United fans, just as he had been with Leeds - represented by the *"Ooh-ah-Cantonah"* chant, first popularised at Elland Road - it then became as familiar a sound on Old Trafford terraces. With Cantona, Giggs and Hughes weaving and carving their way through oppositions' defences, it must have brought back memories to the more senior supporters who had previously witnessed Best, Charlton and Law in action during the 1960s. More success was to follow for Cantona with him helping Manchester to a League and Cup 'double' in 1993/94 season, being the top scorer with 18 goals. His peers formally recognised his hugely entertaining, creative skills at the heart of Manchester's side when Professional Footballers' Association members voted him *Player of the Year* in 1994. In season 1994/95 Manchester again captured the Premier League title; in 1995/96 it was the League and Cup 'double' again! The Manchester faithful crowned Eric the new 'King' of Old Trafford, his record reflecting that up to the end of the 1995/96 season he had made 106 League and Cup appearances, whilst scoring 53 goals in the process.

However, despite this success there was always his temperament - Eric's disciplinary record on the field was very fragile - the most infamous incident whilst being sent off on 25 January 1995 against Crystal Palace at Selhurst Park for retaliation. On leaving the pitch Cantona jumped over a barrier to assault Matthew Simmons, a Crystal Palace alleged 'fan' who had hurled what was described at the time as 'a stream of volatile racist abuse' at him! Being the high profile and newsworthy character that he was, meant repeated press and broadcast news continuation of the issue - mostly very unfavourable to Cantona, for many weeks. The club acted with a certain haste in announcing that the player was to be fined the maximum his contract would allow, plus being suspended from all first team matches until the end of that season. That February a F.A. Commission extended the club's ban to include *all* competitive matches until the end of September together with a further fine of £10,000. That, of course, was not all - though the authorities did stop short of boiling him in garlic butter - as the governing body F.I.F.A. extended the ban world-wide. The French F.A. removed him from captaining the French national side, virtually ending his international career.

In March the legal system acted by convicting him of *common assault* and sentencing him to 2 weeks in gaol. A public outcry, claiming that Eric was hardly a danger to the public, ensued and his sentence was reduced on appeal to 120 hours' *community service*. The 'bad boy' image had again risen to the surface but Manchester kept faith with Eric by offering him a new three-year contract, in March 1995, so success could continue to be made. In the 1996/97 season, disappointed by his own slipping standards, he took over captaincy from Steve Bruce and led Manchester to the semi-final of the European Cup and the club's fourth Premier League title in five years. Then, simply one week after the season had started, he decided to retire from the game and returned home to France. Cantona had influenced and transformed United from simply a good side to a truly great one!

Eric's career record, France: 1981-1991, England 1991-1997; France International 43 appearances, 19 goals. Major club honours - (England) Football League Champions Leeds: 1991/92; Premier League Champions Manchester

United: 1992/93, 1993/94, 1995/96, 1996/97; F.A. Cup winners 1993/94 (finalists only 1994/95) and 1995/96; P.F.A. Player of the Year 1994.

Frank Brennan: Airdrie and Newcastle United, centre half, joining the latter from the former in May 1946 and proved to be a superb servant for United. For example his performance in the 1951 Cup Final against Blackpool was truly committed, never putting a foot wrong. The legendary Stan Mortenson was prevented from shining as 'Big Frank', as he was fondly known, out-fought, out-ran and out-played the classy striker - a classic 'Big Frank' performance!

From 1946 to 1956, he made 347 appearances for United (scoring 3 times) with 7 Scottish appearances, before a totally dissatisfactory split with Newcastle -  which led to his release and move to North Shields as a player/coach. By way of background to this, I understand that MD Stan Seymour was less than pleased with the competition posed to his own by Frank's sports shop - how petty can you get! In those days of no freedom of contract for players, Frank put himself out of the game by signing for non-league North Shields, as an alternative to having to accept the transfer arranged "for" him to Plymouth Argyle. Was it any coincidence that this just happened to be the furthest away League club, from that of Newcastle United? Remember, this had occurred after Wilf Mannion's famous capitulation but before George Eastham finally managed to break the system - please see chapter 11 for details. Understandable then, that the Geordies were in complete uproar about this, as one of their favourite defenders had been let down by the club he had served with great distinction - a sad end to a distinguished career.

Raich Carter: Sunderland, Derby County and Hull City, inside left; Christened Horatio Stratten Carter, Raich was born in Sunderland and became a classic inside forward. Quote: "The finest inside forward of his generation", per Charles Buchan, whom Carter eventually replaced several years after Buchan's move to Arsenal in 1925. Leicester City, not Sunderland, was the first to secure him, but in 1931 (somewhat inexplicably) he returned to Sunderland, where he was to stay for the next 14 years. After the war his career was resurrected at Derby County, performing well, then later in 1948 at Hull City. He became manager at Boothferry Park, Hull and Elland Road, Leeds (see closing part of chapter 13), later taking charge at both Mansfield and Middlesbrough.

Raich's career record 1932 - 1953: League & Cup 512 appearances, 242 goals. England 13 appearances, 7 goals. Major club honours - Football League Champions 1936; F.A. Cup Winners 1937 (Sunderland), 1946 (Derby County).

Charlie Hurley: Millwall, Sunderland, Bolton Wanderers, centre half/centre forward. Born in 04 October 1936 in Cork, Republic of Ireland, arriving in this country at 7 years old to live in Essex (Hornchurch). Millwall scout, Bill Voisey, identified him as a promising youngster which led to Charlie signing-up for "The Lions". During this first stage in his professional career he made 105 appearances before leaving "The Den" to join SAFC at Roker, on 26 September 1957, at a transfer fee of £18,000 (he was certainly one of "Brownies'" better buys - so he can't be all bad after all - despite taking the side down twice). By this time he had already made his first full appearance, at the age of 20, for the Republic of Ireland - a World Cup qualifier against England, having previously been denied this honour due to injury.

Unfortunately his first Sunderland appearance was something of a disaster for Charlie and the side, losing 7-0 to Blackpool - as, oh dear, he made the score sheet but with an own goal. Even the second game produced a bad result, causing many fans to wonder just what kind of centre half Alan Brown had procured - Burnley beating SAFC 6-0 - but as is now history, Charlie proved himself over the next 12 seasons. He became one of the top centre halves in the country at that time.

In season 1963-64 Charlie helped Sunderland return to the First Division, ending the season as runners-up to Leeds United. It also proved to be a personally highly satisfactory one, as he was the runner-up to the late England captain Bobby Moore as Football Writers' Player of the Year - again, testament to the fact that there was no classier centre half in English soccer.

To his adoring fans he became known as "King Charlie" and went on to make 457 appearances achieving a relatively modest 47 goals - but most of them being crucial strikes like the late one against Norwich City in a fifth round F.A. Cup match, February 1961. Charlie's last goal for SAFC was a typical header against Arsenal in April 1968; his final appearance was a year later, at Turf Moor, Burnley. A free transfer came shortly afterwards, in June 1969, to the "Trotters", Bolton Wanderers, where he completed a further 46 appearances. Following this he was appointed manager of Reading in January 1972 and succeeded in winning promotion for the club by the 1975-76 season - for the first time in fifty years - by finishing third in the Fourth Division! Sadly Reading were relegated the following year causing Charlie to resign.

Internationally, he gained 40 caps for the Republic of Ireland and later he also became their player manager. Even long after his retirement, Charlie's fans remain ardently loyal, as shown by the result of the SAFC supporters' "Player of the Century" accolade!

Charlie's career record 1953-1972: League & Cup 105 appearances (Millwall); 402 appearances, 26 goals (Sunderland); 46 appearances (Bolton Wanderers). Republic of Ireland 40 appearances. Major club honours - Second Division champions 1962-63.

Arthur Wright: Sunderland, wing half-back; a Wearsider through-and-through, Arthur joined SAFC straight from Castletown school in September 1936. An England Schoolboy International, he made his debut in April 1938, as an 18 year old, against Leeds United but the result was a goalless draw. In the 1938-39 season he played 12 games in the early part, losing his place to Alex Hastings who had joined SAFC from Stenhousemuir in 1930. In my opinion, he goes down in English football's history as one of *the* best ever, uncapped players. There is no question in my mind that he should have been capped. I can only surmise that this situation was yet another example of the remoteness, at that time, of the Northeast in pre-television days.

Following the outbreak of hostilities, Arthur played a number of wartime games; over the next 8 seasons after the war he missed very few matches. Indeed, during the 1948-49 season he was an ever-present part of the side that finished eighth in Division One. Arthur played his last game for Sunderland in March 1955 against Sheffield United, at Bramwell Lane, following which he took on the job of club's trainer/coach.

Arthur's career record 1938-1955: League & Cup 283 appearances, scoring 14 goals.

Billy Elliott: Bradford PA., Burnley, Sunderland; winger outside-left, left back, left half; a native of Bradford, Billy joined our home team Bradford PA., as an amateur during the second world war and signed professional forms in March 1942. Nine years later, in the summer of 1951, he moved across the Pennines to become Burnley's record signing for a fee of £25,000. At Bradford he had made some 176 appearances, scoring 21 goals. Naturally, Billy became a regular mainstay in Burnley's First Division side; so good was his game in the top flight that he was chosen for England's European tour of May 1952, receiving his first full cap against Italy in Florence with a 1-1 score line. Many believe he was at the peak of his career in the following season, winning three more international caps and scoring goals on 3 occasions. That same season Billy represented the Football League also on 3 occasions. His last game at Turf Moor was in April of 1953 when, unfortunately, Burnley destroyed us at SAFC 5-1. Two months later, in June 1953, he was transferred to Roker Park for another, then-record, fee of £26,000 so joining what became the most expensive club side assembled in England.

Billy made his debut at Roker on the opening day of the 1953-54 season - in a 5-3 defeat at Charlton Athletic. Not the most auspicious start but, during the next 5 seasons he made 212 League & Cup appearances, scoring 26 goals. He made one more representative appearance whilst with SAFC, scoring in the 4-2 win for the Football League against the Irish League at Anfield. Again, a victim of the geographical, football wilderness that was the Northeast in those days. As is only too well known along Wearside, success at club level was somewhat more illusive, even though in 1955 SAFC was positioned fourth in the First Division and we played in the semi-finals of the F.A. Cup in 1955 and 1956. The disaster (Alan Brown), in the 1957-58 season Sunderland were relegated into the Second Division for the *first* time in history. Billy's last playing season in League football was then spent at

"Ell" & "Shack" - no threat to chorus girls anywhere! *(Len Shackleton Collection)*

Roker Park; then followed a short spell with non-League Wisbeck Town. Billy went out to Tripoli to take-up the post of National Coach to the Libyan F.A. (my column at the time remarked that Billy had gone to coach 'blanket defence' to the Bedouins), prior to a variety of coaching and managerial appointments. Preceded by an earlier five-year period as trainer-coach at Roker Park, in 1978 returning from Norway, Billy replaced Jimmy Adamson as SAFC's caretaker manager. In 1979 he steered the club to within a point of promotion back to the First Division. Sadly, this did not secure the manager's job on a permanent basis and he left to spend his remaining professional years, twenty five miles or so down the road, as manager at Feethams, Darlington.

Billy's career record 1942-1958: League & Cup 388 appearances, 47 goals; England 4 appearances, 3 goals. Major club honours, none (*cf* my comments in the opening section above concerning Eric Cantona and the belief that luck or fate often *does* play a decisive role in the shape of a players career).

Billy Bremner: Leeds United, Hull City, Doncaster Rovers, midfield; born December 1942 at Raplock, Sterling. His father was a knowledgeable soccer enthusiast and ran a local team and coached his son - Billy acknowledged that his footballing success, particularly his ball control skills, were a product of this upbringing - his father's coaching combined with his own dedication and practice.

Whilst playing for Scotland Boys many clubs became interested and trials followed at Arsenal and Chelsea - but exactly as my own experiences at Arsenal - Billy was considered too small! December 1959 saw Billy join Leeds United, following impressive performances against England Schoolboys. First he made it into the reserve side at Elland Road, then later his first team debut came with a win of 3-1 against Chelsea in January 1960. This was playing on the right wing alongside Don Revie, their names later to become the focus of football news in the late 1960s and early 1970s.

His nickname of "chalky" indicated the contrast between his complexion and his red hair, the latter hinting at a hot-tempered discipline problem. Soon it was that he was forever losing control of himself, having a go at other players and arguing with referees; fines and suspensions were many. However, with assistance from Billy Collins and Johnny Giles (possibly the greatest midfield partnership of all time), along with the award of captaincy from Don Revie, he became more disciplined as he matured - though he never lost his competitive, give-no-quarter spirit.

Season 1963-64 was the turning point for Bremner and Leeds *and* great rivals SAFC with promotion to Division One. Whereas Leeds were Division Two champions, in both home & away meetings between them, Sunderland had the edge: 1-1 at Elland Road and 2-1 to SAFC at Roker! Unfortunately for Bremner, but not so for Roker fans, a decade later saw this rivalry in the high profile 1973 Wembley F.A. Cup Final - SAFC's victory being the stuff of legends and all the more impressive over the 'red hot' favourites!

A shock to the football world was experienced with Billy's premature death from a heart attack, two days short of his fifty fifth birthday. His memory at Leeds United and the world over is one of the game's greatest midfielders, an inspirational captain and a player of skill and commitment greater than his stature would suggest. In the words of Jack Charlton, his former team mate: "He *was* the spirit of Leeds United". The club honoured him with a bronze statue outside the gates of the ground at Elland Road.

Billy's career record 1959-1978: League & Cup 752 appearances, 115 goals (Leeds only). Scotland 54 appearances - just one short of Dennis Law's record 55 and still today Leeds United's most capped player. Major club honours - League Division Two Champions 1964; League Division One Champions 1969, 1974; F.A. Cup Winners (100th. F.A. Cup Final) 1972; F.A. Cup Finalists 1970-1973; League Cup Winners 1968; European Inter Cities Fairs Cup 1968-1971; European Cup Winners Cup Finalists 1973; Footballer of the Year 1970.

Stan Anderson: Sunderland, Newcastle United and Middlesbrough, right half-back; born at Horden in 1934, Stan joined SAFC in October 1952 and was virtually ever-present for the next 11 seasons. Widely recognised as a tough-tackling wing half - a midfield terrier with an eye for the goal. In November 1963 he moved-on to Newcastle United for a fee of £19,000 much to the dismay of the Roker faithful, not least as they were then soon to see SAFC promoted back to the First Division by a reversal of the earlier Alan Brown disaster. Stan's leadership qualities were immediately recognised at Newcastle and he was quickly made team captain. Often described as a 'gentleman' and very knowledgeable where football matters were concerned, he had a strong and forceful character that took United to the Second Division Championship in 1965.

Stan joined Middlesbrough, first as a player then, in April 1966, he became manager - bringing a revival at Ayresome Park - but sadly this came just too late to avoid relegation. In 1966-67 he led Middlesbrough back into the Second Division; after twice going very near to further promotion, he ventured abroad to manage AEK Athens. He later returned home and had short associations with QPR, Manchester City and Doncaster Rovers. He joined Bolton Wanderers as a coach under the manager-ship of Ian Greaves. Soon after that Stan became the manager when, in January 1981, Greaves was dismissed. Bolton were relegated at the end of the season and in March 1981 - with results not improving - another former SAFC favourite, George Mulhall returned as Stan's assistant. The latter coincided with Bolton's run to safety and in May of that year Stan's management contract was unfortunately terminated with some 2 years remaining. Still, Stan's record remains unique, as a North Easterner, having captained each of the region's premier clubs: Sunderland, Newcastle and Middlesbrough! Internationally, capped only twice in 1962 for England against Austria & Scotland; also four, under-twenty three appearances. But a sending-off against Bulgaria may be said to have blighted his career - as the Selectors regarded him (*totally* incorrectly) as too quick-tempered, although something about 'babies and bath water' springs to mind here - still, as we all realise, they *always* know best - even when they don't!

Stan's career record: (Sunderland) League & Cup 447 appearances, 2 F.A. Cup semi-finals, 35 goals. (Newcastle United) 84 League & Cup appearances, 14 goals, Second Division Champions 1965. England 2 appearances; U-23, 4 appearances.

Billy Bingham: Glentoran, Sunderland, Luton Town, Everton, Port Vale; winger outside-right. Billy's football career started with Glentoran in the Irish League but it was Sunderland who brought him into the English League in 1950. His first game at Roker was in a 1-1 draw against Stoke City on 02 December, 1950.

Billy was a very able dribbler and crosser of the ball; he loved nothing better than to take on an opponent in a one-to-one situation. Within two years of being at SAFC he established a permanent position in the Northern Ireland team, winning 56 caps - which equalled Danny Blanchflower's record until it was surpassed by Terry Neill. The highlight of Billy's international career was helping Northern Ireland reach the quarter-finals of the World Cup in Sweden, in 1958.

In the summer of 1958, Billy left Roker to join Luton Town for a fee of £15,000; in October 1960 he moved to Goodison Park, Everton where he won a League Championship medal in the season of 1962-63. He later moved-on to Port Vale where, sadly, a broken leg brought an end to his playing career. He moved into management at Southport with great success, leading them to promotion for the first time in their history! Billy then had spells of managing Plymouth and Lingfield, later moving further abroad to manage the Greek national team. He returned to Everton as manager in May 1973 - taking a team in need of major rebuilding to seventh place in the First Division. In season 1974-75 Everton achieved fourth place but in January 1977 with the 'Blues' in thirteenth place, he was dismissed. He later took charge of Mansfield Town and took the Northern Ireland side to the World Cup Finals of 1982 and 1986. I would like to class Billy as a mate of mine - and I feel that every properly-balanced side should have a Billy Bingham!

Billy's career record: League & Cup 227 appearances, 47 goals (Sunderland). Northern Ireland 56 appearances. Major club honours - F.A. Cup Loser's medal 1958-59 (Luton Town); League Championship medal 1962-63 (Everton).

Jackie Milburn: Newcastle United, outside right/centre forward. John Edward Thompson Milburn born in Ashington into a large footballing family - amongst others, uncle to the Charlton bothers Jack and Bobby - fondly known to the Geordie faithful as 'Wor Jackie'. Regarded as a Geordie God, *the* most idolised player to have worn United's colours. Jackie was exceptionally fast - being a Powderhall sprinter - more or less as his initials suggest, like a J.E.T.! To the 'Magpie' faithful during their 1950s glory days, 'Wor Jackie' was exciting to watch; he could be awesome with the ball at his feet, not least because he had a ferocious shot with either!

Jackie joined United, before my arrival, during 1945 and it was his only Football League club, remaining at St. James' Park until 1957. He was a three-times winner of a F.A. Cup medal during the early nineteen fifties in the last of which, 1955, he recorded the *fastest ever* goal scored in a Wembley final - a looping header over Bert Trautmann from a corner kick in 55 seconds! Newcastle beat Manchester City by 3-1 but the irony of that was Jackie rarely headed the ball and, even more remarkably, he was nearly left off the side due to his general lack of good form at the time. It took some forty two years for Jackie's record to be broken when the Italian international Roberto Di Mattio scored after only 47 seconds for Chelsea against Middlesbrough in 1997. Interestingly their Dutch player/manager Ruud Gullit became the first foreign coach to win an English trophy and it was he who subsequently became United's manager - in 1998 taking-over from Kenny Dalglish, later to be replaced by another Northeast favourite Bobby Robson during 1999.

Offered a lucrative contract by Linfield in 1957, Jackie went into club management, continued to actively play and was voted Ulster Footballer of the Year in 1958. In the same year Linfield were runners-up in the Irish Cup. In 1960 Linfield eventually gained cup success under Jackie's leadership but November of that year saw him move to Yiewsley as player/manager where he stayed for two years. Jackie took a brief coaching job with Reading, then moved back to home territory to coach Ashington. In November 1963 he moved to Ipswich Town as manager, taking-over from Alf Ramsey (who became England manager). Whilst making very few mistakes as a player, accepting the job as manager was probably Jackie's worst career move of all. Having a poor playing staff and no funds, Ipswich were on a downward spiral in the League and eventually relegated into the Second Division. Jackie remained a few months, returning to his native Northeast by September 1963 to manage Gateshead. Later followed some years prior to retirement proper, as a Northeast sports journalist like myself. We often worked alongside each other and remained great friends, which position I regard as the greatest personal privilege. This most marvellous, native Northeastern soccer idol sadly passed-away after a characteristically brave fight against illness in October 1989.

And you don't need me to tell you that his name will *always* be synonymous (as one of *the* 'good guys' as well as one of the *greats*) with Newcastle United and its faithful followers as 'Wor Jackie'!

Jackie's career record: League & Cup 436 appearances, 214 goals. England 13 appearances. 10 goals. Major club honours - F.A. Cup Winner's medal 1951, 1952 & 1955.

Tommy Lawton: Burnley, Everton, Chelsea, Notts County, Brentford, Arsenal, centre forward. It is not surprising that Tommy is considered one of England's greatest ever centre forwards. Most devastating as a header of the ball, he was also brilliant on the deck - with both feet! One of Britain's natural idols - but in an age before television - and it is certainly true to say that he was a hero amongst his contemporaries like myself. The image of the tall, well built Lawton (with his sleek, black hair parted in the middle) rising high above the defence, hanging there to steer the ball into the net, must remain as one of the truly vintage footballing memories from the years just before and immediately following the second war.

Born in October 1919 at Bolton, at the age of 16 Tommy made his debut for Burnley and scored a 'hat trick' in his first professional game against Tottenham Hotspur. In 1936 he joined Everton for a fee of £6,500, the biggest fee for a 17 year-old at that time. He eventually took over from the legendary Dixie Dean in the first team but always modestly held the view that he could never head the ball as powerfully as Dixie - who had a metaphorical brow of cast iron with which he would destroy defences!

In season 1937-38 Tommy was the First Division's leading scorer with 28 goals - a record which improved the following year. In October 1938 he made his international debut against Wales as the youngest player ever to pull on an England shirt. The Second World War then intervened and, as many a footballing pundit has speculated, what would Tommy have achieved in those lost years? Notwithstanding, he is still thought by many in addition to myself to be one of the greatest England centre forwards to have played, having scored 22 goals in 23 appearances!

More or less immediately after that war, Tommy signed (November 1945) for Chelsea - organizing the transfer himself for a record fee of £11,500 – the first player to realise his own worth. He rapidly became a Stamford Bridge favourite but in 1947 astounded the football-following world by transferring to Third Division Notts County, but again for a record fee of £20,000. Tommy was still appearing in an England shirt alongside the other great names of the time (and occasionally myself), Stan Matthews, Tom Finney and Wilf Mannion but, perhaps because of playing Third Division football, he gradually faded out of the England limelight and played his last international for England in October 1948 - a goal-less draw against Denmark in Copenhagen.

Tommy spent four and a half years at Notts County, scoring 90 goals in 151 games and profited the club greatly by lifting the average home gate from 9 to 35,000. In 1950 the club gained promotion to the Second Division. 1952 saw a transfer to Brentford, as a Second Division player/manager, for a fee of £12,000. In the following year Tommy returned to play in the First Division for Arsenal at a fee of £4,500, where he stayed for two seasons. But, by this time, injury was plaguing his playing and by 1956 he became player/manager again but at non-league Kettering Town. Off the field Tommy was never to have the same force or drive as he had on it. He was appointed manager of Notts County in 1957 but, sadly, he could not prevent their relegation and after a year in the post he left by mutual consent and quit the game. In 1969 he returned very briefly as a scout for Notts County.

Even more sadly as it was to turn out, given such an illustrious playing career and having never been booked or sent off, Tommy Lawton gained very little financially from the game. Certainly nothing at all approaching the level of his true worth. In 1972, unemployed and in debt, he pleaded guilty to six charges of obtaining money and falsifying cheques and was sentenced to 3 years on probation. Later in 1972 his footballing colleagues arranged a testimonial match: Everton v Great Britain XI. This helped his financial position but in 1974 he was again in trouble, this time for deception. He was given 200 hours' community service. It was the mark of the man that he was able to talk about his fallen circumstances - and the consideration of suicide - but being the true gentleman that he was, he blamed no one but himself for his situation. In November 1996 Tommy's death was announced; he was 77 years old. The press and media paid many tributes:-

"England centre forward who ranks with the very best was an inspiration to all."
"He was a lion of English football."

Tom Finney, former Preston and England forward said of Tommy Lawton:-
"He was very talented indeed, one of *the* greats. The best centre forward I played with in an England side. Just look at his record of scoring 22 goals in 23 games for England - and that's overlooking the fact that he probably lost his best years. He was right at his peak when the war broke out."

Tommy's career record 1935-1956: League only 390 appearances, 231 goals. England 23 appearances, 22 goals. Major club honours - F.A. First Division Champions (Everton) 1939, Top Scorer 35 goals; F.A. Third Division Champions (Notts County) 1950.

Nat Lofthouse: Bolton Wanderers, centre forward. In September 1939, the day after war broke out, Nathaniel Lofthouse joined Bolton Wanderers from schools football and played his first game when still only 15 years old. He had been given two, white 'fivers' as the fee for signing-on!

Nat must be 'a classic' English centre forward; direct, fearless, uncompromisingly hard but fair; a very determined leader of an attack. During the war years he worked down the pit; fortunately it made him extremely fit, lean and hard - all the necessary support requirements for a centre forward to lead the attack.

In 1950 he received his first England International Cap, playing against Yugoslavia he netted two goals! May 1952 saw Nat earn his nickname "The Lion of Vienna". England were playing Austria in Vienna and Austria had been crashing goals past most European defences on a regular basis. They had beaten Scotland both home and away and held England to a draw at Wembley. The match was billed as the Championship of Europe, the city of Vienna was still under post-war Allied occupation and was tense with expectation. There was some 2,000 British troops in the 60,000 crowd, England opened the score after 20 minutes, Lofthouse scoring with a volley from a cross and by half-time the score was level at 2-2. In the second half, Austria pressurised the England defence into working overtime. The winner came eight minutes from time when Tom Finney received a ball from goalkeeper Gil Merrick. The England winger drew the only Austrian defender, slipped the ball to Lofthouse, releasing him on a 50 yards' run. A dual between the Austrian goalkeeper climaxed when Nat shot as they collided and was knocked-out cold when the ball hit the back of the net! He was stretchered-off the field but returned to help England protect their lead. Hobbling on the wing, he still managed to crash a shot against the post. At the final whistle, khaki-clad servicemen invaded the pitch to shoulder-off the England players!

Domestically, another highlight in Nat's career, albeit tinged with controversy, was the 1958 Cup Final. Bolton played Manchester United, the latter still recovering from the Munich air disaster horror. Bolton put paid to United's dream, winning 2-0 with goals scored by Lofthouse - in one of which he shoulder-charged Harry Gregg, the United goalkeeper, into the net. No sentiment was given by either Lofthouse or Bolton. However, as might be expected, the press and media made considerable debate as to the legality of the shoulder-charge on a goalkeeper. It may not have looked pretty but proved effective for Bolton - who had been narrowly beaten a few years earlier, by Blackpool 2-3, in the 1953 Final known as the "Matthews Cup Final".

Nat's favourite player, Tom Finney, played 20 internationals with him, 18 times Tom supplied the pass from which Nat scored. His last game at Burnden Park (now known as the *Reebok Stadium*) was in 1960, playing at inside right to ease-in a 16 year old making his debut, who supplied the cross for Nat to score. His name was Francis Lee, who went on to forge an illustrious international career for himself with England as well as domestically with Bolton and Manchester City. Nat is one of the very few footballers to have been a one-team player, still being associated with the Wanderers to this day. In this 60 years' period he has virtually been involved in every capacity, i.e. player, coach, manager, scout and now honoured as their president - such dedication is indeed a rarity in *any* era, not least today!

Nat's career record 1945-1961: League & Cup 503 appearances, 285 goals. England 33 appearances, 30 goals. Major club honours - F.A. Cup Winners 1958, F.A. Cup Finalists 1953.

John Charles: Leeds United, Juventos, Leeds United, Roma, Cardiff City, centre half. First appeared for Leeds when only 17 years old in 1949, then as an International for Wales when aged 18. John was a player not only of great talent and delicate touches but also the coolest of temperaments - especially for such a big player. Not surprisingly, therefore, known as the 'gentle giant'. He moved very effectively from centre-half to centre-forward - and back again - throughout his career. In 1957 he was taken to Italy by Juventos for a then record fee of £65,000 where he soon became enormously popular, was given the nickname 'Il Buon Gigante' and then voted 'Player of the Year' in his first season!

He scored 108 goals for Juventos before returning to Elland Road in 1962, then on to Roma before finishing his playing days at Cardiff City. Eminent sports writer Michael Parkinson for *The Daily Telegraph* recently stated: "There was a time when every football fan knew that John Charles was the best centre-half in the world as well as the best centre-forward." So, a true footballing giant who was never booked or sent off during his *entire* career!

John's career record 1949-1965: League only 374 appearances, 172 goals. Wales 38 appearances, 15 goals. Major club honours - Italian League Champions 1958-1960, 1961; Italian Cup Winners 1959, 1960.

Brian H. Clough: Middlesbrough, Sunderland, centre forward. Born in March 1935 at Middlesbrough, one of nine children; as an 18 year old Brian played centre forward for Billingham Synthonia, having signed from Great Broughton seven days after Harry Sharratt signed for Bishop Auckland. He made his League debut in September 1955 (two years after signing for his home town), against Barnsley but not scoring until one month later versus Leicester City; Brian was on his way to his multitude of goals!

Considered as one of the greatest marksmen at Middlesbrough with 204 goals in 222 appearances. And in the Second Division for three consecutive seasons, he scored 40 goals or more *every* season from 1956 to 1960. In achieving this Brian emulated his 1920s predecessor, George Camsell, by leading the Division Two goal scorers (in 1958-59 season) with 42 goals. By his third season he averaged a goal a game and reached 100 League goals in quicker time than *any* player previously!

No wonder SAFC went after him - in July 1961 he signed for them for a fee of £45,000. His debut was against Walsall on the opening day of the 1961-62 season but this was unfortunately a 4-3 defeat. However, 'Cloughie' went on to be the top scorer that season with 29 goals in 34 games, netting 4 'hat tricks' in the process! In addition to these League appearances, he completed another 'hat trick' in the 5-2 League Cup win over Walsall at Roker. His season's total in 43 matches was 34 goals! Following this, perhaps it is not so surprising that he went on, in 1962-63, to produce 28 goals in 28 games which included 'hat tricks' against Southampton and Grimsby Town. On Boxing Day of that season, playing against Bury, he chased a ball into the penalty area and collided with 'The Shakers' goalkeeper Chris Harker. He was stretchered off the park with the now infamous severe knee injury which effectively - and tragically - marked the end of this most promising of all goal scoring careers. On retirement his scoring tally at SAFC was 63 goals in 74 games!

There is no question that he was an extraordinary player - playing for Middlesbrough and Sunderland he scored 267 goals in 296 appearances and Brian himself *claims* that his record will not ever be beaten!

Internationally, he only received two England caps, uncharacteristically failing to score in either game. But surely this is yet another example of the Northeast's remoteness in those days, where learned fans (backed-up by his 'stats' as above), feel he should certainly have earned very many more. On 23 September 1959 he scored all 5 goals for the Football League in a 5-0 defeat of the Irish League at Belfast.

Managerially what can one say - one hell of a lot - after a short spell on Sunderland's coaching staff, Brian became the youngest manager in the Football League when along with Peter Taylor he took charge of Hartlepool United in October 1965 (cross reference end of chapter 5) and led them to promotion. In 1967 he moved to the *Baseball Ground*, Derby County and led *The Rams* to the Second Division championship and by 1972 the Division One championship - for the first time in their history! 1972-73 saw the club reach the semi-finals of the European Cup, losing to the renowned Juventos. But, as a result of a 'falling-out' with chairman Longson, Brian and Peter took-up an offer to manage Third Division Brighton. This did not work out well and 'Cloughie' left by July 1974 to join Leeds United. However, he only lasted 44 days in charge before being sacked - the shortest tenure of management in the Football League! January 1975 saw him famously join Nottingham Forest and over the successive 18 years Brian was to produce a team whose achievements included: League Division One Champions (1977-78), two European Cup wins (1978-79 and 1979-80), four League Cup wins (1977-78, 1978-79, 1988-89, 1989-90). Of all the achievements to allude him was the F.A. Cup. One unique distinction (though a matter of mixed emotions now, again see chapter 10 reference to commercialism all but gone mad), is the fact that in 1978-79 'Cloughie' paid the first ever £1m transfer fee - for Trevor Francis from Birmingham City. Brian said farewell to his adoring fans at the City ground, 01 May 1993. It was Forest's last home match, they were beaten (by Sheffield United 2-0) but this was of little matter as they were relegated from the Premier League to Division One. Brian's state of health at the time also sadly matched that outcome. Like myself, 'Cloughie' was often labelled a showman and an individualist and, to some, a maverick but he was always the centre of great debate. This is surely all part of being truly alive and in other respects both his playing and managerial honours all speak for themselves! To close, perhaps I can do no better than to quote Martin O'Neill: - "As a manager, he was magical. Some dismiss him as a loud-mouthed pratt, while others rate him alongside Shankley, Busby and Stein; others regard him as a working class hero!" To the majority of those at the City Ground Forest - and none more so than fans in the Northeast - Brian H. Clough was *the* one and only!

~ Chapter 13 ~
The Football League
100 League Legends marking the
1998/9 Centenary

Towards the end of March 1999, whilst still in Tenerife, I was surprised and delighted to learn of my inclusion on the League's Centenary List. What a chance to renew acquaintance with old friends like Jimmy Armfield, John Charles, Tom Finney, Trevor Ford, Nat Lofthouse, Malcolm McDonald, Wilf Mannion, Stan Matthews and Terry Paine (who even flew in specially from South Africa) - plus many more - a few of whom cannot be named because they were the ones that kicked me when I was playing! This was especially the case because we are all widely dispersed geographically and many have lost touch over the years. Sadly, there were also many who could not be there but also one or two very pleasant surprises, such as meeting Beryl Franklin, Neil's widow, and Pat Carter*, Raich's widow.

The official invitation, issued by the Football League's then Chief Executive, Richard Scudamore, explained the nature of the occasion:-

*"...At the start of this season, the 100th League Championship, you were recognised as being one of the 100 best players ever to have graced professional football in this country. The **100 League Legends** were honoured for their individual contribution to the game and to mark this achievement the Centenary Season culminates in a celebration **"Evening of Legends"** (London Hilton, evening of 13th May 1999). This will be a unique gathering, never again will so many of football's greatest ever players join together to honour our national game..."*

"...The focal point of this special occasion will be... ...an audio visual tribute, the climax of which will be the award of a specially commissioned gold medal to each legend. Only 100 players in the world will ever receive this accolade..."

Appendix I illustrates all 100 players courtesy of the Football League.
(* See footnote at end of this chapter)

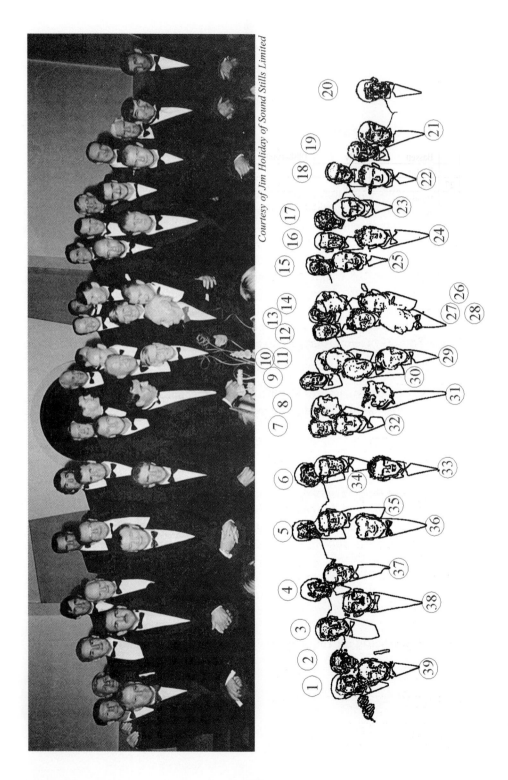

Courtesy of Jim Holiday of Sound Stills Limited

	Adams	Tony	1983-1998	Arsenal.
	Allchurch	Ivor	1948-1964	Swansea City, Newport County, Cardiff City.
39	Ardiles	Ossie	1978-1990	Tottenham Hotspur, Blackburn Rovers, QPR, Swindon Town.
18	Armfield	Jimmy	1954-1971	Blackpool.
1	Ball	Alan	1962-1984	Blackpool, Everton, Arsenal, Southampton, Bristol Rovers.
	Banks	Gordon	1958-1973	Chesterfield, Leicester City, Stoke City.
13	Barnes	John	1981-1998	Watford, Liverpool, Newcastle United.
	Bassett	Billy	1888-1900	West Bromwich.
	Bastin	Cliff	1927-1948	Exeter City, Arsenal.
27	Bell	Colin	1963-1979	Bury, Manchester City.
	Bergkamp	Denis	1995-1998	Arsenal.
	Best	George	1963-1983	Manchester United, Stockport County, Fulham, AFC Bournemouth.
	Blanchflower	Danny	1948-1964	Barnsley, Aston Villa, Tottenham Hotspur.
	Bloomer	Steve	1892-1915	Derby County, Middlesbrough.
12	Brady	Liam	1973-1990	Arsenal, West Ham United.
	Bremner	Billy	1959-1982	Leeds United, Hull City, Doncaster Rovers.
	Buchan	Charles	1910-1929	Sunderland, Arsenal.
	Camsell	George	1924-1939	Durham, Middlesbrough.
	Cantona	Eric	1991-1997	Leeds United, Manchester United.
	Carey	John	1937-1954	Manchester United.
	Carter	Raich	1932-1953	Sunderland, Derby County, Hull City.
9	Charles	John	1948-1966	Swansea City, Leeds United, Cardiff City.
	Charlton	Bobby	1956-1975	Manchester United, Preston North End.
5	Clemence	Ray	1965-1988	Scunthorpe United, Liverpool, Tottenham Hotspur.
	Common	Alf	1900-1915	Sunderland, Sheffield, Middlesbrough, Arsenal, Preston North End.
	Copping	Wilf	1930-1939	Leeds United, Arsenal.
	Compton	Bob	1896-1921	Blackburn Rovers.
4	Dalglish	Kenny	1977-1990	Liverpool.
	Dean	Dixie	1923-1939	Tranmere Rovers, Everton, Notts County.
	Dickinson	Jim	1946-1965	Portsmouth.
	Doherty	Peter	1933-1954	Blackpool, Manchester City, Derby County, Huddersfield Town, Doncaster Rovers.
	Drake	Ted	1931-1939	Southampton, Arsenal.
	Edwards	Duncan	1953-1958	Manchester United.
37	Finney	Tom	1946-1960	Preston North End.
2	Ford	Trevor	1946-1961	Swansea City, Aston Villa, Sunderland, Cardiff City, Newport County.
	Foulke	Billy	1894-1908	Sheffield United, Chelsea, Bradford City.
32	Francis	Trevor	1970-1995	Birmingham City, Nottingham Forest, Manchester City, QPR, Sheffield Wednesday.
	Franklin	Neil	1946-1958	Stoke City, Hull City, Crewe Alex., Stockport Co.
	Gallacher	Hughie	1925-1939	Newcastle United, Chelsea, Derby County, Notts County, Grimsby Town, Gateshead.
26	Gascoigne	Paul	1984-1998	Newcastle United, Tottenham Hotspur, Middlesbrough.
	Giggs	Ryan	1990-1998	Manchester United.
33	Giles	Johnny	1959-1977	Manchester United, Leeds United, West

				Bromwich Albion.
	Goodall	John	1888-1904	Preston North End, Derby County, New Brighton, Glossop.
	Greaves	Jimmy	1957-1971	Chelsea, Tottenham Hotspur, West Ham United.
	Hansen	Alan	1977-1990	Liverpool.
	Hapgood	Eddie	1927-1939	Arsenal.
11	Hardwick	George	1937-1956	Middlesbrough, Oldham Athletic.
	Hardy	Sam	1902-1926	Chesterfield, Liverpool, Aston Villa, Nottingham Forest.
7	Haynes	Johnny	1952-1970	Fulham.
	Hibbs	Harry	1925-1939	Birmingham City.
8	Hoddle	Glenn	1974-1996	Tottenham Hotspur, Swindon Town, Chelsea.
	Hunter	Archie	1888-1891	Aston Villa.
15	Hunter	Norman	1962-1983	Leeds United, Bristol City, Barnsley.
24	Hurst	Geoff	1959-1976	West Ham United, Stoke City, West Bromwich Albion.
	Jack	David	1920-1935	Plymouth Argyle, Bolton Wanderers, Arsenal.
	James	Alex	1925-1938	Preston North End, Arsenal.
6	Jennings	Pat	1962-1985	Watford, Tottenham Hotspur, Arsenal.
	Jones	Cliff	1952-1970	Swansea City, Tottenham Hotspur, Fulham.
	Keegan	Kevin	1968-1984	Scunthorpe United, Liverpool, Southampton, Newcastle United.
	Law	Denis	1956-1974	Huddersfield Town, Manchester City, Manchester United.
	Lawton	Tommy	1935-1957	Burnley, Everton, Chelsea, Notts County, Brentford Arsenal.
	Liddell	Billy	1946-1961	Liverpool.
	Lineker	Gary	1978-1993	Leicester City, Everton, Tottenham Hotspur.
30	Lofthouse	Nat	1946-1961	Bolton Wanderers.
3	Mackay	Dave	1958-1972	Tottenham Hotspur, Derby County, Swindon Town.
29	Mannion	Wilf	1936-1956	Middlesbrough, Hull City.
28	Matthews	Stanley	1931-1966	Stoke City, Blackpool.
	McCracken	Bill	1904-1924	Newcastle United.
21	McDonald	Malcolm	1968-1977	Fulham, Luton Town, Newcastle United, Arsenal.
25	McGrath	Paul	1981-1998	Manchester United, Aston Villa, Derby County.
	McIlroy	Jimmy	1950-1968	Burnley, Stoke City, Oldham Athletic.
34	McLintock	Frank	1959-1977	Leicester City, Arsenal, QPR.
	Mercer	Joe	1932-1954	Everton, Arsenal.
	Meredith	Billy	1893-1925	Norwich Vic., Manchester City, Manchester Utd.
	Milburn	Jackie	1946-1957	Newcastle United.
	Moore	Bobby	1958-1977	West Ham United, Fulham.
	Mortensen	Stan	1938-1958	Blackpool, Hull City, Southport.
17	Mullery	Alan	1958-1976	Fulham, Tottenham Hotspur.
16	Paine	Terry	1956-1977	Southampton, Hereford United.
14	Peters	Martin	1960-1981	West Ham United, Tottenham Hotspur, Norwich City, Sheffield United.
	Ramsey	Alf	1946-1955	Southampton, Tottenham Hotspur.
20	Robson	Bryan	1974-1997	West Bromwich Albion, Manchester United, Middlebrough.
35	Rowley	Arthur	1946-1965	West Bromwich Albion, Fulham, Leicester City, Shrewsbury Town.
23	Rush	Ian	1978-1990	Chester City, Liverpool, Leeds United, Newcastle

				United, Sheffield.
	Schmeichel	Peter	1991-1998	Manchester United.
	Scott	Elisha	1912-1934	Liverpool.
19	Shackleton	Len	1946-1958	Bradford Park Avenue, Newcastle United, Sunderland.
22	Shearer	Alan	1987-1998	Southampton, Blackburn Rovers, Newcastle United.
31	Shilton	Peter	1965-1997	Leicester City, Stockport County, Nottingham Forest, Southampton, Derby County, Plymouth Argyle, Bolton Wanderers, Leyton Orient.
	Swift	Frank	1933-1951	Manchester City.
36	Smith	Tommy	1962-1979	Liverpool, Swansea City.
	Souness	Graeme	1972-1984	Middlesbrough, Liverpool.
38	Southall	Neville	1980-1998	Bury, Port Vale, Everton, Stoke City.
	Stephenson	Clem	1910-1930	Aston Villa, Huddersfield Town.
	Stiles	Nobby	1959-1974	Manchester United, Middlesbrough, Preston North End.
	Taylor	Tommy	1950-1958	Barnsley, Manchester United.
	Trautmann	Bert	1949-1964	Manchester City.
	Woodward	Viv	1908-1915	Tottenham Hotspur, Chelsea.
	Wright	Billy	1946-1959	Wolverhampton Wanderers.
	Young	Alex	1960-1969	Everton, Stockport County.

* I am sometimes reminded of the contrast in terms and conditions between 'then' and 'now' in unexpected ways. One example of this was in 1994 when I received a very nice letter from Raich Carter's widow, Pat. Raich was a good friend; a native of Sunderland (Hendon, I think). He played inside-forward for Sunderland and Derby County and, of course, England. He was slightly older than I and was, more or less finishing his time at Sunderland when I arrived there. We kept in contact and he went on to manage Leeds United, Hull City and Middlesbrough. The last time I saw Raich was at SAFC's 'night of nostalgia' in about May 1993. In the September of that year he suffered a severe stroke which Pat reports he, sadly, never properly recovered from. She sent the letter to our apartment in Tenerife and recalled the time, in 1956, when Leeds United won promotion, the club gave Raich the 'massive bonus' of £350 which the couple spent on a cruise to Madeira and Tenerife. What a contrast, such a small payment for gaining so much for the club, compared to the truly massive financial rewards available to those involved in today's game - even given the now 'historical' nature of Raich's payment, it does seem almost derisory!

SAFC Night of Nostalgia c. May 1993. Front row 'old timers': Bob Stokoe, Bobby Gurney, Raich Carter, LFS, Johnny Mapson. Back row: Cecil Irwin, Jimmy Montgomery, Ron Guthrie, Jimmy McNab, Charlie Hurley, Bobby Kerr, David Young, Dick Malone, Billy Hughes, Vic Hallom, Dennis Tueart, Dave Watson, Ian Porterfield. *(Courtesy of the Sunderland Echo)*

Bibliography, Research & Source Material Acknowledgements

Many works have been used as reference for checking facts, 'background' and other details to the stories in this book. Perhaps the major 'source' is articles in newspapers. These both from visits to their own library archives - in an attempt to cross-reference the many clippings accumulated in my 'scrapbook' - together with the 'scrapbook' collection itself.

The collection was started by my mother, Martha, in our native Bradford in the mid-nineteen thirties - when a young 'Shack' first made public appearances in print. It has been added-to over the years by various family members, armed with scissors, paste bottle and brush. However, it was not until the 1990s that it became an organized-whole. My friend John Feast, a retired Royal Mail manager and collector of memorabilia from nearby Heysham, undertook the rather daunting task of sorting through a 'mountain' of accumulated cardboard boxes full of clippings, old photographs, match programmes and the like. They had been stored in the attic of more than one house. Their sorting was something I had always intended to get around to 'one day' but somehow there was always something (e.g. a game of golf) that seemed to warrant higher priority. At first, John's task must have seemed hopeless but the results of his labours are now eight large, ring-binder volumes. John's indefatigable efforts have proved priceless in the job of assembling raw material and prompting the recollection of otherwise long-forgotten memories. Thank you again John, for your willingness to help and the tenacity to see the job well and truly done!

Unfortunately many 'clippings' and photographs were without their exact date or newspaper title details. Once photos and clippings have been stuck-in, the job of identification becomes very problematic. Considerable efforts have been made by family members involved in this self-publishing project but it has not always been possible to identify the exact source(s). I have attempted, where necessary and possible, to identify original source and so obtain appropriate consent for use. No discourtesy is intended either to any inadvertently overlooked, or where the search has been stopped for reasons of praxis. Apologies are, therefore, proffered in advance to anyone not adequately acknowledged for material referred to or otherwise included in this book. At the time of writing I am in my 79th year. Because a truly exhaustive research effort only seems possible against an expected life-span extending to nearer a hundred years old, I thought it time to call a halt in the interests of achieving completion - literally before it was too late!

A number of newspapers have been very willing to assist and I am particularly grateful for the helpful co-operation I have received in general, more particularly to the editors and staff of: Northeast Press Limited (Sunderland Echo), Newcastle Chronicle & Journal Limited, Bradford & District Newspapers (Telegraph & Argus), Express Newspapers Limited and The People.

I would also like to take this opportunity to thank Geoff and Ian Metcalfe, of Sunderland's Metcalfe Components Ltd, for both their financial and enthusiastic personal support, which came at a vital stage in the production of this book - enabling it to reach completion - thanks again, you're true supporters!

However, other 'source material' has been drawn upon, namely books and miscellaneous articles listed below:

I LEAD THE ATTACK - Trevor Ford, 1957- Stanley Paul & Co. Ltd., London, W. 1.

SOCCER WITH THE STARS - Billy Bingham, 1964 - The Soccer Book Club, London W. C. 2.

THE AVENUE - BRADFORD PARK AVENUE (Pictorial History & Club Record) - Malcolm Hartley and Tim Clapham, 1987 - Temple Nostalgia Press, Nottingham.

Stanley Matthews - David Miller (The Authorized Biography), 1989 - Pavilion Books Limited, London W. C. 2H.

JACKIE MILBURN in Black & White - Mike Kirkup (A Biography), 1990 - Stanley Paul & Co. Ltd., Random Century House, London S. W. IV.

HIS WAY - THE BRIAN CLOUGH STORY - Patrick Murphy, 1993 - Robson Books Ltd., London W. 1P.

Others:

Guinness Football Encyclopedia.
Sunday Times Illustrated History of Football.
Ha'way The Lads, The Road to Wembley (The Story of SAFC and its Supporters 1879 to 1973).
The St. James's Encyclopedia (an A to Z of NUFC).
Determined To Win, George Eastham (Arsenal and England).
Book of Football All Time Greats.
The Greats from the Golden Age of Soccer.
The Daily Telegraph Football Chronicle - Norman Barrett.
The Old Trafford Encyclopaedia (An A to Z of Man United) - Stephen F. Kelly.
Sunderland Football Club (An A to Z) - Dean Hayes.
The Anfield Encyclopaedia (An A to Z of Liverpool FC) - Stephen F. Kelly.
The Highbury Encyclopaedia (An A to Z of Arsenal FC) - Stephen F. Kelly.

The Concise Encyclopaedia of World Football edited by Glen Moore - Colour Library Direct 1998.
Sporting Profiles - Michael Parkinson, Pavillion Books Limited, 1995.
The One Hundred Greatest Footballers - Tim Vigon, Generation Publications.
Bremner! - The Legend of Billy Bremner. - Bernard Bale, Andre Deutsch Ltd

Sponsors:

Sunderland AFC.
Metcalfe Components (Sunderland) Ltd.
Ted Little (Unidirect).
Norman J. Freeman.
North East Press Limited.
Newcastle Chronicle & Journal Ltd.

Collectors' List

1. Robin, Gill, Claire & David Webster, Grange-over-Sands.
2. David & Maureen Mallin, Fatfield, Houghton-le-Spring.
3. The Wyatt Family, Yarm.
4. Raymond Jameson, Witherslack.
5. Derek Roberts, Allithwaite.
6. June Sayer, Croxdale.
7. The Johnston Family.
8. Geoff Metcalfe, Whitburn.
9. Ian Metcalfe, Washington.
10. Metcalfe Components, Sunderland.
11. Metcalfe Components, Sunderland.
12. Metcalfe Components, Sunderland.
13. Metcalfe Components, Sunderland.
14. Metcalfe Components, Sunderland.
15. Metcalfe Components, Sunderland.
16. Mr T.J. Nicholson, Corbridge on Tyne.
17. Fin Adams, Haltwhistle.
18. M. G. Westgarth-Taylor, Stokesly.
19. T. M. Baker, Rickmanswoth.
20. Steve Taylor, Durham City.
21. Norman Linsley, Sunderland.
22. Geoff Heron, Belmont.
23. Rob Lowes, Ingelby Barwick.
24. Gavin Belcher, Headington, Oxford.
25. Ian Belcher, Headington, Oxford.
26. Ellen Birtwistle, Blackburn.
27. June Carine, Oakley, Basingstoke.
28. Frank P. Feast, Abingdon.
29. Scott Feast, Blackburn.
30. Michael Grunshaw, Blackburn.
31. Terry Hargreaves, Quinton Green.
32. Michelle Hargreaves, Quinton Green.
33. Andrew Horwood, Marlborough.
34. Simon Horwood, Marlborough.
35. Gladys Lipscombe, Hatch End, Pinner.
36. Simon Lipscombe, Oakville, Ontario.
37. Andrew Mavin, Cullercoats.
38. Duncan Mavin, Cullercoats.
39. Roger Errington, Whalley.
40. Ivor Bennett, Boldon
41. Peter Halliday, South Shields.
42. Richard Halliday, South Shields.
43. Gerald Sparrow, Barnard Castle.
44. Paul Briggs, South End-on-Sea.
45. Peter Kelly, Sunderland.
46. Andy Moon, Sunderland.
47. Andrew Hetherington, Gateshead.
48. Gerard Armstrong, Brandon.
49. Trevor Lynn, Howden-le-Wear.
50. Daniel Byrne, Fullerton, Nr Andover, Hants.
51. Stephen Simm and son Jack, Sunderland.
52. P.B. Frame, Seven Oaks.
53. Fred Fowler, Fulwell, Sunderland.
54. Kevin McCormick, Birtley
55. Peter Ede, Sunderland.
56. Jack Hunter, Silksworth.
57. Kent Davinson, Craghead.
58. Mark Lloyd Thompson, South Hylton.
59. D. Hamblin, Sunderland.
60. J.G. Bouch, East Boldon.
61. D.G. Hitchcock, Seaham.
62. John Hetherington, South Shields.
63. Rex Lancaster, Grange-over-Sands.
64. Reg Parker, Grange-over-Sands.
65. John Williams, Grange-over-Sands.
66. Mr J. Newby Jnr, Sunderland.
67. P. Days, Chester-le-Street.
68. J.M. Cowley, Sunderland.

69. Joseph D. Stokoe, Brandon.
70. The West Family, Gilesgate Moor, Durham.
71. Keith Moulden, Reading.
72. Ian Pearson, Redcar.
73. Brian Allan, Pinner.
74. Mr Paul Webb, Rainham, Essex.
75. Mr Barrie Fox, Upminster, Essex.
76. Mr Paul Dodds, Newbiggin-by-the-Sea.
77. Howard W. Greenwood, Winlaton.
78. Mark Anthony Barry, South Shields.
79. Mark McIntyre, Bradford Park Avenue F.C.
80. A & G Postlethwaite, Grange-over-Sands.
81. Fred and Linda Foster, Grange-over-Sands.
82. Jeff Scott, Brighton.
83. A. Scott, Tadley.
84. E. Hardy, Washington Village.
85. Brian Capstick, Wardley.
86. Graham Scott, Hebburn.
87. W A Walby, Consett.
88. J. Hunter, South Shields.
89. Des Stook, Stockton-on-Tees.
90. Sue Smith, Shipley.
91. J. Simpson, Stockport.
92. Jerry Pearson, Sunderland.
93 John Trevor Stewart, Thornley.
94. The Gibson Family, Heighington.
95. John Partridge, Houghton-le-Spring.
96. Robert M Jordan, Boldon.
97. Lynn Robinson, Gilsland.
98. Bill Sewell, New Herrington.
99. Allan Bailey, Heighington.
100. George Kastanas, Greece.
101. Geoff Northin.
102. Paul J. Grayson - Bradford Park Avenue.
103. Bradford Park Avenue.
104. Bradford Park Avenue.
105. Mr Frank Thornton - Bradford Park Avenue.
106. Richard Stevens, London.
107. John McHenry, Wideopen.
108. Richard Hockridge, Sunderland.
109. Edward Bartell, Jarrow.
110. Rowland Mizen, South Shields.
111. James Derek Willis, Bradford.
112. Niel Spanton, Reading.
113. Norman Freeman, Cleadon.
114. Len F. Newton, Fulwell.
115. Ian, Andrea and Dillon, Darlington.
116. Paul Michael Hawkins, Durham.
117. J. Carlin, South Shields.
118. Brian Eagles, Durham.
119. Andrew and Sheila Toes, Durham City.
120. Mr Roland Smith, Durham.
121. Paul O'Shea.
122. Alan K. Moore.
123. Jeremy Bassett, Cleobury Mortimer.
124. Julian Elcock, Bridgenorth.
125. Dave Morrell, Swindon.
126. Mr Alfred Carney, Sunderland
127. ALS Publications, Sunderland
128. Alec McFadden Snr & Jnr, Sunderland
129. Richard 'Dick' Wallbank, Morcambe
130. Doug Hall, Sunderland
131. Malcolm Allinson, Beckenham
132. Michael Appleby, Coruna, Spain
133. Eddie Kirkaldy, High Barnes, Sunderland.
134. Ian R. Menzies, Calcot, Reading
135. Tom Conlin, Tunbridge Wells
136. James Henry Broadbent, Sunderland
137. Malcolm Fallow, Wingate
138. Jan & Shane, Kendal
139. Ralph Young, Billingham
140. George Watson, Chester-le-Street
141. David & Lisa Shannon, Strawberry Bank, Sunderland

142. Brian Reed, Shildon
143. Mr P. O'Donnell, Leeds
144. Peter Routledge, Carlisle
145. Mr William Lambert, Witton Gilbert
146. Keith Charlton, Boldon
147. Keith Charles O'Brien, Sunderland
148. Ronnie O'Brien, Sunderland
149. Charles Oliver O'Brien, Sunderland
150. John Chambers, Waterhouses
151. Edward James Jackson, Sunderland
152. Bernard Buckley, Southmoor, Stanley
153. Robert Jeffery Johnson, Penge.
154. Peter Blacklock, Durham.
155. Mr. John Richardson, Lanchester.
156. Bill Wilson, Chester-le-Street.
158. Michael Austin, Whitburn.
160. David Gibson, South Shields.
200. Stephen Wood, Tarleton.
201. Ernest Wood, Sunderland.
410. Dick and Marie Stamp, Helmsdale.
419. Alan V. Taylor, Maidenhead.
1000. Neville Evans

Subscribers' List

1. David & Susanna Mycock, Grange-over-Sands
2. Ken Taylor.
3. Grace Whitaker, Grange-over-Sands
4. G. Lavery, Horden.
5. Arthur Barratclough, Sunderland.
6. Ronald Hayman, Sunderland.
7. F.M. King, Sunderland.
8. Mark McIntyre, Bradford Park Avenue F.C.
9. Alan Simpson, Stockport.
10. Gemma, Matthew, Joshua and Joseph Phillips, Darlington.
11. D.T. Love, Houghton-le- Spring.
12. W H Calvert, Barrow-in-Furness.
13 to 37 Bradford Park Avenue.
38. Peter Berry, Bradford.
39. Peter King, Durham.
40. Stuart Graham, Caterham.
41. Ton Foley, Halesowen.
42 to 1041 Sunderland AFC.
1042. James Shanks, Sunderland.
1043. Geoff Norris, Bolton.
1044. Alan R. White, Newcastle.
1045. Mrs. J. Stone, High Wycombe.
1046. Rebecca Howell, Allithwaite.
1047. Keith Wilson.
1048. Malcolm Pratt, Chester-le-Street.
1049. Mr. W.K. Robinson, Heaton.

GHKN Publishing Limited, Durham City, September 2000.

206

Watercolour action study by Jim Harker of City Art, Sunderland & Durham City.

~ Appendix I ~
100 League Legends

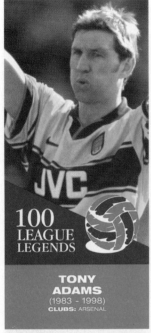

TONY ADAMS
(1983 - 1998)
CLUBS: ARSENAL

IVOR ALLCHURCH
(1948 - 1964)
CLUBS: SWANSEA CITY,
NEWPORT COUNTY, CARDIFF CITY

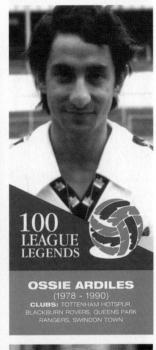

OSSIE ARDILES
(1978 - 1990)
CLUBS: TOTTENHAM HOTSPUR,
BLACKBURN ROVERS, QUEENS PARK
RANGERS, SWINDON TOWN

JIMMY ARMFIELD
(1954 - 1971)
CLUBS: BLACKPOOL

ALAN BALL
(1962 - 1984)
CLUBS: BLACKPOOL, EVERTON,
ARSENAL, SOUTHAMPTON,
BRISTOL ROVERS

GORDON BANKS
(1958 - 1973)
CLUBS: CHESTERFIELD,
LEICESTER CITY, STOKE CITY

100 LEAGUE LEGENDS

JOHN BARNES
(1981 - 1998)
CLUBS: WATFORD, LIVERPOOL, NEWCASTLE UNITED

100 LEAGUE LEGENDS

BILLY BASSETT
(1888 - 1900)
CLUBS: WEST BROMWICH ALBION

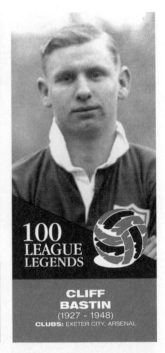

100 LEAGUE LEGENDS

CLIFF BASTIN
(1927 - 1948)
CLUBS: EXETER CITY, ARSENAL

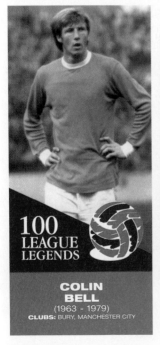

100 LEAGUE LEGENDS

COLIN BELL
(1963 - 1979)
CLUBS: BURY, MANCHESTER CITY

100 LEAGUE LEGENDS

DENNIS BERGKAMP
(1995 - 1998)
CLUBS: ARSENAL

100 LEAGUE LEGENDS

GEORGE BEST
(1963 - 1983)
CLUBS: MANCHESTER UNITED, STOCKPORT COUNTY, FULHAM, AFC BOURNEMOUTH

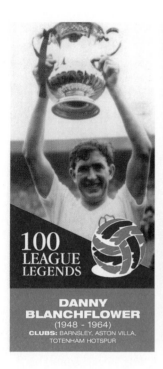

100 LEAGUE LEGENDS

DANNY BLANCHFLOWER
(1948 - 1964)
CLUBS: BARNSLEY, ASTON VILLA, TOTENHAM HOTSPUR

100 LEAGUE LEGENDS

STEVE BLOOMER
(1892 - 1915)
CLUBS: DERBY COUNTY, MIDDLESBROUGH

100 LEAGUE LEGENDS

LIAM BRADY
(1973 - 1990)
CLUBS: ARSENAL, WEST HAM UNITED

100 LEAGUE LEGENDS

BILLY BREMNER
(1959 - 1982)
CLUBS: LEEDS UNITED, HULL CITY, DONCASTER ROVERS

100 LEAGUE LEGENDS

CHARLES BUCHAN
(1910 - 1929)
CLUBS: SUNDERLAND, ARSENAL

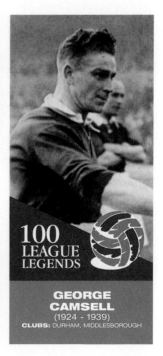

100 LEAGUE LEGENDS

GEORGE CAMSELL
(1924 - 1939)
CLUBS: DURHAM, MIDDLESBOROUGH

100 LEAGUE LEGENDS

ERIC CANTONA
(1991 - 1997)
CLUBS: LEEDS UNITED, MANCHESTER UNITED

100 LEAGUE LEGENDS

JOHN CAREY
(1937 - 1954)
CLUBS: MANCHESTER UNITED

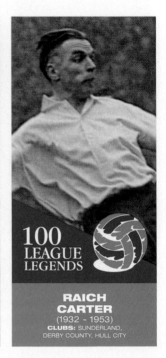

100 LEAGUE LEGENDS

RAICH CARTER
(1932 - 1953)
CLUBS: SUNDERLAND, DERBY COUNTY, HULL CITY

100 LEAGUE LEGENDS

JOHN CHARLES
(1948 - 1966)
CLUBS: SWANSEA CITY, LEEDS UNITED, CARDIFF CITY

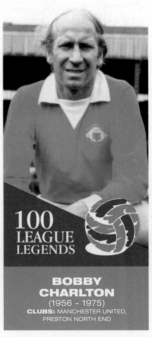

100 LEAGUE LEGENDS

BOBBY CHARLTON
(1956 - 1975)
CLUBS: MANCHESTER UNITED, PRESTON NORTH END

100 LEAGUE LEGENDS

RAY CLEMENCE
(1965 - 1988)
CLUBS: SCUNTHORPE UNITED, LIVERPOOL, TOTTENHAM HOTSPUR

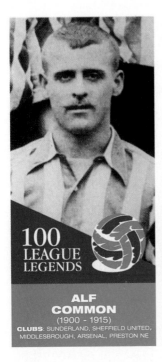

100 LEAGUE LEGENDS

ALF COMMON
(1900 - 1915)
CLUBS: SUNDERLAND, SHEFFIELD UNITED, MIDDLESBROUGH, ARSENAL, PRESTON NE

100 LEAGUE LEGENDS

WILF COPPING
(1930 - 1939)
CLUBS: LEEDS UNITED, ARSENAL

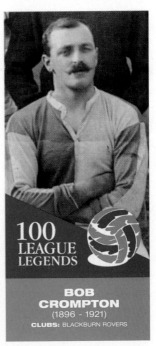

100 LEAGUE LEGENDS

BOB CROMPTON
(1896 - 1921)
CLUBS: BLACKBURN ROVERS

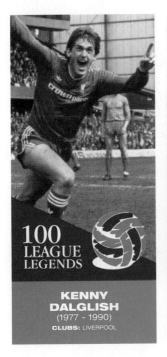

100 LEAGUE LEGENDS

KENNY DALGLISH
(1977 - 1990)
CLUBS: LIVERPOOL

100 LEAGUE LEGENDS

DIXIE DEAN
(1923 - 1939)
CLUBS: TRANMERE ROVERS, EVERTON, NOTTS COUNTY

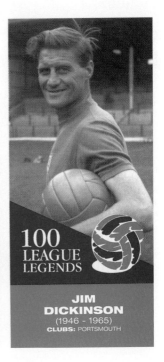

100 LEAGUE LEGENDS

JIM DICKINSON
(1946 - 1965)
CLUBS: PORTSMOUTH

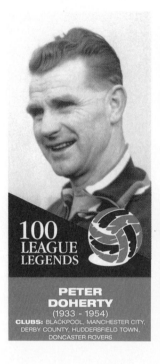

100 LEAGUE LEGENDS

PETER DOHERTY
(1933 - 1954)
CLUBS: BLACKPOOL, MANCHESTER CITY, DERBY COUNTY, HUDDERSFIELD TOWN, DONCASTER ROVERS

100 LEAGUE LEGENDS

TED DRAKE
(1931 - 1939)
CLUBS: SOUTHAMPTON, ARSENAL

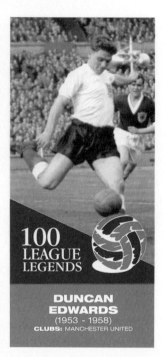

100 LEAGUE LEGENDS

DUNCAN EDWARDS
(1953 - 1958)
CLUBS: MANCHESTER UNITED

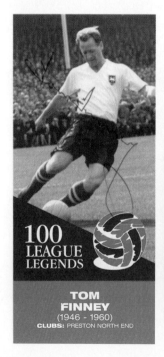

100 LEAGUE LEGENDS

TOM FINNEY
(1946 - 1960)
CLUBS: PRESTON NORTH END

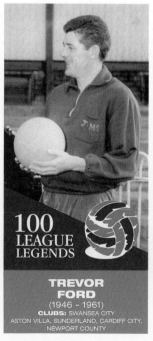

100 LEAGUE LEGENDS

TREVOR FORD
(1946 - 1961)
CLUBS: SWANSEA CITY ASTON VILLA, SUNDERLAND, CARDIFF CITY, NEWPORT COUNTY

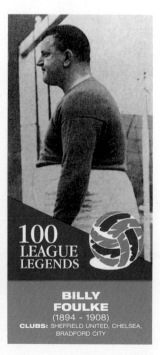

100 LEAGUE LEGENDS

BILLY FOULKE
(1894 - 1908)
CLUBS: SHEFFIELD UNITED, CHELSEA, BRADFORD CITY

100 LEAGUE LEGENDS

TREVOR FRANCIS
(1970 - 1995)
CLUBS: BIRMINGHAM CITY, NOTTINGHAM FOREST, MANCHESTER CITY, QUEENS PARK RANGERS, SHEFFIELD WEDNESDAY

100 LEAGUE LEGENDS

NEIL FRANKLIN
(1946 - 1958)
CLUBS: STOKE CITY, HULL CITY, CREWE ALEXANDRA, STOCKPORT COUNTY

100 LEAGUE LEGENDS

HUGHIE GALLACHER
(1925 - 1939)
CLUBS: NEWCASTLE UNITED, CHELSEA, DERBY COUNTY, NOTTS COUNTY, GRIMSBY TOWN, GATESHEAD

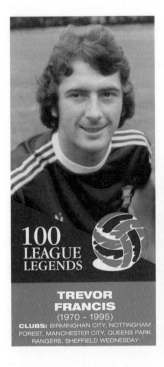

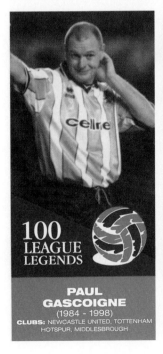

100 LEAGUE LEGENDS

PAUL GASCOIGNE
(1984 - 1998)
CLUBS: NEWCASTLE UNITED, TOTTENHAM HOTSPUR, MIDDLESBROUGH

100 LEAGUE LEGENDS

RYAN GIGGS
(1990 - 1998)
CLUBS: MANCHESTER UNITED

100 LEAGUE LEGENDS

JOHNNY GILES
(1959 - 1977)
CLUBS: MANCHESTER UNITED, LEEDS UNITED, WEST BROMWICH ALBION

100 LEAGUE LEGENDS

JOHN GOODALL
(1888 - 1904)
CLUBS: PRESTON NORTH END, DERBY COUNTY, NEW BRIGHTON, GLOSSOP

100 LEAGUE LEGENDS

JIMMY GREAVES
(1957 - 1971)
CLUBS: CHELSEA, TOTTENHAM HOTSPUR, WEST HAM UNITED

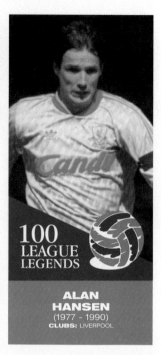

100 LEAGUE LEGENDS

ALAN HANSEN
(1977 - 1990)
CLUBS: LIVERPOOL

100 LEAGUE LEGENDS

EDDIE HAPGOOD
(1927 - 1939)
CLUBS: ARSENAL

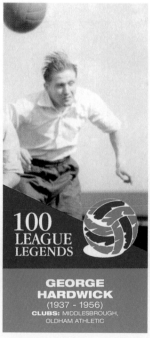

100 LEAGUE LEGENDS

GEORGE HARDWICK
(1937 - 1956)
CLUBS: MIDDLESBROUGH, OLDHAM ATHLETIC

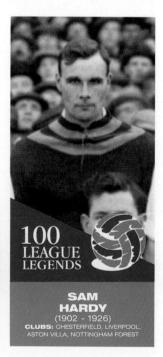

100 LEAGUE LEGENDS

SAM HARDY
(1902 - 1926)
CLUBS: CHESTERFIELD, LIVERPOOL, ASTON VILLA, NOTTINGHAM FOREST

100 LEAGUE LEGENDS

JOHNNY HAYNES
(1952 - 1970)
CLUBS: FULHAM

100 LEAGUE LEGENDS

HARRY HIBBS
(1925 - 1939)
CLUBS: BIRMINGHAM CITY

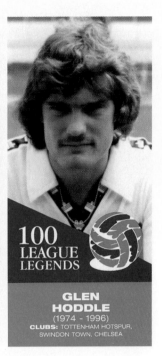

100 LEAGUE LEGENDS

GLEN HODDLE
(1974 - 1996)
CLUBS: TOTTENHAM HOTSPUR,
SWINDON TOWN, CHELSEA

100 LEAGUE LEGENDS

ARCHIE HUNTER
(1888 - 1891)
CLUBS: ASTON VILLA

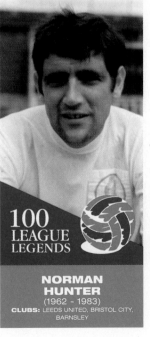

100 LEAGUE LEGENDS

NORMAN HUNTER
(1962 - 1983)
CLUBS: LEEDS UNITED, BRISTOL CITY,
BARNSLEY

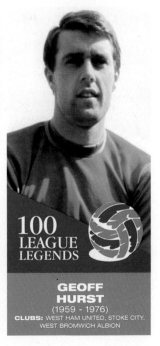

100 LEAGUE LEGENDS

GEOFF HURST
(1959 - 1976)
CLUBS: WEST HAM UNITED, STOKE CITY,
WEST BROMWICH ALBION

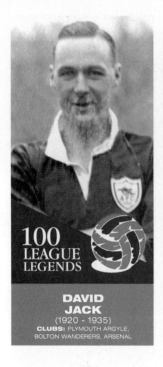

100 LEAGUE LEGENDS

DAVID JACK
(1920 - 1935)
CLUBS: PLYMOUTH ARGYLE,
BOLTON WANDERERS, ARSENAL

100 LEAGUE LEGENDS

ALEX JAMES
(1925 - 1938)
CLUBS: PRESTON NORTH END,
ARSENAL

100 LEAGUE LEGENDS

PAT JENNINGS
(1962 - 1985)
CLUBS: WATFORD,
TOTTENHAM HOTSPUR, ARSENAL

100 LEAGUE LEGENDS

CLIFF JONES
(1952 - 1970)
CLUBS: SWANSEA CITY,
TOTTENHAM HOTSPUR, FULHAM

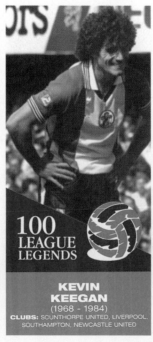

100 LEAGUE LEGENDS

KEVIN KEEGAN
(1968 - 1984)
CLUBS: SCUNTHORPE UNITED, LIVERPOOL,
SOUTHAMPTON, NEWCASTLE UNITED

100 LEAGUE LEGENDS

DENIS LAW
(1956 - 1974)
CLUBS: HUDDERSFIELD TOWN,
MANCHESTER CITY,
MANCHESTER UNITED

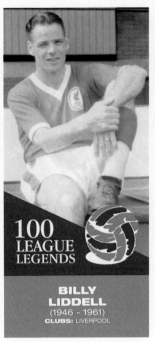

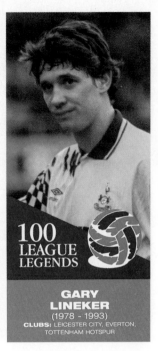

100 LEAGUE LEGENDS

TOMMY LAWTON
(1935 - 1957)
CLUBS: BURNLEY, EVERTON, CHELSEA, NOTTS COUNTY, BRENTFORD, ARSENAL

100 LEAGUE LEGENDS

BILLY LIDDELL
(1946 - 1961)
CLUBS: LIVERPOOL

100 LEAGUE LEGENDS

GARY LINEKER
(1978 - 1993)
CLUBS: LEICESTER CITY, EVERTON, TOTTENHAM HOTSPUR

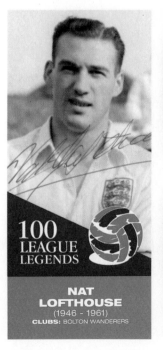

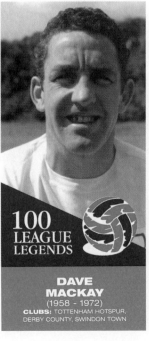

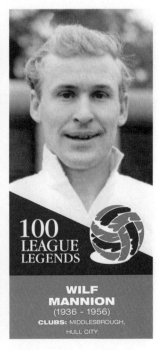

100 LEAGUE LEGENDS

NAT LOFTHOUSE
(1946 - 1961)
CLUBS: BOLTON WANDERERS

100 LEAGUE LEGENDS

DAVE MACKAY
(1958 - 1972)
CLUBS: TOTTENHAM HOTSPUR, DERBY COUNTY, SWINDON TOWN

100 LEAGUE LEGENDS

WILF MANNION
(1936 - 1956)
CLUBS: MIDDLESBROUGH, HULL CITY

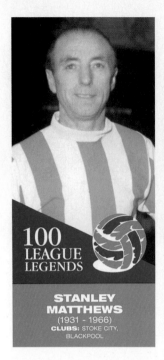

100 LEAGUE LEGENDS

STANLEY MATTHEWS
(1931 - 1966)
CLUBS: STOKE CITY, BLACKPOOL

100 LEAGUE LEGENDS

BILL McCRACKEN
(1904 - 1924)
CLUBS: NEWCASTLE UNITED

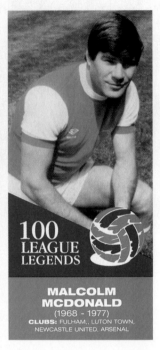

100 LEAGUE LEGENDS

MALCOLM MCDONALD
(1968 - 1977)
CLUBS: FULHAM., LUTON TOWN, NEWCASTLE UNITED, ARSENAL

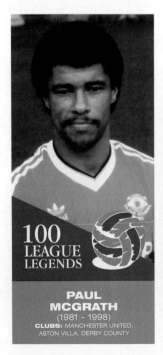

100 LEAGUE LEGENDS

PAUL McGRATH
(1981 - 1998)
CLUBS: MANCHESTER UNITED, ASTON VILLA, DERBY COUNTY

100 LEAGUE LEGENDS

JIMMY MCILROY
(1950 - 1968)
CLUBS: BURNLEY, STOKE CITY, OLDHAM ATHLETIC

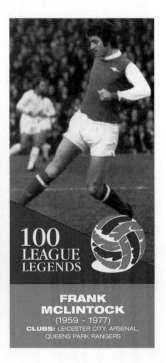

100 LEAGUE LEGENDS

FRANK MCLINTOCK
(1959 - 1977)
CLUBS: LEICESTER CITY, ARSENAL, QUEENS PARK RANGERS

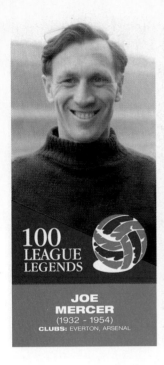

100 LEAGUE LEGENDS

JOE MERCER
(1932 - 1954)
CLUBS: EVERTON, ARSENAL

100 LEAGUE LEGENDS

BILLY MEREDITH
(1893 - 1925)
CLUBS: NORWICH VICTORIA,
MANCHESTER CITY, MANCHESTER UNITED

100 LEAGUE LEGENDS

JACKIE MILBURN
(1946 - 1957)
CLUBS: NEWCASTLE UNITED

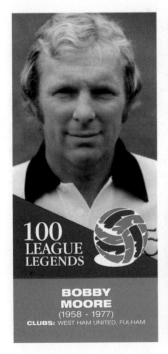

100 LEAGUE LEGENDS

BOBBY MOORE
(1958 - 1977)
CLUBS: WEST HAM UNITED, FULHAM

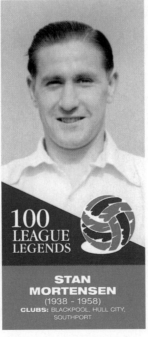

100 LEAGUE LEGENDS

STAN MORTENSEN
(1938 - 1958)
CLUBS: BLACKPOOL, HULL CITY,
SOUTHPORT

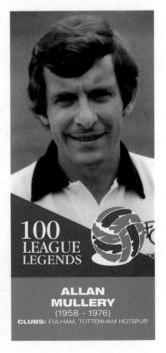

100 LEAGUE LEGENDS

ALLAN MULLERY
(1958 - 1976)
CLUBS: FULHAM, TOTTENHAM HOTSPUR

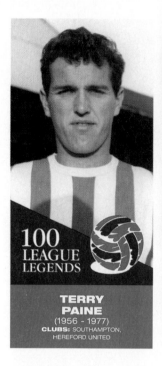

100 LEAGUE LEGENDS

TERRY PAINE
(1956 - 1977)
CLUBS: SOUTHAMPTON, HEREFORD UNITED

100 LEAGUE LEGENDS

MARTIN PETERS
(1960 - 1981)
CLUBS: WEST HAM UNITED, TOTTENHAM, NORWICH CITY, SHEFFIELD UNITED

100 LEAGUE LEGENDS

ALF RAMSEY
(1946 - 1955)
CLUBS: SOUTHAMPTON, TOTTENHAM HOTSPUR

100 LEAGUE LEGENDS

BRYAN ROBSON
(1974 - 1997)
CLUBS: WEST BROMWICH ALBION, MANCHESTER UNITED, MIDDLESBROUGH

100 LEAGUE LEGENDS

ARTHUR ROWLEY
(1946 - 1965)
CLUBS: WEST BROMWICH ALBION FULHAM, LEICESTER CITY, SHREWSBURY TOWN

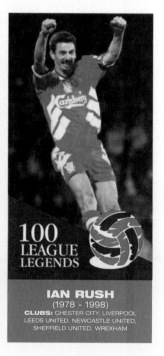

100 LEAGUE LEGENDS

IAN RUSH
(1978 - 1998)
CLUBS: CHESTER CITY, LIVERPOOL, LEEDS UNITED, NEWCASTLE UNITED, SHEFFIELD UNITED, WREXHAM

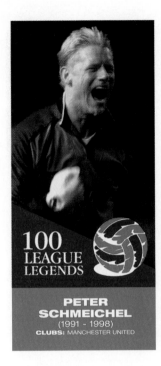

100 LEAGUE LEGENDS

PETER SCHMEICHEL
(1991 - 1998)
CLUBS: MANCHESTER UNITED

100 LEAGUE LEGENDS

ELISHA SCOTT
(1912 - 1934)
CLUBS: LIVERPOOL

100 LEAGUE LEGENDS

LEN SHACKLETON
(1946 - 1958)
CLUBS: BRADFORD PARK AVENUE,
NEWCASTLE UNITED, SUNDERLAND

100 LEAGUE LEGENDS

ALAN SHEARER
(1987 - 1998)
CLUBS: SOUTHAMPTON, BLACKBURN
ROVERS, NEWCASTLE UNITED

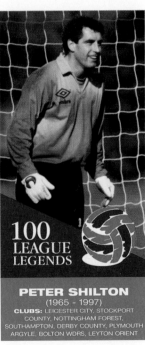

100 LEAGUE LEGENDS

PETER SHILTON
(1965 - 1997)
CLUBS: LEICESTER CITY, STOCKPORT
COUNTY, NOTTINGHAM FOREST,
SOUTHAMPTON, DERBY COUNTY, PLYMOUTH
ARGYLE, BOLTON WDRS, LEYTON ORIENT

100 LEAGUE LEGENDS

FRANK SWIFT
(1933 - 1951)
CLUBS: MANCHESTER CITY

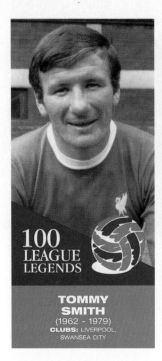

100 LEAGUE LEGENDS

TOMMY SMITH
(1962 - 1979)
CLUBS: LIVERPOOL,
SWANSEA CITY

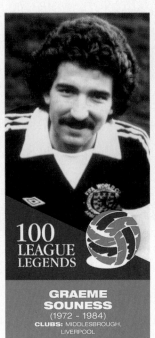

100 LEAGUE LEGENDS

GRAEME SOUNESS
(1972 - 1984)
CLUBS: MIDDLESBROUGH,
LIVERPOOL

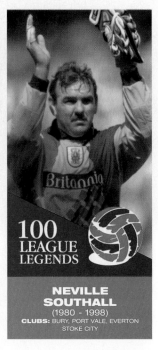

100 LEAGUE LEGENDS

NEVILLE SOUTHALL
(1980 - 1998)
CLUBS: BURY, PORT VALE, EVERTON
STOKE CITY

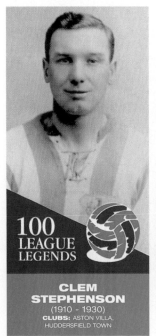

100 LEAGUE LEGENDS

CLEM STEPHENSON
(1910 - 1930)
CLUBS: ASTON VILLA,
HUDDERSFIELD TOWN

100 LEAGUE LEGENDS

NOBBY STILES
(1959 - 1974)
CLUBS: MANCHESTER UNITED,
MIDDLESBROUGH,
PRESTON NORTH END

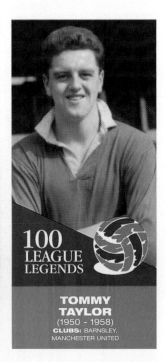

100 LEAGUE LEGENDS

TOMMY TAYLOR
(1950 - 1958)
CLUBS: BARNSLEY,
MANCHESTER UNITED

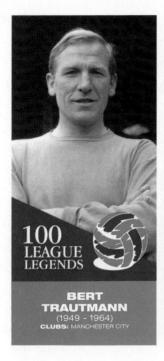

100 LEAGUE LEGENDS

BERT TRAUTMANN
(1949 - 1964)
CLUBS: MANCHESTER CITY

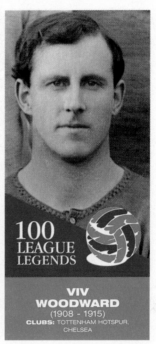

100 LEAGUE LEGENDS

VIV WOODWARD
(1908 - 1915)
CLUBS: TOTTENHAM HOTSPUR, CHELSEA

100 LEAGUE LEGENDS

BILLY WRIGHT
(1946 - 1959)
CLUBS: WOLVERHAMPTON WANDERERS

100 LEAGUE LEGENDS

ALEX YOUNG
(1960 - 1969)
CLUBS EVERTON, STOCKPORT COUNTY

~ Appendix II ~
Editor's 'out-takes'

1985 'Spoof' back page retirement presentation from which this book's title is derived
(courtesy of the Sunday People)

Tenerife plumbing gone berserk - just like top players' demands - see Chapter 10 (author top left).
(courtesy of Colin Saxton)

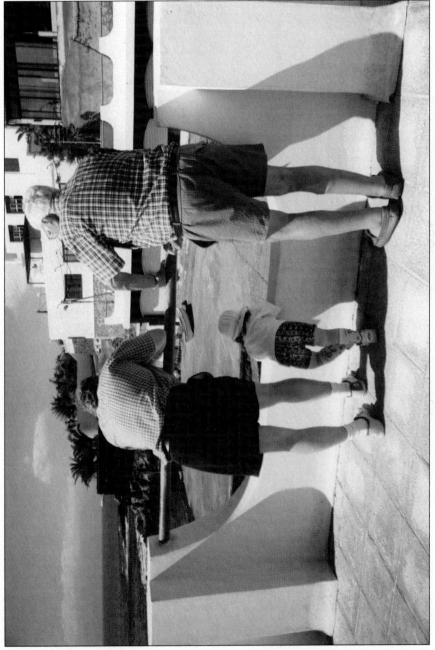

Early 1999 pre-production meeting (R to L) LFS, the 'H' of GHKN and the editor *(courtesy of Catherine Shackleton)*

Author and editor 'hard' at work in the sub tropical heat - life's a bitch - May 2000 *(courtesy of Colin Saxton)*

SS Jaguar 100, made in 1938 when the author joined Arsenal - yes, a long time ago but did international caps really come with goggles? *(courtesy of Gordon Amory)*

SAFC Roker Park Jubilee (1898-1948) with 1948-1949 players (courtesy of the Sunderland Echo)

1979 centenary with survivors: Bingham, Hall, Stelling, Aitken, Reynolds, Shackleton *(courtesy of the Sunderland Echo)*

~ Appendix III ~

Clown Prince of Soccer (1955)

Contemporary Press reviews

"None who opens this remarkable book with all its vitriolic outbursts and revealing sidelights on so many aspects of the game, will lay it aside until the last page has been read."

YORKSHIRE SPORTS ARGUS

"This is easily the best book yet by a footballer and Shackleton may have done the games a service by putting into print what so many players think, but have been afraid to say."

PRESS AND JOURNAL, ABERDEEN

"I agree with much of what Shackleton has to say and - since he has no intention of seeking a living from soccer once he has hung up his boots - I agree he was right to say it. For too long we have suffered the anaemic autobiographies of star footballers who were downright scared to be forthright in their disclosures."

FOOTBALL NEWS, NOTTS.

"There will never be another Shackleton on the football field: there will never be another autobiography such as Shack's."

SPORTS GAZETTE, SOUTH SHIELDS.

"Shackleton is so right to have seen that his book was written this way. He has said things which will not please a good many people, but it is certainly time that they *were* said."

SPORTS EXPRESS.

"The book will undoubtedly lose Shackleton some of his friends in football, but he may gain some new ones from people who like an outspoken man."

EVENING NEWS, LONDON.

"Our old friend Len Shackleton 'has a go' at football and its high-ups in a manner which cannot fail to interest and still more, to entertain."

NEWCASTLE JOURNAL.

"This book is eminently readable. It will be devoured by everyone connected with the game - players, officials, managers and spectators. 'Soccer's Frankest Book?' asks the wrapper - and the reply must be an unequivocal, 'Yes'."

EVENING GAZETTE, MIDDLESBROUGH.

"No one has ever played football quite like Len Shackleton, and no footballer has ever written a book quite like his. In print, as so often on the field, he has produced something at once unorthodox, sensational, and controversial."

EVENING CHRONICLE, NEWCASTLE.

"Len Shankleton, erstwhile England inside-forward - he never wants to play for England again - has written the most bitter attack on Soccer I have ever read."

DAILY MAIL.

"Points Shack puts forward about coaching are that great players who cannot talk will not do; nor will great talkers who cannot play. Shack has certainly proved he is in neither of these categories."

REYNOLDS NEWS.

"All the critics seem to have forgotten one thing, that in his book Len really tries to do something for Britain's national game. He reveals abuses and neglect which show just why Britain's reputation is now so low among the footballing nations."

SUNDAY SUN.

"Yes, this is a controversial book, strong meat to player and spectator alike - and decidedly 'different'."

SATURDAY SPORTS NEWS, WORCESTER.

"Professor Len Shackleton, the Sunderland & England wayward genius, who split the soccer atom in his sensational book, finds himself scorched by the flames of his own honesty. His outspoken comments on the game have raised a real rumpus and revealed 'the jester' as a challenging champion of the rights of professional footballers."

SUNDAY PICTORIAL.

The Author

LEN SHACKLETON

Clown Prince of Soccer

HIS AUTOBIOGRAPHY

Edited by David R. Jack
With pen-and-ink sketches by Mickey Durling
and thirty-seven photographs

Introduction

by BILL MURRAY

(Manager - Sunderland AFC)

Leonard Francis Shackleton - the 'Clown Prince of Soccer' - is the most controversial footballer of his generation, the player who has delighted supporters one minute and disgusted them the next, with the aplomb of an artist who *cares little for praise or damnation.* He is a player who seems to be prompted by an imp of mischief - and how that imp has let him down on occasions!

With all his ability, his wonderful ball control, he could have been a truly great player if that imp of mischief had let him play straightforward football; but then he would have been an orthodox player, and orthodoxy is far removed from his make-up.

It was so typical of him to ask me to write this introduction after he had received a dressing-down. Having discussed football and players' conditions with him so often, I know him to be just as unorthodox in his theories as in his game, and some of his ideas are quite revolutionary.

This life story is Len, in his most provocative mood, and like his play on the field it will emphasise his reputation as *the* controversial player of his generation, either on or off the field.

ROKER PARK, *1955*

Contents

Chapter 1   'Resurrected' by England selectors, I nearly turn them down. Wales and Germany at Wembley, 1954-5,

Chapter 2   The footballer's contract, an evil document. Transfers - public auctions with human beings under the hammer.
My first experience of big fee bargaining.

Chapter 3   Trainers, indispensable men as injury healers-and dressing-room sweepers.

Chapter 4   My introduction to soccer. Early days in the game. Selected for England as a schoolboy international.

Chapter 5   Signed by Arsenal as a boy. Sacked by Arsenal - still a boy.

Chapter 6   I never want to play for England again. International selectors and their shortcomings.

Chapter 7   I sign professional for Bradford and discover soccer glamour is a myth. War-time football. My first representative honours.

Chapter 8   FA and Football League meanness with money. The scandal of Cup Final payments. Ticket problems.

Chapter 9   The average director's knowledge of football.

Chapter 10   Trouble at St James' Park. I go on strike. How NOT to run a football club.

Chapter 11   1 leave Newcastle United for £20,050. My cricket career. The thrill of a first international cap.

Chapter 12   Football pools - another FA blunder.

Chapter 13   Sunderland's buying spree. Trevor Ford is signed, and sold. We just miss relegation.

Chapter 14   Coaching, where we fall down in Britain. My solution.

Chapter 15   Overseas tours. I visit Turkey, Austria, Holland and Denmark.

Chapter 16   Managers who do not manage - and a couple who do!

Chapter 17   Focus on each playing position - and great players in these positions.

Chapter 18   Referees - candid comments.

Chapter 19   'Buried' again by England selectors - the price paid for 'laying an egg' in the Cup replay against the 'Swans'.

Chapter 1

'Resurrected' by England selectors, I nearly turn them down. Wales and Germany at Wembley, 1954-5.

They never come back - in boxing. In football, however, we sometimes do - as I discovered in the autumn of 1954. Rejected by international selectors since playing for England against Wales in October 1949, 1 had made up my mind that, at the age of 32 - after five years without a cap - I was finished with international football. It is no secret that a player is in his prime between his 26th and 32nd birthdays and, as I had failed to impress selectors during my best years, I considered it unlikely that they would reinstate me in my 33rd year.

At that time, perhaps, I did not realise that the men who pick England's international teams do not reason in this way. I should have suspected it, of course, because they were the same men who dispensed with the services of Stanley Matthews in his 30's, and recalled him when the Blackpool genius was nearing 40.

Five years out of international soccer is a long time. During my spell in the 'wilderness' I was keen, keener than most football folk imagine, to wear the white shirt of England; like every other follower of the game, I was disappointed at World Cup failures in Brazil and Switzerland, humiliated to read and hear of those two thrashings inflicted on England by Hungary. I was eager to meet the alleged supermen of South America and the Continent of Europe on the football field - to find out, for myself, just how good they were.

It was like watching a house burn down and being denied the right to contribute the bucket of water in my hand. I did not flatter myself I could extinguish the flames - the Football Association had spread the paraffin too widely - but I wanted to have the opportunity of helping.

Had England been well served in the inside-forward positions - as in the days of Raich Carter and Wilf Mannion - no fair-minded player would have expected international promotion, but there was so much chopping and changing in those two positions that it seemed selectors were picking names out of a top hat. And, as with a conjurer on the stage, we never quite knew what would emerge next from the hat.

My wife Marjorie and I would keep our fingers crossed as team after team was selected and it became customary for her to ask, 'Which pair of inside-forwards are they trying on for size this time?'

Remember the assortment? Jackie Sewell, Red Froggat and Albert Quixall from Sheffield Wednesday, Len Phillips (Portsmouth), Tommy Thompson (Aston Villa), Eddie Bally (Spurs), Stan Mortensen and Ernie Taylor (Blackpool), Don Revie (Manchester City), Wilf Mannion (Middlesbrough), Roy Bentley (Chelsea), Johnny Morris (Derby County), Stan Pearson (Manchester United), Harold Hassall (Bolton Wanderers), Johnny Nicholls (West Brom), Johnny Haynes (Fulham). They even picked wing-half-cum-centre-half Billy Wright as inside forward for the Austrian match at Wembley in *1951,* and although Billy would probably have performed capably at inside right, injuries, fortunately, sabotaged that particular brainwave.

As the years went by, Marjorie and I uncrossed our fingers... 'lock-jaw of the knuckles' might have set in while awaiting the pleasure of selectors; we listened less attentively to England team announcements, and eventually decided that England expected every inside man bar 'Shack' to do his duty, and the men at Lancaster Gate were prepared to try the lot. To say I was disappointed is putting it too mildly; in fact in 1954, when the World Cup party was announced following the Hungarian hiding in Budapest, I told Marjorie, 'If selectors call on me after this lot is over, I won't bother to play.'

I had lost the taste for international football: such things do happen, just as a hungry man, eager for the feast, loses his appetite if kept waiting too long. The taste, the appetite, the eagerness, had died during those five years.

At the start of the 1954-5 season, I was still in that frame of mind. It did not affect my game for my club: I think I was playing quite well, though certainly no better than in previous years, and I was only mildly interested when the Football League picked Don Revie and Johnny Haynes for the 'Dublin Picnic' - the match against the League of Ireland in September.

Don and Johnny must have satisfied selectors, because they were promoted to the England side for the first international game of the season, against Ireland at Belfast. After that game, the Press really gave England the hammer and, with probably the most important international engagement in our history - the meeting with the German World Championship winners at Wembley - looming up, many team changes were forecast.

The next big game - it was really a trial for the full internationals with Wales and Germany - was Football League *v* Irish League at Liverpool. A few days before the match, a newspaper reporter 'phoned me and said, 'You'll be pleased to know you're in the League XI to play the Irishmen.'

Pleased? If only that reporter could have known my thoughts, he would have had a wonderful story. Had he heard the conversation that followed, the story would have been even better.

I told Marjorie, 'They've resurrected me. With my best football days behind me, I'm on trial for an England cap.' Knowing very well how I felt about the international set-up, Marjorie enquired, 'What will you do? You won't play, will you?'

It was a moment of decision. On the one hand I was determined to stick to my resolution that England, having managed without my services for so long, could carry on without me: the urge to refuse the Football League invitation was very strong. On the other hand, though having little interest in the Irish League affair or even the full international with Wales, I was desperately keen to have a crack at the World Champions. I wanted to meet the Germans at Wembley, to try and prove in my own small way that it was not the prerogative of every footballing nation to rub the Englishman's nose in the dirt.

Some would call my feelings a conflict between pig-headedness and patriotism but the issue went much deeper than that. Not knowing which way to jump, I went to a good friend, George Childs, for advice. George, the other director in my company, looked at it partly from the business angle and suggested: 'You play for the League if you want to be picked for the Welsh and German matches. Your new hairdressing salon is due to open around the same time as the game against Germany, and that publicity would give the business a wonderful send-off!'

He was right. Why not use the favour of selectors to launch the barber's shop? I decided to play, and it still amuses me to imagine what the feelings of the Football Association would have been had they known that I represented England for the sake of publicity as much as for the honour of wearing the international shirt!

First, however, I had to serve my ninety minutes' apprenticeship against the Irish League. Sunderland were at Everton on the Saturday before that match, so Marjorie and I decided to stay with friends in Lancashire over the week-end, remaining for the inter-League affair on the Wednesday.

In the Everton match I picked up a groin injury which meant a change of plans and a return to Roker Park for treatment on the Sunday morning. As soon as the Sunderland masseur, Alex Wilson, examined the injury, he shook his head and told me, 'You won't play on Wednesday; in fact this looks like a fortnight's job.'

The big decision about whether to play or not had been taken out of my hands by this unexpected twist. I was disappointed because, knowing the sort of opposition likely to be provided by the Irishmen, I had been looking forward to the game. On paper, they were a poor lot, and I expected the sort of match in which I could 'try something on', in other words display my wares in front of the people who mattered, the boys from the FA.

Perhaps I was not as disappointed as other players might have been. I was in two minds about playing anyway, and would not have lost any sleep about missing Ireland and Wales, so long as I could win a place in the team for the German battle.

Marjorie stayed in Liverpool for the inter-League match and her report to me was, 'This is the first time you've had any luck in a representative game. It was a real shambles, and you were fortunate to have missed it.'

Her verdict was endorsed by the Press who decided almost unanimously that West Ham's outside-right Harry Hooper was the only League forward to show anything approaching international form at Liverpool.

Events might easily have gone the other way. Had Eddie Baily and Harold Hassall, the League inside pair, turned in 'blinders', I have no illusions about how quickly I would have been consigned to the scrap heap. As it happened, I played myself into the party for the international against Wales by *not* playing!

While doing a spot of gardening at home one evening, a neighbour, George Stafford, called over to me, 'Congratulations Len. You've been picked to play against Wales at Wembley.' I refused to believe him until my *Newcastle Journal* carried the team the next morning. It was: Wood; Staniforth, Byrne; Phillips, Wright, Slater; Matthews, Bentley, Lofthouse, Shackleton and Mien.

I had been told, off the record, that my long absence from international football was caused by selectors' reluctance to play individualists: they wanted to pick men who would part with the ball quickly, and I understand it was an unforgivable sin for a player like Stan Matthews or myself to beat an opponent by employing any skill we might possess as ball players.

With Germany still on my mind, I decided just before the Welsh game that if that was the way the FA wanted me to play, I would string along with them and follow their strange ideas - even though I had been picked on my club games as an individualist. Pre-match instructions included the use of 'push and run' methods from the inside-forwards, so, for once, I was doing the right thing.

England beat Wales 3 - 2, with an exhibition of football which would never be labelled brilliant, but I think we did a reasonable job of work against a hard-fighting, inspired, enthusiastic team. Although not happy about my own game - knowing that I had disappointed those spectators who had gone to Wembley expecting to see me 'try something on' - I had evidently played my cards correctly. A selector's opinion was, 'Shack played just as we wanted him to. Why can't he always play that way?' The prospect horrifies me!

People who really knew me were full of questions afterwards. I met David Jack, the *Empire News* sporting columnist, and he was blunt enough when he asked, 'What made you play that sort of game, Len? You parted with the ball as though it were red hot - a thing I've never seen you do before. Was it a tactical instruction?'

I could not explain my reasons at that time, but told him:

'Wait until the Germany match. I might show you something that day, and explain all about the Welsh game.' Friends in Sunderland thought I had sold myself for the sake of England caps, that I was content to become just another 'straight up - and - down inside mans in order to stay in the good books of the selectors. They were right, of course - but that shadow of 'Shack' was created for one game only.

It may be against selectors' principles to retain the same team for two successive matches and, even though no more than three weeks separated the meetings with Wales and Germany, they made two changes. Bert Williams and Tom Finney took over from Ray Wood and Frank Blunstone, the Chelsea boy who had been selected when Nat Lofthouse withdrew from the Welsh game.

Due, perhaps, to an oversight, I was kept in, but the axe had to fall on somebody and Ray and Frank, both youngsters, were the chosen two.

The German World Champions, badly hit by injury and illness, fielded a side against England at Wembley on 2nd December *1954,* which was only a shadow of the one which had shocked Hungary in the World Cup Final a few months previously. The Press had written off the match as a walk-over for England: even Herr Sepp Herberger, manager of the German team, stated, 'My team will have no chance, but we hope to keep the score down to a reasonable size.'

Being a little on the suspicious side - I had heard those sort of stories before - I imagined the Germans were trying 'kidology', and made up my mind to treat the game with all the respect due to a meeting with the World Champions. This was very much a prestige game; there was everything at stake, and until I really got the feel of the opposition, there would be no room for clowning. Providing Germany were as bad as they claimed to be, England might snap into a two or three goal lead in the first half, and that would give me the chance to pull a few tricks out of the bag.

That is why I started, as in the Welsh game, playing straightforward stuff, refusing to let myself go, and generally toeing the line by serving up synthetic soccer for selectors' satisfaction. I played ball by not playing *with* the ball, but after half an hour I was fed up, and decided the pretence had gone on long enough. From that moment I played my normal game - and enjoyed it.

Roy Bentley put England one goal up in the first half. The Germans were so poor that we would have won the game by the interval, had all the scoring chances been turned into goals. I give a lot of credit to the visiting goalkeeper, Fritz Herkenrath, for keeping us out when we threatened to overrun Germany, and although some critics claimed he blocked shot after shot more by good fortune than good judgement, I think they did him an injustice.

Every time England looked like scoring, which was often, Fritz would dash out to narrow the angle. His anticipation was uncanny, and I decided he could be beaten only by dribbling the ball round him or - more difficult - by chipping it over his head. Shots he could not reach went wide. Those on the target bounced off his arms, legs, chest and other parts of his awkward Aryan anatomy.

Ronnie Allen had given England a 2-0 lead, reduced by a surprise German goal in a breakaway, when I had my chance to clinch the game for England. Picking up a pass, I beat one man, sold a dummy to a second, fooled a third, and looked up to see the advancing Fritz Herkenrath standing between me and the empty goal. I managed to dribble past him, only to lose control of the ball and rush desperately to the goal line without catching up with it.

A few minutes later I had a similar opportunity. This time, I thought, the second method of beating goalkeeper Herkenrath must be employed. True to type, he ran out to meet me but, just as he was about to pounce, I produced my right-foot 'mashie niblick' and was relieved to see the ball float over his head into the untenanted goal.

That goal was, perhaps, my most memorable scoring effort in a lifetime of soccer. It is not easy to explain, but I felt a keen satisfaction - not because the goal made our victory over Germany certain, but because I had decided exactly how to go about scoring it long before the chance presented itself. Anticipation and fulfilment.

For the first time for many years the Press were perfectly happy about an England international side. 'A great England team' was their verdict, while misguided scribes who had previously shown their lack of knowledge by criticising Stanley Matthews, had to use every superlative in the book to describe the wonderful performance given that day by 'Scintillating Stanley'.

The newspapers were even kind to me - in fact one of them suggested I was the inside-forward for whom England had been searching for so many years. The score of 3-1 may not look very impressive, but it is no exaggeration to claim it might have been 7-1 if we had been a little luckier with our shooting. The Football Association, reeling under the impact of such a spontaneous and unaccustomed vote of approval, were even tempted to suggest that their successful team might be kept together during the season, assembling at various times in preparation for the next match - against Scotland four months later.

Knowing my selectors, I took all the tales about retaining a settled team with a large pinch of salt: when a friend insisted that the selectors would not dare disturb such a good international **XI,** I told him, 'Six or seven members of that England team will be dropped before the next match.' Six changes were, in fact, made.

I was dropped - but not because I transgressed regulations by talking to a journalist after the match against Germany. He was a foreigner - Swiss, I believe, and I felt sorry for him as he asked his questions in broken English and received only non-committal replies for his pains.

He approached me in the Wembley dressing room, saying, 'Pliss Mr Shack. Will you tell to me why Germany was losing the game?'

I wonder if my Swiss friend realised his leg was being pulled when I answered, 'I think the Germans used the square ball too often. That's dangerous, and it's very painful when you head it.'

Chapter 2

The footballer's contract is an evil document. Transfers - public auctions with human beings under the hammer. My first experience of big fee bargaining.

The professional footballer's contract is an evil document. Of that I am certain, so certain, in fact, that I am quite amazed that such a hopelessly one-sided document has survived the tremendous amount of criticism hurled at it by so many people in these enlightened days. Questions have been asked about it in the House of Commons. Public indignation has been voiced, yet the canker remains with us - causing unrest and dissatisfaction to spread through soccer, season after season.

We have often heard such words as serfs or slaves applied descriptively to footballers but until every player in the game has suffered soccer serfdom and raised his voice against it, I am afraid these descriptions will never be taken seriously. Let's face it - the average pro appears to have a pretty good life, with a possible £15 a week wage, plus bonuses, the hope of a £750 benefit (less tax) every five years, a nest egg of nine per cent of all his football earnings when he retires, a house in which to live, and a congenial working day.

That seems reasonable enough up to a point, but on closer examination many flaws may be spotted in the set-up. In the first place, no more than twenty-five per cent of League players draw the maximum £15 wage. Benefits are unheard of in many clubs, while in others they are halved, or even more drastically mutilated at the whim of the directors. Eviction from club houses is automatic when clubs decide to dispense with players' services, and the 'pretty good life' is over usually long before a man's fortieth birthday - providing injury has not curtailed it even earlier. It was, in fact, stated once that the average playing life of a professional footballer is seven years, causing more than one of us to comment, 'That's a career, that was.'

Estimating the average retiring age at *35,* the professional footballer finds himself, in the prime of life, jobless, homeless, with a few hundred pounds from the Benevolent Fund and no training for a trade or profession. He sometimes queues up for his turn on the guillotine of a managerial career, or for the menial duties of a team trainer, but there are obviously not enough jobs in football to accommodate every player wishing to stay in the game.

It is all very depressing to anyone hoping for security - and who does not? - but these are the sole 'rewards' of the successful players; those who have remained free from injury and been permitted to serve their allotted span as good club servants.

What happens to the unlucky ones? The contract they sign when joining a League club ties them to that particular club for life, if that is the desire of the club, yet it can be terminated without notice if the manager or directors wish it. No more one-sided agreement was ever fashioned in the mind of man.

Professional players are no better than professional puppets, dancing on the end of elastic contracts held securely in the grip of their lords and masters. Sometimes the elastic is severed... always from above, never from below.

Assuming a player has good grounds for wanting a move from his club - his manager may have a particular grudge against him, he might have fallen out with his playing colleagues, or perhaps he detests the town in which he lives - he asks for a transfer. Then the fun starts.

The application may be treated favourably, to all intents and purposes, and the club agree to transfer the player to any other prepared to pay, say, £15,000 for him. To most, that figure is prohibitive, which means our disgruntled soccer star must stay put. On the other hand the Board Room verdict could be, 'We are not parting with you,' meaning, once again, that he stays where he is.

No other form of civil employment places such restrictions on the movements of individuals, while, at the same time, retaining the power to dismiss them summarily. If a man is able to better himself in a job elsewhere, he should be free to take that job on - providing he has fulfilled his contract. It happens in every walk of life, but not in football. Tom Finney, Preston North End's international outside-right, was told he would be a rich man for life *if* he spent five years playing football on the Italian Riviera. Whether or not Tom was keen to accept this offer - made by an Italian prince - it would surely have been a waste of his time to consider it because Preston would hardly think of allowing him to say 'Yes'.

Another Italian club, Juventus, were anxious to sign the Teesside marvel, Wilf Mannion, and went so far as to propose to lodge £15,000 in Wilf's banking account on completion of the transfer. Mannion could not capitalise on his ability, because he was tied to Middlesbrough. I could have made a lot of money, much more than is dreamed of in English football, by joining a club in Turkey, but even after the expiry of my seasonal contract, I would not have been permitted to sample this particular Turkish delight.

One restriction after another haunts the footballer of today. Rules are enumerated in neat little coloured books issued to players by the majority of clubs. These books are usually entitled, 'Players' Instructions and Training Rules,' or 'Guidance and Discipline for the Players of "X" Club,' but I think it would be more appropriate to label them, 'Seventeen Pillars of Serfdom,' or maybe, 'Thirty-Nine False Steps.'

Opening one of these moronic manuals we are instantly informed that the booklet must be carried at all times and shown to the Commissionaire at all home matches: this is no doubt a vital instruction, because it would be embarrassing to turn up for a home game and be refused admittance by a uniformed flunkey!

Then follows a dismal dogma of 'don'ts', insisting that players must not ride motor cycles, dance between Wednesday and Saturday, talk to the Press, wear anything but uniform blazers and flannels for away matches, reside in a place not approved by the club, or spend a week-end away from home. In addition they have to submit to medical examinations whenever required.

There must be very sound reasoning behind each one of these restrictions - although I cannot think what it is, offhand - but the important aspect of the business is, how many other workers, excluding those in the armed forces, have to comply with such regulations in £15-a-week jobs? Penalties for transgression of rules, too, include the stoppage of wages *pro rata* . . . whatever that may mean to the average player! It says so in the book.

No fair-minded person would quibble about toeing the line in his contract, or submitting to irksome restrictions, providing he was getting a reasonably honest deal in return, but there is nothing honest about the player's contract - placing, as it does, all the trump cards in one hand. What is needed is a new form of agreement, allowing players freedom of movement once they have fulfilled their obligations to any particular club. I think the Players' Union are working on the right lines but their reasoning is rejected, their suggestions are scorned, their arguments annulled, at every frustrating meeting with the tradition-bound rulers of football. It is difficult to visualise any change until the staid gentry of Preston and Lancaster Gate are superseded by younger, more realistically-minded men.

Why not run football like any other business, with each player coming to his own agreement with his club about wages, length of contract, benefit payments and any other relevant items? If Stanley Matthews is worth £50 a week to Blackpool, let the club pay him that figure, and if a Blackpool reserve player is rated at £5 weekly he should receive his paltry flyer. If the poorly paid player feels he is being shabbily treated, he can only blame himself - if £5 is the figure he accepted.

The Football League answer is, 'Football is a team game, and differences in wages would cause disharmony.' That is sheer nonsense, if the position in Scotland - where there is no maximum - is examined for guidance.

The Hibernian star right-winger Gordon Smith may be earning £20 a week, while a team-mate is probably on half that figure, yet Gordon has not experienced any animosity, bad feeling, or refusal to co-operate on the field.

A stage show is a team game, but an actress like Mary Martin is surely entitled to a bigger salary than the 'Wacs' who helped her to 'wash that man right out of her hair' in *South Pacific*. The extras, like the soccer reserves, are vital - but not quite so vital as the Mary Martins or Stanley Matthews.

What other arguments are put forward by the League against the abolition of the maximum wage? There is the suggestion that, if this were done, all the good players would join the wealthy clubs, leaving the 'also-rans' for the Second and Third Division. In other words they want to hamper enterprise, and bring every team down to the level of the League's least successful members.

There must, however, be some difference in playing standards, and I cannot see how the League imagine they avoid that. If a wealthy man owns a nice house he expects to fill it with expensive things, but average people do not usually feel aggrieved at having no marble pillars in the bathroom.

Wealthy clubs collar all the best players now anyway: Newcastle United have better players than Newport County, Wolves more talent than Wrexham, Manchester City more than Mansfield Town; yet each of the clubs mentioned is permitted to pay players the same wage.

All the advantages lie with the big clubs: they have the resources to pay larger fees for players, employ more scouts, own bigger grounds - and that means more revenue, have more men on top money, treat benefit payments as an obligation not as a joke, provide more lavish housing accommodation, and interest international selectors much more frequently than smaller clubs. Would it make such a tremendous difference if they were also permitted to pay wages above the present maximum?

Let us examine another Football League 'bleat', trusting they will appreciate my efforts to present their case, as opposed to mine! They stated, before a Ministry of Labour investigation, that in the Scottish League, where there was no maximum wage, the championship had been won by two clubs between them no fewer than forty-one times. On the other hand, in a sequence of fifty-one seasons, no English First Division club had won the championship more than six times.

That sounds a convincing case, but it was not mentioned that there are only sixteen teams in the Scottish 'A' Division, or that only three or four of them are really well supported. In England we have twenty-two First Division clubs - and twenty-one of them draw large enough attendances to enable them to make transfer offers of £20,000-plus. Money invariably brings soccer success, and that money is distributed so evenly in England that no club is wealthy enough to corner the market in players. In Scotland, Rangers and Celtic have practically all the cash - so they win the Leagues and the Cups with monotonous regularity, a state of affairs, which could never occur South of the Border.

Abolish the maximum wage, and you also abolish illegal payments, signing-on presents, and back-door bargaining, all of which the FA and League sincerely want to stamp out. If a player signs a club contract for five years at £2,000 a year, both he and the club are satisfied with the terms, which obviate any necessity to bolster up his wages with mythical jobs and lucrative part-time pursuits.

Wilf Mannion once stated that he was offered a £3,000 signing on fee, top wages, and £25 a week for a non-existent outside job **if** he joined a certain club. Tommy Lawton became a typewriter firm representative - a genuine job - when he was transferred from Chelsea to Notts County and, although Tommy was not exceeding the maximum football wage, the move brought him a considerable amount of money from both sources. It was quite legal, of course, but nobody doubted that this was a means of recompensing a brilliant footballer while, at the same time, keeping within the rules of soccer.

I do not intend to delve into the rather sordid business of under-the-counter payments. It seems to me that everyone in football, at some time or another, has made 'sensational' disclosures about such sinning, but they mean nothing if the names are omitted. I am sure there is substance in the stories, and these tales will continue to be told so long as out-of-date legislation withholds permission for football employers to pay good players good money. It would be better to pay a man £40 a week as a footballer than £15 for his football, plus another £25 for 'outside duties'.

Players' benefits, and all the bad feeling associated with them, could also be dispensed with, if individuals were permitted to negotiate their own terms of employment. Too many clubs blatantly ignore their obligations towards loyal club servants, pleading poverty as their excuse for not attending to benefits as they become due. While rules state that benefits *may* rather than *must* be paid, clubs will continue to shirk the issue: that rule leaves a loophole, deliberately, of course, because a large number of clubs have no intention of acting in good faith over benefit payments.

Small clubs could not afford to pay benefits, I am told, yet soccer claims to be self-supporting; if it is not, then I suggest a grant from the football pools promoters would take care of benefit obligations. Is the game really so poverty-stricken as we are led to believe? I doubt it. From all sides I hear pleas for tax relief and talk of bankruptcy, but the captains of these sinking ships, the directors, are very slow to apply the obvious remedy - by voluntarily withdrawing from the League. Any good businessman who is losing money gets out quickly and, however limited their knowledge of football, directors are usually successful businessmen.

It is reminiscent of the TV viewer, who sits in front of his set complaining about the programme he is watching. He can always switch off!

I have studied this business of players' contracts at great length, and cannot discover any flaws in a system whereby a player signs a contract, like any other professional man, for three, four or five years, on terms mutually acceptable to himself and his club. Expiry of the agreement would leave the player free to accept another contract with any club of his choosing.

This would completely abolish the ridiculous transfer system, under-the-counter payments, bitterness over benefits, and complaints that players were being retained against their will. It would also enable ability to be recognised rather than retarded, by making the labourer worthy of his hire.

The auction of human beings in the transfer market still persists in Britain at a time when it has been outlawed by the so-called backward people of Arabia, Persia and North Africa. The Middlesbrough manager, Mr Bob Dennison, had two experiences of it in *1954-5* when he wanted to sign Charlie Wayman from Preston North End and Frank Brennan from Newcastle United. Bob, allowed by Preston to sound Charlie Wayman, gave 'Wee Charlie' the shock of his life when he told him the Deepdale club were prepared to sell him to Middlesbrough.

The Brennan case, of course, was front-page news. Bob Dennison, given permission to approach this loyal club servant, asked Brennan, 'Will you join Middlesbrough?' Frank, flabbergasted, could only ask Dennison, 'Who says I'm for sale?' Such trading in human property, in which clubs do not even consult the 'article on offer', are a disgrace to football. But they are quite permissible.

My very good friend, goalkeeper Jack Fairbrother, received similar treatment after only one season as a Newcastle player. That was in 1947-8, when the Magpies were promoted to the First Division, but Jack is the first to admit he had not displayed his best form at that time.

In the close season Newcastle were on tour in Ireland when Fairbrother was injured - it was a case of a punctured kidney, causing him to spend six weeks in a

Cork hospital. As he lay there, Jack felt Newcastle had just about written him off: 'It seemed to me they regarded me as finished,' said Jack, telling me the story, but he was not prepared for United's next move.

Fairbrother, still a semi-invalid, read in the papers that Bobby Langton, the Blackburn Rovers international winger, was going to be signed by Newcastle for a £19,000 fee - plus goalkeeper Jack Fairbrother. He decided something had to be done about it, made a complete recovery, and was picked to play in Newcastle United's first trial match in August. As the players ran on to the field, Fairbrother spotted the Blackburn Rovers manager Jack Bruton in the St James Park directors' box - proof that the Langton swop was not just newspaper talk. 'I'll show 'em if they're justified in sacking me,' said Jack, and he turned in a 'blinder' for the benefit of the occupants of the directors' box.

After the game - a game which must have pleased the Blackburn representative - Fairbrother was called into the office and asked, 'Well, Jack, what about it - are you going to join Blackburn?'

He feigned ignorance and said, 'What do you mean - join Blackburn? This is the first I've heard about leaving Newcastle. He was asked, 'Don't you read the papers?' to which his obvious reply was, 'We are always told not to believe newspaper stories.'

As it happens, the deal fell through because Bobby Langton did not want to leave Lancashire for Tyneside - and afterwards Fairbrother was told by his club, 'We had no intention of parting with you anyway.' He took that statement at its face value, having previously read in the Lancashire Daily Post, 'It was confidently expected that Jack Fairbrother would agree to return to Blackburn, and the only doubt about the deal going through centred around Mrs Langton's housing requirements.'

Apparently Mrs Fairbrother's housing problems were not worth considering!

My first experience of big fee transfer deals occurred when I left Bradford for Newcastle, a deal which brought Bradford £13,000, a useful profit on a £10 player. My manager, Mr Fred Emery, instructed me to report at a big hotel at two o'clock one afternoon - without giving me any information about the reason for so doing. I turned up, sat in the lounge for an hour without meeting a soul and pretended not to notice the strange looks of a waiter who was hovering around.

Then a stranger came up and said, 'I couldn't get you. The fee is too high.' I suddenly realised what was happening. It was my first intimation that I was about to be transferred.

A crowd of prosperous-looking individuals descended the stairs and one of them, the Bradford chairman, Mr Stanley Waddilove, pointed at me and told a companion, 'there he is. He's all yours, Stan.' The person, to whom the remark was made, shook my hand and introduced himself, 'I'm Mr Seymour of Newcastle United. Would you like to join my club?' I agreed readily enough, but the whole affair left a nasty taste in the mouth: it was too reminiscent of a cattle market . . . with 'Shack' on show as the prize bull!

I may be wrong, but it seems rather absurd to have people bartering in human flesh, without so much as permitting the object of their bids to be present at the sale. Even harem-bound girls were permitted to sum up their prospective employers while the bidding was taking place.

It is also wrong to allow clubs to benefit to the extent of as much as £35,000 when they transfer a player, while the person worth that sum is entitled to nothing more than his £10 signing-on fee. Just dwell on that £35,000 figure for a moment: it may not sound much, spoken quickly, but on reflection, it could buy sixteen semi-detached houses in many places. Some misinformed people actually believe players receive, if not the whole fee, at least a portion of it, which reminds me of the old lady who approached me at Newcastle on the occasion of my first game for United. She congratulated me on my six goals and then said, 'You are a lucky lad getting £13,000 for joining Newcastle.' I wonder if she believed me when I told her my share had been a tenner.

Clubs would be wiser to sign players on contracts at, say, £1,000 a year for five years, include floodlight and friendly match clauses, and fix a benefit payment if desired, than to spend, for example, £10,000 on their transfer. They could employ their popular sliding scale, because I, for one, would not complain about receiving £15 instead of £25 if I lost form and played in the reserve team - so long as I was not out of the first XI through injury.

Perhaps clubs would have to cut down their staffs if the general wage level rose, but I question whether that would really be a bad thing for the game. A number have too many players on their books: to release them would enable smaller clubs to use some of the talent now hidden away in reserve teams.

In any case it is still to be proved that the scheme would be any more costly than the one now in operation. Isolated stars like Stan Matthews would be paid well in excess of the present £15, but - and this is important - several £15 a week novices, would be recompensed in proportion to their ability - on contracts of £400 to £500 yearly. They would have no complaints, if the terms were mutually acceptable to club and player.

While apologising if this chapter delves too deeply into the 'politics' of football, I am sure the question of players' working conditions badly needs airing - not by the Union, not by the Press, but by a player, such as myself.

I have tried to put forward a reasonable case, and hope I have succeeded.

Chapter 3

Trainers, indispensable men as injury healers - and dressing-room sweepers.

To achieve success, a football club must have the right men in the right jobs - on and off the field. It is useless having a great manager to look after a team if the men playing in that team are not intelligent or skilled enough to respond to his management. By the same token, there is little point in assembling eleven soccer stars and placing them in the hands of a manager insufficiently equipped with the better points of the managerial profession - such as they are!

Taking the argument a stage further, skilled players and a manager of proved ability are still only sections of the complicated machine known as a club. Directors, unfortunately, must be considered because nothing upsets the blend of a winning team more than the presence in the board room of the wrong type of men. Players, manager, directors: the machine is almost assembled, but it still requires lubrication to run smoothly, and that is where the trainers come in.

I am convinced that soccer trainers are the real key men in the Football League: without their healing hands and medical knowledge, clubs would be struggling to field one team weekly - let alone the four, five, or six turned out now by most of the important clubs. How do we reward these vital men? In most cases by paying them a miserable pittance of a wage - almost certainly less than that of the players they control - by saddling them with every ignominious task imaginable, and by treating them as the poor relations of football whenever possible. The job has its compensations, I suppose. Trainers survive longer than managers - as they should in view of the difference in pay for services rendered.

It is a gloomy picture, this training business, yet it has been brightened up since the war by some clubs who have made efforts to raise the status of 'the man with the sponge'. These are the clubs who, realising the necessity of maintaining perfect fitness among players, have appointed fully qualified physiotherapists and entrusted them exclusively with the task of looking after injuries.

Such enterprising clubs have been accused of wasting money on one of the luxuries of the game, but I fail to see how a physiotherapist who really knows his job can be classed as a luxury. I know it means one more name on the payroll, but I regard an expert in physiotherapy as a necessity - and he should be paid accordingly.

If such an expert could ensure keeping first team players fit for forty-two League matches, he would soon be included among the fixtures and fittings of every club. That is impossible, of course, but when the physiotherapist gets eight or nine more matches out of players than would an unskilled man, his wages are surely well covered by increased attendances at first XI games?

Another point worth remembering is the damage that might be done - is done, in fact - when serious injuries are 'treated' by trainers whose medical background would hardly qualify them for sweeping out the chimney in a GP's surgery. This is no exaggeration. How many footballers have been put out of the game through clumsy attempts to heal injuries?

There was the incident in which a player received an injury - obviously a nasty one - during a match and, as he lay on the turf, called to an opponent, 'I've broken my leg. Fetch your trainer on. Don't let our bloke touch me.

The player to whom this appeal was made must have remembered the incident vividly later, because he too broke his leg in a match. And he had no doubts about the damage that might be done, because he was evidently terrified of his own trainer when he implored, 'Don't let our fellow catch hold of me.'

True stories, emphasising the damage that is done when unskilled trainers tend injuries. Every footballer, I imagine, has experienced their shoddy work at some time in his career.

Let us not be too harsh. There is a place in every club for an unskilled trainer . . . but that place is not the treatment room. That is why I feel it would be a progressive move if all clubs employed a team trainer *and* a physiotherapist.

Anticipating the 'we could never afford it' cries, and admitting that every club must cut its coat according to its cloth, I still believe that while football directors are prepared to pay thousands of pounds for players, it is in their own interest to have them looked after properly. A god physiotherapist could save a club £20 a week - probably more - and if he is being paid £10 to £15, directors would actually be in pocket.

Is there sufficient work to justify the employment of two men instead of one? I think so. The majority of clubs nowadays expect their trainers to be:

(a) Medical experts to treat injuries
(b) PT instructors to organise training
(c) Team coaches
(d) Assistant managers
(e) Boot cobblers
(f) Dressing room sweepers-up
(g) Private detectives to keep an eye on unruly players
(h) Tea boys (although the chief scout usually looks after this).

It is obviously too much to expect of any one man, yet most of these tasks must be performed by somebody, and that somebody is invariably the trainer. To relieve him of duties connected with the treatment of injuries would still leave enough to keep a team trainer fully occupied.

I am surprised that a club of Sunderland's standing took such a long time to think about appointing a qualified physiotherapist, but when they did make the move they chose the best in the game, Alex Wilson. Alex has the right soccer background - he was Arsenal's goalkeeper in the 1930s and trainer with Brighton & Hove Albion and Birmingham City before moving to Roker Park. In addition Alex has made a study of physiotherapy, passing all his exams with flying colours. Not surprisingly, every player treated by Alex Wilson has implicit confidence in the healing skill of his hands.

I mention Wilson's football background because although this is not essential, it can be very useful when a team manager is looking for guidance or constructive suggestions from his training staff. A case in point is the Jimmy Seed - Jimmy Trotter partnership which has been so successful for Charlton Athletic. Seed is a manager in a million; he must be to have held his job so long in a game which tolerates managers only in small doses and for short periods. But without belittling Seed's achievements at the Valley, I wonder how important a part Jimmy Trotter has played in the Charlton story.

Trotter is more than a trainer ... he is the boss's right-hand man, and, as such, must be almost indispensable to Jimmy Seed. Any manager would welcome a trainer fashioned in the Trotter mould. No wonder he is an almost automatic choice as team attendant to the England international team: even the FA could not fail to recognise Trotter's ability.

One hears many amusing tales about the methods of club trainers. It is surprising how frequently a secret remedy, handed down, perhaps from past generations, succeeds in curing an injury when the more orthodox methods have failed. There must even be some magic healing powers in the mixture of oil and 'tab ash' with which players in one club are massaged, for their trainer always has a cigarette in his mouth and just does not seem to notice if the ash drops on the injury.

Some trainers, rightly or wrongly, pin their faith to remedies which, I imagine, would make illuminating reading for the tenants of Harley Street. I have even heard of one team attendant who claims the best way to clear up a knee injury is to massage it with oil from the tail of a tiger.

I wonder if he also recommends the best way to obtain the co-operation of the tiger!

Chapter 4

My introduction to soccer. Early days in the game.
Selected for England as a schoolboy international.

Ever since I started putting two and two together - and that was a long time ago -
I have had a passionate interest in football. As an elementary school kid, playing no
organised Saturday afternoon soccer, off I would trot with Dad to Valley Parade one
Saturday, Park Avenue the next... dividing my affections equally between the two
Bradford clubs. Footballers normally become spectators when they are too old to
play, but I was a keen fan before starting to play.

Although there was no official football session at school, I spent all my spare time
kicking a ball about in the schoolyard, in the fields near our home and even in the
house, the latter with full parental approval. In the early 1930's, when television was
merely a madman's mirage, when empty pockets put the cinema out of bounds,
youngsters manufactured their own entertainment with a tennis ball. From May to
August we were all budding Herbert Sutcliffes or Hedley Veritys. In the winter we
became Cliff Bastins and Dixie Deans. Even though youngsters stuck to their
seasons religiously, the same tennis ball and pile of coats were utilised for
equipment.

Whenever Mum told me to go on an errand, I would make sure I had a pal to keep
me company, produce the tennis ball the minute we left the house, pass and re-pass
it all the way to the shops and back, and hardly notice I had performed the loathsome
task of shopping. Refusing to be robbed of football time after dark, our gang played
many a 'cup-tie' in front of a well-lit grocery shop - unaware then that we were the
first floodlight footballers in Yorkshire!

Nowadays the younger generation might call me a football fanatic, yet I was
merely doing the same thing as nine out of ten kids from Aberdeen to Aberystwyth,
from Inverness to Ipswich. It was the natural thing to do. How many lads today carry
muddy tennis balls in their jacket pockets, head for the fields and parks the moment
they finish school, or sit through their lessons in shirts soaked with the sweat of half
an hour's honest endeavour in the school playground? Not many. It is no longer

normal to do as we did. There are too many counter-attractions: manufactured merriment for the millions is laid on without our having to search for it.

Is it surprising then, that the days when half a dozen tip-top players queued for each position in England's international side have gone, and in their place we have the possibility - perhaps inevitability - of any good player being capped thirty, forty, or even fifty times by his country? Let us not spin tales about the wonderful football of Hungary, Yugoslavia or Uruguay when, if we faced facts, we would realise that those nations' victories over England were achieved only because Britain's footballers no longer serve their soccer apprenticeship between the ages of six and sixteen.

Like Jimmy Hagan, Wilf Mannion and the other over-30's, I was fortunate enough to be brought up in an age of football enthusiasm. As a seven-year-old, I could not afford real football boots so my Uncle John bought some studs and hammered them into an old pair of shoes. Uncle John always wanted me to be a footballer and he realised how much I would appreciate those studded shoes.

Dad didn't appreciate them so much the first time I tried them out. Every evening, Sundays included - we were not answerable to the Football Association then - the decks were cleared in the Shackleton living room for indoor football. Chairs were removed from the room, while furniture too bulky to evict was pushed into a corner, though as a slight concession to the landlord's windowpanes, a ball of paper bound with elastic bands was substituted for the tennis ball.

Wearing Uncle John's home-made football boots for the first time, I was having the time of my life when the ball rolled under our sideboard. Dad bent down, fished out the ball, I aimed a mighty kick at it... and connected with father's eye. It gave me a fright I shall never forget, yet such was Dad's enthusiasm, he treated the incident as a normal hazard in the football education of son Leonard.

Father was always keen. As an amateur footballer he had sufficient ability to think about taking up the game professionally, until a First World War wound put a stop to his ambitions. Dad's type of football pleased the 'get stuck in' spectators; he revelled in hard tackling and almost made a boast of the fact that he had been sent off the field frequently. All our family regarded sport as an occupation for he-men. David Steward, another uncle of mine, was for fifteen years captain of Bradford Northern Rugby League club - and that's no game for softies. I sometimes wonder whether I would have been a better footballer if possessed of some of the 'devil' of Dad and Uncle David.

Although I hold no brief for the professional player who shirks the tackle, there is always the thought in my mind that I want to play the following Saturday, and when that day comes I want to turn out the week after. Players like Stan Mortensen or young Derek Tapscott, dashers who might be prepared to run into a brick wall for the sake of Blackpool or Arsenal, have their admirers but I have always played this game my way, and that is the way I mean to carry on.

When the time came for me to move from elementary to secondary school, I was given the choice of about half a dozen schools as the prize for passing the scholarship exam. Two were quite near our house while the others were on the opposite side of Bradford. I chose Canton High School - about a twenty minutes' tram ride away - because Carlton had the best schoolboy soccer team in the city. And Dicky Watmough, the famous Preston North End winger, was a former pupil.

At Carlton High I was introduced to organised football as part of the school syllabus: I wondered what game I had been playing previously. As a novice in the finer points of the game, I imagined the inside-right marked the inside-right, the left-back was responsible for the opposing left-back and so on, with everyone on the field - bar the goalkeepers - chasing the ball. In those days youngsters seldom sat at home discussing the tactics of soccer; we were too busy playing it, after our own fashion.

Thanks mainly to the interest and encouragement of my sports master, Mr Walter Hodgson, who must have spotted some natural ability in his new pupil, I was soon wearing the Carlton first XI colours.

Next step from the school side was selection for Bradford Schoolboys against Stoke Boys at the Victoria Ground, home of famous Stoke City. It was a wonderful experience, that first representative match for Bradford, an occasion made even more memorable by the presence of City's international stars, Frank Soo and Stanley Matthews - recruited as linesmen. Had anyone told me that day I should play for England in 1954 with the same Stanley Matthews, it would have seemed too ridiculous for words.

After a few reasonable games for Bradford Schoolboys, Mr Hodgson and another Bradford schoolmaster, Mr Kendall, nominated me for an English international trial, and I was selected to play for the North against the Midlands at York. Boarding the train from Bradford to York, suitcase in hand, I dreamed of travelling by train every Saturday for Utopian-sounding places like Turf Moor, Deepdale, Saltergate or Gigg Lane. How times change! Since then I have done so much travelling, it would suit me never to see another railway carriage.

At York I did well enough to earn a second trial, this time at Walsall, followed by selection for The Rest v England Boys at Kettering. Weighing 6 stone 2 lb, a paltry 4 feet 11 inches tall, I was handicapped physically, in fact I was the smallest boy in that Kettering trial; but I was well enough pleased with my performance to keep my fingers crossed and await the announcement of England's chosen team.

Devouring every column on the sports page of a local evening newspaper, I read the announcement, 'Len Shackleton plays outside-right for England Schoolboys against Wales at Aberdare'. Outside-right? Me? I had never played in the position in my life - but that didn't matter in the least. I had been picked to play for England, a task I would willingly perform - even as a goalkeeper.

On the Wednesday before the international, playing for Carlton High School in a local cup-tie, I suffered every known mental anxiety, as well as physical pain, when an opponent stepped heavily on my big toe. That caused some panic in the Shackleton household: all that night, and the following day, my precious toe was bathed while every few minutes somebody asked, 'Is it any better?'

Friday came, the big match was 24 hours away, and I was still doubtful - but that was a well-kept secret. I had no intention of crying off, or even reporting the injury, as I caught the train for the long journey to South Wales. Once again I admired the grubby third-class carriage and thought: 'This is the life for me'.

1. Len Shackleton congratulated by his school-mates on being chosen for his first international (England Boys v. Wales Boys, 1936).

2. The Bradford Park Avenue team of 1946. Left to right, back row: *Leonard, Ruecroft, Farr, Greenwood, Hepworth, McTaff.* Front row: *Walker, Downie, Shackleton, Gibbons and Smith.*

3. *The author, a sixteen-year-old ama-teur, has a training spin at Highbury during his short career with Arsenal. With him is Bobby Daniel.*

4. *'Shack' photographed in his England shirt and cap.*

5. *Members of the staff of the London Paper Mills who entertained Len Shackleton when he was first selected to play for England.*

In the strange position of outside-right I turned out at Aberdare, scoring two goals in a 6-2 victory. Working a switch with my inside partner, a Birmingham boy called Davis, I spent most of the ninety minutes in my normal inside-right position. I was reminded of that game many years later when I joined Sunderland from Newcastle United, and Sunderland centre-forward Dicky Davis told me he had been my inside-right at Aberdare.

On the Sunday after the match I arrived home in Bradford late at night to be greeted by my father who, traditionally trying to hide his enthusiasm, was obviously as pleased as punch about my first game for England. I showed him my cap: he collared it and made a tour of the whole neighbourhood, knocking on doors, exhibiting the cap, and informing everybody in the district, 'Young Len scored two goals for England against Wales.' In the early hours, Dad crept into the house - still clutching his precious souvenir.

My next outing for England Boys was at famous Villa Park, Birmingham, where a crowd of about 40,000 saw us give Scotland a hiding 4-2. One member of the Scottish side had a good game that day, a wiry left-winger called Billy Liddell, later destined to play many times for the senior Scotland team as well as being Liverpool's outstanding post-war footballer.

Following the Irish international at BeWast Celtic's ground - a game we romped through (8-3) - my career as a schoolboy international had to end. The next season I was too old - at 14. There were occasional opportunities for representative soccer, like the day I played for Bradford Secondary Schools against Glasgow Schools at what is generally regarded as Britain's finest football ground, Hampden Park. Whenever I discuss Hampden I fall out with Scottish friends, but they have never succeeded in making me alter my view. Hampden Park - in the springtime, when most of the big games are staged - is one of the poorest grounds on which I've played. Hard, bumpy, bare of grass in patches, the problems of the pitch are not helped by the notorious 'swirl', the gusty wind, which always rises and falls when least expected.

There is no comparison between Wembley and Hampden Park, the one being an even stretch of beautiful green turf on which even a bowls match might be played successfully, the other... well, I've just described it. Of course Hampden is used every week during the long Scottish soccer season, while Wembley seldom stages more than half a dozen games annually. The North London stadium would possibly be just as poor as Hampden if it received the same sort of treatment.

Still a pupil at Carlton School - in those days schoolboys were permitted to discuss terms with professional clubs - I answered a knock on the door of our house one day and recognised the caller, Billy Hardy, the manager of Bradford Park Avenue. Billy invited me to join Bradford as an amateur. I immediately said, 'Yes', as would any youngster in similar circumstances, but Dad was not so eager. He told Mr Hardy, 'You know I'm a Bradford City supporter and it seems all wrong that our Len should go to Park Avenue and not Valley Parade. What will his uncles say? They're all City fans.'

Objections overcome, however, I signed the forms and was flattered to be told, 'We want you to come to the ground as often as possible - and make sure you train with us every Tuesday and Thursday evening.' It was the first step on the ladder to a career in football, and I made up my mind I was going to have a real crack at climbing that ladder, regardless of all advice warning me against professional football. Plenty of folk were prepared to condemn professional players but I am glad I did not listen to their arguments, including one particular protest from a Sunday School teacher.

There we were, sitting in Sunday School, when our teacher asked each member of the class in turn, 'What would you like to be when you grow up?' It came to my turn, and I told him outright, 'I'm going to be a footballer.' He was not impressed. 'That is no career. There may be some money in it for a few lucky ones, but, you know, footballers take up the game professionally only when they cannot earn their livings at a better job. You would find yourself mixing with all kinds of people - not a course I would recommend.'

No doubt he was passing on the sort of advice anyone would in similar circumstances, but it is time we all forgot the bad old notions of football being a job fit for the cloth cap and muffler brigade, a dead-end occupation for street corner boys and snooker saloon spivs. Since leaving school I have mixed with all kinds and all classes of people - some big, some small - and the most genuine of the lot, my most loyal friends, are professional footballers. Fifty years ago it might have been different, yet it is a fact that among players of recent times may be found many brilliant men: schoolteachers like Bill Slater and Dennis Wilshaw of Wolves and George Robb (Spurs); successful businessmen such as Joe Mercer (ex-Arsenal) and Bert Williams (Wolves); fully-qualified accountants - Billy Kiernan of Charlton Athletic is one; and lads who have found time to dabble, and do reasonably well, in the arts - Len Boyd (Birmingham City), Frank Brennan (Newcastle United) and Jeff Taylor (Brentford) came into the last group. It could also be claimed that many footballers have become successful authors - but I prefer to be truthful about that business!

Chapter 5

Signed by Arsenal as a boy. Sacked by Arsenal - still a boy.

Having read, and heard, so many different versions about my short career as an Arsenal footballer - most of them incorrect - I feel it is about time the true facts of this depressing episode were brought to light. There are still people connected with the Arsenal club ready to deny my story, yet, as the individual most concerned, I feel I know more about it than any of them.

As a fifteen-year-old still at school, I was playing for Kippax United in the Leeds League, while on an amateur form with Bradford Park Avenue. Apart from training sessions on Tuesday and Thursday evenings, I had no close connection with Park Avenue, and there had been no suggestion that I should become a Bradford professional on coming of age. It was taken for granted, though, that I would eventually sign for the club, so it came as a big surprise to be told by Mr John Plows, a schoolmaster who took an interest in Kippax United, 'I have recommended you to Arsenal and they're sending a scout to see you play.'

Arsenal - of all teams. Could it be true? After all, every youngster, at some time or other, imagines himself in an Arsenal shirt, yet the majority must remain content with imagination. I was flattered to think Arsenal were sending a man to have a look at Kippax United - and me.

His report must have been favourable because a few days before the end of the 1937-8 season, a beautiful car pulled up outside our unpretentious residence, neighbours congregated to have a look at the Chrysler - or was it a Rolls? - and out stepped Mr George Allison, secretary-manager of fabulous Arsenal, to ask if I would join his club.

With neighbours still gossiping outside, Mr Allison painted rosy Highbury pictures inside, with Dad, Mum, and 'young Leonard' hanging on every word. He had no need to 'sell' Arsenal to me. At that time, any 15-year-old boy, invited to join the greatest club in the world, would have been out of his mind to think twice. So it was that I accepted his offer of a job on the ground staff and signed as an amateur.

I thought August would never come, but eventually I packed my bags, caught the train to London, and was met at King's Cross by Jack Lambert, centre-forward hero of so many Arsenal triumphs. Jack had finished his playing career but, like other Arsenal servants, had become a staff man, as coach to the younger players. Having been installed in Highbury Hill lodgings, I went with Lambert, for my first peep at the magnificent Arsenal stadium. It was a real eye-opener. Villa Park, on which I had played as a schoolboy international, was my idea of soccer perfection, but even Villa Park appeared shabby as I gazed glassy-eyed at Highbury for the first time.

The mighty stands, the spotlessly-clean terracing, reaching, to my eyes, into the clouds, the emerald green turf: these would have been sufficient to impress the bumpkin from Bradford, but to cap the lot, I saw - and recognised immediately - several of the favoured, fabulous, footballers, who had helped to make Arsenal great, helped, in fact, to make Arsenal 'The' Arsenal. There they were, within hailing distance, Ted Drake, Wilf Copping, Cliff Bastin and George Male, yet I did not dare hail them, even with a 'good afternoon'.

The following morning I was handed my equipment, and it didn't include football boots, shirt or shorts. I was given a pair of overalls and told to follow the motor mower all over the pitch clipping any long grass stalks missed by the mower. A rake was provided too, but never a sign of a football. Enviously, I watched the 'real' players doing their training stint - while I pretended to rake the gravel or cut the turf, without having the heart for either task. Each day a fresh face would join the stalk-shortening squad: among my companions were Les Henley, later to become an Arsenal first team player, Stan Morgan, who contributed so much to Leyton Orient's promotion drive in *1954-5,* Bobby Daniel, brother of Sunderland's Welsh international pivot Ray 'Bebe' Daniel, and Harry Ward, another product of the Leeds League. Bobby Daniel looked like becoming a really great player, until his tragic death in the RAF during the war.

In 1938 Arsenal staggered the football world by signing inside-forward Bryn Jones from Wolverhampton Wanderers for £14,000, a fee described by many a critic as the height of lunacy - but, of course, critics have been saying exactly the same thing since Alf Common moved from Sunderland to Middlesbrough for £1,000. And they will be repeating it when somebody in this country moves for £50,000, which could happen anytime. One newspaper decided it would be a good stunt to get a picture of Bryn, Arsenal's costliest player, alongside their cheapest - and they selected me for the job. In the paper there was a wonderful action picture of Bryn Jones, accompanied by the caption, 'He cost £14,000'. Alongside was 'Muggins', in overalls, stalk-shortening with a pair of grass clippers, and the caption, 'He cost nothing'.

I suppose it made me look a bit of a chump but I did not bear Bryn any malice: though to emphasise what an up-and-down business football is, it is worth mentioning that after the war I was transferred from Newcastle United to Sunderland for a record £20,050 fee at about the same time that Bryn Jones, then a veteran, moved from Highbury to Norwich City in exchange for a relatively small fee - certainly not more than £3,000.

Record fees did not concern me in 1938, however. I was more worried about hiding myself from the Highbury groundsman, Bert Rudd, and with Bobby Daniel and Harry Ward, kicking a tennis ball about the passages, snack bars and empty terraces when we should have been assisting Rudd. It was easy to hide at Highbury: the place is colossal, as our groundsman boss discovered. Bert, incidentally, is still with Arsenal and we always have a chat when Sunderland play there. His usual greeting is, 'Are you still managing to hide yourself?'

One of our hiding-places at Highbury was alongside the asphalt training pitch behind the terracing, and it was there that Bobby, Harry and I sat for hours watching the Arsenal stars train. My particular favourite was Eddie Hapgood, the finest left-back ever to play for England, and even during those not-so-serious antics on asphalt, Eddie seemed head and shoulders above all the other players. Hapgood had such tremendous faith in his own ability that his confidence affected everything he did, and it spread through any team in which he played.

Although I spent a complete season with Arsenal - from August 1938 to May 1939 - I turned out only twice in the famous red shirt, once against Oxford University and once against Bristol Rovers.

Quite a number of the Arsenal youngsters, myself included, were playing Athenian League football for Enfield: there were so many on the ground staff that it would have been impossible to give us all match practice with Arsenal, but, of course, each one kidded himself he was certain to get his chance one day.

Meanwhile I was being paid fifty shillings a week, twenty-seven and sixpence of which went on lodgings and laundry, and ten shillings home to Mum, so that by the time I had paid out a few coppers for odds and ends, I was left with the princely sum of ten shillings a week on which to live in London. It was enough in those days to supply my needs, an occasional evening at the pictures and a nightly dream of Shackleton shining in an Arsenal shirt - which cost me nothing.

Ground staff boys did not mix with the big men of Highbury. I seldom spoke to the Hapgoods, Swindins and Craystons, which is why I was staggered, in the course of a paddock-sweeping manoeuvre, to hear manager Allison shout, 'Go and get stripped. I want you to play outside-left in the trial match.' I did not wait to give him the chance of changing his mind: within five minutes I was in the dressing-room and out again, lining up at outside-left, a position I had never occupied before.

The opposing full-back was George Male, first choice for England; my partner was Gordon Bremner, a brilliant ball player who, but for the war, might well have become the inside-left for whom Arsenal had been searching since the retirement of Alex James. My main worry was a 'doubtful' left foot, or, to be more truthful, a practically useless one.

Yes, in those days I was very much one-footed, in fact as a 5 feet 2 inches youngster, I don't think I had the strength to reach the penalty area from a corner kick *using my good foot,* never mind the left one. Things turned out better than I expected, a state of affairs entirely due to the brilliance of partner Gordon Bremner who, with the minimum of assistance from me, managed to 'paralyse' the normally cool and capable George Male.

It was the only occasion during my 10 months at Highbury that I was able to play football with the stars there.

A week or two before the end of the season, Harry Ward and I were approached by groundsman Rudd and told, 'The boss wants to see you in his office.' We imagined the summons was in connection with some neglect of our ground staff duties: we both hoped it would not be a reprimand relating to the playing side of the job.

In the magnificent managerial mausoleum I stood awkwardly facing Mr Allison, wishing, I don't know why, that the pile on the ankle-deep carpet might grow and keep on growing until it attained a height of 5 feet 2 inches to hide me from the eyes of my manager.

Then followed an interview I shall never forget. With each pronouncement the facts became clearer. I was washed up, was not good enough for the Arsenal - or any other club for that matter; I would have to return to Bradford and become, perhaps, a miner, an engineer, perhaps a commercial traveller - but never a footballer.

Mr Allison could not have been kinder: he handled that interview with diplomacy, repeatedly assuring me that he was advising me in my own interests, and told me not to take the news too badly. One day I would be grateful. He said, 'Go back to Bradford and get a job. You will never make the grade as a professional footballer.' I should have been thankful to have discovered such shortcomings so early in my career, but my only thoughts that day were the shame of returning home a failure, the epitome of 'local boy doesn't make good', and I was not far from tears as Allison's verdict was pronounced.

Something else happened that day. Just before I left the office - the office I should never again see - Mr Allison tried to cheer me up by giving me one last glimpse of the greatness of Arsenal before I returned to the back streets of Bradford. 'Come next door', he said, 'I have something special to show you.' Like a kid in a dream, I accompanied him and was shown... a television set.

Instead of treating the incident as a friendly gesture from the Arsenal manager - what else could it have been? - I was livid, telling myself that I had been shown the television set so that I could go home and tell my 'country-bumpkin' chums in Yorkshire about the miracles of modern science. There is no bitterness now. Time heals all wounds, but should George Allison ever be passing through Sunderland, I will gladly reciprocate and let him have a look at the 17-inch screen TV set in my front room.

During the past few seasons I have been given the title of 'Arsenal's Star Attraction', just because I seem to reserve all my best displays for Sunderland's games against the club that sacked me. There is, of course, an instinctive urge to do well against Arsenal, and there is no denying everything goes right for me when I play at Highbury, but I refuse to admit it is a case of pulling all my tricks out of the bag just to prove Arsenal were wrong.

Every player appearing at Highbury has the incentive to perform a little above normal form. Many of the important people in the game have regular stand-seats and invariably the directors' box contains the FA types who do not journey beyond the limits of Stamford Bridge, White Hart Lane and Highbury. Dressing-room amenities cannot be bettered anywhere in the world - and I have sampled all sorts in many countries - which reminds me of a crack made by a Roker team-mate, Ken Chisholm, when he stepped out of the bath following a Sunderland game at Highbury. It may surprise a lot of people to hear that the dressing-room floors are heated. 'Chiz' was unlucky enough to stand on a spot, which had become over-heated, causing him to jump in the air with pain and babble about his burnt bunions. Said Ken, man of many clubs, 'I've asked for transfers for less than this.' I told him, 'That's nothing. I was given a free transfer here - without complaining about the floor.'

Yes, I can joke about my Arsenal days now, but it was not very funny in May 1939. I was out of a job, faced the prospect of crawling home as a football failure after leaving to a fanfare of trumpets, and wondered how I could face everyone in Bradford.

Harry Ward was in a similar position, so we got together to discuss the next move, determined to do anything rather than catch the train back to Yorkshire. Although we were amateur footballers, we had lost our living through being sacked by Arsenal: there were too many promising youngsters waiting for ground staff jobs to allow the club to retain a couple of 'failures', paying them fifty shillings a week to cut the grass. Then I had a stroke of luck, or, to be more correct, a sample of true generosity on the part of a man I had never met. Somebody tipped me off that anyone capable of playing a reasonable game of football would be fixed up with a job in the London Paper Mills at Dartford - providing he played football for the particular firm. It was a long shot - we could have been misinformed, but Harry and I packed our bags, spent the few shillings in our possession on rail tickets to Dartford, and duly arrived at the London Paper Mills office.

Mr Frank Langan was the man I wanted to meet; it is true to say I *had* to meet him because, with all my belongings in the suitcase and without a penny in the world, I would have been stranded had Mr Langan not been available. He was keen enough to discuss a job when he heard we had arrived from Arsenal, but looked rather doubtful when we explained just what we were capable of doing. We had no trade, we had sunk all our hopes and energies in soccer, and the type of work we could have done was worth no more than 17s. 6d. a week to the Paper Mills. It would not have provided me with a bed.

Then Mr Langan made a proposition for which I shall always remain grateful: 'I'll find you some lodgings, pay you enough money to satisfy the landlady, and give you a few shillings a week on top for spending money.' I jumped at the offer. It was equivalent to double the normal pay for boys of my age on that particular job, and, more important, it saved me from returning home with my tail between my legs.

The soccer season was just about ending, but I played cricket right through the tempestuous summer of 1939 for London Paper Mills, working in the mill, earning enough money to keep going, and stubbornly refusing to believe that I would never be a professional footballer. Still an amateur, I played during the early part of the 1939/40 season for the works football team until, with the 'phoney war' gradually developing into the real thing, I decided to heed Mum's pleading and return to join the rest of the family in Bradford.

It is fashionable to blame the war for a lot of things. Railway chaos, the housing shortage, plus a hundred and one other ills were attributed to it - even ten years after the last bullet was fired. Perhaps that is why the Arsenal verdict on the Shackleton sojourn there, in the words of the present manager Mr Tom Whittaker, is 'Len

Shackleton would be an Arsenal player today, had it not been for the war. He left the club at the start of the war, and decided to settle in Bradford.' Arsenal are entitled to their opinion, but there was no war in progress that day in May when I was called to the manager's office and given marching orders!

There is one story concerning my move to Arsenal which is worth re-telling here. My amateur registration with Bradford was very nearly due to lapse when George Allison asked me to go to Highbury: it may, in fact, have expired, but David Steele, then the manager of Park Avenue, took a dim view of the Arsenal approach and he fired on the Gunners with all the ammunition at the disposal of a small club.

Mr Steele knew I had taken my boots with me - and they were no ordinary boots. They had been specially made, because a 'nipper' like me did not use stock sizes, so the Bradford boss wrote to Arsenal demanding the return of those boots. George Allison sent Park Avenue a cheque for 17s. 6d., in recompense for loss of footwear if not of footballer, a move which has since inspired tales that I was transferred for half a crown short of a pound!

Frank Langan is still with the London Paper Mills and he finds time to send me good luck telegrams whenever I play in big games. I made a sentimental return journey to Dartford in 1946, after playing in the FA *v* Army PT XI international trial match at Wembley - on the day I was picked to play for England for the first time as a senior.

Turning up at the Paper Mills, my wife Marjorie and I were swamped with congratulations, asked to pose for photographs with mill-workers who had played football for the Dartford side when I was there, and made such a fuss of that it was almost embarrassing. I told Frank Langan, 'You have been very kind today, but you were just as generous in 1939 when I was an unwanted nobody. That is why Dartford had to be my first call after England picked me to play against Scotland.'

In football I have discovered it is easy to cultivate friendships; everyone wants to help with favours, and strangers cannot do too much for you - while you are at the top of the tree. How many remain friendly when you slide, when you are no longer held in public esteem, or when luck goes against you? Not many, which is why I am so grateful to men like Frank Langan. He alone saved me the ignominy of scuttling home, a heart-broken flop. Perhaps Frank played as big a part in the football career of Len Shackleton as anyone in this book. So many different things might have happened without his assistance.

Chapter 6

I never want to play for England again.
International selectors and their shortcomings.

Speaking at a well-attended football dinner, a very important personage in the Football League informed the guests that it was not terribly serious if Hungary, Yugoslavia, or even Timbuktu beat England in international matches - so long as League entertainment was being provided for fans in England every Saturday. He pointed out that a million people attended League matches weekly - and those million spectators were more concerned with their local clubs than with international affairs!

Those sentiments provide the key to the international set-up in Great Britain: club first, country second, is the view of many football legislators, and nothing the reasonably progressive Football Association attempts in the way of international reform has an earthly chance against such an uncompromising attitude.

Instead of every interested official pulling in one direction - for England - the two premier bodies, the FA and League, are engaged in a tug o' war which can have only one result, to the detriment of soccer on an international scale. The Association, keen to enter into as many international engagements as possible, continually meets frustration as stick-in-the-mud League legislators protest about too many representative games - or even threaten not to release players. It seems to me English soccer will have to decide very soon whether the domestic affairs of Bolton, Birmingham, Bury, Burnley or Brentford are more important than the international status of the England XI. It is well known that, at present, parochial problems everywhere mean more than national prestige - and until that order of precedence is reversed, we should not expect any real improvement in the standards of the English soccer team.

If an honest census of opinion among League managers and directors were taken, I am certain those individuals would vote overwhelmingly that the League and Cup are more important than international matches. Some directors claim to have the wellbeing of England uppermost in their minds, yet would they endorse that patriotism by backing the FA to the hilt no matter how wide the talent-seeking net were cast? I doubt it.

Could it be that the Football League is now such a huge organisation that it cannot take second place to anything else? Or do so many people make their living out of 'domestic' soccer that any interference with the League system is unthinkable - even though it benefit England?

There are so many things wrong with British international football and so few things right that I can quite honestly state I have no desire to be capped again. I believe, rightly or wrongly, nothing will be done to put our international team where it belongs - at the head of the class - until a few leading players withhold their support as a gesture against poor remuneration, poor team selection, and the various other ills now afflicting our international soccer system.

Author's Apology:- At the time that this was first published, critics seized upon the phrase, "I have no desire to be capped again" but this was taken out of its correct context. It was not my intention to be disrespectful to England, merely to highlight the ills of the game, as described.

However, for the avoidance of doubt, even though I felt strongly at the time – and indeed still do today – that my position was a morally correct and logical view, I take this opportunity to apologise for any apparent lack of patriotism. I say "apparent" because my personal sentiments have always been what I hope most people would accept as conventionally patriotic. Indeed it is because of such patriotic feelings that I was motivated to try and make something of the issue – a positive attempt at a change for the better.

Following "my day", it wasn't until 1966 that England finally triumphed in the World Cup – and even then I think it was despite, not because, of the system. This view is surely corroborated as England has not been able to repeat this achievement in the intervening 30 odd years. One can only hope and conclude that the National side's future fortunes should be increasingly entrusted to the hands of real professionals and not amateur footballing businessmen.

Players like Stanley Matthews, Tom Finney, Jimmy Dickinson, Gil Merrick, Jimmy Hagan, Nat Lofthouse and the rest must realize that the situation in English international soccer is far from perfect. League interference, slap-happy selection, meanness with money, are common topics of conversation among players. That is why I suggest the country's leading players should present football with the ultimatum, 'Put your international affairs in order or we will not play for you.'

I am prepared to do so, and even though this may be purely a one-man stand against inefficiency, I hope it may help, in a small way, to impress upon football followers the seriousness of the situation. I cannot recall any instance of a player refusing to represent England: after all, the rules state you *must* play if selected, but I fancy that rule would be very difficult to enforce!

Should my decision be regarded as unpatriotic, I must stress most sincerely that I have the good of my country at heart, something few of those who may condemn me would be able to claim with honesty. I am desperately keen to see England once again leading the soccer nations of the world and, to achieve that end, something drastic must be done by the people most concerned, the men who wear the famous white shirts.

Undoubtedly the greatest honour soccer can bestow upon a player is national recognition. Except for the favoured few, international caps are difficult to win - as I have discovered - and for that reason, I think the honour should be accompanied by financial remuneration in keeping with such an occasion. When an Englishman plays for his country he is paid £50, a fee which I have heard described as too high - in comparison with the effort expended by the player. It is a different story, however, when that fee is compared with the £50,000 which may be paid by spectators for the privilege of seeing an international match. In terms of percentages, the twenty-two people who attract such mammoth gatherings are paid a little more than two per cent of the money they bring in. In no other branch of the entertainment industry would a paid performer think of accepting similar terms.

If Tommy Trinder attracted a £50,000 audience, would he feel well recompensed with a fee of £1,100? If Don Cockell and Rocky Marciano fought before a crowd, which had paid £50,000 to watch them, would they consider they were overpaid at £550 each? Of course not, yet, so used are we to accepting paltry payments for playing football, that the international match fee of £50 is actually regarded as excessive.

As in the Cup Final - I shall have more to say about that later - there are too many willing horses in soccer: too many so-called professionals who would gladly give their services free of charge. I applaud their patriotic motives, while at the same time deploring the way those motives are exploited by the promoters of show games, the FA and League.

I have read a book written by Billy Wright, England's soccer skipper. Billy states in that book, 'If there was nothing else but the inducement of an international cap, I would be just as eager to play for England'. I consider his sentiments ludicrous, because when a man is playing football for a living, he must be paid in sterling - unless he intends to exist on the trophies the game provides. If Billy Wright and other international players had not been paid for their prowess, I fear we would find all those velvet caps most indigestible when our playing days were ended.

None of us would gain much sustenance from a meal prepared from the following menu, for instance:

> Souvenir Soup, Continental, or Medallion Minestrone.
> Filleted Illuminated Address.
> Stewed White Shirt, Braised Badge, Steamed Velvet Cap,
> Boiled Boot, and Gratuitous Gravy (garnished with Wembley
> Spring Grass).
> Team Tour Tart and Cup Custard.
> Lancaster Gate Cheese (rather high).
> Coffee (Brazilian), optional.

Seriously, though, something must be done to rid soccer's ruling bodies of their inherent meanness, because so long as England can recruit the services of great

6. 'Open the cage!' Bradford colleagues Len Shackleton and Jimmy Stephen begin the descent to the coal face during their days as Bevin Boys.

7. *'Shack' at home with his wife, Marjorie and Whisky, their fox terrier.*

9. *Shackleton, playing for Sunderland against Blackpool, cuts in towards goal but finds centre-half Harry Johnstone blocking the way.*

players like Billy Wright at a negligible cost, legislators will continue to shirk their obligations to the men who bring in the money.

When sums in the region of £50,000 are paid by spectators to see an international match, I feel, on principle, the twenty-two players appearing in those matches should be paid at least £200 each. Could any unbiased person claim that the sum total of £4,400 would be too big a percentage of £50,000 as recompense for the performers in such a game?

Objections? There would be many of course, and I have no doubt the theme of most of them would be, 'Footballers would become very wealthy men if that happened.' I agree, but is not Tommy Trinder wealthy? Is not Sir Gordon Richards financially prosperous? Has not Rocky Marciano been paid fabulous sums for performing professionally? What is the difference?

I recall playing at Highbury Stadium, on Cup Final eve in 1954, as a representative of 'Old' England against Young England in a match which produced not less than £6,000 in receipts. My fee that night was £6. Further comment seems unnecessary, except to state that it was nothing less than an insult to pay a talented artist like Stanley Matthews that sum for the performance he put on for the benefit of the 43,000 spectators at Highbury.

Cheeseparing is taken to ridiculous limits by the FA who, even in these enlightened days, insist on third class travel for players and first class for officials. After helping to attract a record attendance at Wembley for the England v Germany match in 1954, Billy Wright and his Wolverhampton team-mate, Bill Slater, returned from London to Wolverhampton cramped four-a-side in a third class railway carriage. When another occupant of the carriage, who had recognised Billy, asked, 'Can't the FA afford to give you first class tickets?' even the Wolves players must surely have realised how poorly they had been treated.

The reluctance of England men to protest about this sort of meanness is, in my opinion, explained by their anxiety to do nothing which might jeopardise their future selection.

I returned from the Germany game overnight, and, as anyone who has travelled from King's Cross to Sunderland in a third class sleeper will no doubt agree, did not think it was out of place to request a first class sleeper ticket. Assured it would be all right, I was more than a little annoyed to be handed a third class ticket just before attending the after-match banquet.

The excuse was, 'There are no first class sleepers available.' Half an hour before the train was due to leave, I called with two friends at the King's Cross sleeper reservation bureau . . . and had no trouble in purchasing three tickets for a first class sleeping coach.

Not wishing to accuse the FA of deceit, I must assume that I, an ordinary individual - unrecognised by the clerk at the station - had more influence with British Railways than the much-respected, much-travelled Football Association. It would be unjust to suggest that somebody at Lancaster Gate deliberately purchased a third class sleeper, because footballers are not expected to travel first class!

Before playing against Wales and Germany in 1954 the England 'possibles' met frequently for training, sessions being held at Charlton, Chelsea, Villa Park, West

Bromwich, Tottenham and other grounds. That meant quite a lot of travelling for me and, not wishing to sit uncomfortably for five or six hours - or perhaps, stand - I travelled first class on every occasion. I had no regret about spending my own money on a spot of comfort, but is it necessary for players to be faced with the alternative of travelling in crowded conditions, or being transported comfortably by making up the difference from their own pockets?

In all I was £5 out of pocket over the pre-Germany match training: my £50 fee was halved by income tax: I neglected my businesses for long spells, and returned home with the magnificent net sum of £20 after helping to beat the World Champions and assisting to draw £51,000 to the Wembley turnstiles.

I suppose the best story to illustrate the meanness of the Football Association was told by Wilf Mannion. Wilf complained, in a newspaper article, that, after being injured while playing for England against Scotland, he stood all the way from Glasgow to Darlington in the corridor of a train - because the Association had not bothered to book him a seat. Mannion had played the previous day for England against Scotland. Gate receipts, £32,000. Cost of a seat reservation, one shilling!

There are many ways in which the fabulously wealthy FA could spend money on international players without needing to raise the match fees, yet too often they seek methods of keeping expenses down to rock bottom. Two days before we played Germany players were handed tickets for the match: that meant hurried 'phone calls to confirm the hopes of all our friends who had been given half-promises. That was the cue for a Lancaster Gate official - seeing what was going on to warn us, 'I hope you've all paid for your telephone calls. They mustn't go on the bill.'

My wing partner, Tom Finney, told me I should have written weeks before the game for tickets instead of waiting so long, but I doubt whether that would have been fruitful. Having written to the team manager, Walter Winterbottom, for Cup Final tickets the previous season and been refused, I decided there was not much future in requesting tickets from the FA. Incidentally, I wrote again to Walter for tickets for the Manchester City v Newcastle United Final in 1955 and received a reply from Sir Stanley Rous turning me down flat.

Now, with receipts consistently increasing, is the time for the Football League and the Football Association to open the padlocks on their purse strings for the benefit of international soccer.

Having criticised those bodies for their niggardly methods, and the League particularly for putting domestic dampers on the Association's international progress, I have reserved until now the blackest nigger in the woodpile, the biggest fly in the ointment, the ever-present ball and chain restricting the efforts of the England team. I refer to the method of team selection.

Let us look at some of the men on whose shrewd or otherwise *judgement* rests the composition of England's international XI. There is Mr Arthur Drewry, who has connections with the fishing industry in Grimsby; Mr Harold Shentall, wholesale provision merchant from Chesterfield; Mr Harry French, wholesale greengrocer from Middlesbrough; Sir Amos Brookhirst, a Huddersfield solicitor; Mr Arthur Oakley, a retired Wolverhampton businessman, and Mr Joe Mears, a London transport contractor. Those are enough names for the time being. Some may no longer be international selectors - changes are often made on the committee - but each of those named has, at some time or other, had his finger in the England pie - without, in my opinion, materially improving the quality of that dish.

All these gentlemen have one thing in common - the striking absence of any soccer-playing background of note - although I have heard rumours that one once played in goal for an amateur team. Obviously his attainment of such football eminence has been kept a good secret from his selection committee colleagues: there would surely have been no place for him as an England selector had it been known he had actually played football!

For many years the policy has been to ensure that men who have made a big success in football as players shall have no opportunity to use their knowledge of the game as international selectors. Perhaps there is a good reason for this: it could be that somebody at Lancaster Gate knows why greengrocers and lawyers - but never footballers - are best qualified to assess players.

In the meantime I mean no disrespect when I suggest that, by the very nature of his professional occupation, Mr Harry French should be a better selector of cabbages than of footballers; Mr Harold Shentall should know more about gorgonzola than goal-keepers and Mr Joe Mears should be better equipped to pass judgement on boats and buses than on ball players.

When in two minds about buying a certain type of motor car, I call in a motoring expert to help me in my selection: that seems the correct thing to do, although, working on the FA selection system, perhaps I should ask the advice of a deep-sea diver, or a veterinary surgeon.

It is common knowledge in soccer that the selection committee has often picked players who have failed, and if positions as selectors depended upon the consistent success of the teams picked, they would have been out of office years ago. I seem to remember that Mr Stan Seymour, the chairman of Newcastle United, was outspoken enough to state he did not think the right men were selecting the England team - a forthright opinion which merely put into words what everyone was thinking soon after Hungary gave England a hiding at Wembley in 1953.

I also recall being picked to play for the Football League against the League of Ireland in Dublin, at a time when I was going through an off-form spell at Sunderland. Although imagining no decision by the selectors would surprise me, the honour came as such a shock that I told the Roker manager, Billy Murray, 'You know, and I know, I haven't been playing well enough to get in - but I've been picked. Last season, when I was at my best, selectors ignored me.'

As it happened, however, I had a good day, scoring twice in a 5-1 victory. The England team to tour Scandinavia was then announced. It included the other four forwards from the Dublin game, but excluded me - proof, as far as I was concerned, that I would have to play much worse if I wanted to catch the eye of international selectors!

I should have been proud to join the ranks of the really great players like Jimmy Hagan, Raich Carter, Tommy Lawton, and Stan Matthews, all of whom had previously been neglected by those same selectors. Were it not so tragically serious, amusement might be felt at decisions such as the selection of the West Bromwich centre-forward Ronnie Allen for outside-left, the Manchester City centre-forward Don Revie for inside-right; of Billy Wright, playing wing-half for Wolves, as inside-forward; of Johnny Hancocks, right-winger for Wolves, as left-winger for his country; of Roy Bentley, Chelsea centre-forward, as inside-right; and of Johnny Berry, Manchester United outside-right, as outside-left.

There was nothing very funny, though, about the day England were beaten in Stockholm by a side of Swedish amateurs; selectors might have been playing a little joke, at England's expense, when they fielded a forward line which did not contain one recognised inside-forward against those Swedes.

Football fans, sickened by too many international reverses, have ceased to laugh: their feelings, expressed in the Press, emphasise clearly that they have had enough of the amateurish selection efforts of successful businessmen with obscure football-playing ability. I believe it is desirable - even essential - for all selectors to have gone through the top-class soccer grind on the field of play. Is it unreasonable to suggest that selectors' credentials should be based on soccer skill, rather than on fish, fruit or flour?

The type of committee I have in mind would consist of no more than three successful League club managers, men like Arthur Rowe, Jimmy Seed, Joe Smith, Cliff Britton, Ted Drake, Stan Cullis or Tom Whittaker. The chosen three should be offered financial inducements in keeping with such a responsible post - the FA would have no difficulty in paying them £50 a week each - providing they ceased to act as managers and treated the England international XI as a full-time job.

It may seem revolutionary employing football people to perform football functions, but surely the loyal soccer enthusiasts of England deserve such men to safeguard national sporting prestige? Three selectors spotting talent all the time throughout the season could keep tabs on all the players needed for major representative games.

Possibly the three members of the selection committee would find themselves with time on their hands; if so, I suggest they could, in addition to reporting on players, make unbiased assessments of referees - a move which would be applauded by every match official who has been given 'bad marks' by a beaten club and 'good marks' by the winners.

With no club ties, there could never be any suggestion of favouritism, or lobbying for one player's nomination in exchange for that of another, or blatant bullying as instanced by the remark of one selector at an England team-picking session 'If my player Bill So and So isn't selected, I'll have wasted my time coming to this meeting.'

There is too much string-pulling for international caps, too many directors eager to push the claims of their own pet players. It reminds me of a conversation I had with the late Mr George Rutherford, the Newcastle United director who travelled with me to an inter-League match on one occasion. As so often happens, the inter-League affair was a try-out before the full England team was selected. I was playing inside-right, with Newcastle's popular Jackie Milburn as centre-forward, and Mr Rutherford made no bones about his hopes for Jackie when he told me, 'You can get Jackie into the England team, Len. You know the sort of passes he likes. Give them to him all the time, and we'll have Jackie in an England shirt.' Apparently it had never occurred to Mr Rutherford that I, too, had international ambitions; that I might have been there hoping for a good enough share of fortune - and passes - to win attention, too.

Whatever their limitations as football judges, England's selectors are honest men, which is just as well considering the temptations which may be, and have been, put in their way from time to time. An unscrupulous man could do his own club a good turn by declaring certain players were not performing well enough for international duty, thus persuading his co-selectors to pass them over. I am thinking now of the rather ticklish situation before England played Scotland at Hampden Park in 1953/4. At that time, Wolves and West Bromwich Albion were having a tremendous tussle for the First Division Championship, and it was generally anticipated that their League match at The Hawthorns - on the same day as the England v Scotland game - would settle the League Championship.

A director of Wolves, Mr Arthur Oakley, was an England selector. It is unthinkable that Mr Oakley's club connections could in any way have influenced his decisions as a selector - yet an unscrupulous man, so placed, might have been tempted to nominate Albion stars, Ronnie Allen, Johnny Nicholls, Stan Rickaby, and Ray Barlow, while at the same time suggesting certain Wolverhampton players were below England form.

As it happened both Wolves and West Bromwich were robbed of key players for that game. Even so, cases such as this pinpoint the necessity - in fairness to everyone - for international selectors to have no connections with clubs.

Let club directors make a hash of the affairs of their own teams if they must, but spare England the catastrophe of their attentions.

My suggested committee of three would no doubt introduce fresh ideas on the controversial topic of pre-match training - gatherings of international 'possibles' now kept down to a minimum through the Football League's reluctance to release players.

Training spells are certainly not the magic key to international success; it is wrongly assumed that foreign nations achieve supremacy over England solely through hiding away their star players in plushy mountain retreats before important games. Such meetings, however, must be slightly beneficial if only as a method of introducing players on a christian name basis. Had Jimmy Mullen and I, as left-wing partners, trained together before representing England 'B' against Holland 'B' at Newcastle, Jimmy would not have needed to ask our team manager, 'When can I expect Len to pass the ball to me?' Or been given the answer, 'When you least expect it - probably when Len's facing the other way.'

Such are our club commitments that it would be impracticable for the England party to train together for four weeks before a big match. On the Continent that is the normal procedure, because it is considered essential to scrap the League programme for a month when national prestige is at stake.

In Britain we play League matches a few days before turning out for our country, a system which worked well enough before the war - when overseas opponents were so obviously inferior at the game. Since then the opposition has improved a hundred per cent, and that is the best possible reason for us to step up our match preparations to meet the threat.

It could be done without seriously hindering the more parochial activities of the Football League. Pre-match training seemed to pay dividends before the England *v* Germany match in 1954, although four months later England shunned any real preparations... and scored seven goals against Scotland. That humiliation of the Sects, however, must never be used as a reasonable argument against international training sessions. It would be equally unreasonable to suggest Scotland conceded seven goals because they had no extensive pre-Wembley get-together!

In endeavouring to point out that the FA *v* League tug o' war is ruining our international status; that international match payments are ridiculously archaic; that the selection committee should be composed of football experts, I believe my motives for refusing to play for England are, at least, worthy of consideration.

Not until other players take a similar stand will the misrulers of British international football do anything to right those wrongs.

Chapter 7

I sign professional for Bradford and discover soccer glamour is a myth.
War-time football. My first representative honours.

I suppose every footballer remembers with pride the day he signed his first professional form, the day football became a career, a great adventure, a livelihood - not just a game. The big day, for me, came during the Christmas holidays in 1940 - about eighteen months after Arsenal had informed me I would never be good enough to earn my living at soccer.

At the time it seemed a wonderful experience: looking back, now, I realise it was nothing of the sort; in fact, I am still not certain whether I was paid my full £10 signing-on fee - a token payment made to every player on signing for his club.

After spending twelve months with the London Paper Mills at Dartford, I returned to Bradford in April 1940 - hoping Yorkshire friends would have forgotten, by then, my Highbury failure. The Bradford manager, David Steele, the man who had seen me collared by Arsenal as a boy, heard I was back in my home town and invited me to Park Avenue for a chat. The outcome of that talk was my reappearance in the multi-coloured Bradford shirt as an amateur player.

Working on aircraft wireless for GEC during the week, I played two or three games for Bradford in that 1939/40 season, trained all through the summer close season, and decided that the following season would either make or break Len Shackleton.

Still an amateur, I turned out regularly from August until Christmas,. when Steele asked me to sign on as a professional. Had I been guided by my experience at Highbury, I would have refused: but I had sufficient confidence in my ability to make the grade. I took the plunge.

Dad and I walked the four miles from home to Park Avenue where David Steele was waiting with the forms - legal documents which were to change my life completely, but I was not thinking about such things very deeply then. As soon as I had signed, Mr Steele explained to me, 'You should receive £10 from me, but I'm afraid the club haven't got that much money in the kitty.' So I was paid ten shillings, picked up another fifteen shillings a week later, seven and sixpence after that, and sundry other small payments from time to time. Transfer fees are often paid on hire purchase, but I imagine this was the only time a club had paid a signing-on fee on the 'never-never'. There is not much glamour in hire purchase!

By way of celebration I played immediately for Bradford against Leeds United on Christmas morning at Elland Road, had a cup of tea in Leeds, and, at the invitation of Bradford City - Park Avenue's rivals - travelled to Huddersfield as a City guest player in the afternoon. In wartime soccer, of course, players were free to move from club to club. I shall always remember that particular game in City's side because I headed a goal from fifteen yards: it went in like a rocket. It was such a surprise that I have never attempted to repeat the feat - as Roker Park supporters well know, judging by their good-humoured sarcasm whenever my head and the ball come into contact.

Christmas Day 1940 was, then, perhaps the reddest red letter day in my career. I became a professional player, represented two clubs in one day - and actually headed a goal!

Another Christmas Day, incidentally, sticks in my mind even now, because of a remarkable prophecy made by Mr Gibson, the secretary of that famous youth team, South Shields Ex-Schoolboys. I was representing Leeds Boys against the South Shields lads, and had the good fortune to score twice and lay on our third goal in a 3-2 victory. A boy called Stanley Mortensen scored both Shields goals on that cold, frosty day, prompting Gibson to state after the game, 'Both Mortensen and Shackleton will, one day, play for England's full international team.' That was pretty good guesswork on his part.

As a Bradford professional player, I still had to continue the factory work, even though I was itching to spend all my time at the ground working at my real job, as a footballer. I was classed as a skilled worker, and although such good fortune might have suited plenty of Army dodgers, it proved a real hindrance to me. One by one my pals left for the Army, Navy or Air Force and, tired of civilian life, I wanted to join up with them. I volunteered for the RAF, but as soon as the authorities discovered my employment they turned me down. I tried for the Fleet Air Arm, once again meeting frustration because the firm for which I worked refused to release me. At that time I was haunting each recruiting office in Bradford in turn, but when the Army acted like the other Services, I decided I was wasting my time. They preferred to have me assembling radios, and my feelings in the matter were of small account.

I had my football at the weekends: it was war-time substitute soccer, the regional stuff with over-familiar opponents, but at least I was getting more match practice than other players overseas in uniform. It was good fun, war-time football, with little at stake, no reputations to be considered, and nothing more than petty cash as the reward for playing.

I remember leaving the house for Ayresome Park, Middlesbrough, one Saturday morning and being told by Dad, 'I'm in a buster sweep, and I need eight goals from Park Avenue today to win it.' I told him, 'I'll fix it for you.' I was only kidding, of course, but Bradford actually did score eight goals that day, although judging by centre-forward George Ainsley's desperate efforts to score a ninth in the closing minutes, he was deliberately trying to sabotage Dad's buster! For the benefit of the

Football Association, I must put my hand on my heart, look suitably repentant, and admit I told the rest of the Bradford team about the eight goals Dad needed. Perhaps I shall be in trouble for 'fixing' a match!

As the war drew to an end, my firm, GEC, decided to return to their former home in Coventry, and I was asked to go with them. In 1945, with 'real' football just around the corner, I had no desire to leave Bradford, and refused to move to the Midlands. At Park Avenue, David Steele had been quietly building a fine team, including such players as Geoff Walker, who went to Middlesbrough for £8,000, Ron Greenwood - Chelsea signed him from Brentford for £10,000 - Billy Elliott, a £27,000 transfer when he moved from Burnley to Sunderland, Jimmy Stephen, a Scottish international full-back - another five figure transfer man, and John Downie who cost Manchester United £18,000 when he was transferred from Park Avenue.

We were all keen to do well as professional footballers, not as radio mechanics, or pit men, or soldiers, and none of us wanted to leave the club in 1945. In addition, despite playing well at that time, I had attracted the attention of international selectors, and those gentlemen had been blooding me in FA and Football League teams.

Beginning to realise I could make some sort of a name for myself at this football business, the thought of leaving Bradford to do factory work in Coventry did not inspire any enthusiasm in 'Shack'. Having refused GEC's kind offer, I received notification that I would have to join the Army and do National Service. Keen enough during the war, after VJ-Day with all my friends returning on demob leave, I had no desire to join up. And unlike a person doing an ordinary job of work, two or three years' Army service after the war could easily have ruined all my hopes of a career in soccer.

I inquired if there was no alternative, and was told I could state a preference for coal mining. Deciding that, in the pit, I would at least be fairly near home - and Park Avenue football ground - I said I would have a crack at it. My papers to report as a Bevin Boy duly arrived, even though I had warned the postman not to worry if he accidentally mislaid an OHMS envelope addressed to Len Shackleton.

Attempting to look the part, even though I did not feel much like a pitman, I tried on the necessary equipment, overalls, boots, helmet, and even remembered to carry a lamp. Everything fitted perfectly, and I set off for the thirty-odd mile journey from Bradford to Fryston Colliery, near Castleford... with team-mate Jimmy Stephen keeping me company.

I thought it was a severe enough shock having to leave home at six o'clock in the morning, but that was nothing compared to the experience of my first descent in the pit cage. For the benefit of anyone who has not travelled in one of those torture boxes, let me make it quite clear that a pit cage is nothing like a department store lift, although it is rumoured the same principle of operation is employed.

Going down in a pit cage is a terrifying experience: it is like being suspended on a piece of elastic. One minute you are rushing into the bowels of the earth, imagining Brisbane to be the next stop; the next minute you stop suddenly and . . . just dangle. One day at Fryston was sufficient to convince me I had made a real blunder by volunteering for mining, and I soon started investigating ways and means of 'dodging the column' without being reprimanded for absenteeism. To be perfectly frank, I did not overwork myself.

I noticed a big difference in pit life following my transfer to Newcastle United. As a £13,000 'Magpie' I was asked to work at practically every pit in Northumberland and Durham, but was foolish enough to listen to the advice of England international Jackie Milburn, a real pitman, who told me, 'I've got a smashing job in the pit at Gosforth. Come and work with me.'

Imagining one mine to be as bad as another, I decided no harm would be done if I teamed up with likeable Jackie, but it was soon apparent that I had left a wonderful job at Fryston in favour of something quite different at Gosforth. Jackie told me he worked *every* day, from half-past seven until six o'clock, but I had heard those kinds of tales before and did not take him too seriously.

That was another mistake. Keen to make a good impression, and hoping the boss would not expect me to do it often, I reported at the pit dead on time for my first day's work. It was pitch dark, and there was six inches of snow on the ground; but some of my depression lifted when the foreman told me, 'You can work with Jackie Milburn. He'll look after you while you're here.'

It was the winter of the big freeze-up, 1946-7. I was frozen up all right, and fed up into the bargain, but Jackie kept insisting he was on a 'smashing job' so I went along to see what it was all about. 'This way,' said Jackie, leading me into a snow-covered field. The two of us waded through the snow and ice, eventually reaching a half-submerged pile of steel girders. Our 'smashing job' involved lifting those girders and carrying them across the field. Nowadays, whenever I want a good nightmare, I just go to sleep thinking about Gosforth Colliery ...and about my days as a Bevin Boy generally.

I suppose I was not cut out to be a miner, but having sampled the sort of conditions under which they work, I have a lot of admiration for pit men. They work hard, are never lavishly paid, and, in my opinion, are among the most likeable and genuine people one could wish to meet.

I mentioned earlier that my wartime football was interesting the England selectors, and it was a great thrill to know they had set me on the ladder to the England team, when I was asked to represent the Football League against Northern Command at York.

It was my first senior honour in representative soccer, and I well remember the small, wiry, 'unknown' who partnered me at outside-right. His name was Tom Finney, a name destined to join the ranks of the great, a winger in a million, and now the proud possessor of more than fifty England International caps - despite his brilliance.

Another of soccer's great men was on the field of York that day, but not as a player. I refer to the best referee in the world, Arthur Ellis of Halifax - in those days, just a struggling match official who little realised he would eventually whistle his way to fame in every country in which football is played.

The Press were very kind to me in my early days: time after time they nominated me for important matches, and selectors must have read the papers because they gave me plenty of opportunities to prove my worth, or otherwise. The final hurdle before promotion to the England XI was the match at Wembley Stadium between an FA XI and the Army PT side and, although it was presumably an international trial, selectors only stayed for the first half before retiring to pick the England team to meet Scotland at Hampden Park in May 1946. When the players reached their respective dressing rooms they were informed of the selectors' deliberations: for me that meant good news. I was chosen to wear the white shirt of England for the first time.

Before the game against Scotland, the England party stayed at a big hotel in Glasgow and it was there I met, for the first time since he had given me marching orders from Highbury, George Allison, the manager of Arsenal.

On entering the lift to go up to my room, I noticed the only other occupant was Allison. It was a big temptation to point out to him, 'I shall be playing for England against Scotland in a few hours' time. Do you still think I'll never make the grade as a footballer?' instead, I just looked at him, wondering if he would recognise his fellow lift-traveller.

Allison smiled and said, 'You're Shackleton, aren't you?' Not another word was spoken, but, knowing he had recognised me and would be a spectator at the big match, I had one more reason to make sure of doing well at Hampden Park.

England were beaten 1-0, and I had a poor match - endorsing, perhaps, the Arsenal manager's original opinion about my football ability. It was some consolation, however, to know I was in good company, because bigger names than Shackleton were ground in the dust of the wind-swept, bumpy, bowl of Hampden Park at that particular match.

Denis Compton was on the left-wing. He did not play again for England. That wonderful wing-half, Joe Mercer - perhaps the best in his position ever to delight Arsenal fans - also made his international exit when Scotland ended England's successful run of victories in 1946.

It was a sad day for England, as well as for the Shackletons, Comptons and Mercers: the all-conquering war-time international XI was no longer invincible, and selectors had a great time chopping and changing before the next game.

I was out, and not until the game against Denmark three years later was it decided I had paid the appropriate penance for my soccer sins. If any young player doubts my contention that the glamour of soccer is a myth, let him sample the alarming drop and the sickening thud, which follows rejection from the international scene. Now, if only he had the benefit of a trip in a pit cage...

When I was asked to contribute an article to the handbook of the Bradford Schools' Football Association, I went out of my way to point out that headlines were no guarantee against heartaches, that praise would not stave off poverty, that cash in the bank was of more value than caps in the cupboard.

I stressed to the Bradford boys that it would take only a week or two for them to become accustomed to seeing their names in the newspapers. There is no glamour in that. The headline, 'Shack had a great game', will not buy my kiddies their food and clothes. I cannot take a glowing match report to my grocer and ask him to accept it in settlement of his account.

This is not bitterness: soccer has been good to me, and I have no regrets about taking it up as a living, but I believe there is some common sense in stripping the game of part of its glamour.

Any footballer who has been paid his signing-on fee in very small instalments should know just where he stands in this game. I was lucky enough to learn when I was at the right age.

Chapter 8

FA and Football League meanness with money.
The scandal of Cup Final payments.
Ticket problems.

There is a lot of money in football. That fact cannot be questioned, even though it has become fashionable for about seventy-five per cent of the clubs in the Football League to hoist annual distress signals, claiming they are enduring a hand-to-mouth existence. Isolated cases of hardship there may be, but as the biggest entertainment money-spinner in the British Isles, soccer - in the hands of the right legislators - could and should pay its way handsomely.

Without intending to disparage or slander a most loyal body of sporting enthusiasts, it must surely be admitted that the average soccer fan is easy meat for anyone wishing to raise a few thousand pounds with the minimum of effort. It has been proved repeatedly that star names attract star attendances, and that the right Press build-up for the right occasion brings in the right sort of receipts.

That is why, when the Football League, in a magnanimous gesture to assist the needy of soccer, instituted their oft-slandered Jubilee Benevolent Fund in the late summer of 1938, they had no doubts about their ability to raise just as much cash as was required whenever it was needed.

The Jubilee Fund was a wonderful scheme providing, as it did, the first real hope of security for anyone who had fallen by the soccer wayside. Launched with a fanfare of trumpets, welcomed by everyone in the game, it was regarded as a tremendous step forward - all the more praiseworthy because it was instituted by a body unused to moving in that direction.

I have no doubt the late Charles Sutcliffe, President of the Football League, was full of good intentions in 1938 when he claimed, 'The Jubilee Fund will, in my judgement, remove any suspicion or suggestion that players are left either stranded... or not reasonably provided for, after their playing days are over. The scheme must continue as long as the League itself continues, and must embrace, not only players, but also trainers, managers and even directors who have fallen on bad times.'

Although I refuse to believe there is such a phenomenon in soccer as a hard-up director, the rest of Mr Sutcliffe's statement was nevertheless an unexpected gesture of good faith and sound common sense. Money would be raised from football, and it would be spent on football folk. It was gathered in quickly enough, but the trouble is, the League did not spend much of it.

One week before the official opening of the 1938-9 season, a series of local derby games were put on as pipe-openers for cricket-weary spectators, with all profits passing into the Jubilee Fund. Spurs played Arsenal, Blackpool met Preston, Cardiff City and Swansea Town provided a Welsh contribution, the two Manchester clubs played each other, and so on. A year later the money-minting operation was repeated, the two efforts furnishing the sum of about £50,000, raised in the space of twelve months. Which proves my contention that a football follower and his money are easily parted. In the circumstances it is not surprising that the Football League had hopes of building up the Fund to half a million pounds.

The war came, football was forgotten, and the more serious military matches against Germany, Italy and Japan dragged on until 1945 - providing the League with the best possible excuse for freezing their Jubilee Fund fortunes. Wisely invested, the money yielded regular dividends, causing the secretary, Mr Fred Howarth, to state, in 1943, 'It must be obvious that the Fund, which since the war has been earning very useful interest, will be an invaluable aid to the League administrators in their efforts to aid players.'

There were a few payments from the Fund during the war, but to all intents and purposes expenditure was nil. After the end of hostilities, many players who had been in the 27 to 31 age group in 1939 returned to their clubs as veterans, or has-beens, and were faced with the anxiety and hardship common to anyone deprived of his living. Those players could so easily have been set on their feet, established in businesses, or at least helped on their way by the Jubilee Fund. What a marvellous opportunity to use these resources in the cause of vocational training. The chance was neglected: as in war-time, grants were isolated and small, and the suspicion - fostered entirely by League conduct - that the trustees of the Fund were not going to distribute on a large scale the bounty in their care took root. The pledge of the late League President that soccer's unfortunates would no longer be in need was hardly fulfilled.

The Players' Union, unfairly libelled as the 'Ball Game Bulganins' by some legislators, invariably placed the Jubilee Fund on their agenda for meetings, and made regular protests that the League did not dip deeply enough into the interest, let alone the capital.

While disagreeing with the Union on several issues, I have no doubts about the sincerity and sound reasoning behind a 1948 appeal from the secretary, Jimmy Guthrie, in which he suggested, 'The League should hand over about £30,000 from the Jubilee Fund to the Union where it would be placed into a common fund to help everyone needing assistance.'

I have met many fallen soccer stars, seen them trying to cadge half a crown 'for a packet of fags'; felt ashamed to see great footballers, unknown and unwanted, outside every big ground in the country. So has Jimmy Guthrie. I believe that, had he been tempted to distribute the *entire* £30,000 among such men, his action would have been in keeping with what I understand the aims of the Jubilee Fund to be.

The Union, for instance, would have done something about a former Millwall player who had fallen on hard times, pocketed his pride, and written to the Football League begging for a grant - as injury had ended his playing days. The League did nothing about that unfortunate player, pointing out, 'The trustees of the Jubilee Fund have decided that only those players and officials who were in active service of the League or clubs on 30th May 1938, are eligible for benefit from the Fund.' Rules, regulations and red tape; these prevented a needy ex-player from being helped on his way; the soccer-lamed dog was not assisted over the stile.

Even had it been necessary to deviate slightly from 'the rules' to assist him - and I question the necessity - would not the Jubilee Fund trustees have been justified in doing so?

For whom it may concern, I repeat the pledge of Mr Sutcliffe. 'It (the Fund) will, in my judgement, remove any suspicion or suggestion that players are left stranded after their playing days are over.

Were the suspicions or suggestions removed when George Cryle, the former Reading player, applied for a grant for a course in physiotherapy - and was refused? Or when Jim Twomey, Leeds United's Irish international goalkeeper, applied for money from the Jubilee Benevolent Fund - and received not a pennyworth of benevolence to cause jubilation?

When the Fund was started, the football public were not aware of any rigid rules about qualification dates; in fact, as I write, I have before me the 1938 Souvenir Brochure in which three objects are defined.

They are: -

1. Assistance to necessitous players and ex-players of Association Football and their dependents.
2. Assistance to necessitous club officials and other officials connected with the League or clubs.
3. Educational and Vocational training for players of Association Football.

Admirable motives all, yet how sadly they have failed. Can anyone blame the soccer straggler for feeling bitterness and scorn when he reads in the Brochure, as I have done, 'The League spirit is meant to strike an effective blow at meanness and selfishness'?

Was there no evidence of meanness - or at least over-caution - in October 1947 when, with the Jubilee Fund standing at *£65,000,* it was officially stated that only eight footballers had received benefits from it - with a £300 payment to the former Arsenal winger, Alf Kirchen, as the largest individual grant? Or the admission a few months later that during the first ten years of the Jubilee Fund's existence, grants had totalled a mere £1,725?

Attempting to justify such figures, a League spokesman claimed:

'It is a healthy sign that there have been so few applications from players for assistance.' Perhaps there would be fewer signs of good health if a list of applications received, and refused, had also been published.

No doubt the Fund trustees are perturbed in case they should take their relatively minute pitchers too often to the well; yet, as I mentioned before, they need have no fears about soccer's ability to prose that there's plenty more where that came from. In addition, football pools promoters have made generous offers of assistance including one of £5,000 a year for twenty years when the Fund was launched in 1938. At that time Mr Sutcliffe said, 'I should take pools money for this Fund without any qualms of conscience,' but he was not allowed to touch such 'tainted' cash, unfortunately. I say 'unfortunately' because, had he done so, the League might now have another £100,000 not to spend.

How is the Jubilee corpse faring in its compound interest coffin in this season of 1955-6? A balance sheet, kindly supplied to me by Mr Fred Howarth, the secretary of the Football League, makes interesting reading.

It indicates that £60,130 has been invested in eighteen different undertakings; that, in one year, £2,000 was received as income from these investments and that, despite the payment of nearly £3,000 in benevolent and vocational training grants, the actual amount of money at the disposal of the Fund shows no signs of being exhausted through such channels as help for the needy.

Mr Howarth is an honest, hard-working, sincere servant of soccer, and I am certain he, like most of us, is anxious to see the maximum amount of benefit derived from his employers' Jubilee Benevolent Fund. Other great men of football claim to have similar sentiments. That is why I would like to suggest that *everyone* connected with soccer who needs financial assistance - I exclude the cranks whose claims would not stand scrutiny - should write to the Football League direct... applying for a grant from the Jubilee Fund.

The League, by their response, could immediately give the lie to prevalent suspicions that this money must remain all but untouched: they could demonstrate their good faith by acting generously in this test of League sincerity.

Perhaps I am wrong to be pessimistic about the result, but judging by previous cases, I fear each application would be pulled to pieces with the finest tooth-comb in Preston market. If the League decided not to assist these players with money raised by players for the benefit of players, their attitude would then be branded as scandalous by all observers.

While money is the root of all evil, the lack of money is probably at the root of most of the troubles afflicting modern soccer. There are too many officials determined not to spend money: we are overloaded with regulations prohibiting even generous clubs from doing what they want with their own bank balances.

Why, for instance, should a beaten semi-final cup team be restricted to a maximum of £330 talent money when they reward their players for gallant performances in the knock-out competition? Let us assume sixteen players are needed to take a club that far, and the club plays eight cup games in all: every player can expect about £20... or a sum of £2 10s. for each game. The Cup run could have produced £45,000 in gate receipts: the footballers who attracted such a colossal amount of cash are allowed to receive a total of £330. I can think of no more convincing demonstration of the Football League's assessment of the worth of its paid performers.

Talent money is distributed equally lavishly for success in the League. The champions of the First Division are accorded the privilege of recompensing the lads who have fought successfully from August to May - so long as the reward does not exceed £550. That would probably work out at something like £27 for each player with first team experience, or thirteen shillings per game for anyone with an ever-present record. Clubs should not be blamed for making such miserly payments: many, I know, would like to increase their financial obligations to their players, but meanness at League headquarters restricts them.

Others, of course, are only too pleased to keep talent money at a minimum, as I discovered in Newcastle United's promotion year, 1947-8. I was at Sunderland when Newcastle finally made certain of promotion to the First Division, but having played twenty-five games for United before being transferred, I considered I had made at least some contribution towards the Magpies' great achievement. I was not paid a penny from the talent money grant, and although my share would hardly have reached double figures, I feel, on principle, Newcastle should have made the gesture.

Wembley Stadium provides the setting for the greatest games in English football. It has also, as soccer's show-piece stadium, a magnetic attraction for enormous crowds of football fans who are willing to pay sky-high prices. The FA Cup Final at Wembley is the classic event of the season - as the Derby is to racing, as Wimbledon is to lawn tennis, as Henley is to rowing, and as the Open Championship is to golf.

Obviously the FA Cup Final at Wembley provides football legislators with a glorious opportunity to display their meanness to best advantage! This is done through the bonus system, at present based on the figure of £20 per man for the winning team, and nothing at all for the unlucky losers. A normal Cup Final attendance yields about £50,000, yet the twenty-two or twenty-four men whose skill has attracted such a mint of money, receive an aggregate of £240. I am told that in a recent Final, the massed bands were paid £320 for filling in spare time before the game and during the interval - £80 more than was allotted to the real entertainers, the players in both teams.

Anyone who has ever watched the losing team dragging their weary feet off the spongy Wembley turf knows just how depressed and miserable each player feels. The winners get the glory: the losers get, if you will pardon the expression, a slap in the face with a wet kipper. For the criminal folly of being beaten they are given losers' medals, reduced talent money, no bonus, and derision from disappointed supporters and directors - as if broken hearts were not enough. I have heard stories about 'celebration' Cup Final banquets for losing finalists; it would be difficult to imagine more dismal functions.

If the Cup Final at Wembley is a show game - which it obviously is - I suggest there should be no difference in bonus payments, regardless of the result. Let the twenty-four players involved, including one reserve from each team, be paid at least £100 a man, and before that suggestion is ridiculed, just examine what this would mean. It would cause some £2,400 to be diverted from £50,000 . . . into the pockets of the men who put on the show. Do 100,000 spectators go to Wembley to see a soccer match - or to watch the massed bands? The question should not require answering, although, knowing the type of people who get hold of precious Cup Final tickets, I am not even so sure about that.

What percentage of a big fight gate is paid to the top of the bill boxers? How much does the winning jockey in the Grand National receive? What proportion of professional tennis tournament receipts goes to men like Jack Kramer, Frank Sedgman and Pancho Gonzales? Boxers, jockeys, tennis stars... would they be satisfied with £240 if they had attracted £50,000?

Of course they would not, yet footballers - who can raise more money than any other sportsmen in Britain - are presumed to be well recompensed with such a percentage.

A player can turn out at Wembley for England against Scotland and be paid £50, win or lose. Yet he can play there a few weeks later before just as large an attendance, producing identical receipts, in the Cup Final - and be paid nothing. It prompts me to wonder if the Final really is the classic engagement of the football season.

There is no mystery about players' willingness to play for such a paltry percentage: every performer in the game would give his right arm to turn out in the Cup Final, and would almost certainly play without payment. That is why there are so few quibbles, and that is where the FA and League hold all the trump cards: even so, I think it is most unfair to take advantage of the fact that there is an endless supply of willing horses.

Footballers know there is no money in the Cup Final for the losers, and precious little for the winners: that is why they must try and cash in on the honour with side lines such as newspaper articles, phoney testimonials for advertisers and the harshly condemned practice of selling Wembley tickets at inflated prices. Nobody would attempt to justify the last course, but it has been fostered by the authorities themselves, whose reluctance to give players legitimate rewards has forced Cup Finalists to seek such means of recompense.

In 1952, following Newcastle United's Cup Final victory over Arsenal, the United skipper, Joe Harvey, was unfortunate enough to be involved in a court case over ticket sales, and, soon after, the Football Association imposed a limit of twelve tickets for each player. Obviously some restrictions had to be imposed when, year after year, players were buying up to a hundred tickets, keeping a dozen, and making a handsome profit on the rest in the black market.

What a pity similar restrictions were not placed on club directors. There is not much difference in a footballer selling half a dozen guinea tickets for £20, and a director giving away a similar number to a business contact, knowing well that their value will be more than repaid by increased business.

I know such things happen because, in my own small way, I have had experience of the effect that sort of favour can have on dealings in commerce. A customer of mine - he is an ex-customer now - placed a small weekly order at my off-licence for a few bottles of beer and minerals. Before a 1954-5 Cup-tie he phoned me and asked for tickets for the match but, much as I would like to have helped him, I just did not have the tickets to pass on. When I explained the position, he was very upset; his disappointment turned to rudeness, and he told me, 'Cancel my weekly order from now on.' It did not worry me at all, as the order was not big enough to affect my off-licence receipts to any extent, but I thought then that a club director - with perhaps 500 Wembley tickets in his pocket - could make himself very popular in business by distributing them shrewdly.

That is why, if it is a bad thing for a player to have 100 tickets, it is equally wrong for a director to get 500. Or, to be more correct, five times worse!

In soccer it is well known that Cup Final tickets are inequitably distributed: apart from any abuse by clubs, the Football Association system is out of date, full of loopholes for the spiv, and aimed, so it seems, at ensuring that genuine supporters of the two clubs concerned are the last to be considered. Unfortunately the Cup Final at Wembley is no longer treated as a football match: it is a social occasion with all the trimmings - soccer's answer to Ascot, Wimbledon and Lord's - and, as befits such a gala day, *must* be attended by everyone who is anyone in Society circles.

The competing clubs had to be content with a total of twenty-five per cent of the tickets until 1955 when, finally moved by public opinion, the Football Association increased the percentage slightly by deciding to allocate 15,000 tickets to each. Lancaster Gate still, however, diverts something like 40,000 tickets to the County Associations for distribution among minor clubs who would appear to have no real interest in the big match at Wembley.

In theory the FA Cup competition is not entirely a Football League show, yet how many of the non-League and amateur teams coming under the banner of the County Associations have ever reached Wembley? None. And none ever will.

Year after year, however, tickets desperately wanted by supporters of the Cup Finalists, find their way - via the county FA's - to comic teams who go to Wembley in morbid curiosity for a day out. I know the secretary of one club who has a laugh every year when he receives his allocation: it is a good joke, really, because the club was disbanded years ago! That is only one example of the ticket leakage. Multiply it a hundred times, and it is easy to understand how real soccer supporters are deprived of the chance to see their favourite clubs in the most important game of the season.

As in so many other walks of life, it is not *what* you know but *whom* you know that counts. When Preston North End played West Bromwich Albion in the 1954 Final, I was to be in London for the weekend - staying over from the Friday night 'Young' England *v* 'Old' England match at Highbury. Naturally I was keen to see what would have been my first Cup Final, so I wrote to the Football Association asking for a ticket for my wife and myself. My application was refused.

Realizing that a professional footballer should not expect to get tickets - after all he knows something about the game - I immediately telephoned a pal of mine in the fishery business and asked if he could let me have two tickets for Wembley. They were sent by registered post the following day.

In case anyone wonders how this pal could obtain and give away Cup Final tickets, I should mention that he supplies freshly caught fish regularly from the coast to a gentleman in the FA. This is not as 'fishy' as might be imagined because the FA can distribute tickets where they wish, but I would rather see them diverted to supporters of the clubs at Wembley.

When Newcastle United met Arsenal at Wembley in *1952,* some of the smartest spivs from the seamy side of the city of Newcastle occupied the best seats behind the Royal Box. But when Jimmy Nelson, Scottish international full-back who had

10. *One of the goals which featured Shackleton's high-scoring* début *for Newcastle United is on its way here. Attempting to intervene is Norman Low, the Newport County centre-half.*

11. *A great Newcastle United team.* Back row: *Harvey, Burke, Swinburne, Corbett, Brennan, Wright.* Front row: *Stobbart, Bentley, Wayman, Shackleton, Pearson. In the white coat is trainer Norman Smith.*

14. Making contact with the outside of the foot.

13. Feinting to the left to deceive the goalkeeper.

12. Run up to the ball.

TAKING A FREE KICK THE SHACKLETON WAY

15. *Not an optical illusion as 'Shack's' boot follows through at right angles to the ball.*

16. *The ball speeds towards the goalkeeper's left.*

17. *Caught in two minds, the goalkeeper has still not begun to move.*

TAKING A FREE KICK THE SHACKLETON WAY

296

18. This is the penalty kick described by the author with which he beat the Manchester City goalkeeper, Bert Trautmann.

19. Another Shackleton effort—but this time Trautmann has it well covered.

captained Newcastle in their 1932 Final against Arsenal, wrote to United for a ticket, he received an impersonal telegram informing him bluntly that he could not have one. That telegram has not been destroyed. It should be framed. It reads like this: 'NELSON ROYAL GEORGE HOTEL MACKINTOSH PLACE CARDIFF. REGRET NONE AVAILABLE. NEWCASTLE UNITED.'

Jimmy Richardson, who became Leyton Orient's trainer, was the Newcastle outside-right in that 1932 Cup Final: Jimmy, in fact, centred the ball which Jack Allen converted for the Magpies' equalising goal - a goal still disputed in soccer circles. Richardson also has a 1952 Cup Final souvenir, a postal order for six shillings, returned to him by Newcastle after he had applied for two of the cheapest tickets. No wonder Jimmy Nelson refused to destroy the telegram and Jimmy Richardson kept the postal order!

Few people know even now of the terrible row that took place at Newcastle's Weybridge headquarters the night before the 1951 Final against Blackpool: they may be shocked to learn that it was touch and go whether the United lads would even turn up at Wembley the following day. The trouble was caused by the method of allocating tickets, which Newcastle officials excused as an accident.

Despite their intense interest in the Final against Blackpool, the Newcastle players' wives had been given tickets! One complimentary ticket each was the ration for the womenfolk, who had been told they would all be together near the Royal Box to see their husbands shaking hands with the late King George VI after the game. Ida Harvey, wife of United's captain, Joe Harvey, 'phoned her husband at headquarters twenty-four hours before kick-off time to tell him that the players' wives were not near the Royal Box, their seats were scattered all over the stadium, and some of them were not even under cover.

The balloon went up. Players demanded a showdown with directors, and not until they were promised better accommodation for their wives did they agree to turn out and win the Cup from Blackpool.

It may be argued that players' wives should not expect preferential treatment, but if the wives of the men playing in the Cup Final are not entitled to such a privilege, then nobody should be. 'It was all a mistake,' claimed the Newcastle officials, but, even after the 'mistake' had been rectified, Ida Harvey was not near enough to see Joe presented with the Cup by His Majesty.

Obviously it would be pointless to put the spotlight on the shameful shambles of a ticket distribution scheme now operating, were I not prepared to offer a reasonable alternative. Many plans have been suggested by the Press, and it is no compliment to the FA when I say that the poorest of these schemes is still a big improvement on the present practice.

I was tempted to suggest that each competing club should be allowed 50,000 tickets, thus filling Wembley with the same people who would normally watch the clubs play in a League game. It would, however, mean too much of a closed shop, while abuse would still be likely - with so few clubs able to boast 50,000 regular supporters.

As sponsors of the competition, the Football Association should be entitled to a few tickets: so should the Wembley Stadium authorities . . . after all, it is their ground. Clubs in the League, too, should get a small number each; while, for services to the game, I would make sure one ticket was issued to every referee on the full list - including all those whose decisions continue to perplex rather than please!

My quota to the County FA's would be shared out on the basis of two tickets for each, and even that allocation might be too generous.

The two clubs playing at Wembley should, in contrast to the present system, receive the major share of tickets. Each team's allocation should be equal to seventy-five per cent of the average home attendance. Should the Wembley clubs be Sunderland and Sheffield United, that would account for, perhaps, 52,000 tickets, leaving the very considerable number of 48,000 for the titled ladies, film stars, friends of the FA, and even a few followers of football. There would still be enough for the fresh-fish men, thus giving me a chance of a couple of seats!

Seriously, though, my suggestion would make sure that three-quarters of the people who regularly support both Final teams would be looked after (provided that directors, officials and players were content with a dozen or so apiece).

It is a simple system, designed to ensure that the right people receive the tickets. That is why, although it could mean one club getting twice as many tickets as their opponents, I suggest using the average home gate as a yardstick. When a club is watched regularly by about 17,000 spectators, that club could hardly claim 25,000 'regular' supporters when asking for Wembley tickets.

Whatever solution is decided upon - and, personally, I do not think the Football Association are really looking for one - tickets will continue to be a nightmare for players, a headache for officials, and usually non-existent for fans.

It reminds me of the day I was approached in the Sunderland General Post Office by a complete stranger who slapped me on the back and said, 'How are you, Shack? I haven't seen you for a while. Let me have two tickets for the Burnley Cup-tie, will you?'

I looked at him, and asked him quite seriously, 'How many tickets do you imagine I get?' When he suggested half a dozen, I put this point to him: 'If I get six tickets, do you think it is reasonable for me to give you, a complete stranger, one third of my allocation?'

Apparently he had not looked at it that way. Maybe he thought footballers should not have wives, families or friends - or, if they did, the wives and children would not be interested in watching their men folk play.

Chapter 9

*The average director's knowledge of football. **

Chapter 10

Trouble at St James' Park.
I go on strike.
How NOT *to run a football club.*

My style of football has often been criticised and from all levels. Once during my lengthy spell of international inactivity a journalist asked an England selector: 'Why is Len Shackleton consistently left out of the England team?' The answer was smart enough; in fact, I suppose I should have been flattered: 'Because we play at Wembley Stadium, not the London Palladium!' Spectators, too, have not always taken to my particular methods, but I am not alone in earning their disapproval. Invariably when a player holds the ball in an effort to do something intelligent with it - rather than passing the buck to a team mate - he comes in for advice from the knowledgeable ones on the terraces. Ball players, call them jugglers if you like, must expect to antagonise the 'get rid of it' faction while trying to inject fresh ideas into the bloodstream of modern mass-production soccer.

I encountered my share of barracking even in the early days, this being chiefly responsible for my transfer from Bradford to Newcastle United. At any rate, I was helped on my way by the bob-enders. The great Stanley Matthews, writing in a Sunday newspaper, was unusually aggressive when he said, 'The £13,000 transfer of Len Shackleton from Bradford to Newcastle United is another proof of the harm unsporting spectators can do to players and clubs.'

Actually I had already decided by then that my football future would take me far from Park Avenue, Bradford, for even as a 24-year-old I was seeking security for my family - the sort of security which can only be gained through a big club. Call me callous if you will but Bradford was just a stepping-stone for me. I had other ideas.

That is why I made several trips to the office of the manager, Fred Emery - each time asking for a move, and constantly being told, 'The Board will consider your request.' Their deliberations produced exactly nothing, until I received my summons to meet the Newcastle United party and sign for the Magpies.

Imagining that I was joining a great club, I was determined to stay to the end of my playing days at St James' Park. Yet though the best laid schemes of mice and men and professional footballers frequently go awry, I am convinced to this day that my stormy couple of seasons with Newcastle United could have been avoided had the club been run more efficiently.

I could not have had a better send-off. My opening match was against Newport County at Newcastle and as I ran on to that great playing arena I felt somehow that Newport County just had to be another chopping-block in the career of Len Shackleton. Looking back now, I know the match could not have been more successful had I planned the entire ninety minutes before it started. Newcastle United won 13-0, I scored six goals, and was declared Public Hero Number One when the final whistle blew.

What a forward line we had at Newcastle! It read Jackie Milburn, Roy Bentley, Charlie Wayman, myself and Tommy Pearson. Milburn is the only one still with the Magpies, the others deciding there were better clubs in the game than Newcastle United - and for that I blame the United officials.

We were a happy bunch against Newport County, though. The ball ran well for us, and after Charlie Wayman had missed a penalty in the first five minutes, he went on to score four times; Jackie Milburn weighed in with two goals and Roy Bentley scored one.

As Marjorie was still living in Bradford - she was expecting a baby and we had decided not to move until she and the child were well enough - I could not really celebrate on the night of the match. So I was keen to get home to everyone in Bradford as I boarded my train from Newcastle on the Sunday morning, keen to hear what they thought about the game and about my new nickname, 'Six Goal Shack'.

Yes, I was anxious for Marjorie's verdict on the Newport fireworks, but I was even more eager to get my father's opinion - knowing him to be my most severe critic. Never once has he told me I have played well and I think Dad's attitude has helped me to keep my feet on the ground and my head out of the clouds.

I well remember playing for Bradford against Hull City during the war, on one of those days when everything came off for me. Bradford won *5-0* and I scored all five goals. At home that evening Father sat in his armchair staring at the fire. This, I thought, is one day he will *have* to compliment his son on a notable performance, but Dad was silent, not even mentioning the game - let alone my nap hand of goals. I could not stand it any longer and had to ask, 'Don't you think I had a good match?' He thought a long while before answering. Then came this broadside: 'Your sister Irene could have backheeled another three into the net.'

That is why, on returning from my six goal *debut* for Newcastle, I was not surprised to be greeted with silence from Dad: as long as he was uncomplaining, I was satisfied I had done everything expected of me.

My first three games with Newcastle were successful but I came down to earth with the fourth - against my old club Bradford at Park Avenue. Marjorie, by now overdue with her baby, went to the match against doctor's orders, sat with all our Bradford friends and assured them, 'My Len will hit the headlines today.' I did, I missed a penalty kick, Newcastle were beaten, and Marjorie was terribly disappointed, yet I still managed to salvage a valuable lesson from the wreckage. I learned that day that no footballer can expect to be on top all the time; the rough and the smooth go hand in hand. It is a lesson which should be driven home to every player - preferably when he is young enough to appreciate it. There are some, of course, who firmly believe they never have a bad game. They should stop kidding themselves.

There is a story behind my missed penalty at Park Avenue. In the Bradford goal was my old friend and former team-mate, Chick Farr, the same Chick who had spent hours with me practising penalty kicks... but this was the first time we had faced each other in a League match. I normally hit a penalty with my right foot - to the goalkeeper's right - but I thought Chick would expect that, so I would aim for his left. Suddenly I thought he would expect me to change my normal kick - so I had better not. I was undecided, in a dither, and as I ran up to the ball I had still not settled on its destination. Not surprisingly, Farr saved easily.

The lesson I would impress on all penalty takers is: always make up your mind where the ball is going *before* you start your run. Never change your decision, and never fall for the obvious invitation from the goalkeeper to put it where he wants it. That great German goalkeeper Bert Trautmann once tried to kid me into shooting for the spot *he* had selected: he positioned for my penalty about midway between the centre of his goal and his left-hand upright. I had the alternative of shooting for the wide open space on his right or squeezing the ball between Trautmann and the left post. I looked to his right and shot to his left, while Bert dived in the direction nine out of ten penalty takers would have chosen to place the ball. Trautmann changed direction in mid-air but even his amazing agility could not prevent the ball entering the net.

Newcastle United did well in my first season, 1946-7, reaching the FA Cup Semi-final after licking the Cup favourites, Sheffield United, at Bramall Lane in the sixth round. During the long break between the sixth round and the Semi-final the team were constantly in special training at Seahouses on the Northumberland coast; closeted away like a bunch of atom scientists, permitted to break camp for League matches once a week. About this time some of the smooth rhythm seemed to leave our game, and though it was obvious several players should have been rested, the directors, who were running the team themselves, were determined to keep the Cup team intact, if possible. That is where they blundered.

I am certain Charlie Wayman would have benefited from a rest, but he was selected week after week, struggling all the time to recover lost form. Eventually the directors decided to leave out Charlie - but they chose the wrong match to change the side.

Only a few days before the Semi-final against Charlton Athletic at Elland Road, Leeds, it was announced that George Stobbart would replace Wayman. Trust Newcastle to make headline news with a bombshell like that just before the most important match of the season, a match in which we were humbled 4-0. Nobody blamed popular Charlie Wayman for asking for a transfer; he had every right to complain at such treatment.

There was more trouble in the Newcastle camp at Seahouses. For months I had been pestering the board to honour their promise to me about housing accommodation, a promise that I would be permitted to rent a semi-detached house similar to the one I had given up in Bradford. The club had let me down and I decided, regardless of the Semi-final result, to stay in Yorkshire after the match, until something was done about my house. Our skipper Joe Harvey was experiencing similar difficulties, so Joe made up his mind to go on strike as well.

What a story that was for the newspapers. It was no idle threat either. After we had been hammered 4-0 by Charlton, the team returned to Newcastle minus Len Shackleton and Joe Harvey and, convinced that I had a good case, I waited in Bradford for Newcastle to make the first move. The opening gambit was an order to appear before the directors on the Thursday following the Semi-final. Entering the room, facing the stern-looking collection of businessmen turned soccer sages, I kept telling myself, 'You are in the right. You have nothing to fear.'

Mr Willie McKeag, a solicitor, later to become Lord Mayor of Newcastle, assuming the role of chief questioner, pointed out the waywardness of my sins in authentic court-room fashion.

I had to hand it to him. In no time at all I started thinking I was entirely in the wrong - the villain of the piece - while the club, not 'Shack', had been treated scurvily. Then Mr John Lee, who was a very good friend of all the United players, suggested that there was really only one relevant point to be cleared up. He suggested that the meeting should be adjourned for the Board to obtain from Mr Stan Seymour either confirmation or denial of my story. The issue would be settled one way or the other on Mr Seymour's version of my contention that I had been promised the tenancy of a semi-detached house.

That night at home I was worried, knowing that if Stan Seymour denied making that promise, I was in serious trouble. After all it was only his word against mine, and what chance has a professional footballer in a straight battle with a club director?

Joe Harvey and I were temporarily suspended, which meant we missed the Good Friday match against Birmingham City at St James' Park, but I went along as a spectator and happened to meet Mr Seymour outside the ground. He winked and said, 'You'll be all right, Len.' After the game there was a directors' meeting and John Lee, the first director to leave, came up and said, 'You shall have your house, Len. It is up to us to keep our word.' They did too.

Of course, a club as big and mighty as Newcastle United could never afford to let supporters think that a couple of players had put one over on them and that is why a club-sponsored statement was produced for Joe and me to approve.

It was an official handout to the Press, reading something like, 'Len Shackleton and Joe Harvey have had a meeting with the Board of Directors, both players have apologised, and their housing difficulties will be settled.' The wording may be a little out but I remember the bit about our 'apology'. I told the directors that I would agree to anything so long as I got a house.

It appeared on the surface as if Harvey and I had been in the wrong, the club had been sinned against, and we had apologised for our misdemeanours; yet the fact that Newcastle took my wife and me house-hunting within minutes of the end of the meeting, and that we were installed in a new place at Gosforth by the following Wednesday, proved, I think, the justice of my case.

The next brush between Newcastle United and me occurred before Christmas 1948 when we were again on the special training pantomime' - this time at Letchworth. Marjorie was spending Christmas with friends at Leicester and I had been given permission to join her after our match on the Saturday.

The FA Cup draw was made (Third Round) and United were again faced with the prospect of meeting Charlton Athletic, away from home. Over the Christmas holiday our Cup opponents had a League game with Middlesbrough at Ayresome Park, and our manager, George Martin, informed the lads that they were all going to Middlesbrough to have a look at the Charlton team. Pointing out that I had been given permission to go to Leicester, I said, 'I'm not spending Christmas in Middlesbrough.'

The Newcastle goalkeeper, Jack Fairbrother, my best friend in football, had also arranged to spend Christmas with his family, and he told Mr Martin he was not going to let them down. Manager Martin seemed to think we had taken leave of our senses, insisting that football was our bread and butter and we could not afford to forget it.

Jack Fairbrother snapped back, 'The only reason we want the bread and butter is so that we can look after our wives and families. Unless they are happy, this whole football business is meaningless.' We stayed with our families during the holiday, but it did not make Jack and 'Shack' very popular with Newcastle United. The events of Christmas 1947 had the effect of widening the gap already opened between the club and myself.

On the Wednesday before the Third Round Cup-tie at Charlton, players were booked for golf at Tynemouth, but before leaving the house I was perturbed to discover Graham, my lad, then fifteen months old, was unwell. Although I 'phoned for the doctor, I imagined he was suffering from just another childish complaint. The next day he looked worse, necessitating another visit from the doctor. On Friday morning the team were due at Newcastle station at 9.45 for the ten o'clock train to London. That morning, Graham was in a terrible state, screaming, pulling his knees up to his chin, and refusing to leave his mother's knee. I rang the doctor and told him, 'Come immediately. This is very serious.'

Had we been playing a League match I would have awaited the doctor's arrival, but not wishing to clash again with the club, I left home and headed for Central Station, arriving just before the train was due to leave. Anticipating a reprimand for being late, I was so keyed up that morning I am certain I would have told Newcastle United what they could do with their Cup-tie - had I been told off. Surprisingly there was not a word and the train left on what seemed to be my longest-ever journey to London.

Immediately I arrived at King's Cross I rang Marjorie, to be told Graham had been taken to hospital and that our doctor would keep in constant touch with the hotel in London. Between mid-afternoon and bed-time he 'phoned several times, but as I went to my room, I knew there would be no sleep that night.

At 2 a.m. the telephone rang again and the voice at the other end said, 'Your son has had an emergency operation, but it is too early to let you know the result.' There were other calls during that terrible night: with each message I felt relief - because the youngster was still living. In the morning I was undecided about my movements.

Should I return to Newcastle for what could well be a last look at my son, or should I play in the match at Charlton? I informed George Martin that I would turn out for the Magpies providing I caught the *5.35* train from King's Cross to Newcastle. The Valley is not an easy ground from which to get away on a match day and it was imperative that I should have a taxi waiting when the final whistle blew. Martin promised this would be arranged, so I took the field for that vital Cup-tie, reassured just before the start that Graham was still alive, yet worried about catching my train.

At half-time I asked Mr Martin if the taxi was ordered and he told me, 'Don't worry, I'll fix it'. That was not good enough for me. I had to be certain transport was laid on, and if my insistence appears unreasonable in retrospect, it was caused solely by mounting anxiety about my little boy.

Although Mr Martin, no doubt, had every intention of getting that taxi, I dashed out of the dressing-room in football strip, explained my anxiety to a Charlton official, and was assured, 'The taxi will be ready when you are'. It was - after Newcastle had been beaten 2-1. The driver did a great job threading his way through the busy streets of London to King's Cross where I caught my train. Reaching Newcastle, I dashed straight to the hospital to be met by Marjorie who warned me, 'The operation was a success; the crisis is over - but you are not to be shocked when you see our boy.' He was surrounded by glass screens, had both legs in splints and both arms spread-eagled, and looked terrible. But I was happier when the doctor told me, 'In the language of the layman, we have untied a knot in the intestine. We were only just in time: another hour and it might have been too late.' He explained that Graham's 'stringing-up' was intended merely to stop him scratching.

At St James' Park on the Monday, Joe Harvey gave the Cup players a pound note each for their theatre ticket, taxi fare, and a meal in London. Joe told me, 'I've been told not to pay you, Len.' Newcastle were quite right, of course. I had not stayed over on the Saturday night and I was not entitled to the money, but it seemed very mean to withhold this single pound note just because I had rushed home to my boy in hospital.

I also had trouble getting my taxi fare - twenty-five shillings plus a half-a-crown tip. That is exactly the amount for which I asked. There were hints that I was over-charging. I am no saint, and in any other circumstances I admit I might have asked for more than I had actually spent, but this was different - a case of illness. I wanted no profit from that.

Twenty-five shillings means nothing to a football club - let alone the Bank of England club - so the dispute over the taxi fare was obviously just one more effort by Newcastle to antagonise me. The song tells us, 'Little things mean a lot,' and between 1946 and 1948 plenty of little, nasty things were happening at St James' Park: they meant a lot, too, judging by frequent transfer requests from players who, on the surface, should have been contented.

Even Tommy Pearson, loveable Tommy, who in dressing-room discussions invariably went out of his way to be fair to the directors, was being treated badly. It was hinted that there was a troublesome clique at Newcastle and, of all people, Pearson was supposed to be the ringleader.

If I point out that Tommy Pearson was the player who always preached about club loyalty, who told young players exactly what he thought - not what they wanted him to say - it will be appreciated how unfair United were to treat Pearson as a trouble-maker. If I were manager of a football club - though I'm not that crazy! - I would go out of my way to sign a player of Tommy's temperament. His influence in the dressing-room was worth thousands to Newcastle, yet even Pearson had his loyalty shattered by the shabby treatment he received at the hands of the club. Like the others, he was transferred - returning to his native Scotland as an Aberdeen player.

Convinced that I would never be happy with Newcastle, wondering whether I would be able to get away, I was out one day when a Newcastle official called me over and said, 'Get wise, Len. There's only one way to make money in football.'

Having said that, he walked away leaving me scratching my head at such unexpected 'advice'. What did he mean? What was the implication? I told Jack Fairbrother about it, and Jack said, 'He's advising you to ask for a transfer and he'll help you get it.'

I'm still a little puzzled, even now, but I decided it was about time I found a club which knew how to treat its players properly and I knew then any transfer request from me would stand a good chance of being granted. I even told the rest of the lads - many of whom were hesitating about asking for transfers - that I would be away from St James' Park within a week of asking for a move. And I was!

The excuse was presented to me when, following a club defeat, I was dropped from the first team. In went my request for a transfer, on to the scene came Sunderland, and within a matter of days I joined the grandest club in soccer.

Chapter 11

I leave Newcastle United for £20,050.
My cricket career.
The thrill of a first international cap.

January and February 1948 were stormy months in my career - and in the affairs of Newcastle United. Those were the days when, among other strange happenings, the entire United forward line - the highest-scoring line in soccer - was dropped at somebody's whim, and almost every player of note on the club's books had either asked for a move or was thinking of doing so. In times like those, any sort of relaxation is welcome, and many of the Newcastle lads, myself included, found peace of mind at Tynemouth Golf Club, driving, chipping, putting, and hacking our way round eighteen frustrating holes.

Tommy Pearson, Jack Fairbrother and I had some wonderful times on the golf course: Jack and I always played together, receiving a generous start from scratch man Pearson, but it made no difference... Tommy always licked us. The Scottish left-winger took his game of golf very seriously, looking upon the clowning of his two opponents as something near to sacrilege, and always making sure he had the very best of equipment money could buy. Despairing of ever making an impression on such a great golfer, Jack said to Tommy one day, 'No wonder you always beat Len and me. You've got about twenty steel-shafted match clubs, and I'm playing with half a dozen old wooden things, most of them warped.' Tommy's immediate response was, 'I'll take yours and you take mine.' Bags were exchanged - and Tommy won just as easily.

So earnestly did Tommy Pearson take his golf, I feel sure he would have played all night if it meant finishing a game rather than abandoning it; in fact we nearly did carry on through the night at Letchworth during a spell of special training.

It was nearing teatime on a winter afternoon, dusk was closing in, and the Shackleton-Fairbrother partnership was once again trying to unseat the reigning champion, Pearson. We were one up at the sixteenth hole, and it was getting darker every minute, so I told Tommy, That's it. We've beaten you at last.' 'Not at all,' said Tommy, 'we must play out the round.'

Somehow or other we played the next hole, won by Pearson to square the match, by which time it was pitch dark. As Tommy placed his ball on the tee to drive off at the eighteenth hole, it was so dark he couldn't see the head of his club, but Tommy cracked it straight and true into the gloom of the fairway. Jack followed with a drive - not so straight or so true - and lost his ball. 'Cats-eyes' Pearson strode down the course and, as if guided by radar, walked straight to his ball, which was then dispatched green-wards with a No. 4 iron. Deciding that the winner of this hole would be the man who didn't lose his ball, I tapped mine laboriously up the fairway in ten-yard bursts, arriving at the green in about thirty-seven shots, to discover Tommy Pearson searching for a lost ball. About four putts took me to the pin, and just as I sank the precious white sphere, a lorry swung round the corner, its headlights turning night into day. Ever since that crazy night, I have wondered what the lorry driver thought of the three madmen playing golf in the dark: he may never know that he was privileged to get a glimpse of the eclipse of Tommy Pearson - the Ben Hogan of St James' Park.

To complete the story I should mention that Tommy went out looking for his ball before breakfast next morning... and discovered it in a bunker beside the green, not fifteen yards from the pin. He had made two wonderful shots in complete darkness, the sort of shots, which have brought Tommy Pearson many offers to take up the game professionally.

He is now doing nicely as a soccer and golf reporter in Aberdeen, where Jack and I hope, one day, to accept an offer of a golfing holiday. For Tommy's benefit, I will pass on the news that Jack Fairbrother has now bought a new set of match clubs, but he is willing to dig out the 'old contemptibles' for old time's sake, as soon as our holiday is fixed.

On a cold February day at the Tynemouth course - it was the day I was transferred from Newcastle United to Sunderland - Pearson, Fairbrother and Shackleton were performing when two professionals passed through, each making a spanking drive and marching off as if such things were commonplace. I can still visualise one of those experts, away in the distance, about to play his second shot, as Jack teed up for his old faithful number three iron (Jack never could use wooden clubs). The Pro must have been as shocked as we were when Jack's drive whistled over his head causing him to duck in terror. He turned and shook his fist, which immediately brought the response from Fairbrother, 'You'd shake your fist a lot more if you knew I'd used a No. 3 iron for that shot.'

We soon sobered up when a messenger from the clubhouse approached with the news, 'Mr Shackleton must report immediately to St James' Park.' We finished the remaining seventeen holes with mixed feelings, knowing that the message would almost certainly mean my transfer from United, and facing up to the grim fact that this would be our last game of golf together for some time.

Tommy Pearson drove me in his car to the ground and, as we parted, said, 'You're doing the right thing, Len. I will probably follow you soon.' I realised then just how badly Newcastle United players were being handled because, although it does not matter very much when a player of my temperament wants to move, there must be something seriously wrong if a loyal club man like Tommy Pearson decides he has had enough.

I suppose the Shackletons, the Fords and the Lawtons can always be relied on for a few headlines, but the good club servants, the one-club types, are the people who really make this game of football tick. I was flattered, just before leaving Newcastle, to know that workers in the mighty Vickers Armstrong factory were staging a 'Keep "Shack"' protest meeting, and it was encouraging to read the hundreds of sympathetic letters in the local Press, but what a pity such demonstrations seldom accompany the departure of a Tommy Pearson.

No fewer than twelve clubs had been mentioned as interested in me, and the fee for my transfer was confidently expected to reach £20,000, a figure which, to my mind, was nothing short of fantastic.

One paper reported that Arsenal were ready to pay £20,000, a statement I found most amusing after having been kicked out of Highbury nine years previously when Arsenal could have signed me for nothing. In addition to the Gunners, Hull City, Portsmouth, Blackpool, Bolton Wanderers, Liverpool, Manchester City, Bury, Aston Villa, and Sunderland had been linked with my name. Enough there for even the most finicky footballer, but the club in which I was most interested was Sunderland: at Roker Park I would be able to retain all my north-east connections. A move to Sunderland would enable me to go on living among the grand folk in Northumberland and Durham - the best people in the world.

That is why, as I entered the Newcastle office on that February day, I had my fingers crossed, hoping the Wearside club had not withdrawn from the public auction for my services. A Newcastle official told me, 'We have accepted an offer from Sunderland. Now it is up to you to have a chat with their representatives, Colonel Prior, Mr Collings and Mr Murray.' I could not have had better news, though at that time I knew nothing of the late Colonel Prior's business acumen which had given Sunderland the edge on all other bidding clubs.

Joe Prior, as he was affectionately known in football, imagined the bidding would start around £17,000, with all the interested clubs prepared to go to £20,000, and he guessed - so rightly - they would all be frightened off if they heard Sunderland's opening bid was *more than* £20,000. He tossed in an extra £50, giving the Roker club a clear field to sign me for £20,050.

My interview with the trio from Sunderland did not last long, which may have been disappointing to Mr Syd Collings who confided to me, 'It's quite a thrill to be in on this signing. I am a new director, and after reading so much about players being transferred for big money, it's nice to see what actually goes on.'

Guided by previous painful experience - the housing business following my move from Bradford to Newcastle - I insisted on taking the Sunderland officials to see Marjorie at our Gosforth home, telling them when I arrived there, 'I want you to see the house I'm living in. Now tell my wife we will be able to rent one just as nice in Sunderland.' Maybe I was out of place talking that way to my new directors and manager; I cannot imagine many players doing such a thing, but while clubs are prepared to pay a king's ransom for a piece of soccer property on two legs, the object of their attentions is entitled to make his own demands, providing these do not transgress League regulations. There is such a thing as bartered pride!

The new boss, Mr Billy Murray, being a good sort assured my wife, 'You can look at half a dozen houses and turn down the lot if you like. And you needn't give your reasons either.' I knew then there would be no more 'strike action': obviously this was one club which knew the right way to treat players.

It was agreed I should stay in my house at Gosforth until I found a place in Sunderland, but even that small concession must have upset Newcastle because I was continually being asked, 'When are you going to move? When can we have your house?'

A week or two of that sort of nagging was enough for me, so for my own peace of mind, I moved to a friend's house in Newcastle and carried on house hunting in Sunderland. Looking back now, the Newcastle United insistence on 'reclaiming' their house seems even more petty than it did then. They signed me for £13,000, had eighteen months service from me, and transferred me at a profit of *£7,050*. Yet they still wanted to throw me out of my home.

First impressions are often misleading - which is just as well, because my first day at Sunderland Football Club was not at all favourable: I thought, in fact, I had jumped out of the frying pan into the fire. Arriving at Roker Park, I was introduced to all the lads - not one of them making any cracks about the colossal figure paid out for my transfer - and was just imagining I was among friends when a member of the staff looked me up and down, as if I were an exhibit in an agricultural show, and said, 'You needn't expect any special favours from me.'

My first reaction was 'Shackleton won't stay with this club long', a feeling endorsed by the following conversation between me and the man who was going to withhold his favours:

'The players are on road work. You'd better go with them.'

'I haven't got any equipment - no sweaters or old flannels.'

'Then go in what you're wearing, that suit is all right.'

'If you think I'm running around Sunderland in a good suit, with clothes on the ration, you've got another think coming.'

We compromised when my 'friend' suggested I should do some lapping on the ground in a pair of borrowed shorts, but as I trotted round Roker Park, quite alone, on that first day as a Sunderland player, I kept asking myself, 'What sort of a club have I joined?'

There was no need to worry: although I would never have guessed it that day, I had joined the best club in football. I had made a move which was to give me everything I had ever wanted from soccer - the chance to branch out in business, a house of my own in the best part of the town, generous and considerate treatment from my employers, and the opportunity of finding favour once again with those hard-to-please gentlemen of the Football Association, the international selectors.

Not since 1946, when the wreckage of a once invincible England team had been torn to shreds and scattered on the bumpy battlefield of Hampden Park by Scotland, had my services been required in the international arena. That did not worry me, because the men occupying the inside-forward positions were Raich Carter and Wilf Mannion, and there was no reason at all why Len Shackleton should be preferred to either of those geniuses.

In the autumn of 1948, Carter was on the way out - at least in the eyes of selectors, while Wilf Mannion had decided to stage a stop-cut strike, forsaking the roar of the Ayresome crowd in favour of a job as a dispenser of dairy produce in Oldham. That meant changes in the England side for the international against Denmark in Copenhagen, changes which gave that prince among inside-forwards, Jimmy Hagan, his solitary England cap, with me occupying the other inside position.

The shelving of Hagan for so many years is just one of the many blunders made by the selectors of post-war international teams, but that one cap against Denmark provided Jimmy's team mates with some of the funniest off-the-field hoaxes ever perpetrated in soccer.

We were never safe when Jimmy was around, and more than one well-known England player, if asked to recall his most embarrassing moment, might think back to some of the leg-pulls perpetrated by Jimmy Hagan on the Danish trip. The subtlety, the effervescence, the artistry which mocks convention - all so obvious in Hagan's football - do not desert this cheery character when he leases the field of play. Frank Swift, himself acknowledged as one of the few real soccer humorists, said once, 'Jimmy Hagan is football's greatest mimic - bar none.'

The actual match against Denmark was not so funny, in fact the England captain, Billy Wright, has gone so far as to describe it as England's poorest international, though the 0-0 draw may not look so depressing as some other results in the record book.

Of course we should have won - those Danes were never great - but it is surely unfair to class them as just a bunch of amateurs, suggesting inferiors, when the same side was good enough to reach the final of the 1948 Olympic Games football tournament at Wembley. But the critics put us on the dissecting table, an operation which caused, among other things, the end of Tommy Lawton's international career. Even the gentlemen of the FA used strong words to describe the Copenhagen Catastrophe, the late Mr Harry Huband, a well-loved football figure, pointing out that 'Our amateur team scored three goals against Denmark. The professionals couldn't get one.'

I thought I had scored about five minutes after the start, when I showed the ball to a full-back, feinted one way and went the other, took it up to the goalkeeper, walked round him and, with the empty goal facing me, side-footed the ball along the carpet. I turned to shake hands with my team-mates, heard a roar from the crowd, and swung round to see that my 'goal' had stopped on the line - stuck in the mud, for a Danish defender to rush in and kick clear.

As that match started so it continued, with nothing going right for England, with one player after another tarnishing whatever claims he had to an international reputation. Tommy Lawton was made chief scapegoat, and no matter how well he played subsequently, Tommy was never given another international cap. It was perhaps a match better forgotten.

I could not forget, though, the great time we all had in Denmark, including a profitable excursion to a race track near Copenhagen. All the England lads stood in a group, wondering which nag we ought to lose our money on, when the horses trotted past on their way to the starting tapes. An English jockey guided his horse over to the rails, leaned down, and introduced himself to us thus: 'I'm going to win this race. Have a few kroner on my mount.'

There was a solid rush to the betting-window - I think every one of us was in on the tip - and then... the race. Halfway round the course our jockey pal took his mount to the front and opened up such a gap between himself and the rest of the field that he approached the winning-post easing up - with the second horse fifteen lengths behind. Just as he crossed the line the jockey pulled himself erect, looked across at the England party and bowed solemnly to us. The queue at the pay-out window seemed composed entirely of tourists in England international blazers, but we did not win a fortune. Our wagers were in keeping with the liberal spending allowance permitted by the FA.

This being my first full international match, I was keen to collect a few souvenirs, which is why I asked in the dressing-room after the game if I could retain my football shirt. 'No, you can't have it,' was the pleasant reply dictated, I imagine, more by the team's poor showing than by FA policy.

International matches certainly do not provide me with the happiest of sporting memories. Perhaps my most enjoyable days have been spent during the close season, on the cricket field where I can relax and treat the summer game as a game.

My introduction to first-class cricket - and by that I do not mean County Cricket - was in the no-holds-barred atmosphere of the Bradford League, during the war. At Lidgett Green, I was thrilled to be playing with, and against, such famous men as George Pope, Leslie Ames, Cyril Washbrook, Cliff Gladwin, Bill Copson and the man who has twice led his country to Test series victories against Australia, the England skipper Len Hutton.

Unlike other youngsters in the Bradford League, I had no real ambitions to be invited to Headingley, no desire to represent Yorkshire as a county cricketer - should they consider my efforts worthy of such elevation. I was dedicated to soccer, and no matter what others may think about it, I am certain League football and county cricket can never be combined without neglecting, even slightly, one or the other. In modern times Denis Compton. Arthur Milton, Willie Watson and others have done very well at both games, but how much better would they have been had they specialized in cricket - or football?

Take Denis Compton. Denis, in my opinion, could have been one of the greatest left-wingers soccer has ever seen, had he been a one-game man. And just ask the MCC if football has had any effect on Denis's cricket career! What about my former Sunderland team-mate Willie Watson, capped by his country at both games, and suggested, maybe, as the very man to disprove my ideas about soccer and cricket not getting on together? I believe Willie Watson had sufficient natural ability to become a world-beater at either football or cricket, but he could never become such a superman with his affections equally divided. Arthur Milton, at 23 the pride of Arsenal and England's outside-right against Austria, was transferred to a Third Division club before he was 27. Who knows what heights fair-haired Arthur may have reached as a footballer - had he not been a good cricketer.

I do not recommend giving up entirely either football or cricket, but I would advise any youngsters gifted at the summer and winter games, to treat one seriously

- it does not matter which - and the other as a pleasant recreation.

That is the way I tackled this problem and I have never regretted any decisions on that score. Football is number one as far as I am concerned. I take my soccer seriously – usually - and spend the summer relaxing in club cricket, keeping my mind off football and, most important, staying fit.

County cricket did interest me for a while, but even in the Minor Counties Championship as an all-rounder - a description covering a multitude of sins - for both Northumberland and Durham, I found two-day matches a mental and physical strain - and there's enough of that in the winter.

As a Newcastle United footballer, I played cricket for Benwell with a fair amount of success; one of my most prized sporting souvenirs is a ball presented to me after scoring 117 not out and taking 8 wickets for 35 runs in a local derby against Benwell Hill. Since joining Sunderland, Wearmouth has been my only cricket club, and I hope to play for them for a long time.

I have often been asked if I believe in clowning at cricket and to that one I must reply, 'Definitely not.' Mind you, it is often disconcerting for the batsmen when I look at one wicket and throw the ball at the other while fielding at cover point. It may not be cricket, but I think the crowd like it!

21. *A souvenir from abroad which seems to win the family's approval.*

22. *Wearing the multicoloured shirt of Bradford Park Avenue, the author makes an opposing goalkeeper dive the wrong way as he prepares to chip the ball with the outside of his foot.*

20. *'Keep your eye on the ball'—always good advice— as demonstrated in this action picture of the author.*

23. The Three Musketeers of Newcastle United — Tommy Pearson (left), master golfer, Jack Fairbrother (centre), a moderate golfer, and 'Shack', who made up the number.

24. The author talking to Alex Coxon, the former Yorkshire County cricketer, as he was about to lead a Sunderland football - cricket team on to the field.

1 X 2

Chapter 12

Football pools - another FA blunder.

Ever since 1936 - when Football Pools betting first began to develop into a major industry for promoters and punters - the ruling bodies of soccer have been at war with the pools people. For most of the time it has been a cold war, periodically breaking out into skirmishes with no holds barred from the lists. In the main the Football League and Football Association tolerate the pools because they have no choice in the matter, but never let it be said that those august bodies condone them.

FA Rule 43 states: 'An official of an Association or Club, Referee, Linesman or Player, proved to have taken part in Coupon Football Betting shall be permanently suspended from taking any part in Football or Football Management.'

That rule, of course, is broken more often than any yet devised by the Association: it is abused even more frequently than the one prohibiting amateur clubs from paying their players. For confirmation of this, I would recommend the FA to listen to the after-match conversations in any dressing room, the disappointed discussions of the draw-dabblers as their coach leaves an away ground, the blatant checking of coupons by players as soon as results are announced. Of course footballers do the pools - about ninety per cent do anyway - but the fact that they append the names of their wives or other relations on the actual coupons makes it all quite legal and in keeping with the rules of the Association. Reducing the percentage slightly, the practice also applies to referees, managers and directors.

Does it do any harm? Certainly not, although the FA seems in two minds about the effect coupon betting has on the game. In April 1936, in a circular to Members of Parliament, the Association condemned football pools on these grounds:

1. They caused players to be barracked, thus making them unhappy.
2. There was the danger that football would be used more for gambling than for sport.
3. Attendance slumped at amateur and junior games because spectators spent all their money on pools.

4. People gambled on pools with money they could not afford to lose, causing family hardship.
5. Junior club secretaries were being bribed with free jerseys if they distributed pools coupons.

What a terrible state of affairs to have this Monster from the Mersey spreading its ugly tentacles over the lives of British citizens, and - we must shudder at the thought - maybe causing corruption on the field when players require certain teams to win or lose! That last suggestion has been put forward seriously by the anti-pools brigade, yet in 1949 the FA stated, 'There is no reason to believe that pools can in any way affect the result of any individual or group of games.'

How right they are. Looking at it logically, and accepting the 'Three Draws' as the minimum requirement for forecasting, no fewer than sixty-six players would have to be squared if I, for instance, wanted to make certain of a winning line on the coupon. Were it at all possible for players to be bribed in this way, I would be the first to condemn Football Pools.

So would such distinguished football personalities as Mr Robert Smith, the chairman of Manchester City for many years, who once said, 'The idea that pools, by creating inducement to corruption, could harmfully influence the results of matches is utterly stupid. Pools today are too big to give an unscrupulous person a ghost of a chance to load the dice in his own favour.'

Or that doyen of referees, J. T. Howcroft, who said, 'It is the height of absurdity to suggest it.'

Another interesting opinion on the pools menace, discovered in a newspaper cuttings library, was this statement by Mr C. T. O'Brien, a director of Stockport County Football Club in 1936. 'Pools are the finest advertisement football has ever had. More people are interested in the game today than ever - because of the pools.

Such sentiments present us with a completely different angle on the controversy: they suggest that not only is pools betting harmless, it is actually a benefit to soccer - a view endorsed by an investigation of pools activities on the Continent of Europe.

In Norway, for instance, about £300,000 a year is granted to sport from the State Pools profits, the same profits which also yield three quarters of a million pounds for scientific research. Biggest shareholders in this pools company are the Norwegian FA and Norway's Sporting Association (cries of 'Shame!' from Lancaster Gate).

Move from Norway to Finland, a country which sent 172 representatives to London for the 1948 Olympic Games on the proceeds of the football pools, a source of revenue which also provided financial backing for the staging of the 1952 Olympics in Helsinki.

Italy's state-controlled football pools provide the National Olympic Committee with twenty-two per cent of their profits for division between football clubs and a fund for financing other sporting activities.

In Berlin in 1949 a bankrupt city government decided to legalise pools and, within two months, profited by £7,000 a month, the money being spent on welfare work.

The 1952-3 soccer season in Britain, utilised sensibly by pools organisers in

Switzerland, caused nearly half a million pounds to be diverted to Swiss sports organisations. Dutch Olympic Committees share in pools profits. In Spain forty-five per cent of pools takings go to charity.

The Continental list seems endless - then we return home and read the following, which contains a faint note of regret, in the FA Bulletin: 'It is known that Football League matches played in England are used as a basis for the pools in several countries and that a share of the profit is returned to sport. Sport in England receives no share of the profits made by English pools firms.'

It seems everybody is doing very nicely, through the pools, out of British soccer - except the people responsible for it, the players, clubs and ruling bodies.

It is indeed a strange state of affairs, but I do not blame the pools promoters - most of whom have made generous and genuine offers to the FA and League, and been snubbed for their pains. In case memories are dim, let me point out what happened in 1936 when the pools people made their first offer of help to soccer.

The suggested figure was £50,000 a year, to be paid for at least ten years; but, following a meeting of clubs in the League, the helping hand was spurned. Instead, on April 1st - a day, singularly enough, reserved for celebrating All Fools' Anniversaries - a Football Association circular stated, 'Football should be protected from the parasitical outside organisations that fasten upon it for the sake of profit.' While prepared to admit there are parasites in this great game of football, yet I question whether they are all connected with betting.

Moving forward seven years, that same Football Association advocated the use of pools money to benefit sport, a suggestion which brought the immediate response from League headquarters in Preston, 'We will have nothing to do with such an idea.'

By this time, of course, any self-respecting pools organiser would have been entitled to feel he was under no obligation to soccer: as a parasite he would be tolerated, but as a benefactor, he was shown the door. The promoters' persistence brought yet another offer of financial assistance to the game when, in 1945, they doubled their first bid with a suggested payment of £100,000 annually - and more as times became normal.

That was the signal for the various clubs and individuals to say their pieces, and a lot of sound common sense was spoken, including a remark from Wagstaff Simmons, speaking for Tottenham Hotspur, who was courageous enough to say, 'We firmly hold that some of the pools profits should come into League football.' On all sides there was agreement that soccer should receive a share of the pools money, so League clubs gathered in Manchester and, with fingers unerringly on the pulse of public opinion, rejected this manna from Merseyside by thirty-nine votes to nine.

Lancaster Gate, however, looks at this business more sensibly than Preston. Certain important people in the Association believe the day will come when we shall have to recognise soccer betting and, rather than ignore it, gain some benefit from what is now a national institution. The secretary, Sir Stanley Rous, for instance, was once quoted as saying, 'I know pools money is regarded in football circles as bad money, but why not turn this bad money into good money by dedicating it to the encouragement of sport? The Swiss and the Swedes do it - betting on our soccer -

and I would say that not only ought we to make use of some of this money: we have got to use it.'

That, surely, is the sensible attitude. Dr Tommy Thompson, who ran that great Pegasus side of *real* amateurs is also in favour of using pools money, as is the Players' Union chairman, Jimmy Guthrie, who insists, 'A contribution of only one per cent from the pools could be the saving of football.'

Does then the drowning man - and let nobody doubt that some clubs are coming up for the last time - feel he can survive without clutching the stout straws offered by Littlewoods, Vernons, Copes, Shermans, and the rest of the so-called parasites? I think not; in fact, at a time when danger threatened so many overdraft-conscious clubs, in *1954-5,* it was agreed by the forty-eight members of the Third Division that pools firms should be approached for the sum of £400,000 yearly.

To me that was the equivalent of locking the stable door after the parasitical horse had been allowed to bolt, but I still regard it as a step in the right direction.

What is the right direction? In my opinion a national pool, on the lines of the one in Norway, is long overdue, and I feel soccer missed a wonderful opportunity of starting such a scheme just after the war when a group of businessmen in the Midlands were prepared to launch it. These philanthropists - and I use the word seriously - intended handing over eighty per cent of their profits to football clubs, players, and amateur sport.

They suggested using the money to increase pay for players, maintain players' wages during injury and illness, finance insurance policies, provide pensions for wives and children as well as players, set up players in business, build stadiums, training schools, soccer holiday camps and, in addition to all these benefits, alleviate amateur sport's number one headache by assisting in financing the Olympic Games.

Almost every problem facing sport in Britain could have been eased and, should anyone question it, I could do no better than refer them to Norway where unbelievable results have been achieved on one twentieth of the money staked in Britain.

The British National Football Pool could have been a success, but what chance was there when the FA General Purposes Committee went to the trouble of stating that benefits from such a pool could not be received by organisations and individuals under their control? And what hope had organisers when the Football League president, the late Will Cuff, said, not for the first time, 'I think the pools are a social evil'? Not surprisingly the National Pool controversy produced more fan mail at Players' Union headquarters than had ever been experienced. Not surprisingly, too, the promoters decided to suspend the whole idea, following so much antagonism from the game's ruling bodies.

The anti-pools brigade would do anything rather than condone gambling in soccer, but their efforts to kill the pools have all failed dismally. Soccer still remembers 'Sutcliffe's Folly' in 1936, when, as League vice-president, the late C.E. Sutcliffe decided to abolish the fixture list and keep matches secret until forty-eight hours before kick-off time. Letters and telegrams were dispatched, allowing clubs practically no time to arrange travel and hotel accommodation, killing completely many journeys for supporters and producing the ridiculous state of affairs when prominent League clubs telephoned newspapers to ask whom they were playing.

One club, Plymouth Argyle, lost £1,000 on the first Saturday of 'secret fixtures', while attendances were disastrously hit all over England and Wales. The League president, John McKenna, refusing to believe that his organization had made a blunder of the first magnitude, blamed the gate slump on the weather; but it was not the weather that caused clubs to arrange a protest meeting in Leeds and revert to the normal fixture list after only two Saturdays of League chaos.

'Sutcliffe's Folly,' however, provides the perfect example of the Football League's abhorrence of the pools: it emphasises what little chance - far less a Treble Chance! - there is of a swing in the other direction. Let a county cricket club make £10,000 in one season from a privately run football pool; allow poorly-supported non-League soccer sides to benefit by as much as £300 weekly from Supporters Clubs' pontoons; permit pools promoters, their employees, winning punters, newspapers and, of course, a tax-conscious government to cash in on the pools - but, at all costs, never let soccer itself derive any benefits from the Football Pools industry. It is an uncompromising attitude which could not be affected even by the Chancellor of the Exchequer, Mr R.A. Butler, who said in the House of Commons, 'I am ready to examine a submission that some of the profits of football pools should be used for physical education.'

The Chancellor does very nicely with his various nibbles at the pools pie: postage stamps, postal order poundage, colossal taxes on profits - all must help to convince him that the government would be ill-advised to pay too much attention to any and every move to ban gambling on soccer. Football's rulers apparently have become more high-minded than the nation's rulers.

I repeat again and again, I regard it as a crime that so much money should be generated by the soccer dynamo, the greater part of it diverted in every direction but the logical one. What right had the League and Association to refuse the generous offers of the pools promoters? Did they imagine soccer had no need of the money? If so, I could name a dozen good causes which might benefit from it, including the erection of a super stadium in which all show games could be staged - thus keeping in football large sums of money now being paid to such organisations as Wembley Stadium Ltd.

It may be suggested that my ideas on football pools are unreasonable, that the Football Association and Football League should continue their ostrich act of treating the pools as if they did not exist. On the other hand these ideas may make sense. I think they do.

Let us remember that some of the strongest arguments against the pools in the 1930's were advanced by the churches, yet many of those churches now run their own pools and pontoons. Enlightenment? Desecration? Or just common sense?

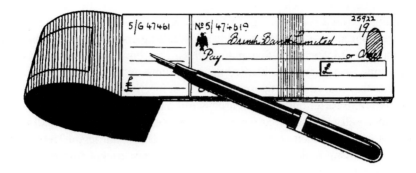

Chapter 13

Sunderland's buying spree.
Trevor Ford is signed, and sold.
We just miss relegation.

Sunderland Football Club have always had progressive ideas. Like Arsenal, Newcastle United, and, in earlier days, Aston Villa, they work on the assumption that only the best is good enough - and to get the best, Sunderland often make front page news. The Wearside club have always been among the most active participants in the transfer market, this activity frequently being condemned and even ridiculed by lesser clubs.

Between 1948 and 1955 Sunderland shocked the soccer world by casting their transfer nets - regardless of expense - for the most fancied fish in the soccer sea. The haul produced such specimens as Ivor Broadis, Trevor Ford, George Aitken, Jimmy Cowan, Ray Daniel, Billy Elliott, Billy Watson, Ken Chisholm, Tommy Wright - and me!

From Plainmoor to Pittodrie, football's Lands End and John O' Groats, the Sunderland manager Billy Murray and his free-spending directors were abused; they were accused of attempting to buy the honours of the game with a cheque book. The criticism turned to amusement as our Bank of England XI sank into the doldrums - from where a clear view of the Second Division can be seen on any Spring Saturday. Sunderland were the laughing stock of soccer, and the saying 'you can't buy success' was hammered home to us with each successive defeat. As if determined to demonstrate their contempt for public opinion, the Sunderland Board bought bigger and bigger, until only one first team player - right-half Stan Anderson - had been signed without payment of a colossal fee.

Nobody in his right senses would condone indiscriminate buying, and there is no doubt my club made some regrettable signings through not making a thorough investigation of the material for which they were prepared to pay such fabulous amounts. Directors rightly denied that team spirit was affected, but in the dressing room we knew well enough that the wheat would have to be sorted from the chaff before Sunderland started winning matches.

In addition, we were not a team in the true sense of the word. When eleven famous footballers, each an individual star in his own right, are suddenly thrown together and expected to fit in as a machine, there is bound to be some discord. It takes time to harness and control a team of thoroughbreds. It took time to achieve the blend at Roker Park.

Team spirit, though, did not suffer, and there was plenty of leg pulling as each new face arrived at Roker Park. I remember talking to Ray Daniel and Billy Elliott (both £27,000 signings) one day when South African Ted Purdon (signed for £12,000) arrived on the scene. I kidded Ted, 'You mustn't mix with us. Go and talk to the other serfs and peasants.'

Ray Daniel is a great character... as well as being a great centre-half. He can crack a joke, and take a joke, but there was nothing funny about his first season at Roker Park: the directors, who had paid such a staggering sum to Arsenal for him, had little cause to smile about the Daniel deal, then.

Ray just could not hit the form which had brought him fame as pivot for Arsenal and Wales: he insisted on playing football, substituting science for stopping - a most refreshing outlook from a centre-half, but one which in Ray's first season did not pay the expected dividends. Our £27,000 star was relegated to the reserve team while the man he had come to displace, 33-year-old Fred Hall, took over in the first XI. We used to joke to 'Bebe' - Ray's nickname - about his misfortune, and he, in turn, often chaffed directors about the money they had spent on him. One day 'Bebe' went up to the chairman and requested, 'Tell the rest of the lads how much you paid for me, Mr Ditchburn.' At that time the money Sunderland had paid for Daniel was the last thing about which Mr Ditchburn wanted to be reminded.

Later, looking back on Ray's disappointing first season, I often kidded him, 'Remember that brief bad spell you had, Bebe - from August to April?'

Then there was the Welsh international Trevor Ford, signed by Sunderland for nearly £30,000. Trevor stayed with us three seasons - during which time he was fined £100 for an alleged breach of League rule 67 - and was transferred to Cardiff City, who paid Sunderland a large fee for him. The fining incident was the only real highlight of Fordy's career at Roker Park.

Favourably situated in the heart of football's most fertile talent belt, Sunderland were attacked for not encouraging young locals, but with a dearth of good ones on the Roker books, players had to be bought for first team duty. There was really no alternative.

Obviously, directors would rather sign a player for £10 than £30,000 - ability being on a par - but even the dogmatic disciples of over-rated youth encouragement schemes, like Wolves and Manchester United, find the transfer market a useful medium for occasionally strengthening a team. The recruitment of young players by Wolves has been given a lot of publicity, but it should be remembered that the cheque book also helped to build the successful Molineux side when Bert Williams, Johnny Hancocks and Peter Broadbent were signed. Manchester United, too, were not too youth-minded to feel any pangs of remorse after paying big money for Reg Allen, Johnny Berry and Tommy Taylor.

Sunderland were lavish spenders, but the businessmen on the Board of Directors did not pour money down the drain. They treated it as an investment, and even though the return in the way of dividends may not have been apparent on the playing field, it was certainly reflected at the turnstile.

Whether Sunderland were right or wrong, there is no denying that the buying spree was responsible for Roker Park's boasting one of the highest average attendances in football: in addition, we invariably drew big gates away from home, a state of affairs much appreciated by the clubs we visited.

Similarly, when Tommy Lawton left Chelsea for Third Division Notts County, it was freely prophesied that Notts were committing financial suicide by paying £20,000 for his transfer. Yet there was nothing suicidal about increasing a normal 15,000 gate to an average of 29,000, and smashing the Meadow Lane ground record within a month of Lawton's signing. In soccer, as in any other profession, money attracts money.

Of course there is a lot of luck involved. Some clubs catch a cold by signing the wrong stars, perhaps being dazzled by the brilliance of these individuals for ninety minutes on the actual field of play, and not bothering to enquire about their less attractive background - which must be tolerated for the remainder of the week. Luck plays an important part because, to my mind, a footballer must have fifty per cent ability plus fifty per cent good luck if he is to be successful.

That was proved by Sunderland in 1953-4 and in 1954-5. In the earlier season we were struggling constantly; we were, in fact, candidates for the Second Division practically all the time. A year later we were favourites for both the Cup and the League - with the same players on duty. The difference was almost entirely due to our having the run of the ball, without which the greatest teams in the world can do nothing. In addition, the expensive players had achieved harmony... they had come to know each other better.

Skilful buying ensures the recruitment of soccer ability, but even the wealthiest club in the world could never sign a cheque big enough to buy good fortune. There is no premium on the run of the ball, and that is just as well.

I give our manager Billy Murray credit for usually insisting on signing ball artists rather than 'straight up-and-downers'. His policy makes no allowances for crude workmen, but that does not mean Mr Murray inclines towards non-progressive fiddlers.

Scientific soccer is nice to watch, but a place must always be found for goal-minded dashers with the ability to finish off the approach work of the ball manipulators. That is why players like Trevor Ford and Ken Chisholm - neither of whom dresses up his game with the frills of football - were introduced at Roker Park.

Some clubs, realising the value of the Ford-Mortensen-Milburn-Chisholm style of tearaway play, have built their teams on those lines - with considerable success, too. The most consistently successful club in post-war football, Wolverhampton Wanderers, provide the classic example: with the possible exception of Sammy Smyth and Peter Broadbent, Wolves practically dispensed with the services of classic ball players and obtained results.

The Molineux style has often been criticised. Tradition dies hard, and there are many students of soccer who feel Wolves, and teams with similar tactics, are killing football as a spectacle. But their manager, Stanley Cullis's answer to his critics is, 'Look at the League table. Results count - and Wolves get results.' With ten per cent artistry, and ninety per cent enthusiasm - call it guts if you like - Wolverhampton Wanderers are a match for any team, as Russia's Spartak and Hungary's Honved discovered in the autumn of 1954. Each player in the Wolves battering-ram brigade is imbued with a fanatical team spirit and the will to win - a state of mind which induces them all to work like horses from the start to the final whistle.

Every team to its own taste, of course, and without claiming to be entirely right or wrong, Sunderland have no fancy for the Wolves style. Looking back on some of the big names attracted to Roker Park, the accent has always been on individual ability. Brains rather than brawn have influenced most signings, and I do not think Wearside supporters would have it any other way. Jackie Robinson, Billy Watson, Ray Daniel, Ivor Broadis, Billy Bingham, Billy Elliott, Charlie Fleming - every one of these players has the ability to do something with the ball and confidence that the ball will obey.

Then there was that player signed from Newcastle United for £20,050 in 1948. I know he would never have suited Wolves!

Newcastle United won the Cup twice in successive years, with a team of direct, go-ahead players, although Ernie Taylor and Bobby Mitchell helped to relieve the monotony to some extent. Perhaps Newcastle's plan was inspired by the director who once told the United lads, 'Kick the ball as hard as you can - and chase like mad after it.' That particular director was, in my opinion, qualifying to be an England international selector.

It is incorrect to assume 'crash-bang-wallop' tactics are always successful; by the same token I would not suggest that sheer football artistry is certain to pay off. Like Sunderland, there are clubs such as Middlesbrough, Plymouth Argyle, Liverpool and Preston North End who have insisted on embellishing their game with trimmings, and, although some have been successful, others have paid for the privilege of taking pot shots at perfection.

Unfortunately for clubs, and football in general, there has been a serious shortage of first-class ball players since pre-war years of abundance: hence the big fees paid out whenever their services are available in the transfer market. While admitting it is not conducive to a settled dressing-room atmosphere to read stories about such-and-such a player being wanted by, say, Sunderland, I am certain any player of proved ability would be welcomed if his talent could be harnessed to help the club win matches.

Sunderland seldom broadcast their intentions before making a big signing. That is where Newcastle made so many mistakes in their free-spending campaign to recruit players. Week after week, when I was at St James' Park, it was stated in the Press - and, believe it or not, professional footballers can read - that manager George Martin and director Stan Seymour were hoping to recruit certain players. United were doing well enough to cause the players in possession to ask, 'What more do the club want? Why are they trying to replace us while we're winning matches?'

At Roker it is comforting to know that, providing each player is doing his job satisfactorily, his place is secure. Healthy rivalry there must be, for I am sure there is no room for a player who fails to respond to another's challenge for his position. Where there is no incentive there is nothing, and when the cheque book and the star-signing provide that incentive, they need not be criticised.

Supporters of Sunderland, from Seaham to Shields, from Whitburn to Washington, would never recommend the scrapping of the star system: it means quite a lot to them to know that many of the big names of soccer play for 'the local club' every Saturday.

It reminds me of a message I received from a friend of mine, Jock Smith, a male sister at Monkwearmouth Hospital in Sunderland. Jock told me, 'There is a young boy called Bobby Wallace in the hospital here. He is suffering from polio, he's football-daft, and never stops talking about "Shack". Will you look in sometime and cheer him up?'

I went, not once, but many times, and in an endeavour to provide young Bobby with the incentive to get well quickly, promised to take him to Roker Park as soon as he was well enough to go out. I also assured him he would be allowed in the Sunderland dressing-room to meet the 'Star Gang'.

Bobby improved every week as the season progressed, and was well enough just in time to be brought to Roker for the last home game of that season. Carried upstairs to a seat in the directors' box, he thoroughly enjoyed a match against Wolves, afterwards meeting all the famous players in the, normally, very private dressing-room.

Later I was told by a Monkwearmouth doctor, 'The improvement in Bobby Wallace's health since you started taking an interest in him is unbelievable. His fifteen minutes with the Sunderland players did more good than six months' medical treatment.'

Stars may dazzle...but that is not always a bad thing.

Neither is it out of place for the 'glamour boys' of soccer to tell stories against themselves - as happened during a tactics talk given to the Sunderland team by Billy Murray just before a big match. Mr Murray was explaining to Ken Chisholm and me, as inside-forwards, that he wanted us to prevent the opposing wing-halves coming through with the ball.

I told him, 'If we miss them coming through, we can always catch up with them when they come back.' That was the cue for centre-half Ray Daniel to chip in with, 'I always catch up with the centre-forward as he comes back - when everyone's shaking hands with him.'

Chapter 14

Coaching, where we fall down in Britain. My solution.

Coaching plays a big part in football these days. More money, in fact, is being spent by the Football Association than was ever dreamed of in pre-war soccer, practically every club having its quota of fully-qualified instructors, each armed with the appropriate certificate. Where is all this getting us? Has the standard of soccer improved since coaching was made available to the masses? Plenty of food for thought is provided if that question is answered truthfully.

Let's be blunt. Football in Britain between 1948 and *1955* reached an all-time low: players between the ages of 30 and 40 were able, not only to hold their places, but to outshine the postwar products of calculated coaching. It may seem unfair to draw comparisons, but it is a fact that real artists like Stanley Matthews, Tommy Lawton, Wilf Mannion and Jimmy Hagan were denied the benefits of coaching in their younger days, yet each one of them - self-taught - climbed to the top of the football ladder.

It would be easy enough to make out a case against coaching of every description, but I am not going to do that. Coaches may not be indispensable, but they have a valuable contribution to make, providing they go about the job in the correct way.

In this connection I would emphasise that soccer instruction must be limited solely to young players. If a man has achieved first team status with a Football League club, if he is earning a living at the game in his middle twenties, he should not require any assistance from a teacher.

I mention that because it came to my ears that Newcastle United, putting the accent on coaching in *1954-5,* held one session at which every player on the club's books - many of them internationals - was taught to kick the ball correctly. I can just picture my old team-mate Jackie Milburn being told how to shoot... after scoring more goals than his instructor had probably ever dreamed of.

Newcastle are not an isolated case. The FA-inspired coaching fetish seems to have swept right through football and I could name many clubs who imagine their senior players will improve in the hands of a qualified coach. Yet some of these coaches - young men - would be unable to command a place in the teams represented by their pupils.

That is a very important point. If a coach has not made a success in football as a player, there must inevitably be a feeling in his class that the coach has no right to be talking about the game. I have always maintained that a person who cannot play football - and play it well - is not qualified to assume the responsibility of passing on his knowledge to others. A case of the blind leading the blind, in fact. After all a man who teaches football is presumed to be a football expert: every other type of teacher must be master of his subject before being permitted to instruct others. Yet in this great soccer game it is possible for anyone to pass out as a coach - with the blessing of Lancaster Gate - before he is a real footballer. How can such a state of affairs be condoned?

Some of Britain's top coaches, men regarded as experts by the PA, were mediocre - if not complete flops - as players. Why should this be? The answer of officialdom, a very convincing point of view, is that limitation of the coaching certificate to successful players would lead to a serious shortage of recruits: it might even mean the total collapse of all organised coaching in Britain.

Therefore we must compromise. We must tolerate the influx of many of the puerile professors, hoping they will know enough, at least, to be of some benefit to schoolboys and novice players, while trusting they will not be too well versed in theory to mislead any of their charges possessed of natural playing ability.

Having made that concession, I feel we should insist that the men at the top, the key men from whom coaching directives, ideas, and schemes emanate, should be first-class footballers - and convincing talkers. I believe it is essential for the chief instructors to be able to demonstrate, with all the confidence of an expert, every skill in the science of soccer... every trick in the book.

In England the number one coach is Walter Winterbottom, director of coaching at the Football Association. Walter is a popular figure, he has the knack of being able to make friends with everyone - even odd characters like me. His wonderful gift for passing on verbally all the things that matter in football make him the envy of every leading coach in the world; he is a soccer student whose life is dedicated to the game.

Winterbottom is the epitome of the perfect coach in every aspect of the game save, in my opinion, the ability to demonstrate perfect control of the ball in the manner of, for instance, Peter Doherty or Wilf Mannion.

Not for one minute do I suggest England's leading coach must be a great international player, but he should have sufficient ball control and proficiency in the skills of the game to be able to demonstrate competently *with the ball*. I could name dozens of players who could do that, yet not one of them would be able to succeed in Winterbottom's job - because they could not match his verbal delivery. None of them are masters of the English language for it is true to say most of them 'talk with their talented feet'.

To be a first-class coach, a man must have sufficient playing skill to command respect from his pupils, and he must be able to convey his ideas effectively to those under his command. Practice and theory: each is vital in the make-up of the ideal coach. Where one is missing, coaching suffers.

It is as simple as that, yet I am certain the officials responsible for coaching in

25. *Ball control, as demonstrated by two masters of the art, Tom Finney and Len Shackleton.*

26. A record transfer goes through. The author signs for Sunderland for £20,050. Also in the picture are the late Colonel Joe Prior, Mr Sidney Collings and Mr Billy Murray.

27. Len Shackleton, in the Sunderland shirt, attempts to force his way past two Bolton Wanderers defenders.

Britain will have none of it. Should they require an example to illustrate my point, I would mention the name of Willie Cook, the former Everton and Ireland full-back, who was, without question, expert in both sides of this coaching business. That made him almost unique, and it meant he often had to do twice as much work as other coaches because of his playing ability. His colleagues handled their classes confidently while they were talking about the game, but as soon as it became necessary to demonstrate their theories with the ball, the cry went up, 'Send for Willie.' Had those talking teachers been on their own, with no Willie Cook available, they would have been really struggling.

I can anticipate the next protest from Lancaster Gate. It will be claimed that some of the most successful coaches on the Continent of Europe were just ordinary players during their Football League days, and I am willing to concede that few headlines distinguished the playing careers of such men as George Raynor (Sweden) and Duggie Livingstone (Belgium). Even so, Raynor and Livingstone were playing at a time when standards in England were much higher, in the days when almost every player in the land had to be an expert to hold a first team place with his club.

In addition, coaches on the Continent are handling material infinitely more responsive than that in this country. During the past few years we have had ample evidence of the foreigner's eagerness for soccer education, his slave-like willingness to master this game: a state of affairs which must give any coach a wonderful opportunity to do his job well. It is essential to have willing subjects, for even the best coaching is wasted when students refuse to absorb knowledge. On the Continent players submit willingly. Here they do not.

However, it should be the aim of the FA to press on with the good work, hoping just a few of their scattered seeds of soccer science will avoid the stony ground. But to do that, their whole coaching system might profitably be revised.

It would be desirable to have a man at the top with Walter Winterbottom's grounding in theory, and the practical skill of a Peter Doherty. My ideal, and I had to do a lot of searching, would be Jimmy Hogan, the man who taught such nations as Hungary and Austria how to play football.

Ageless Jimmy Hogan - people guess his age as anything between *65* and *75* - *is* the greatest coach football has ever known. In 1912, while a player with Bolton Wanderers, he first went to the Continent to spread the soccer gospel and from that time he has accepted engagements in Germany, France, Czechoslovakia, Holland, Switzerland, Italy, Spain, Portugal, Algiers, Sweden, Austria and Hungary. No, I don't think Hogan coached in Albania... which is probably why that country is seldom prominent in international football!

For years he has been a 'wanted' man all over the world - except in his own country, England. Hogan's off-the-field activities at home have been divided between a number of clubs: he was Fulham's manager, Aston Villa's manager, Brentford's coach, Southend United's coach, Glasgow Celtic's coach, and is now coach with the club he used to manage, Aston Villa. This great football sage has been driven from pillar to post, proving once again what a tremendous struggle faces even the best coaches who try to make a living with League clubs in Britain.

Possibly the greatest tribute paid to Jimmy Hogan (which was also something of a smack in the eye for the FA!) was a statement by Sandor Barcs, the Hungarian FA director following 'Black Wednesday' at Wembley when Hungary humiliated England 6-3:

'Jimmy Hogan taught us everything we know about football. If I may say so, England could, with advantage, take to themselves some of the hints Mr Hogan gave Hungary.

A man like Jimmy Hogan would never pass out some of the novices now in possession of FA coaching badges. Perhaps he would do something about a system which allows many great players to be rejected as unacceptable, while poor players are given the Lancaster Gate blessing to pass on their doubtful knowledge.

Come to think of it, I might still be an Arsenal player had the Gunners been blessed with a man like Jimmy Hogan to coach their younger players. The late Jack Lambert was in charge of the young Highbury lads while I was there, but Lambert, despite his success as a goal-scoring centre-forward - flanked on either side by David Jack and Alex James - was not the ideal type of footballer for a responsible position as coach to a great club. Even as a 16-year-old, I imagine I had certain potentialities which might have been spotted by a David Jack, an Alex James or a Jimmy Hogan, although missed by a Lambert.

I sometimes wonder if we are putting too much emphasis on coaching - a dangerous practice when, as sometimes happens, it changes natural style, curbs individual ability or tends to make the pupil think through the mind of his coach rather than go ahead with his own ideas. Which reminds me of a Yorkshire cricket story about a natural young batting genius who played three successive 'cow shots' which, nevertheless, yielded a six each time. After the third delivery had been dispatched to the boundary the coach - it might have been Will Rhodes or George Hirst - protested to his young protégé, 'Just look where your feet are.' Said the lad, 'Ay - but look where the ball is.' He was right of course. Any cricket coach, for instance, could find fault technically with the strokes of Denis Compton, but would they dare question his brilliance with the bat? Denis does the wrong thing right, as do many footballers.

Such natural ability, though, is rare, which is why coaching still plays such a valuable part in the moulding of young football brains. Let us, then, have the best men controlling coaching, make do with the not-so-bright boys in minor positions, and bear in mind these points:

1. A man who cannot teach himself how to play football has no right to teach others.
2. Great players who cannot talk will not do.
3. Great talkers who cannot play will not do.
4. A compromise between 2 and 3 is unfortunately inevitable - but not at the top of the coaching tree.

In conclusion, here is a point worth thinking over. There has never been such a shortage of good players. There has never been such a glut of coaches.

Chapter 15

Overseas tours. I visit Turkey, Austria, Holland and Denmark.

Overseas tours in the close season are the dessert following the feast of football; invariably pleasant to take, yet frequently served up after the soccer appetite has been amply satisfied. That is why so many footballers treat these trips as part of their normal job, another wearisome task which must be performed in the cause of England, home and booty. Yes, there is booty to be picked up on many tours, in fact I could name clubs which have shown a healthy seasonal credit balance - due chiefly to these safaris in the sun.

Tours can, broadly, be placed in two categories. Those which take a club into the football-crazy areas of South America and mid-Europe where attendances are colossal, sometimes reaching six figures, and where equally colossal cheques are so often the payment for a sound thrashing. Or the other type of tour, the 'everything found' holiday jaunt to the beauty spots of Scandinavia, South Africa or the West Indies where expenses are just covered, match opposition is rarely troublesome and everyone has a good time - because that is the real object of the tour.

In the years following the last war, Arsenal, Portsmouth and Southampton braved the tedious travelling, unfamiliar conditions, slightly shady tactics and first-class opposition of football in South America. Courageous ventures all, yet profitable only from the financial angle. And to think the author of *Charley's Aunt* told us the nuts came from Brazil!

On the other hand my own club, Sunderland, have been to Turkey, and Middlesbrough toured Norway; Canada and the United States always attract a queue of clubs, while a Burnley party spent a few weeks on the island of Mauritius and had a wonderful time. These are the sensible excursions and, in my opinion, players who condemn them are obviously incapable of appreciating anything.

I certainly enjoyed the Sunderland tour of Turkey in the spring of *1950*. First stop after taking off from London airport was Rome, a city packed with pilgrims from all over the world, a city which was the hub of an amazing twelve months' demonstration of devotion by Roman Catholics. It was Holy Year.

Every hotel, boarding-house and private dwelling in Rome was used to accommodate the thousands of visiting worshippers and we, a party of professional footballers from Wearside, felt almost like interlopers, party gate-crashers who had turned up without our invitation cards. But the warmth of our welcome was so genuine it was impossible to feel that way for long.

The Sunderland team were quartered at a converted hospital, just one of the many buildings brought into use to deal with the influx of visitors. That 'hotel' must have been almost unique: it was staffed entirely by nuns. One nun booked us in, others waited at table; they even performed the menial duties of chamber-maids and dish-washers. They were so efficient and gracious to the lads that we were all rather sorry Rome - and that particular hotel - provided only a twenty-four hours' break in our trip to Turkey.

Of course accidents are inevitable, and soon after I had retired to bed a frightening crash, followed by the sound of glass breaking, had everybody wondering what had happened. Was it an anti-British brick heaved through a window? A hotel brawl? Or, more serious, an assassin's bullet? It did not take long to find out. Reg Scotson, the Sunderland right-hall, had been deceived by a double window! Reg, on opening the window of his room, had attempted to put his head out, and thrust it right through a second pane of glass. That was casualty number one - and we had not played our first match.

It was not serious and Reg was fit enough to take his place in our party for a visit to the Vatican and other religious and historical places which every visitor to the Italian capital must undertake. I was not keen to go, but I'm glad I did.

I have no strong religious leanings, yet the sight of St Peter's, surely the most beautiful place of worship in the world, provided me with an experience never to be forgotten. Perhaps I was envious of the faith shown by the hundreds of Catholics queuing up to file past a statue, kiss its feet, and drop money into a box. They believed. So, I think, did I as I watched them. That is why I was in no mood to smile at the remark of a cash-conscious member of the Sunderland party who licked his lips, surveyed the mounting pile of coins and notes in the collection box, and said, 'I'll bet they take a canny few quid here in a day.' In different surroundings, at some other time, it would have been funny. But nobody laughed in St Peter's.

The two Roker players who most enjoyed their stop in Rome were Johnny Mapson, the evergreen goalkeeper who served the club so well for so many years, and little Tommy Reynolds, the left-winger with the tiny feet and the outsize heart. Mapson and Reynolds are Catholics, and I know what St Peter's must have meant to them.

We flew eastwards from Rome. Istanbul was our destination. None of the Sunderland party had ever been there before; to most of us it was vaguely a mysterious city of the East, a collection of mosques and mud huts and harems, where the women covered their faces with veils and the men wore funny little round hats and natives sprawled in the sun chewing jelly confectionery dipped in powder.

Of course it was nothing like that. There were no cases of sunstroke as we stepped out of the plane: instead we met overcoat and muffler weather, more reminiscent of Tyneside in February than Turkey in May. When I complained about the temperature

I was assured by a local, 'The weather will come soon, any day in fact.' I hoped we would remain there long enough for it to arrive!

The Sunderland party had all the tour trimmings including special, rather hideous light blue blazers, and I was not surprised when a rich Yorkshire voice greeted us with, 'I've come to meet a football team - not Harry Roy's band.' I realised just how small a world it was when I met the owner of the voice, Pat Molloy, a former Bradford City player, a fellow-townsman of mine and an old pal I had not met for years. Pat, now trainer at Watford, was coach of the crack Turkish team Galatta Saray.

VIP treatment was accorded us at the airport - bunches of flowers, presents, Press interviews, the third degree from photographers. Then a vintage bus which even my Sunderland team-mate Billy Elliott, a spare-time car salesman, would have had difficulty in recommending, took us along some shocking roads towards the hotel. Passing through Turkish villages and hamlets, it was soon apparent that here was a country in which poverty prevailed. Those impressions were confirmed during my stay.

In Turkey there is no middle class as we know it in Britain. The poor people are very poor - to the extent of having no shoes for their feet, clothing patched so much that the patches claim preference over the original material, and habitations which would have been condemned even at the turn of the century in England.

On the other hand, Turks with money are really loaded! A wealthy man in Turkey lives a luxurious life. He has a palatial home, eats and drinks of the best and, as I discovered on tour, dispenses hospitality generously.

The coach journey from the airport took us to the very shores of the Bosphorus, in fact it seemed almost as if the driver intended trying a submariner's performance as the water lapped the front wheels of his bus. It was a relief to discover he was driving on to a couple of planks which led to the ferry boat, but rather terrifying to look out of the side windows and see there was only an inch or two's clearance between the tyre wall and the plank edge. The boat moved off. We reached our headquarters, the Moda Palace hotel, and all agreed we had done well to survive the journey.

First impressions of the Moda Palace were not favourable. An old-fashioned place, it was like a castle in the Middle Ages and we all expected to find four-poster beds in our rooms. When we went up after a hash of a meal we found... four-poster beds. One of the players wanted to organize a return home immediately - but what a difference a day made.

In the morning I drew back the curtains, was dazzled by a wonderful view of the Bosphorus, blinded by glorious sunshine, and decided that Turkey, after all, was not so bad. Moreover, the Moda food improved: strawberries and cream, sufficient for a family of four, were served to each of us twice a day throughout our stay.

At the team's first training session I met my 'shadow'. He hardly left my side for three weeks. A stocky customer wearing the Turkish 'uniform' of rags and patches, with a Jerry Lewis haircut, the 'shadow' attended every match, was present at all training work-outs, sat like a faithful dog on the hotel steps, appeared in our dressing-room before each game, and I even spotted him helping to load hampers as we set out for a picnic. After a few days the uninvited guest started talking to me; he told me he wanted to go back to England with us. I wonder if he ever managed it.

Four matches were played in the first fortnight, all of which we won. Pitches were as hard as concrete, the opposition was roughly English Third Division, and there were only a couple of incidents to mar an otherwise peaceful tour.

I was concerned in both. In the opening game a ball was centred from the right-wing and instead of bringing it down and steadying myself for a shot, I decided to crack it on the volley. Just as I was about to make contact, a Turk headed the ball at about waist-height, and although I managed to draw back, I still connected with his chin and drew enough blood to make the injury appear more serious than it really was.

In an instant he was on his feet heaping his Turkish tantrums on me, and using repeatedly the only three words of English he knew, 'You no gentleman.' That annoyed me. After all, his attempt to head that cross was dangerous; in addition, I had taken most of the sting out of my kick. I decided to pull his leg. I put my arm round his shoulder, looked suitably repentant, and assured him, 'I should have kicked your head off instead of drawing back.' The Turk took the bait, smiled, shook hands, and ran off - convinced I had apologised for the incident.

A few minutes before the end of our final match, I was running with the ball when I had my legs whipped from under me. The whistle blew and my assailant was ordered off the field. Up ran the referee to apologise for the incident and assure me, 'That player will be suspended for three months from today.' Such a harsh penalty for a tripping offence was out of all proportion, and after the final whistle, I visited the Turks' dressing room to plead for an annulment of the suspension. The ordered-off player winked at me and said, 'Do not worry. There are no more matches for three months.'

We should have returned home after that game, but our hosts had other ideas. Hull City, who had been touring Palestine, were contacted by the Turks and agreed to play against Sunderland in Istanbul. Billy Murray, our manager, refused - quite rightly too. We had played four matches in a fortnight, fulfilled our contract to the letter, and were eager to return home. 'Sorry, your plane has gone,' he was told. 'You must wait - and while you are here you can play Hull City.' Mr Murray still refused.

Daily he called on the airline people, badgered the sponsors of the tour, and even approached the Turkish government with the warning, 'There are eighteen British citizens being kept in Istanbul against their wishes. This will be treated as a serious international incident at home.' After seven days of parties, picnics, swimming and sunbathing - but no football - the "plane" was produced.

While waiting to take off, the pilot told us, 'I should really make the journey in two stages with a halt for refuelling but, with luck, I can reach London in one hop - if I skim the Alps.' We managed it without a stop, and worried all the way about our rapidly emptying fuel tanks. Making the approach to London Airport, the plane was suddenly enveloped in fog, but the pilot made a perfect landing and as our 'plane-load of sun-tanned tourists inhaled those first breaths of London fog, none doubted they were at last home.

A different type of tour took Sunderland to Austria at a time when Austrian soccer was, without a doubt, the best in Europe. Initial opposition was provided by Rapide FC whose ground in the Soviet zone of Vienna compared favourably, as far as playing conditions were concerned, with Wembley Stadium.

That is important because there was never any question of conditions causing the chaos in our side which led to a 5-1 hammering by Rapide. Playing for the Austrians were Ernst Ocwirk and Gerard Hannapi, two of the finest artists in soccer, and their efforts, coupled with the fact that Sunderland were out of training - it was a month after the end of the English season - made this a most unhappy day for the Wearsiders. A large proportion of the spectators were Russian soldiers, most of whom had rifles or light machine-guns on their knees, so there was not much sympathy from that quarter when our tongues started hanging out after half an hour's play.

Prestige counts for a lot in these affairs and every member of the Sunderland team felt he had let down the old country. We held an informal meeting and decided to run till we dropped in the next game against FC Austria; the supreme effort would have to be made if the smirks were to be removed from the faces of the Russian soldiers. It was not just talk either. The lads played really well, held a 3-1 lead twenty minutes from full time and were so much on top I ran up to Arthur Wright and said, 'Thank goodness we won't be "done" by five goals this time.' Then FC Austria scored four goals, missed a penalty kick, and finished victors 5-4.

I am not a drinker, though occasionally I have a drop to be matey, but following the FC Austria outing - remember, Sunderland had conceded ten goals in two matches - I suggested to my good friend Tommy McLain, one of the hardest-working, hardest-tackling wing-halves I know, that we should, if not drown our sorrows, at least damp them a little.

In an old-fashioned beer-cellar, not unlike an English country pub, Tommy and I were sipping a drink at the bar when a rather noisy party seated round a corner table recognised us by our blazers, and invited us to join them. We were not keen but, not wishing to appear rude, decided to play our small part in cementing Anglo-Austrian relations.

One character, dressed in engine-driver overalls, was about 6 ft. 4 in. tall. We thought we had better keep him on our side during the party but it was not easy. The big fellow had been a sailor on a German submarine during the war; he had been captured and kept in a prisoner-of-war camp near Portsmouth and, if we could believe his story, had been treated abominably while in British hands. I soon realised he was getting hostile. Then, out of the blue, he stumped me with the question, 'What is your honest opinion of Adolf Hitler?' Tommy and I were searching for a suitable answer when everyone at the table jumped up, gave the Nazi salute and shouted, 'Heil Hitler'. That really made our day! In a matter of minutes we had excused ourselves to seek the sanctuary of the garlic-scented Hotel Fuchs, Sunderland's headquarters. We were glad to be among friends again.

Sunderland's final game on the Austrian trip was against Graz FC. They had as much ability as a Sunday School XI. On a normal day we would have licked Graz 10-0 but again we were beaten, this time 2-0. It was that sort of a game. And that sort of a tour.

In the cause of football I have visited many countries, and all have contributed something towards my education: I have pleasant memories, others not-so-pleasant, but without any shadow of doubt, I must put Holland right at the top of the list for hospitality. In Amsterdam the Sunderland party stayed at a most luxurious hotel - I was told the terms were about £4 a day plus meals - the food was fabulous, and our hosts couldn't do too much for us.

During our stay, Mr Leo Brunt, the secretary of the Netherlands Football Association, a man as important in his own country as is Sir Stanley Rous in England, went out of his way to supervise personally all the arrangements for our comfort. Mr Brunt, to us, was not Holland's most esteemed soccer legislator - he was our personal friend. Chatting to him one day I mentioned the wonderful impression made on me by Dutch hospitality, and asked if he could help me arrange for my wife Marjorie and sister Irene to spend a holiday in Holland. I was not referred to an underling. Mr Brunt insisted, 'Leave it to me. Tell me when they wish to come and I will see they have an enjoyable time.'

He was a man of his word. When Marjorie and Irene arrived at the airport Mr and Mrs Brunt were there to meet them; what is more, the Brunts took the Shackletons touring all over Holland and provided them with a holiday which could never have been even contemplated on the normal overseas allowance. To this day I have corresponded with Mr Brunt and I sincerely hope he will allow Marjorie and me to repay his wonderful hospitality when his football globe-trotting permits. The Seaburn invitation will always remain open.

In Amsterdam Sunderland played the Netherlands 'B' international team, and won 7-3. We had a field day, one of those days when everything comes off, the sort of match which tempts me to 'try a few things on', whatever anyone else may feel about my efforts. I think we were about four goals up when I had a nice run through, drew the Dutch goalkeeper, walked round him and put my foot on the ball just before it crossed the goal line. It seemed too easy tapping it into the net so I pushed the ball out again, ran clear, and watched Trevor Ford come charging in to crash home a spectacular shot. That sort of thing accounts for the label of 'clown' bestowed on me, but that is the way I play my football. Call me queer if you like - plenty of people do - but in Amsterdam I got more satisfaction out of watching Ford blast through that goal than I would if I had tapped it in myself. And so did the crowd.

I was reprimanded later by a Roker director who, after first congratulating me on my game, handed out these solemn words of advice: 'It is not a bit of use playing well if you don't figure among the goal-scorers. In years to come, when the record books are brought out, your contribution to this 7-3 victory will not get a mention'. I told him I didn't give a damn and, anyway, how could I score goals if I spent my time laying them on for 'Fordy'.

That director always imagined I was rather odd. He must have been certain of it then.

Pent up, longing to go out but compelled, through empty pockets, to sit around the hotel lounge, the Sunderland players were not a very bright bunch on the evening of our last day in Holland - until Mr Brunt walked in.

We did not let on but he soon guessed the reason for our confinement; it was obvious, I suppose, from the non-committal shrug of our shoulders when Mr Brunt inquired, 'Why are you not out enjoying the bright lights?' He said, 'There can be only one reason, so I insist every one of you comes out with me.' We did and had a magnificent night, taking in all the best night clubs, eating and drinking whatever we fancied.

It was a wonderful gesture from a great man of soccer. How fortunate are the Dutch to have such a person controlling their football affairs.

Sweden, Denmark and Norway are always popular nations for League clubs on tour. The journey is short, the climate equable, attendances good, the opposition fairly strong and, perhaps most important, the hospitality genuine and generous. Quartered in Copenhagen - yes, it really is 'Wonderful Copenhagen' - the Sunderland party touring Scandinavia went by river steamer to Malmö in Sweden for the first match, a match which we had no illusions about, regarding the strength of the Swedish side. Champions of Sweden and undefeated by any touring team, Malmö were a club with a reputation on the Continent. But Sunderland also have something of a reputation. It was the Swedes who finished with their record tarnished: we beat them 5-3, despite the handicap of a makeshift goalkeeper, right-winger Tommy Wright, who took over when Harry Threadgold received a nasty kick in the face. I scored three goals and Tommy Wright performed so well that the rest of the team were not at all sure it was a good idea to cable home for Johnny Mapson who flew out as Threadgold's replacement.

Returning to Copenhagen by boat, we were scheduled to pass the Danish yacht with King Frederick aboard, but there was nothing on the itinerary to indicate what would actually happen as the royal craft approached. Not being very optimistic about our chances of seeing the King - after all, none of us had anticipated consorting with the monarchy - we were flabbergasted and flattered to see every member of the royal crew lined up on deck and Denmark's ruler himself on the bridge, saluting the English visitors to his country. We were indeed honoured.

Pulling back a three goal deficit to draw 3-3 with Gothenburg Alliance in the second match of that tour, the Sunderland lads were determined to do well in the last game, against a Danish representative XI in Copenhagen, thus preserving an unbeaten record. Pre-match orders were, 'Get stuck in. No letting up. Hit them for six goals if possible.' We took those instructions too seriously. It was a hard tussle, we won 2-0 and were helped off the field with a chorus of boos and a shower of orange peel. In the dressing-room, Sunderland directors were furious and one, who was naturally perturbed at the way we had aroused the hostility of our hosts, kept asking, 'Why, oh why, did you have to get stuck in?' I suppose you cannot please everyone!

Tour memories are worth cherishing, although one player, who went to Spain with Sunderland before the war may not agree. Travelling on a night train, he took out his false teeth and put them in a glass of water clouded with some cleaning preparation. His sleeping-berth companion was up early the next morning and, wanting a drink, threw what he imagined to be just dirty water out of the window.

When the toothless traveller awoke and discovered what had happened, he asked at what time his teeth had left the train, tried to estimate the train's speed, and worked out with pencil and paper how many miles behind he might find the missing molars.

It was useless. He completed the tour without them - and was nicknamed the grand old man of English football.

I have had some wonderful trips - appreciated by nobody more than my young son Graham, who always expects his quota of presents when I get back. No wonder Graham surveyed his battered toys before I went to America, gave me an old-fashioned look, and enquired, 'Isn't it time you went abroad again, Dad?'

Chapter 16

Managers who do not manage - and a couple who do!

I have often been asked if I would fancy going in for the managerial side of soccer when my playing days are over. The prospect appals me. Offhand I can think of no more precarious occupation, no quicker method of ruining my health, no sound reason at all why anyone should want to become a football manager. The job is supposed to be financially rewarding, but even that supposition is untrue because a man earning £30 a week for three years - the average *'life'* of a manager - is surely not so well off as one earning £10 a week for life, in a more humdrum occupation.

It is high time managers started to manage, instead of being content to bow and scrape like glorified office-boys while directors gratuitously, and usually unsuccessfully, perform the managerial functions. Some managers, of course, have attempted to assert their authority by resisting the subtle, scheming suggestions from the board room overlords. For their pains they have been dismissed - or to be technically accurate, have been asked to tender their resignations.

A very few managers, too, really manage their clubs but for every Matt Busby, Cliff Britton, Bill Murray or Bert Tann there are ten office-boy types who have no more control over the club than their ground-staff lads. Managers accept this unsatisfactory state of affairs - are frank enough to admit it exists, and actually boast they are being paid good salaries for not managing.

I once congratulated a former player on being appointed manager of a famous club, but enquired if he would be able to handle his interfering chairman. He told me, 'I know the exact set-up. The chairman will buy and sell players, pick the team, and hand me a nice cheque every month.'

Another club 'boss' was asked if he had any team changes an hour or so before the kick-off time. His answer? 'That's my team in the programme, but I cannot vouch for its taking the field.' He had hardly finished speaking when loudspeakers announced two changes in the team, causing him to shrug his shoulders and remark, 'See what I mean?'

A former club-mate of mine told me how he was upset a few years ago when his club dropped him from the first team, so he approached his manager for an explanation. He was told, 'Don't blame me, son. I don't pick the team.'

What satisfaction do these managers get out of soccer? They have sold their self-respect for a monthly cheque: they can never really feel a sense of achievement, even though their team may be topping the League or heading for the Cup Final.

Human nature being what it is, directors feel that as they are responsible for the financial problems of their clubs, they should have some say in the way clubs are run. But would it not be more honest to come out in the open about their intentions, as Preston North End and Newcastle United did for many years, and do away with a manager? There is no place for hypocrisy in soccer, yet managers are continually being appointed by men who do not want them to manage.

Although I feel it would be more satisfactory to have no managers than nominal managers, if soccer decided to rely on directors' knowledge the game would be in a chaotic state inside twelve months. I have had plenty of experience of the almost unbelievable lack of knowledge in the board room: so have my playing colleagues, who often compare, in the dressing-room, their own pet stories about directors - just for a good laugh before we take the field.

In my early days I met one director who came into the dressing-rooms before the start of a match and, after asking if my 'spikes' were comfortable, said, 'It's going to be very windy today, so keep the ball up in the air.' I laughed. He didn't. The sun was shining and there was quite a nip in the air, causing another visitor from the board room to clap his hands and roar, 'It's a perfect day for football.' I said, 'What about the gale blowing straight down the pitch?' - but apparently he had not thought that would affect the game. Then, of course, there is the classic story about Arsenal playing against Manchester United at Old Trafford - and being two of three goals down at half-time. An Arsenal director observed, 'I hope we can keep up this form in the second half.' Someone disillusioned him by pointing out that Arsenal were playing in white shirts, having had to change because their red clashed with Manchester United's colours.

He knew as much about the game as a Midlands club chairman who instructed his club coach to make all players kick, not with the instep but with the toe - to make the ball travel farther.

I shall never forget some half-time advice administered by a director to the wing-half of one team in which I played. This director who, by the way, had never played football, said, 'You should stop marking the opposing inside-forward from behind. Stand in front - and you can stop the ball reaching him.' Fortunately my team-mate was experienced enough to laugh about it after the misguided man had departed, but a youngster might have felt compelled to obey such tactical trash - and teams can lose matches that way.

In my opinion ninety per cent of directors know nothing about football, while the odd ten per cent are even more of a hindrance to the manager because they know sufficient to command attention from players. Yet there is no denying that football is controlled almost entirely by directors, at club level in the international arena and in the lobbies of legislation where these novices are transformed into experts; and heaven help any manager standing in their way.

28. Some of Sunderland's 'international brigade' ready for training.
Left to right: *Ray Daniel, Jimmy Cowan, Billy Elliott, Tommy Wright,*
George Aitken, Billy Bingham, Trevor Ford and Len Shackleton.

29. *Footballer turned businessman. The author has to reprimand his son*
Graham for dipping into the sweets in his father's confectionery shop.

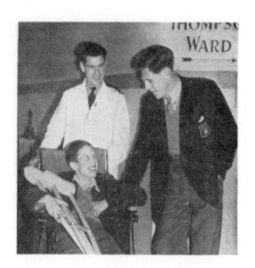

30. *The boy who recovered from illness because he loved football. Bobby Wallace chats with the author in Monkwearmouth Hospital, Sunderland.*

31. *Young Graham's tadpole jar and comic hat provide his father with some amusement.*

32. *An unusual picture of Shackleton, who makes no secret of his contention that football should be played with the feet. He goes to head the ball on this occasion.*

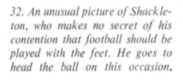

Remember what happened to Johnny Duncan, the man who took Second Division Leicester City to the FA Cup Final in 1949, after completely reorganising the club following the war. Duncan, a man who really knew his job, was appointed in Leicester's darkest days: things were so bad, in fact, he paid a club debt of £50 out of his own pocket until City were in a position to reimburse him.

Johnny Duncan worked twelve hours a day at the football ground, even neglecting the public house business which he wisely kept on after the directors had appealed to him to manage Leicester. On a limited budget, he signed players who were to bring honour and glory to the club and themselves. He ignored the insults of one director who laughed when Duncan suggested he could sell one young player for £10,000 - a player who has since moved twice at £20,000 fees, an England international called Don Revie! Then, only a few months after Johnny Duncan had marched Leicester City on to the green Wembley turf, for the Cup Final against Wolves, a player went up to him and said, 'You have been sacked by the directors.'

A few weeks later Johnny Duncan parted company with Leicester City and returned, a disillusioned ex-soccer manager, to his Turk's Head Hotel in the shadow of Leicester gaol... to reflect, maybe, on the comparative freedom of the prison's inmates as opposed to that of football managers.

There are far too many dismissals for any manager's peace of mind, yet so used is everyone to these constant upheavals that it is now regarded as most unusual for a man to retain his job while the team is doing badly. I hold no brief for the dud manager: if he is a proved failure, then he is entitled to be dismissed - but how many deposed managers are entirely responsible for their club's troubles?

If a team boss has been given his head, if he has had complete control of the team without displaying any talent for success, let him take his medicine. On the other hand, if he has been nothing more than a stooge for the financial fuehrers, he should not be expected to accept responsibility for their errors. If he knows his job, has full control, and reasonable luck - most essential that - he will be successful.

I think it is worth defining my idea of the duties of a manager - if only for the benefit of directors, most of whom will be horrified by such suggestions.

First, he should select his teams, allowing assistants to advise him on the form and capabilities of candidates in all but the first XI.

He should have complete charge of appointments to the training and scouting staff because, unless he works in harmony with trainers and scouts, he will be badly handicapped.

He should have the last word on players being bought or sold - providing he keeps within the club's financial limits - and should draw up the end-of-season retain and transfer lists, again subject to pecuniary considerations.

Let him concentrate on those tasks, leaving all the clerical work to the club secretary, and the 'big business' problems to the men who know all about them - the directors. Surely this is not such a revolutionary idea. It seems reasonable for a secretary to do the secretarial work, a team manager to manage the team, and businessmen to look after the business side.

That is the way Bradford Park Avenue was run when I first became a professional footballer, and if results mean anything, David Steele was an outstanding success in his job as manager. I am sure Steele would have been one of our greatest managers - with the right club - but he paid the penalty for insisting on doing things his way, and there can be only one loser when manager and directors clash.

I recall one incident when the Park Avenue team stopped at a roadside hotel for a meal following an away game. In walked the waiter with the soup for the Bradford directors, but he nearly upset the lot in their laps when Steele yelled, 'Never mind serving them. Attend to the players first. They haven't had a proper meal since breakfast.' He was quite right, of course, but directors do not like being treated that way.

I suppose David Steele would be classed as a players' manager, but I prefer to call him a club manager. Always his motive was to do the best thing for the club, and that should not be a punishable offence! He always got the best out of his team because we respected him as a man who, in addition to telling us what to do, was able to do it himself - in training or even in actual match play.

Yes, Mr Steele played with me in regional football for Bradford, and, although turned 50, he was still as good as any right-winger on the Park Avenue books. That reminds me of a game at Lincoln in which the boss played. All through the first half he was shouting at us, telling us when we made mistakes, and acting exactly as though he were sitting on the bench.

At half-time Chick Farr, Bob Danskin, George Stabb and I had a confab and decided to give Mr Steele the ball every time he called for it - taking care to push it inside the opposing full-back so the 'gaffer' would have to run. The plan worked perfectly - we were all in on it - and after he had chased about a dozen passes to the corner flag, his tongue was just about hanging down to his knees.

That didn't leave him any breath to have a go at us, but he failed to realise what was happening, even when we were doubled up with laughing as each pass sped to the right-wing.

Another incident in David Steele's managerial career concerned me personally; I think it emphasises his conscientiousness and earnest endeavour to do everything possible for the sake of his club. I was laid up with a bad ankle injury when he called at my house in the early hours of one morning. He woke me up and said, 'I've been out in the fields for an hour collecting herbs for a poultice, and I'm not leaving your side until that ankle is fit for Saturday.'

He was as good as his word, working hour after hour to reduce the swelling, but he was really trying to do the impossible. That kind of injury takes weeks, not days, to heal, but I had recovered sufficiently on the Saturday to limp out and play on my manager's instruction. I had a shocking match, but had to laugh in the dressing-room afterwards when Mr Steele, the man who had insisted on getting me on the field, told me, 'You should never have played with that ankle injury.'

He had done his best, as he always did, for Bradford, and I was really sorry to see the boss leave Park Avenue to take over the Huddersfield Town managership. I doubt whether he was anxious to go, in fact he told me before leaving, 'I am happy with Bradford, I have full control, and the money is reasonable - but, as an old Huddersfield player, I consider it a great honour to be invited back to my old club as manager.'

At Huddersfield, David Steele set to work clearing out all the old players, cutting away the dead wood, and building for the future. His forthright methods were apparently not appreciated, and Huddersfield lost a great manager when Steele drifted to the Bradford City club. He was not there very long before leaving to take over a public house, near Pudsey. What a tragedy that there is so little room in soccer for managers who really manage - men like David Steele.

I suppose the late Herbert Chapman and Major Frank Buckley are two of the greatest soccer has ever known, yet they were never the most popular of men. Chapman, the man who built the modern Arsenal, is now a legendary figure; there is even a bust of him in the imposing marble entrance hall at Highbury, but the players he controlled did not regard Chapman as a lovable character. Ruthless to a degree, he was sometimes accused of being a tyrant - yet Herbert Chapman was always the boss, he got amazing results, and he was respected as a successful manager.

There is nothing easy-going about Buckley, either; in fact Billy Wright has referred to him as the man who wielded the big stick, but Billy insists it did him no harm to serve under such a disciplinarian. Ken Chisholm tells a good story about the Major, who managed Leeds United while Ken was a player with that club.

Buckley knew there were great possibilities in 'Big Chiz', but he decided they could be improved with a course of commando training. That is why he told him, 'Jump out of bed at six o'clock, have a round of golf, then a good breakfast and a hard morning's training at the ground. After lunch, train all afternoon, have your tea, follow it with a rest, then a long walk, and go to bed at nine o'clock. Stick to that routine and I'll have you in the Scottish international team inside a month.'

Ken, who, although one of the most diligent of trainers, likes his share of the good things of life, replied, 'No you won't. I'd be in my grave in a week.'

Chapman and Buckley earned the mantle of greatness, but there are many managers in football who are so incompetent it is a mystery to me how they are able to retain any position of responsibility. There are clubs controlled by men who cannot even write a letter, while others pay big salaries to semi-illiterates with no command of the Queen's English.

There was the case of one manager taking his team to play against Aston Villa and solemnly informing them at the start of the journey, 'There will be a convenience waiting to take you from Birmingham station to Villa Park.'

Army sergeant-majors are credited with the invention of many strange words and phrases - there was one who, following the 1940 collapse of Belgium, announced to the sergeants' mess, 'King Leopard's catapulted.' His misuse of the language might be compared to that of the football manager whose club was beaten in the race for the First Division championship. That manager, seeing his side tail off after looking like champions, said, 'What a pity we could not win a converted trophy like the Championship Cup.'

He had been appointed manager solely on his ability as a football player, with never a thought to his capabilities on the managerial side. Here again, directors must shoulder the blame for ignorance in dealing with applications, and carelessness in examining the administrative background of men who are, after all, club ambassadors.

Some of their appointments are so baffling that it is obvious they know nothing about the men they employ. It reminds me of a conversation I had with the chairman of a Northern Third Division club, soon after he and his board had taken on a new manager - a former international player.

Asked if I had ever met the new manager, I answered that I knew him very well. Then followed the question, 'What do you think of him?' I said, 'He's a nice chap, and I think he'll do your club a lot of good.' I was shocked when this chairman told me, 'I'm glad you said that. You see, we don't know much about him.'

Since the war there has been a trend towards the appointment of player-managers but, like so many other bright innovations, this one has been getting out of hand. It worked well at first, with great international players like Peter Doherty, Raich Carter and George Hardwick steering Third Division clubs Doncaster Rovers, Hull City and Oldham Athletic to promotion. That set the ball rolling for, with all due respect to the proved managerial ability of Peter, Raich and George, the biggest single factor in their clubs' success was the playing prowess of these international stars.

Other clubs had similar ideas, encouraged often by the generosity of wealthy teams who allowed ageing soccer stars to join Third and Second Division outfits as player-managers on free transfers or at nominal fees. Good clubs like Manchester United or Charlton Athletic, anxious to reward fine servants like Jack Rowley and Benny Fenton, set them on managerial careers with Plymouth Argyle and Colchester United by cutting the transfer fees which would normally have been paid.

Any good businessman - and I give most directors credit for business acumen - is interested in getting something for nothing. The player-manager racket is a case in point, with the lure of a career - don't take that word too seriously - to tempt the big football fish into the tangled net of managerial misery.

Not so long ago, I commented to a club secretary, 'You've done well to get so-and-so as player-manager. He should do you a power of good on the field, but what about his capabilities as a manager?' Quite blatantly I was informed, 'I don't think he'll ever make a manager, but we've signed a darned good footballer without having to pay for him.'

No wonder experienced managers are finding it increasingly difficult to get jobs in soccer: most of them are too old to play for their pay.

There have been moves recently to recognise the extra work undertaken by player-managers by permitting them to receive more than the maximum playing wage; I am certain that such a course would simply open the door to more abuse. Every star player would be a nominal player-manager, if only for the opportunity to increase his weekly wage.

If the rumours I hear are correct - and who would deny them? - player-managers do very nicely already, with nest eggs paid monthly for future withdrawal, short-term insurance policies, and deeds of houses which are bought by the club but sold by the player-manager.

Far better to tighten restrictions on player-managerships than ease them. In the long run it would benefit players who accept these appointments only to discover, too late, that they have often been engaged for just as long as they remain fit to play.

The Welsh international wing-half, Ivor Powell, dismissed from his post as player-manager of Bradford City, made no secret of his view that the loss of the managerial job and an injury which ended his playing career were closely connected.

Again, could the public be blamed if they put two and two together when that great Arsenal and England full-back, Laurie Scott, was sacked from the Crystal Palace manager's position after injury cut short his days as a player?

Perhaps the only sound method of curbing the small club's abuse of the player-manager arrangement is for wealthy teams to insist on payment of the full transfer fee when they are asked to release anyone. That would scare off the 'something-for-nothing' merchants, at the cost of hindering the ambitions of managerial-minded players. But as those ambitions invariably lead to a blind alley, it might not be such a bad thing.

Although the perils of soccer management are legend, I daresay plenty of people will dismiss my views as exaggerated, but before they do, I feel they should take the trouble to interview some of the unfortunate ex-managers whose experiences are fact - not fiction. I did and, if anything, the seamy side of it all has been toned down in this chapter. Let the doubters talk to Bob Brocklebank (ex-Birmingham City), David Jack (ex-Middlesbrough) Jimmy Rae (ex-Plymouth Argyle), Norman Bullock (ex-Leicester City) or any more of the 'ex' brigade, disillusioned occupants of the managerial electric chair.

Why should a manager with a very big salary, enjoying complete control of a club at the top of the League, suddenly decide to walk out of football? That is the question I asked Jack Fairbrother when, in 1954, he startled the soccer world by resigning from his lucrative post with Coventry City. His answers to me differed from statements put out by himself and by Coventry - that he had resigned because he wanted a long rest, following the tragic death of his wife.

I know Jack was badly cut up about the loss of Belle, but there were other reasons including, inevitably, attempted board room interference in the running of the team - despite earlier guarantees that Jack should have complete control. The real story has never been told. Here it is, in Fairbrother's own words:

'I was only in League football a month or two as a manager before I realised what a heart-breaking occupation it is. Managers in general were being treated shamefully and I often wondered if I was right to console myself with the thought that I, at least, was not being pushed around.

'Was I so different? Certainly not. I knew, somehow, that the day would come when I would be struggling for survival like so many others, and I vowed to get out immediately the first signs appeared. I love this great game of football, but I was determined not to become a physical wreck in its service.

'The warning lights were flashed at the start of my second season with Coventry, when subtle suggestions were made about such-and-such a player being left out of my team when he should have been in.

'I would not alter the line-up. I had full control over team selection. Then the suggestions became in my view more blatant. I began to wonder what it would be like if Coventry were at the bottom of the League, instead of the top. The answer to that was obvious, and the outlook was not cheerful. There were no harsh words, no scenes, no recriminations. I decided I was not going to wait for trouble, so I just walked out of one of the best jobs in the game.

'Football management is the most precarious racket in life - and the word racket is not out of place. That is my opinion, and it's not "sour grapes". I could have made plenty of money writing newspaper articles for the benefit of some Fleet Street circulation in Coventry, but I preferred to safeguard my own circulation... by getting out quickly, and quietly.'

That is Jack's story: it is different from most, because he acted like a condemned prisoner who escapes before entering his cell. Perhaps he was wrong to anticipate hard labour, or even the hangman's noose - but I doubt it.

Managers have even less security than players: they get all the bad breaks in soccer, yet seldom collect the credit when things are going well. No one knows that better than the manager of a club promoted from the Third to the Second Division a few years after the war. It was a real rags-to-riches story, so he kidded one of his directors by suggesting, 'I think you should celebrate promotion by voting your manager a nice bonus. I feel ten years older after this struggle for the League.'

The director, quite seriously, told him, 'Of course we appreciate your efforts, but the credit is not due to you, the trainers, or even the players. We directors formulated a promotion plan three years ago, and it succeeded. Promotion was inevitable.'

I shall be interested to see whether the directors are as quick to accept responsibility when that particular club experiences the sort of bad season which comes to us all at some time or other.

There are not enough directors in football with the progressive approach of the Sunderland Board. Men like Mr Billy Ditchburn, Mr W. S. Martin and their colleagues go out of their way to investigate the rights and wrongs of soccer, and Mr Ditchburn, backed by the Sunderland club, regularly advances suggestions for improving the game - and the conditions of its paid servants. Unfortunately, few managers experience the pleasure of working under such directors.

All the kicks. None of the glory. That is the prospect facing nearly every manager in British football. Why, then, should scores of applicants line up as each vacancy occurs? That's one question I cannot answer.

Chapter 17

Focus on each playing position - and great players in these positions.

Picking teams is a popular hobby. The Press indulge in it, not always successfully, from August to May; the man in the pub picks his best eleven as he drinks his pint; footballer-authors count it a 'must' when they assemble their memoirs and, of course, the gentlemen of the Football Association must get a tremendous amount of fun when they gather at Lancaster Gate to select full international teams, 'B' teams, Intermediate sides, and those rather odd mixtures of professionals, amateurs, and others labelled FA XIs.

The names put forward are many and varied. That is unimportant. What is essential is the reason behind each nomination, because unless we know exactly what we are looking for, we will never be in a position to judge one player's ability against another's. *If,* for example, the search is on for a goalkeeper, and the goalkeeper's number one virtue in the eyes of the team picker is his ability to kick a dead ball, nobody should be surprised if he throws three goals in his own net - in between taking goal kicks which travel three-quarters the length of the pitch.

Exaggeration? Not a bit of it! There was the true story, told to me by one who was present, of the Second Division club directors' meeting at which certain directors doubted the wisdom of signing a full-back because he was on the small side. One of them jumped to his feet to inform the meeting, 'It doesn't matter how small he is so long as he gets us plenty of goals.'

With directors scouting for goal-scoring full-backs, it was not really surprising to see that particular club relegated to the Third Division (see Chapter 9).

I have my own ideas about the different virtues and vices of each particular playing position - and the players I would like to see in those positions if I had the running of a team. Some suggestions, perhaps most of them, will seem strange to a lot of football folk, but allow me to present my case before you find me guilty.

GOAL. Pity the poor goalkeeper! Ten-a-penny in the eyes of many football managers, but just ask some of them without a good goalkeeper what they would pay for one. The goalkeeper is the odd man out, the fellow in the green jersey who goes along to make up the number: his football knowledge is obviously non-existent and there is no doubt he must have toppled from his high chair in baby days to acquire the correct mental approach for the task of keeping goal. A most under-rated, yet vital, member of the team, he holds within his hands the winning or losing of every match. My boy Graham summed up perfectly all the nefarious notions on goalkeepers when I asked him if he wanted to be a footballer. 'No, Dad,' he said, 'I would rather be a goalkeeper.'

I would list the goalkeeping merit table in this order:

1. Anticipation and positional play
2. A safe pair of hands
3. Cool nerves, correct temperament
4. Physique (accent on height more than weight)
5. Agility
6. Kicking (never turn down a goalkeeper on this).

I trust I will not be accused of bias when I name my good friend Jack Fairbrother as the outstanding British goalkeeper of the past twenty years, as far as positional play goes - and, for my money, that is more important than all the other points put together. Few would nominate Fairbrother for a team of all stars: he seldom made the sort of saves which delight the Press photographer; he was never a favourite of international selectors; his name was not often to be found in the headlines of a match report. But Jack Fairbrother never played a poor game and I know of no other goalkeeper of whom that could be said.

Fairbrother's secret was geometrical. He knew his angles well enough to compete with Pythagoras on equilateral terms! Jack would watch the approach of an opposing forward, time his move to meet him perfectly, come out just far enough - and leave the rest to the man with the ball. Invariably a shot would be attempted. If the shot was on target - the goal - it would hit Jack somewhere on the body; if only a foot to right or left and out of Jack's reach, it went wide of the upright; if too high for him to touch, it must clear the cross bar. The only chance for the forward, in fact, is a mashie niblick shot, a gentle chip, over Fairbrother's head and under the bar. And how many contemporary players are capable of that?

Jack Fairbrother never made spectacular saves - he didn't need to. That is why he was never capped by his country, an omission which, to my mind, merely endorses my views on the football knowledge of selectors.

Remember this point. Spectacular goalkeeping is the result of bad positional play.

FULL BACKS. What would I look for in a full-back? Contrary to the opinion of my manager Billy Murray - himself a former back - I consider this the easiest job in the team; in fact there is no reason why a brainy full-back should not play until he is 40. If his positional play is good enough he can save his legs a lot of work.

My list of attributes:

1. Positional play

2. Tackling ability (knowing *when* to go in rather than *how* to go in)
3. Ball control (proficiency in this department is uncommon)
4. Speed
5. Heading ability.

Call me hard to please, if you like, but I have yet to see my ideal full-back. The ones excelling in positional play and ball control seldom have speed, while the 'quickies' invariably lack positional sense. It should be stressed that my memory takes me back no more than twenty years. No doubt there were several backs measuring up to the standards I have set playing between 1900 and 1935, or earlier. My choice is limited but I have no hesitation in nominating All' Ramsey and Eddie Hapgood as the outstanding pair of my day.

Two of a type? Undoubtedly: they might even have been fashioned in the same mould. I never saw Ramsey or Hapgood rush an opponent, miss his tackle and land his team in trouble. Neither did they believe in clearing the ball recklessly, kicking into touch or making spectacular sliding tackles. As a forward, I like to meet precocious full-backs, types who come rushing in like contestants on the field of Balaclava rather than Bramall Lane, Burnden Park or Bloomfield Road. It is easy to have a fullback on toast if he puts all his eggs in one basket - the full-blooded tackle. Walter Winterbottom, so often criticised as the England team manager, is absolutely right in his ideas of 'funnelling defences' in which full-backs and half-backs retreat towards their own goal, jockeying the approaching opponent, keeping their feet and timing their tackle for the opportune moment. These are sound tactics seldom appreciated by spectators who offer the gratuitous advice to 'Get stuck in'.

AW Ramsey and Eddie Hapgood were footballers in every sense of the word; neither could be called quick but they had sufficient natural ability to overcome failings in that direction.

WING-HALVES. The key men in every team. It is often claimed that inside-forwards fill the most important positions. I disagree. No inside-forward could do his job successfully without the essential prompting of a good wing-half, and by that I do not mean a wing-half always in the public eye through spectacular runs with the ball, the man to whom possession is nine points of the law. He may look the part but he is not necessarily doing his job correctly. Time after time I have seen a wing-half come out of a tackle with the ball, carry it fifteen to twenty yards instead of slipping it to an inside man who has run into the open space, part with it too late - and start galloping back hopelessly out of position. The iniquitous part of it is that the inside-forward is often blamed, after having been crowded out and easily robbed.

In a wing-half I would look for:

1. Strength in the tackle
2. Intelligent distribution (knowledge of the right time to part)
3. Ball control
4. Stamina (more essential than actual speed).

Not being particularly keen on half-backs who hold the ball, I nominate Ken Willingham, of Huddersfield Town and England, for the right-half position. Ken did not believe in carrying the ball half the length of the field; he was seldom tempted to beat a man, but it must have been a wonderful experience playing in front of him as an inside-right or right-winger. He would make a quick, accurate pass, run on for the return, and having seen the wing pair on their way, return to his position ready to do his job again when required. It was all so quiet, hardly noticed - but wonderfully effective.

My left-half would be Joe Mercer, when he was past his prime. No, that is not a misprint. I am convinced that Joe, as an Arsenal-player between his thirtieth and fortieth birthdays, was a far better wing-half than in his younger days as an Everton and England player. When Joe Mercer discovered his legs would not allow him to run all over the field, when his physical condition hampered him, when he played almost entirely in his own half of the field, he was great. The service of wonderful passes that flowed from this spindly bow-legged genius was, I am certain, fifty per cent of the reason for Arsenal's post-war successes. How Joe was missed when a broken leg ended his long, illustrious career.

Before leaving the wing-half positions, I would like to pay a personal tribute to my Sunderland colleague Arthur Wright by naming him as the best uncapped half-back in soccer. Joe Mercer excepted, I did not see a finer wing-half in post-war football. Neither did the selectors of the England team!

CENTRE-HALF. Searching for the ideal centre-half I put safety-first play at the top of the list of qualities: come to think of it, that particular virtue might be first, second and third because, to my mind, it overshadows all other requirements in a pivot. Never mind distribution, neat heading to the wing-halves, impressive runs upfield. Let anybody else in the team play football - but not the centre-half. If a pivot tries to beat a man or make a short pass, and the move comes unstuck, the ball can be in the back of the net in an instant. Teams with good defensive records usually install the labourer in preference to the artist at centre-half: after all, team-building can be likened to house building, and the finest architecture in the world counts for nothing if the foundations lack solidity. The centre-half is, of course, the foundation, the rock on which a side stands or falls.

My points for pivots are:

1. Ability to block up the middle - allied to kicking and heading proficiency
2. Physique (very important in this position)
3. No inclination to play with the ball
4. Strength in the tackle.

Who measures up to these requirements better than my old Newcastle United club-mate Frank Brennan? I am not suggesting by my choice that Big Frank is lacking in the soccer skills. He knows how to use a ball as well as the next man, but Brennan takes the field for every match with one idea on his mind - the subjugation of all attacking moves down the centre of the field. And what a magnificent job he makes of it.

WINGERS. Here we have two schools of thought; one favours the speedy, direct type of wing man, the other prefers the ball artist. I am old-fashioned enough to think there is just a little too much so-called direct soccer without the trimmings in Britain today, and when we decide we can get along without the ball manipulators we may well find ourselves trying to get along without support from the turnstiles. Let's face it. Footballers are entertainers and when they resort to kick and rush they cease to entertain.

That is why I feel wingers should possess:

1. Ball control
2. Speed (in particular the initial burst over short distances)
3. Shooting ability.

This is where we come to the Matthews - Finney controversy, possibly football's favourite talking point. While admitting Tom Finney's game embodies more of each type of wing play, so that, according to my requirements, Preston's Peerless Plumber would look the better bet, I must nominate Stanley Matthews for the outside-right position in my team. Why? Because he's. . . Stanley Matthews.

It is easy to criticize a man playing Matthews' type of game. Many, indeed, have condemned him for holding up the forward line, thus giving an opposing team time to cover and recover. I could pull the Stanley Matthews game to pieces in theory yet, despite the plausible preaching of so many coaches, I still believe matches are won and lost on the field of play - not with blackboard and chalk. No, it is not for me to criticize Stanley Matthews. He is a perfectionist.

Stanley Matthews has terrific speed over the first vital ten yards, out-of-this-world ball manipulation, precision passing, a natural body swerve, and two good feet. And this is the man shunned for years by the selectors of the England international team - at a time when England had few players of real class. Further comment seems unnecessary.

Matthews for the right-wing: who for outside-left? This is a real teaser, in fact it had me so stumped I decided to follow the course adopted by international selectors, and put forward the name of an outside-right, Tom Finney. In post-war soccer Billy Liddell and Jimmy Mullen stand out as the pick of outside-lefts, but neither would get my vote in preference to Finney. Acknowledging that Finney is only half the player on the left flank he is on the right, I would still find room for him - and that is no compliment to the hundreds of players who have occupied the left-wing position in club football over the past twenty years. There is a depressing lack of talent for this berth. Why should that be? Could it be that this is the one position in which a 'cork' left leg cannot be hidden? Most of us are naturally right-footed: that is no real handicap at left-back, left-half or inside-left, but an outside-left trying to hide his 'dummy' has no chance. If he cannot cross the ball on the run without bringing it on to his right foot, his effectiveness is shattered.

One last word on the Matthews-Finney business. Why should the Preston North End player always be the unlucky one selected to play out of position? I know Tom has often wondered why Stan has not been accorded the 'privilege' of taking over as

England's outside-left. I do not condemn the FA for finding room for both these truly great artists but I do criticize them for being unfair to Finney and always picking on him to make the switch.

INSIDE-FORWARDS. This is my special department. In the circumstances I feel I can write with some authority because, whatever deficiencies there may be in my game, I know which virtues should be featured in it.

1. Ball control
2. Initial burst of speed
3. Shooting ability
4. Two good feet - without which a player could hardly fulfil (1)
5. Capacity for hard work and graft (this would kill my chances immediately).

Let me put forward four names: Wilf Mannion, Peter Doherty. Jimmy Hagan, and Raich Carter. Apart from natural football ability, what have they all in common? They are all ball jugglers, complete masters of the tool of their trade - and each is twofooted. As inside-forwards, they are supreme in the era under discussion. Mannion, Doherty, Hagan and Carter may have individual styles, but they all lead to the one end. Each has the ability to size up a situation and adopt the right course instinctively, and my biggest headache is to place them in order of merit.

In discarding maestro Raich Carter and mercurial Jimmy Hagan in favour of Ireland's pride, Peter Doherty, and blonde, bewitching Will' Mannion, I am probably inviting protests from Sunderland and Sheffield - but I have very sound reasons for so doing.

Peter Doherty was surely the genius among geniuses. Possessor of the most baffling body swerve in football, able to perform all the tricks with the ball, owning a shot like the kick of a mule, and, with all this, having such tremendous enthusiasm for the game that he would work like a horse for ninety minutes. That was pipe-smoking Peter Doherty, the Irish redhead who, I am convinced, had enough football skill to stroll through a game smoking that pipe - and still make the other twenty-one players appear second-raters. But of course Peter never strolled through anything. His energy had to be seen to be appreciated.

I recall a war-time match in which Doherty, then appearing as a guest-player with Lincoln City, turned out against my team, Bradford Park Avenue. Peter brought the ball from the half-way line, beating man after man until finally, on the edge of the penalty area, he cracked in a shot which no goalkeeper had an earthly chance of saving. Chick Farr, the Bradford goalkeeper, could do no more than dive desperately... and pick the ball out of the net. A few minutes later the move was repeated: Doherty reached the eighteen yards line and drew back his right foot for the pay-off punt - but he didn't shoot. It was the perfect dummy, clever enough to induce Chick Farr to dive - while Peter calmly trotted on and walked the ball over the goal line. I realised that day I was on the field with a master footballer. It was a privilege.

Wilf Mannion, for many years the hero of Teesside, gets the other inside-forward

33. Shackleton, the Istanbul Police goalkeeper, and the ball, all in the net. But it was a goal—during Sunderland's tour of Turkey.

34. Off the field the Sunderland players had a wonderful time on their Turkish trip. In this picture Tommy McLain, Len Shackleton and Tommy Reynolds are being entertained at a party in Istanbul.

35. 'Shack', taking time off from his sick-bed, has fun in the snow with Sunderland colleagues Ken Chisholm, Billy Bingham and Ted Purdon, just before their Cup-tie with Swansea Town.

36. Another kind of fun. Drawing-room heading, for the family's amusement.

berth in my team of all the talents because he has very nearly everything on a par with Peter Doherty. And that is sufficient recommendation.

I did not play with Mannion very often, but on the few occasions we did get together, I was impressed, more than anything else, by his positional skill. In other words Will' is an easy player to get along with: he knows instinctively where to find the open space and wastes no time running into it; he sees in a second whether to give a quick pass or hold the ball, and spends so much time doing the academically correct thing that colleagues around him can hardly fail to fall into the scheme of things, thus elevating their own games on Mannion's prompting.

On the evening before the *1954* West Bromwich Albion *v* Preston North End Cup Final, Wilf and I were inside-forwards in an England side which licked Young England at Highbury Stadium. The average age of our team was 35 and, at 31, I was the 'baby' of the bunch. Several of our young opponents were included in Continental tour and World Cup 'possibles', while our sole representative currently favoured by selectors was our promising right-winger - a boy called Stanley Matthews. I thoroughly enjoyed the match because it confirmed what I have always believed... that a pass at the right time, and the use of guile rather than speed, save a lot of dashing about. In a side such as the one fielded by 'Old' England that night, chasing was unnecessary. Mannion, at inside-right, was brilliant - and he made my game that much easier.

Raich Carter was not quite in the Mannion-Doherty class as a ball juggler, but he made up for that by being quick-thinking and quick-moving. If only Carter could have had Mannion's ball control, he would have been the greatest player this game of football has ever seen.

CENTRE-FORWARD. The orthodox centre-forward, that is, the spearhead of the attack in a five-up forward line, has one mission in his soccer life - the scoring of goals. That is his only job. Let the inside men and the wingers weave the pretty patterns and create the openings. The centre-forward is there solely for the purpose of finishing off the job, and that means getting the ball, by some means or other, into the net. I think his equipment should be:

1. Two good feet, providing him with the ability to shoot from all angles
2. Proficiency with his head
3. Speed
4. Ball control
5. Enthusiasm (call it guts if you like)
6. Physique.

Plenty of players with limited ability - in the artistic sense - have made a success of this job. I could name one who has been capped many times by his country, yet, so far as pure soccer skills are concerned, he is still a novice. In almost every game centre-forwards are presented with at least two or three goal-scoring chances, and providing they are able to think quickly and shoot hard with both feet, they can get by with nothing else in their favour - and be hailed as a success. Even so, some of the greatest names in football have filled the centre-forward position and the best of them, in my time, was Tommy Lawton. Tommy, in his prime, had everything required of a centre-forward. A terrific shot with either foot, strength and accuracy with his head, the perfect physique, wonderful positional sense and a quickness off the mark that was unexpected in one of his build.

In addition, Tommy Lawton possessed tremendous confidence in his own ability, a mental lift which seems common to all the players mentioned in this chapter.

What of the unorthodox centre-forward, the deep-lying leader who patrols the area between the half-way line and the edge of the penalty box? Is he here to stay, or does he come under the heading of temporary tactics? I think the deep-lying centre-forward, Don Revie, who has made a great success of this task for Manchester City, is the obvious answer to the stopper centre-half, and while I am not entirely in favour of this manoeuvre, I feel we should take note of anything new in a game which must never be permitted to stand still.

Is the employment of a 'rover' really a new idea? I doubt it, in fact the loose man must be the nearest approach to the attacking centre-half we have seen for many years. A ball player in mid-field feeding two thrustful inside-forwards lying well up, provides attractive football for spectators. And for that reason alone, I applaud Manchester City and other clubs playing that way.

So much for the requirements of the various positions on the field and the men I would nominate to fill them. My team reads:

Fairbrother; Ramsey, Hapgood; Willingham, Brennan, Mercer; Matthews, Marmion, Lawton, Doherty, Finney.

I've a hunch it would win more matches than it would lose.

Chapter 18

Referees – candid comments

The soccer referee and the fair-ground Aunt Sally have a lot in common: both are on public show to be shot at by everyone, and having been assaulted from so many different directions, both are expected to present to the world at large a happy countenance - while awaiting the next salvo. Of course referees get paid more than Aunt Sallys, but, in many grades of football, such payment is negligible.

I sympathise with the men with the whistles. They have to be as fit, mentally and physically, as the men they control; they must accept insults as other men would accept the time of day; they must submit to biased assessments of their ability by club directors; their grasp of the diplomatic art must be at least on a par with that of a cabinet minister, lest one word in the wrong place should bring banishment from Lancaster Gate or Preston. Referees must indeed be virtuous virtuosi until, at the age of 47, by which time they have just about mastered the job, they are no longer considered suitable for it - and are compelled to volunteer for retirement to the League list.

That compulsory retirement should be abolished. Were we blessed with a preponderance of top-class referees, we could afford to consign good men to the scrap heap at 47, but I am sure soccer cannot spare men like Bill Evans (Liverpool) and Reg Mortimer (Huddersfield) who were 'struck off the books' of the Football League simply because they celebrated a particular birthday. Referees, like goalkeepers, improve with age - providing their physical condition shows no deterioration. Year after year the whistler gains in experience, picks up new 'wrinkles', and learns something extra about controlling odd characters like me.

I would not advocate the introduction of medical examinations for referees at the age of 47, because that sort of idea could spread to players, and if that happened, I might not be allowed to play at all. No, any physical failings would surely be noted by those who report on referees: it is not easy to hide lumbago, failing eyesight, gout or middle-age spread!

What about the standard of refereeing in the Football League? I think it could be improved but, comparing it with standards in other countries, we have not much to grumble about. With a few exceptions, foreign referees are very, very poor.

There are some queer ones in Britain, too, and without mentioning names, I feel they all fall into certain categories, consistently making similar mistakes.

First let us take the 'two wrongs do make a right' type. This is the fellow who omits to award a penalty, free kick, or what-have-you, when he should - then, a few minutes later, gives one when it is unnecessary. In his interpretation this is a compensatory wiping of the slate, but I call it mental cowardice.

Another coward is the 'no penalty at any price' type. He is on view almost every week, awarding free kicks anything from one to twelve inches outside the penalty box, when it is plain to everyone that the transgression took place inches - perhaps feet - inside the box. His usual excuse to himself is that the offence did not warrant so serious a disciplinary move as a penalty kick, yet the laws of the game make no provision for such doubtful discretion.

A group with whom I have had several altercations might be classified as the 'anticipation is everything, whistle-happy' types. Let me explain. Playing for Sunderland once, I managed to break through on my own with the ball, walked it round the opposing goalkeeper, and just as I was about to run it into the goal, stopped the ball on the line and shouted to him, 'Hey, George. It's not over the line yet.' There he was scrambling on hands and knees in the mud, trying to reach it. Meanwhile the referee, from some distance away, had blown his whistle and pointed to the centre, awarding a goal. Not making allowances for people like me, that referee naturally expected the ball to enter the net once I had rounded the goalkeeper, but his anticipation and eagerness to blow the whistle caused a goal to be given before it was scored.

I had a similar experience in a match when Sunderland were being well beaten with only a few minutes left for play. All on my own on the left-wing, I received a pass and, with nothing more important on my mind, decided to 'try something on'. I rolled the ball along the touchline with the inside of my right foot - it was like a police test for a drunken man, but I was sober enough - and, although I swear to this day the ball did not once cross the line, the linesman's flag and the referee's whistle gave our opponents a throw-in. A ball running along the touchline is expected to go out of play so, on that assumption, up had gone the flag.

Anticipation is a great virtue in a referee providing it is not overdone, which brings me to another officious official, the 'I'll stop any trouble before it starts' type. This one is probably the number one culprit when matches are spoiled for spectators and players, the one who assumes he is handling twenty-two cut-throats when, as everyone knows, we modern professional players are the gentlest of souls.

He is usually an early starter: within a minute or two of the kick-off he will blow for a foul, rush up to the offending player and, armed with the deadly, pointed finger of accusation, murmur a pleasantry like 'Just try that once more and you're off the field. I know all about you, so behave yourself.' It happens often; in fact a reporter friend at one match - it was a clean game, too - listed the number of times the referee reprimanded players and showed me the totals of eleven (first half) and six (second half). The official had even spoken to players without penalising them.

Of course, I realise the necessity for discipline - especially in local 'derby' matches - and it is no help to a referee endeavouring to keep twenty-two players under control when some of us try to make his duties even more complicated than necessary. That reminds me of one meeting between Newcastle United and Sunderland in which I played. Newcastle's goalkeeper was Jack Fairbrother and we still laugh about the time he gathered a ball just as I was running towards him. I aimed a mighty mock kick at Jack and jumped over his head. The whistle blew, up scooted the referee who, finger outstretched, admonished me, 'Raise your boot once more to the goalkeeper and off you go.' Jack thought it was funny but, with a hurt look on his face, told the ref., 'Never mind the next time: he ought to go off now. Shackleton's a killer.'

That whistler had seen what looked like a nasty incident and, quite rightly, had stepped in with his warning; but he must have received a shock when big Frank Brennan took him aside to tell him, 'They're pulling your leg, ref. Those are the two best pals in football.'

Last on my list of 'types' is the 'homer', the official who never makes the mistake of erring in favour of the visiting team, the one who endears himself to the home crowd by making biased decisions - with the bias always on the same side. This species, thank heavens, is almost extinct, but I have met a few of them.

On one occasion the refereeing was so obviously in favour of the home team - I was playing for the away team - that I said, whenever I was within earshot of the man with the whistle, 'Oh Mr Khayyam.' It happened many times during the match, so I was not surprised to be tackled by the referee as we entered the tunnel at the end of the game. Putting his arm round me, he said, 'I have often been called names by footballers, but what's all this "Mr Khayyam" business?' I told him, 'Mr Khayyam was a Persian philosopher and poet - and you know what his Christian name was.' The referee went up in my estimation when he roared his head off, because he could so easily have taken it the other way - and booked me for insolence.

I like to meet a referee with a sense of humour: perhaps his possession of that quality is behind Arthur Ellis's popularity with officials, players, Press and public. Mr Ellis is, in my opinion, the finest referee in soccer because he is liked yet respected; he is one of us but always the governor.

Referees who cannot see the funny side of life might have reacted differently from Ellis when I had a bit of fun with him before taking a free kick just outside the penalty area in a Roker game. As a protection against frost, the pitch had been covered with peat moss and straw the previous night, so, gathering a few lumps of peat moss left behind by the sweepers-up, I made a tee on which to perch the ball. Arthur Ellis spotted what I was doing, ran over, and swept aside my tee with his boot. Laboriously I started gathering up the peat moss again, informing Ellis, 'There's nowt in't rules to say players can't tee-up the ball on peat moss.' Quick as a flash, Ellis kicked down my peat castle for the second time, saying, 'No - and there's nowt in't rules to say players can.'

Ellis is the official who, ignoring my remarks of 'Terrible decision' several times during a match, waited until I had missed an open goal, then ran past saying, 'Terrible shot.'

Paddy Power of York is another referee who doesn't object to a bit of leg pulling. He was talking to a group of Sunderland players on Stalybridge railway station one night when up came a blind man, his white stick tap-tapping along the platform. I pulled Mr Power and a couple of the players out of the blind man's way with the warning, 'Stand aside. There's a referee coming.' Ever since that night, whenever Paddy Power and I have met, his greeting has been, 'I've left my white stick at home.'

Looking back on other memories of referees, I find some were not so funny - like the time I played for Bradford on the day that Jackie Gibbons, the England amateur international forward, incurred the wrath of the whistler.

Following an opposition goal, Gibbons and I were lining up ready for the kick-off, but Jackie was making sure the referee knew all about the injustice of that goal. The official lifted his finger and shouted over, 'Come here, Gibbons.' I whispered to Jackie, 'He cannot force you to go to him. I know this law backwards, and he won't be able to do a thing if you stay put.' Jackie did not move. Following another 'come hither' order from the ref., he took two steps forward, thought better of it, and again stood his ground. Of course the referee, like Mohammed, had to come - and he promptly sent Jackie off the field. As our disconsolate centre-forward started that long, humiliating walk to the dressing-room, he passed me and I told him, 'He can't do that, Jackie.' He looked up and, like a teacher addressing an immature pupil, informed me, 'He's done it, Len.'

An oft-mooted idea concerns the employment of former professional footballers as referees, and although players are now welcomed into refereeing circles, few of them have come forward - which reluctance might profitably be investigated by the authorities. Referees have a standing joke that it takes such a long time to reach the top of the tree - unless branches are being pulled - that compulsory retirement usually follows promotion to the top class.

It is not as bad as that, of course, but there is no denying that a former player taking up the job of match official at the age of, say, *35,* would be unlikely to reach the full League list before his fortieth birthday. Why not, in view of their playing experience, allow ex-players to by-pass the monotonous years of slow promotion through minor leagues and give them full status after about two seasons in amateur soccer?

Safeguards against incompetence could be assured through the medium of an examination paper, plus reports on practical ability.

Legislation on former players as referees should not be held to imply that all referees must have played the game. That, in my view, is not essential... but it is a big help.

Another suggestion I recommend to the ruling bodies is the employment of refereeing teams, comprising a referee and two linesmen from the same district who could work together every Saturday, learning, through experience, each other's idiosyncrasies and methods of match control. It is not a new idea but, until logical arguments against its use are put forward, it will remain a good one.

A new deal for soccer referees is long overdue. They perform a thankless job, and for the most part - exceptions analysed above - do it honestly, conscientiously and competently. Let the match fees of the leading men be raised from five guineas to ten as a token attempt to remunerate the most important man on the football field in proportion to his position.

But should fees be scrapped entirely, there would still be a queue of applicants for this thankless task, which causes me to observe that it takes all kinds to make a world. And that's just as well.

Chapter 19

'Buried' again by England selectors - the price paid for 'laying an eggs in the Cup replay against the 'Swans'.

Having opened this book with the tale of my 'resurrection' by England international selectors, it would not be complete without recounting the 'Shack' burial ceremony performed for the match against Scotland on 2nd April *1955*.

I was quite satisfied with my game against Germany in December, and, barring injury, felt capable of retaining my England place - despite the four months' break before the Scottish affair. So did Ron Staniforth, Bill Slater, Ronnie Allen, Roy Bentley, and Tom Finney, but that quintet, their deeds against the Germans soon forgotten, joined me on the international scrap heap in April.

The *1954-5* season hammered home to me the truth of the maxim that soccer is a game of ups and downs. At one stage of the season I was re-established as an England player and my club, Sunderland, were at the top of the First Division. Later we needed just one FA Cup victory - in the Semi-final against Manchester City - to be certain of playing in the Final at Wembley.

The Press were writing most flattering articles about me: I even wrote a series myself on the lines of, '"How I came back", by England's forgotten man.' A journalist friend went so far as to joke about the possibility of Len Shackleton being elected 'Footballer of the Year'. If ever a footballer was on top of the world, I was at that time... but it did not last very long.

By the end of the season, I had been dropped by Sunderland for the first time in my career, cast aside by England selectors, lost my chance of a Cup medal, and also given up hope of a League Championship medal as Sunderland faded so suddenly in March and April.

I know well enough the reasons for my temporary personal decline; they coincided with the fifth round Cup-ties against Swansea Town on 19th and 23rd February, the replay on the 23rd still being a talking point in Sunderland long after the season had ended.

I must start the troublesome tale with a home League game against Charlton

Athletic on 12th February, a match I would have been happier to miss had I realised what it would eventually cost me. On that Saturday morning, I awoke with a filthy cold, sneezing, coughing, head aching, and possessed of just about every discomfort inflicted on mankind by the inconsiderate bug.

A check by the Sunderland club doctor established that my temperature was a little below normal and, assured by the thermometer that I was imagining my illness, I played against the London side. Sunderland lost their first home game of the season that day.

I went straight home to bed - and stayed there until the following Thursday when the Roker party left for Porthcawl, the Welsh seaside resort chosen as our headquarters for the Swansea Cup-tie at Vetch Field.

The next morning in Porthcawl I felt a little better, did an hour's training, and returned to the hotel for another miserable afternoon in bed. I was well enough to play in a 2-2 drawn match on the Saturday but still feeling seedy on returning to Sunderland, I was once again confined to bed. The replay was scheduled for the following Wednesday at Roker Park, but I was in no condition to train on the Monday or Tuesday.

So it was that, having done a matter of one hour's training in the eleven days preceding the vital Swansea replay, I lined up with the rest of the Sunderland lads, hoping I could somehow snap out of my lethargy as the match progressed.

Sunderland won and I make no secret of my own shortcomings; I agree they won despite Len Shackleton. It is possible I have had poorer games, but I doubt it: that Cup replay against Swansea Town was a nightmare for me; it seemed the longest game ever staged, and I could not have run about to save my life. Of course it looked bad from the stands and terraces, and not being the most understanding spectators in football, the Roker Park fans gave me the bird mercilessly. Mentally and physically unwell, I played like a man in a dream, and was far enough removed from the events of that day to leave the field at the end without noticing my own supporters were booing me into the tunnel.

While not wishing to make excuses for such a putrid performance, I feel entitled to present my side of this story of a game which left a nasty taste in the mouths of some Sunderland supporters. I deny, most strongly, that I was a non-trier against Swansea Town: only a fool or a scoundrel would deliberately attempt to hold himself back on an occasion like a fifth-round Cup replay.

The Press spread far and wide the tidings of 'Shack's Shocker', as was their duty. On the day after the match, a local paper put me in the stocks, firing all the ammunition in the journalistic armoury at me. After reading that particular report, I put down the paper and told Marjorie, 'That's a well-written story.'

Perhaps a more sensitive player would have been in tears: other types would have felt they were being treated unfairly, but I knew better than anyone that I had 'laid an egg' against the Swans. Not knowing of my physical condition, or lack of training, reporters were entitled to believe the evidence of their own eyes - and it was pretty damning evidence. I do not plead 'Not Guilty'. I merely present my side of the story, never previously told. That is the condemned man's privilege.

After that dismal, depressing, display, I went to see manager Mr Billy Murray in his office and, after apologising for the game, told him, 'I don't know why, but I couldn't get my teeth into the match. In the circumstances I'm not doing myself or the team justice, and I think it would be a good move to leave me out of the first team on Saturday and give me a chance to find my feet in the reserves against Blackhall Colliery.' Mr Murray promised to think about it.

The request was granted, and I was left out of the first XI. Once again I was in the headlines, but I was not very happy about the way my relegation was handled by the Press. They made no mention of my request for a rest in the reserve side. Len Shackleton had been dropped by Sunderland for the first time since he had joined the club, and that was a good enough story, without delving too deeply into the facts behind it.

Reinstated after one reserve match, I played against Bolton Wanderers at Burnden Park, collecting an ankle injury which kept me out of the league games against Cardiff City and Arsenal, and also the sixth round Cup-tie with Wolves at Roker.

All this time, I seemed to be on the receiving end of an attack from one newspaper, and suggestions were made that, even when I was fit again, there would be no room in the team for me. That was when I was given a most encouraging demonstration of loyalty from my fans. They wrote to the papers appealing for a square deal for me, and I was flattered to discover there were dozens of 'pro-Shack' letters for every one against me.

A week before the Cup Semi-final against Manchester City, I reported fit, but it was decided not to introduce me for the Arsenal League match - a game which would have given me valuable match practice before the more serious affair at Villa Park seven days later. Against Arsenal, unfortunately for Sunderland, but perhaps fortunately for me, our forward line did not do as well as expected. I was brought back for the big game, ace goal-snatcher Ken Chisholm being left out, and although City beat us 1-0, I knew that in that Semi-final I had played as well as I am ever likely to play.

My performance that day did not interest any England selectors: presumably they had already written me off as an England player on the strength of that one bad performance against Swansea and my one appearance as a reserve team player.

In the space of a few months I had 'come-back', I had 'gone back', been 'resurrected', been 're-buried', had visions of Wembley, and had a rude awakening. As the director of a Yorkshire club once said, 'Football's a funny game - but it's not supposed to be.'

~ INDEX ~

A.

ABRAM, Ken: 173
ADAMSON, Jimmy: 185
ALLCHURCH, Ivor: 124
ALLISON, George: 14, 75,
ALLEN, Ronnie: 95, 124
ARMFIELD, Jimmy: 13-30, 178, 195
ANDERSON, Jack: 117-118
ANDERSON, Stan: 167, 186-187
ASHURST, Len: 130

B.

BAILEY, George: 130-131
BALL, Alan: 176
BANKS, Gordon: 102
BANKS, Tommy: 49
BASTIN, Cliff: 163, 168-169
BATTY, David: 167
BAXTER, Jim: 178
BEARDSLEY, Peter: 179
BENTLEY, Roy: 77, 78, 95, 124
BEST, George: 163, 165, 171-172, 181
BINGHAM, Billy: 19, 21, 24, 51, 86-94, 167, 187-188
BISHOP, Bob: 171
BLANCHFLOWER, Danny: 188
BOSMAN, Jean-Marc: 157-158
BREMNER, Billy: 50, 167, 185-186
BRENNAN, Frank: 77, 86, 165, 182
BROADIS, Ivor: 90
BROWN, Alan: 57, 58, 183, 184, 187
BRUCE, Steve: 182
BUCHAN, Charles: 182
BULL, David: 7
BURRICHAGA, Jorge: 172
BUSBY, Matt: 171, 172, 193

C.

CAMSELL, George: 192
CANTONA, Eric: 164, 165, 180-182, 185
CARTER, Raich: 165, 182-183, 195, 199, 200
CHAPMAN, Herbert: 168, 169
CHARLES, John: 124, 167, 168, 192, 195
CHARLTON, Bobby: 176, 177, 180, 181, 188
CHARLTON, Jackie: 186, 188
CHILDS, George: 126, 129
CHISHOLM, Ken: 19, 31, 32, 35, 48, 55, 111, 114-116, 160, 167
CLAPHAM, Tim: 75
CLAY, Ernie: 82, 153-157
CLOSE, Brian: 128, 165, 179, 192-193
CLOUGH, Brian: 75, 95-99, 147-148, 150
COCKELL, Don: 35
COLLINS, Billy: 186
COLLINGS, Syd: 56, 58
COMPTON, Dennis: 26, 119
COPPING, Wilf: 163, 169-170
COWAN, Jimmy: 20
COWELL, Bobby: 18, 77
CRAWFORD, Joan: 35
CROSSLEY, Mark: 179
CROWE, Charlie: 83

D.

DALGLISH, Kenny: 188
DANIEL, Bobby: 15
DANIEL, Ray: 19, 20, 23, 24, 31, 32, 48, 49, 52, 111-114,
DAVIS, Don: 168
DEAN, Dixie: 150, 189
DEMPSEY, Jack: 32
DIFFIN, Jack: 84-85
DiMATTIO, Roberto: 188
DITCHBURN, Bill: 56, 114
DITCHBURN, Ted: 114
DOHERTY, Peter: 163, 173
DOIG, Eric: 161
DOIG, Teddy: 161
DRAKE, Ted: 150, 153, 164, 167, 170, 177

E.

EASTHAM, George: 153-157, 182
ELLIOTT, Billy: 18, 19, 20, 26, 50, 166, 184-185
EMERY, Fred: 14

F.

FAIRBROTHER, Jack: 77, 120-122
FARR, Chick: 14
FEAST, John: 7
FERGUSON, Alex: 180
FINNEY, Tom: 43, 48, 83, 163, 165, 173-175, 190, 191, 195
FLEMING, Charlie: 19
FORD, Trevor: 20, 87-91, 195
FRANCIS, Trevor: 193
FRANKLIN, Neil: 26, 195

G.

GALLACHER, Hughie: 173
GASCOIGNE, Paul: 27, 147, 163, 165, 179
GAYNE, Arthur: 101,102
GIBSON, John: 135, 137
GIGGS, Ryan: 181
GILES, Johnny: 186
GLADWIN, Cliff: 131
GREENWOOD, Ron: 14, 176
GREGG, Harry: 191
GEORGE, Rodger: 58
GRAY, George: 116
GREAVES, Jimmy: 164, 177-178, 187
GREEN, Geoffrey: 94
GULLIT, Ruud: 188
GURNEY, Bobby: 200
GUTHRIE, Ron: 200

H.

HALL, Jack: 44
HALLOM, Vic: 200
HAGAN, Jimmy: 25, 94
HANNAH, George: 77
HAPGOOD, Eddie: 163, 169
HARDAKER, Alan: 53
HARDISTY, Bob: 119
HARDWICK, George: 135
HARKER, Chris: 192
HARMER, Tommy: 143
HARPERS, Gerd: 94
HARRIS, Peter: 54
HARTLEY, Jim: 159
HARTLEY, Malcolm: 75
HARVEY, Joe: 77, 78, 79, 86, 130
HASTINGS, Alex: 184
HOUGHTON, Frank: 77
HUGHES, Billy: 200
HUNTER, Norman: 50
HURLEY, Charlie: 165, 166, 183, 200
HURST, Geoff: 164, 175-177, 178

I.

IRWIN, Cecil: 200

J.

JACK, David: 7, 53
JAMES, Alex: 163, 168
JOHNSTON, Bert: 35, 36-37, 38-39, 111
JOHNSTON, Harry: 54
JONES, Keith: 93

K.

KEANE, Roy: 50, 166, 167
KERR, Bobby: 200
KIRKUP, Mike: 77-83
KOHLMEYER, Werner: 94

L.

LANGTON, Bobby: 25
LAW, Dennis: 165, 178, 181, 186
LAWTON, Tommy: 19, 25, 26, 76, 94, 150, 167, 189-190
LEE, Francis: 191
LENG. Brian: 7, 43-59, 94
LESTAR, Bert: 177
LINEKER, Gary: 164, 165, 173, 179-180
LITTLE, Ted: 7
LESNOVITCH, Gus: 35
LOFTHOUSE, Nat: 43, 167, 190-191, 195
LONGSON, Sam: 97, 193
LLOYD, Cliff: 156

M.

MALE, George: 163-169
MALONE, Dick: 200
MANNION, Wilf: 43, 48, 83, 143, 156, 182, 195
MAPSON, Johnny: 116, 117, 200
MARADONNA, Diego: 163, 164, 172-173
MARCIANO, Rocky: 35
MARTIN, George: 79
MATTHAW, Walter: 119
MATTHEWS, Jack: 95
MATTHEWS, Stanley: 25, 26, 43, 48, 92, 94-95, 118, 175, 180, 190, 191, 195
MAXWELL, Bob: 7
McDONALD, Joe: 55, 56
McDONALD, Malcolm: 195
McDOUGAL, Jock: 36
McKEAG, William: 135-138
McMICHAEL, Alf: 77, 86
McNAB, Jimmy: 200
MEE, Bertie: 153
MENOTTI, Cesar: 172
MEREDITH, Billy: 171
MERRICK, Gil: 191
MERVIN, Tommy: 119
MILBURN, Jackie: 30, 43, 77-83, 94, 124, 130, 167, 188-189
MILLER, David: 94-95
MILLS, Freddie: 35
MILTON, Arthur: 119
MITCHELL, Bobby: 77, 86,
MITCHELL, Tommy: 131
MONROE, Marilyn: 32

MONTGOMERY, Jimmy: 200
MOORE, Bobby: 176
MORTENSON, Stan: 82, 182
MORTON, Billy: 124
MULHALL, George: 187
MURPHY, Patrick: 95
MURRAY, Bill: 8, 36, 44, 50, 51, 52, 53, 56, 86, 91, 111, 114, 149
MURRAY, Bob: 7, 9, 10, 11, 148-149

N.

NEILL, Terry: 188
NICHOLSON, Bill: 178
NORMANTON, Skinner: 141

O.

OLDROYD, Eleanor: 13
O'NEILL, Martin: 193
ORD, Ernest: 95
OWEN, Michael: 164

P.

PAINE, Terry: 195
PAISLEY, Bob: 159
PARKER, Jack: 58
PARKINSON, Michael: 5, 141-143, 192
PAUL, Roy: 48, 50
PEARSON, Tommy: 79, 83, 120-121
PELE: 171
PETERS, Martin: 178
PHILLIPS, Kevin: 148
PORTERFIELD, Ian: 200
PURDON, Ted: 19, 31, 32, 35, 48, 49,
PRIOR, Joe: 45, 148

R.

RAMSAY, Alf: 176, 178, 188
RAMSDEN, Barney: 11, 37, 159-162
RAMSDEN, John Charles: 162
REDHEAD, Brian: 14
REVIE, Don: 52, 167, 186
RITSON, Stanley: 112
RIVALDO: 150
ROBLEDO, George & Ted: 77, 86
ROBSON, Bobby: 149-150, 179, 188
RONALDO: 150
ROUS, Stanley: 68, 73
RUTHERFORD, George: 17

S.

SCOTT, Laurie: 26
SCUDAMORE, Richard: 195
SEYMOUR, Stan: 16, 17, 77, 82, 145, 182
SHACKLETON, John: 117
SHANKLEY, Bill: 145, 193
SHARRATT, Harry: 192
SHEARER, Alan: 150, 165, 167
SILLET, Peter: 27
SMITH, Dennis: 119
ST JOHN, Ian: 178
STEIN, Jock: 193
STELLING, Jackie: 46
STEPHEN, Jimmy: 126
STOKOE, Bob: 18, 21, 27, 77, 130, 200
STUBBINS, Albert: 16, 19
SWIFT, Frank: 14, 25, 54,
SWINDON, George: 22, 51

T.

TAPSCOTT, Derek: 21
TAYLOR, Ernie: 118, 124
TAYLOR, Graham: 179
TAYLOR, Peter: 95, 193
TAYLOR, Wilf: 17, 19
TREADGOLD, Harry: 116
TRAUTMANN, Bert: 188
TUEART, Dennis: 200

V.

VIOLET, Dennis: 105
VOISEY, Bill: 183

W.

WADDINGTON, Tony: 101-105, 177
WATSON, Dave: 200
WATSON, Vic: 177
WATSON, Willie: 92, 119-120, 128
WAYMAN, Charlie: 77
WEBSTER, Colin H: 108-109
WESTWOOD, Eric: 54
WHITTINGHAM, Bob: 63, 64, 67, 71
WILKINSON, Howard: 180
WINTERBOTTOM, Walter: 25, 54, 82-83, 94,
WOODFIELD, Billy: 25
WOLSTENHOLME, Ken: 176
WRIGHT, Arthur: 166, 184
WRIGHT, Billy: 25, 26, 43
WRIGHT. Tommy: 116-118

Y.

YOUNG, David: 200